Nineteenth-Century Spain

CW01500731

Nineteenth-century Spain deserves wider readership. Bedevilled by lost empires, wars, political instability, and frustrated modernisation, the country appeared backward in relation to northern Europe and even in relation to much of its own geographical periphery. This new history, the first survey of its kind in English in more than a hundred years, offers a fresh perspective on this century, showing how and why elements of backwardness and modernity ran in parallel through Spain. Bounded by the military and imperial crises of 1808 and 1898, this study pays special attention to the experience of war on politics and society, and integrates the latest historical debates in its analysis.

Mark Lawrence is Lecturer in History at the University of Kent.

Routledge/Cañada Blanch Studies on Contemporary Spain

Edited by Paul Preston and Sebastian Balfour
*Cañada Blanch Centre for Contemporary Spanish Studies,
London School of Economics, UK*

Claiming the City and Contesting the State
Squatting, Community Formation and Democratization in Spain
(1955–1986)
Inbal Ofer

Guns, Culture and Moors
Racial Perceptions, Cultural Impact and the Moroccan
Participation in the Spanish Civil War (1936–1939)
Ali Al-Tuma

Revolution and the State
Anarchism in the Spanish Civil War, 1936–1939
Danny Evans

Medicine and Conflict
The Spanish Civil War and its Traumatic Legacy
Sebastian Browne

Nineteenth-Century Spain
A New History
Mark Lawrence

Also published in association with the Cañada Blanch Centre:

Spain and the Great Powers in the Twentieth Century
Edited by Sebastian Balfour and Paul Preston

The Politics of Contemporary Spain
Edited by Sebastian Balfour

For a full list of titles in this series, please visit www.routledge.com

Nineteenth-Century Spain

A New History

Mark Lawrence

Routledge
Taylor & Francis Group

LONDON AND NEW YORK

First published 2020
by Routledge
2 Park Square, Milton Park, Abingdon, Oxon OX14 4RN

and by Routledge
605 Third Avenue, New York, NY 10017

First issued in paperback 2021

Routledge is an imprint of the Taylor & Francis Group, an informa business

British Library Cataloguing-in-Publication Data
A catalogue record for this book is available from the British Library

Library of Congress Cataloging-in-Publication Data
A catalog record for this book has been requested

ISBN 13: 978-0-367-78604-5 (pbk)
ISBN 13: 978-0-815-35106-1 (hbk)

Typeset in Garamond
by Apex CoVantage, LLC

MIX
Paper from
responsible sources
FSC™ C013985

Printed in the United Kingdom
by Henry Ling Limited

Contents

Acknowledgements

Researching nineteenth-century Spain can be a lonely business in the English-speaking world. So much Spanish history research and teaching remain tilted towards the twentieth century, and one is fortunate indeed to find an audience for earlier periods. For this reason, my thanks go to Rob Langham, senior publisher at Routledge, who invited me to write a new history of Spain and has been supportive along with his team throughout the process. I thank Charles Esdaile, who read and recommended my initial proposal. I thank Joan-Xavier Quintana i Segalà for his generosity in donating me some of the latest conference publications on historical Carlism arising from the Centre d'Estudis a'Avià. I also thank the following: Guy Thomson for sharing with me his notes relating to his extensive research on General Narváez, Natalia Sobrevilla for her insights into Spanish American militarism, and Gregorio Alonso for reading the final draft manuscript and recommending a number of improvements. Any errors or weaknesses remaining in the text are entirely my own. Above all I thank my wife, Susana, and my daughter, Nicole, for their love and support throughout this process. Este libro está dedicado a ustedes.

Mark Lawrence, Canterbury, February 2019

Introduction

Spain is a country normally seen as a laggard in terms of modernity but vener-able in terms of tradition. Spanish identity is one of the oldest in Europe. As early as the eighth century, the Cult of Santiago grew as a sort of Christian Mohammed, or Holy Warrior, even if the origins of the Santiago myth, just like the adjective *español* (*espagnole*), lay in France rather than Spain.[1] By the time of Spain's 'Golden Age' (*Siglo de Oro*) such famous Spanish artists as Diego de Velázquez and Bartolomé de Murillo occupied the summit of a uni-versally recognised Spanish culture. Spanish 'identity', if not yet nationhood, was formed long before the nineteenth century which occupies this study.[2]

Yet the nineteenth century remains one of the more mysterious periods in Spanish history. Sandwiched between the apparently more significant histo-ries of early modern Spain and the Spanish Civil War, the nineteenth century evokes images of failure, of empires lost, of civil strife, of dynastic clashes, of militarism, and of progress held in check by the forces of tradition. Spain appeared backward in relation to northern Europe and even in relation to much of its own geographical periphery. Opinion in both Spain and abroad deemed the country eccentric from the European mainstream. Philosopher Montesquieu's eighteenth-century critique of despotism modelled Spain as a corrupt, declining state riven with the Inquisition. The nineteenth-century American Hispanist and pioneer of scientific history William H. Prescott pre-sented Spain as the antithesis of American liberty and modernity.[3] Whereas educated Spaniards travelled abroad in search of modernity, other Europeans came to Spain in search of the opposite, Spain having cast a peculiar spell in the century of Romanticism. George Ticknor, Harvard's first professor of modern languages, upon visiting Spain in the early 1800s wrote, 'Imagine a country so deserted and desolate, and with so little travelling and communi-cation, as to have no taverns' that was found wanting for both 'cultivation and refinement'.[4] American poet Henry Wadsworth Longfellow, visiting Spain in the 1820s, remarked, 'There is so little change in the Spanish character, that you find everything as it is said to have been two hundred years ago'.[5] In 1836, the British Protestant missionary George Borrow, arriving in Spain in order to preach the Bible, was struck by the timelessness of Spanish culture and customs instead, especially the gypsies of Andalucía.[6]

Spanish historians writing in the nineteenth century were usually also politicians who were only too aware of foreign impressions of their country, given their periods of exile caused by pendulum swings in Spanish politics and the elite links with European cultural capitals, especially with Paris. Although Spain did not produce a nineteenth-century historian of the grandeur of Ranke, Michelet, or Macaulay, two Spanish names do stand out. Modesto Lafuente, a former priest turned Liberal parliamentarian, published his thirty-volume *Historia general de España* (1850–67) and Antonio Cánovas del Castillo, the architect of conservative liberalism in the last quarter of the century, published his national history in 1890. Lafuente's work stressed the heroism of the Spanish people since ancient history, and Cánovas's work celebrated the centralisation and unity imposed after the Reconquista was completed in 1492. Both men relished the intrinsically 'Spanish' events that forged their country's identity, writing in the Hegelian sense of historicism, suspicious, mournful, but also acutely aware, of other European comparisons, especially for the century of 'failure' in which they were writing.[7] Like their counterparts in the rest of Europe, Spanish historians were marked by the publication of Georg Wilhelm Friedrich Hegel's *Philosophy of History* (1837) which placed the 'centre of Europe' somewhere between England, France, and Germany, symbolically amputating Spain from modernity.[8]

Despite its importance, the nineteenth century remains the 'Cinderella' of Spanish history, attracting nothing like the scholarship lavished on either the Golden Age or the Spanish Civil War. The twentieth-century Jesuit historian Federico Suárez Verdeguer (1917–2005) thought that the sources, pro-liberal bias of his fellow historians, and the century's closeness all rendered an objective account of the nineteenth century impossible.[9] Right-wing views of the nineteenth century under Franco's rule (1939–75) were frequently apocalyptic. Franco himself spoke in 1950 of wanting to 'erase that century' from history for being 'the negation of the Spanish spirit'. Francoist propaganda pointed to the chaos of the nineteenth century as proof that Spaniards needed authoritarian rule.[10]

Twentieth-century historians generally accepted the 'failure' interpretation of modern Spanish history; indeed, several placed the divisions of the nineteenth century at the heart of explanations for the 1930s' civil war.[11] By the 1960s, historians were using modern historical methods of analysis in order to answer the question of what 'went wrong' in the nineteenth century. Marxian historians applied the 'bourgeois revolution' model for measuring the failure of Spain to transition successfully from the old regime to capitalism, always with the sacrosanct model of the French Revolution in the back of their minds.[12] These historians concluded that the Spanish bourgeoisie was too 'weak' to advance the economic revolution adequately, Spain therefore remaining less dynamic and 'modern' than several northern European countries. Over time, however, the 'bourgeois revolution' paradigm was revised, and this revision accelerated in the 1990s with the end of the Cold War. Jesús Cruz argued that Spain lacked a bourgeoisie in any meaningful sense of the word. Liberal political and economic reforms were enacted instead by dynastic elites, who, irrespective of whether they professed radical or conservative sympathies, came from the same social spectrum as those of the eighteenth-century *antiguo régimen*.[13] Historians no longer talk of Spain's 'bourgeois revolution'. But they do talk of the nineteenth-century 'liberal revolution'. During the second half of the twentieth century, there was a 'Pamplona school' of right-wing historians using modern historical methods to argue the superficial, often harmful, and 'foreign' impact of liberalism on a society still wedded to tradition. They were countered by a 'Valencia school' of liberal historians who presented a more optimistic view of liberalism and its role in modernising the Spanish state.

The 'Valencia school' were instrumental in revisiting long-held assumptions about Spanish decline in the nineteenth century. Over the past decades, the 'failure' interpretation has been challenged by a 'normalisation' trend which has viewed Spain's historical development as essentially part of a loosely defined European norm, especially in comparison with the rest of southern Europe.[14] Indeed, some of the most recent research has normalised Spain in new ways by highlighting unremarked peculiarities in other European states, thereby questioning whether a European norm existed to accommodate Spain at all.[15] The cultural impact of Spain's eclipse by the Great Powers, the overhaul of its monarchy and church, and its frequent wars and revolutions, was rich and variegated. The legacy of the old merged with the new, often in a transnational context as Spanish artists and intellectuals immersed themselves in European currents.[16]

Local histories continue to dominate Spanish academic publications, a product of the prevalence both of local publishing houses and regional regulation of universities. By contrast, nationwide survey histories of twentieth-century Spain continue to thrive, a sure sign that students continue to appreciate national histories organised chronologically. This book offers the first English-language survey of nineteenth-century Spain in several decades. This book integrates the international, military, political, and social history of Spain during its 'short' nineteenth century in Spain (1808–98). What historians understand as a century is usually different from simple chronology. They consider the Western nineteenth century 'long', running from 1789 to 1914, or even from 1776 to 1914, whereas the twentieth century they consider 'short', running from 1914 to 1991. A recent, non-Eurocentric study of global history, even stretches the long nineteenth century from 1750 to 1914.[17] Countries also have their own chronologies. Spain was centre stage neither in the French Revolution nor in the First World War, so the dates of its nineteenth century lie outside the European norm, not 1789–1914 but 1808–1898. In 1808, the implosion of Spain's old regime was witnessed, setting in motion a national war against Napoleon, a violent independence process in continental Spanish America, and then a succession of civil wars in Spain itself, all with attendant pendulum swings in political extremes and notions of legitimacy. The year 1898 experienced the *El Desastre*, the loss of Spain's remaining world empire and an attendant transformation in the political and intellectual shape of Spain's new century. As the earliest European example of a post-imperial state, Spain's short nineteenth century is deserving of a survey history of its own.

The nineteenth century also witnessed Spain fitfully transitioning from an old order of noble and clerical estates to a new order of property and laicism, a process enabled by liberal revolutions starting with the Constitution of Cádiz (1812), and achieved against entrenched opposition from the regions, countryside, and forces of Spanish tradition, most evidently during the Carlist Wars of 1833–40 and 1872–76. The Peninsular War (1808–14) created a politically interventionist army fed by generations of unwilling conscripts led by officers with political ambitions. Yet for all the political appeal of militarism, Spanish nation building remained weak, especially during the first half of the century, when it did not have the army as its servant. Military service did not turn peasants into Spaniards. Certainly, the anti-liberal forces of religion and tradition gradually reconciled themselves with the state in the second half of the century. But centralised nation building also had to contend with the growth of regional nationalism, especially in economically advanced Catalonia, even if for most of the nineteenth-century Catalanism was not inherently irreconcilable with the wider Spanish national identity.[18] Historians now accept that national Spanish identity was strong and that nation building was not solely a matter of Madrid imposing its will on the provinces.[19] The historian Juan Pablo Fusi called nineteenth-century Spain a 'country of centralism in theory, but of localism and regionalism in practice'.[20] The regions themselves drove policies and initiatives which reinforced a common Spanish identity as much as they differentiated it. For too long, historians sought to compare the supposed weakness of Spanish nation building with the supposed strength of modern France, substituting Madrid for Paris, *conscripción* for *conscription*, and the *municipio* for the *hôtel de ville*.[21]

Yet comparisons with other European states must be not be taken too far – not because Spain was somehow absent from the European mainstream (as most nineteenth-century contemporaries, both Spanish and foreign, would have held) but because Spain's nineteenth century was highly conflictive despite rather than because of attempts to inculcate a common identity. Whereas other European states also faced a lack of consensus about what constituted legitimate power (Italy, France), Spain's crisis was of a different order. It alone spawned an enduring and insurrectionary legitimist movement in the form of Carlism, and Spain, more than most countries, experienced the dynamic linking patchy economic modernisation with repeated recourse to violence and extremism in politics. Internationally, too, Spain's nineteenth-century decline contrasted with the rise of other large European states. From being a world empire and a still crucial factor in diplomacy at the start of the nineteenth century, by the end Spain had declined to second-rate status, occasional successes in foreign policy and foreign wars over the past century notwithstanding.

Geography, history, and historians

Historians for most of the twentieth century wittingly or unwittingly believed in the 'two Spains'. Modern Spanish history was shaped by modernity frustrated by the forces of reaction. This notion has sometimes been challenged as being rather too stark, but it is one that persisted over time. And certainly the struggle against Napoleon unleashed developments which were conducive to the emergence of political modernity (especially the affirmation of popular sovereignty). For generations, modern Spain's conflictive history was viewed either as *sui generis* or as an outlier to more successful European state building in Britain, France, the Low Countries, and Scandinavia. Spain's apparently patchy historical modernisation and a lack of 'progress' were found wanting compared with northern Europe.

Since the 1990s such Euro-Whiggishness has been revised, albeit with mixed success, by a 'normalisation' trend in the Spanish historiography. The most recent research normalises Spanish history with reference to the persistence of the old order in other European states. For most of the nineteenth century, Britain's aristocracy retained more nominal power and influence, the French repression of the Paris Commune was bloodier than any nineteenth-century Spanish counter-insurgency, and between 1812 and the First World War, Spain was the continental European country with the longest experience of constitutional rule.[22] The European 'model', which inspired and anguished Spanish intellectuals from the nineteenth century onwards, now appears less persuasive. In fact, Spain's nineteenth-century modernisation was fairly consistent with a southern European model: slightly better than Portugal and Greece but rather worse than Italy.

That said, the 'failure' interpretation of Spain's nineteenth century is not entirely wrong, given the conditions imposed by the country's physical environment. Geography shaped much of Spain's history. Extreme temperatures and regular droughts shaped a largely agricultural country with less industry and urbanisation than northern Europe. Apart from the temperate zones of Galicia and the Biscayan coast, most of the country was an arid tableland, where fertile soils and adequate rainfall were seldom found in the same place. Moorish irrigation allowed crops to flourish around Valencia, and agriculture flourished in Navarre, the Basque country, and a few small areas in Andalucía, besides. But Spain productivity was low.[23] Most urban centres (Valladolid, Jaén, Zamora, Cáceres) were market towns for the countryside. Madrid consumed more wealth than it generated, and even though Barcelona, Bilbao,

Seville, and Cádiz were more prosperous, their wealth depended more on sea communications than on the poor roads to the interior.

Ortega y Gasset argued that regional and local loyalties remained fierce over Spain's history thanks in large part to the inaccessible landscape, its poor roads, a lack of navigable rivers, and formidable mountains and plateaus. Indeed, the subordination of politics to geography blurred the 'public' and 'private' spheres in Spain. An institutionally weak monarchy was riven by the competing loyalties of the cities, the enforced autonomies of remote villages, and the competing networks of differing patron–client networks.[24] Edward Banfield developed the theory of 'amoral familialism' to explain how patron–client networks operated in 'partially modernised, generally backward' societies in southern Europe. Politics was the preserve of families securing private interests via corruption and bribery. Politicians claiming to act in the public interest were prone to demagoguery, and the mass of the population valued democracy very little, preferring an authoritarian regime to check the abuses of local power brokers.[25] Banfield studied southern Italy, but his model has been discussed in the context of Spain's local power brokers (*cacique*) in Restoration Spain (1875–1923), where abuses of power were rife despite formal constitutional guarantees of liberty.[26]

For all the political complexities of Spain's topography, the landscape also reinforced the Romantic conception of Spain which dominated foreign impressions, especially during the first half of the century. Historically, Spain's position was even more variegated for two reasons: first, the overlapping jurisdictions weakening the state and, second, its vast overseas empire. Seventeenth-century Spain was characterised by a weak central government and overbearing aristocratic bluebloods, and little changed until Carlos III (1759–88) bore down on the feudal privileges of church and nobility.[27] Before the nineteenth century, the Spanish state was barely visible. It recruited long-serving soldiers (usually by force); taxed its subjects, usually through consumption; delivered post and maintained a few excellent 'royal' roads; but little else besides. To most Spaniards other jurisdictions seemed to hold more sway: the Catholic Church, with its tithes, extensive welfare, and land interests, as well as its political body, the Inquisition; noble landowners with their huge properties worked by serfs and in many areas administered by the nobles' private justice; and the cities and guilds which operated different rights and responsibilities besides.[28]

In the Americas, the Spanish 'state' was much weaker still. Catholicism permeated all aspects of life in Spanish America, as the Spanish Crown retained wide-ranging powers over the church as a direct consequence of the 1492 Reconquista, turning the church, in many, ways into an arm of the king. The *criollos* (American-born whites) of Spanish America did not see themselves as colonised but as equal members of the Spanish monarchy. Nowhere in Spanish America before 1810 were there any *criollo* nations struggling to be free of peninsular rule; rather, the nation was conceived as a totality of hierarchical bodies emanating from kingdoms downwards.[29] Before the Bourbon reforms, Americans from all castes enjoyed a surprising degree of representation. The fourteenth-century origins of the Spanish culture of outwardly obedient disobedience – *se obedece pero no se cumple* (paying lip service to orders) – applied to America even more than the peninsula, as various stakeholders could block unpopular laws or reforms, implementing them only as a last resort, and the Crown until the last third of the eighteenth century showed great leniency. But from the 1760s, the Bourbon reforms eroded Spanish America's autonomy. The imposition of Intendants symbolised this, although one ironic result of the Crown centralising military, political, and judicial control into their local hands was a growth in regionalism. After the Jesuits were expelled from the Spanish Empire in 1767, American governance was increasingly militarised by officers sent from Spain. Spain's 'military monarchy' governed an empire which, by the turn of the century, was in some ways at its peak in terms of territory and Bourbonised administration.[30] But in other ways signs were ominous. Even though Buenos Aires units had twice repelled British attacks in 1806–1807, in so doing they merely underlined their potential for autonomous action without Spain. At the other end of her American empire, Spanish authorities in West Florida and Texas were successfully squeezing American filibusterers' encroachments in Mississippi. But this scenario, just like the British raids in the River Plate, underlined the innate rivalry demonstrated by Anglo imperialism. The Anglo-Spanish alliance against Napoleon in 1808 was a surprise for all concerned.

Notes

1 José Álvarez-Junco, *Spanish Identity in the Age of Nations* (Manchester: Manchester University Press, 2011), pp. 16–20.
2 *Ibid.*, p. 48.
3 Richard L. Kagan, 'Prescott's Paradigm: American Historical Scholarship and the Decline of Spain', *The American Historical Review*, Vol. 101, No. 2 (April 1996), pp. 430–1.
4 George Ticknor, *Life, Letters and Journals of George Ticknor* (Boston: J. R. Osgood, 1876), p. 198.
5 Andrew Hilen, *The Letters of Henry Wadsworth Longfellow*, Vol. 1 (Cambridge, MA: Harvard University Press, 2014), p. 222.
6 Juan Marichal, *El secreto de España* (Madrid: Taurus, 1995), pp. 347–8.
7 Inman Fox, *La invención de España* (Madrid: Cátedra, 1997), pp. 39–42.
8 Javier Krauel, *Imperial Emotions: Cultural Responses to Myths of Empire in fin-de-siècle Spain* (Liverpool: Liverpool University Press, 2013), p. 21.
9 Encarna García Monerris and Josep Escrig Rosa, 'Apologistas y detractores. El primer discurso antiliberal en la historiografía', in Encarna G. Moerris, Ivana Frasquet, and Carmen G. Monerris (eds.), *Cuando todo era posible: liberalismo y antiliberalismo en España e Hispanoamérica (1780–1842)* (Madrid: Sílex Ediciones S. L., 2016), pp. 31–2.
10 Paloma Aguilar Fernández, *Políticas de la memoria y memorias de la política* (Madrid: Alianza Editorial, 2008), p. 25.

11 Gerald Brenan, *The Spanish Labyrinth: An Account of the Social and Political Background of the Spanish Civil War* (London: Cambridge University Press, 1943); Raymond Carr, *Spain, 1808–1939* (Oxford: Oxford University Press, 1966).

12 For example, Miguel Artola-Gallego, *La burguesía revolucionaria* (Madrid: Alianza, 1974); Josep Fontana, *La crisis del antiguo régimen* (Barcelona: Editorial Crítica, 1992); Manuel Tuñón de Lara, *Historia de España* (Madrid: Ámbito, 1988).

13 Jesús Cruz, *Gentlemen, Bourgeois, Revolutionaries: Political Change and Cultural Persistence among the Spanish Dominant Groups* (Cambridge: Cambridge University Press, 1996); *Los notables de Madrid: las bases sociales de la revolución liberal española* (Madrid: Alianza Editorial, 2000).

14 Juan Pablo Fusi and Jordi Palafox, *España: 1808–1996. El desafío de la modernidad* (Madrid: Espasa, 1997); David Ringrose, *Spain, Europe and the 'Spanish Miracle', 1700–1900* (Cambridge: Cambridge University Press, 1998); Adrian Shubert and José Alvarez-Junco (eds.), *Spanish History Since 1808* (New York: Bloomsbury, 2000); Gonzalo Anes and Alvarez de Castrillón (eds.), *Economía, sociedad, política y cultura en la España de Isabel II* (Madrid: Real Academia de Historia, 2004).

15 Nigel Townson (ed.), *Is Spain Different? A Comparative Look at the Nineteenth and Twentieth Centuries* (Sussex: Sussex Academic Press, 2015).

16 Andrew Ginger and Geraldine Lawless, 'Introduction', in Andrew Ginger and Geraldine Lawless (eds.), *Spain in the Nineteenth Century: New Essays on Experiences of Culture and Society* (Manchester: Manchester University Press, 2018), pp. 6–8.

17 Trevor R. Getz, *The Long Nineteenth Century, 1750–1914* (London: Bloomsbury, 2018).

18 Angel Smith, *The Origins of Catalan Nationalism 1770–1898* (Basingstoke: Palgrave Macmillan, 2014), pp. 1–7, 36–8.

19 Mary Vincent, *Spain, 1833–2002: People and State* (Oxford: Oxford University Press, 2002), pp. 3–5.

20 Cit. Guy Thomson, *The Birth of Modern Politics in Spain* (Basingstoke: Palgrave Macmillan, 2009), p. 296.

21 For example, Javier García Fernández, *El orígen del municipio constitucional: autonomía y centralización en Francia y en España* (Madrid: Instituto de Estudios de Administración Local, 1983).

22 Townson (ed.), *Is Spain Different?*.

23 For a more detailed description of Spanish geography, see Gerald Brenan, *The Spanish Labyrinth* (London: Cambridge University Press, 1960), pp. 92–117.

24 Michael Broers, *The Napoleonic Mediterranean: Enlightenment, Revolution and Empire* (London: I. B. Tauris, 2017), p. 8.

25 Edward C. Banfield, *The Moral Economy of a Backward Society* (Chicago: The Free Press, 1958).

26 Robert W. Kern, *Liberals, Caciques, Reformers* (Albuquerque, NM: University of New Mexico Press, 1974), p. 14.

27 Henry Kamen, *The War of Succession in Spain, 1700–1715* (London: Littlehampton Book Services, 1969), pp. 25–41.

28 Diego Palacios Cerezales, 'The State', in Adrian Shubert and José Alvarez-Junco (eds.), *The History of Modern Spain* (London: Bloomsbury, 2018), pp. 308–9.

29 Brian Hamnett, 'Process and Pattern: A Re-examination of the Ibero-American Independence Movements, 1808–1826', *Journal of Latin American Studies*, Vol. 29, No. 2 (May 1997), pp. 279–328, 282.

30 Jaime E. Rodríguez O., *"We are now the True Spaniards": Sovereignty, Revolution, Independence, and the Emergence of the Federal Republic of Mexico, 1808–1824* (Stanford: Stanford University Press, 2012), pp. 7–33.

Chapter 1

1808–14: two Spains?

This chapter explains the social, political, and imperial crisis culminating in the events of 1808 (palace coup and French invasion) and how these helped determine Spain's military failures in the Iberian Peninsula and political failures in the Americas. In Spain the weakness of the Patriot armies was countered by the strength of Europe's strongest guerrilla phenomenon. The peculiar military environment was matched by peculiar political and imperial ramifications. Uniquely in Napoleonic Europe, Spain underwent two processes of political reform at the same time, one under French domination and the other under the Patriots. The Napoleonic Wars also proved uniquely decisive in terminally eroding a European colonial power's control over a vast non-European empire.

Just as in Portugal, Austria, and Naples, the second half of the century saw Spain undergo a series of Enlightenment-inspired social, political, and economic reforms, particularly during the reign of Carlos III (1759–88). Thus, deserted lands were resettled under royal jurisdiction, escaping being entailed in the complex patchwork of ecclesiastical, noble, and other corporate land-ownership with which Spain had been saddled as a result of the Reconquista and over which enlightened absolutism was trying to assert uniform regal control. Meanwhile, the traditional aristocracy of 'right' was being undermined by the creation of an elite of 'merit'. Carlos III had no qualms about raising plebeians and minor nobles into a new aristocracy of service, thus bypassing the grandees. Nevertheless, such enlightened reforms were regularly stymied by traditionalist elites who could rely on administrative inertia and on occasion even raise a crowd when the latter was convinced that popular interests stood to lose. In 1766 riots swept the countryside in protest at Carlos III's 'progressive' abolition of grain controls.[1] Therefore, social tensions simmered throughout the second half of the eighteenth century as the people of Spain were neither ruthlessly modernised so as to raise general living standards nor paternalistically protected by full-blooded feudalism. Only the ubiquitous charity relief provided by the powerful Spanish Church prevented further repeats of 1766 or, still more terrifyingly, the 1773–75 Pugachev revolt in Russia.

Even if Spain's old order could weather the good years of peace, good harvests, and buoyant American bullion, all generally coterminous with Carlos III's reign, the reign of Carlos IV (1788–1808) was marked by natural disasters, harvest failures, war and penury, destabilising the old regime and making it vulnerable to foreign intervention. In 1803, for example, a disastrous harvest led to robberies, assaults on bakers' shops, and curfews. Smitten with hunger, the populace also had to contend with an epidemic of yellow fever that autumn which claimed sixty lives per day in Málaga and reached as far north as Burgos. From Burgos, the Hispanophile Whig, Lady Holland reported the poor to be 'dropping like flies' and abandoning the countryside in desperate search of relief in the towns.[2] Such was the suffering that the kind of paternalistic grain controls which had been in place before 1766 were reintroduced. The hand of God sent an earthquake to Motril, a plague of locusts to Segovia, and a flood killing thousands downstream from a dam breached at Lorca.[3] Famines and disasters made unaffordable cost of war and armed neutrality which Spain had been obliged to sustain in the wake of the French Revolution. Whilst Spain was already no stranger to tithe strikes and anti-conscription riots, the 1793–95 War of the Convention added land riots to this list of manifestations of popular grievances when common lands in the Basque war provinces were sold off to sustain the war effort.

The 1793–95 war dragged Spain's eighteenth-century army into France's nineteenth century. Spain's peninsular army had been neglected in favour of the navy, as the Bourbon 'family compact' imagined no more threat coming from across the Pyrenees but a very lively threat coming from the oceans in the form of Britain's Royal Navy. By the end of the century, the Spanish army was therefore mediocre. It was heavily influenced by the Prussian model, even down to maintaining linear warfare and refusing to experiment with the line and column tactics being practised by the French Army. The troops consisted mainly of line infantry and a supplementary force of provincial militia raised by conscription and mobilised only in times of war. The Spanish cavalry was similarly a conventional force. Two elite guard-cavalry regiments (the Guardia Corps) and twelve line regiments (each of four squadrons) completed the force in 1793. In 1788, there were also three regiments of light infantry and two of light cavalry tasked with carrying our raiding actions against both native bandits and foreign Barbary corsairs. The Spanish Army could also count on irregular forces. The Basque provinces, Navarra and Catalonia, all had homeguard forces to be mobilised in time of war. Armed civilians were mobilised in parish companies led by local worthies against the French in 1793, and in Catalonia, local conscripts fed the *somatén* irregular militia and a slightly different all-volunteer force – the *migueletes* – called to support the regular army in wartime and in Catalonia only. Wartime also led to the local recruitment of varied units of freebooters, often former wrongdoers, in ad hoc units.

These units were led by an officer corps which was far from the old regime monochrome assumed by Marxist historians. Political favouritism could allow for remarkably rapid promotions of humble officers, the case of Godoy being the most extreme example. Non-political promotion was possible for rankers, albeit rare, and hardly ever beyond the rank of captain. In practice, high ranks were reserved for nobles who entered the military estate, often as cadets aged 14, who could end up with commands at both young and inexperienced ages and in territories where they often clashed with regional military and civil authorities.[4] Officers from the rank of captain and above (short of major-general and captain general) had part of their salaries deducted to fund the 'Monte Pío' system of widows' pensions. The female next of kin of officers killed in service received part of the deceased officer's salary until the widow either remarried or became a nun. The children also received money until the age of 18 in the case of boys and in the case of girls until they married or became nuns. In times of relative peace, there was money in the pension fund to be particularly generous (e.g. around 1790). But from 1808, the system would begin to collapse.[5]

Recruitment was designed in two ways, the first (and crudest) being the *leva*. Marginalised and criminal men were forced into military service at regular intervals (the last being in 1787), and this mechanism obviously served a social function in terms of welfare and order. The second, more sophisticated recruitment system was the *sorteo* or *quinta*. The *quinta* raised recruits out of a ballot operating under a system of fixed exemptions which allowed the wealthy and the well-connected to obtain substitutes or more comfortable militia service. Unsurprisingly, this ballot system was deeply unpopular and often produced riots.[6]

The actual Spanish performance against the French between 1793 and 1795 was surprisingly good, leading to a victory at the Battle of Trouillas on 22 September 1793. Reverses thereafter were not catastrophic, as witnessed in the lenient peace terms France offered Spain in 1795. But the extent of war enthusiasm – what historian Richard Herr called 'Spain's levy en masse' of 1793 – has almost certainly been exaggerated. Enthusiasm for war came from the usual suspects (churchmen) rather than the masses as a whole. National identity has to be manufactured over a long period in order for 'people's war' to emerge, and these conditions did not yet exist in Spain.[7] Yet the demands of blood and food certainly caused inchoately political protests. A poor harvest and war in 1793 inspired the mobilisation in La Rioja of hundreds of hungry peasants who marched from village to village offering *vivas* to liberty, equality, and to the French Assembly.[8] But fifteen more years of socio-economic strains caused by either war or armed peace were necessary for the explosion to take place. In the meantime, the old regime appeared to be teetering. Inflation linked to the 'funny money' (*vales reales*) launched by the monarchy to fund the deficit caused strikes in the state-owned tobacco factory at Guadalajara where some four thousand workers had to be suppressed by three thousand troops.[9] Meanwhile, demographic pressures combined with the harshening of Valencia's already-dire feudal regime to cause in 1801 a full-scale peasant rising.[10]

The target of popular ire was Carlos IV's pseudo-dictator, Manuel de Godoy, who, despite his obscure provincial origins, had enjoyed a meteoric rise thanks, firstly, to the Bourbon structural reforms which created a merito-cratic aristocracy of 'service' and, secondly, to the caprice of the wilful queen. Queen María Luisa's physical attraction towards the young Extremaduran proved to be a crowd-pleasing propaganda gift for Godoy's enemies, whose scurrilous pamphlets and rumours suggested that he owed his position to his prowess in the queen's bedchamber. The tourist Lady Holland remarked that the queen's affair was the subject of conversation even amongst muleteers.[11] But what really rallied popular opinion against Godoy was more structural, namely, the fact that he served as the obvious scapegoat for a foreign policy which gave Spain the worst of both worlds: domination by France and the enmity of Britain. In addition to the sale of common lands during the War of the Pyrenees, subsequent penury had obliged Godoy to auction the welfare centres of the Spanish Church (hospitals, poorhouses, orphanages), as well as a portion of Spain's extensive ecclesiastical lands. Their buyers were given *carte blanche* to raise rents as they wished. In 1806 Godoy alienated even more church lands, albeit this time with Papal agreement, in response to being bullied by a Napoleon flush with victory over Prussia into renewing Spain's 'French subsidy' (annual neutrality payments).[12]

Godoy's regalism should have pleased the enlightened young men soon to become known to history as *liberales* (during their phases in power after 1810 Liberals would place the reduction of ecclesiastical power at the heart of their reforms), all the more so because Godoy followed up this objective attack on privilege with another, namely, in the painstaking reductions he made to the overmanned and wasteful Royal Guard. Thus, the traditional aristocracy of 'right' saw one of its remaining outlets for patronage curtailed. But Godoy also tried to conciliate traditional clerical opinion by persecuting such promi-nent Jansenists (anti-Jesuit reformists) and enlightened laymen as Melchor Jovellanos, José Urquijo, and Manuel José Quintana.

The rallying point for opposition to Godoy was the person of Prince Ferdi-nand, who became popularised as the 'desired one' (*el deseado*). The popular classes were becoming radicalised not just by the dire social situation, now intensified by the squeeze on church relief, but also by a surge of propaganda which created expectations of change. This ranged from the intellectual to the pedestrian: from the radical poet Manuel José Qunitana's late-1807 attack on Godoy for keeping Spain 'shackled, oppressed and vilified'[13] to an intensifi-cation of the tavern rumours and pictorial satires with which the favourite had had to contend since 1798. Thus, when the El Escorial plot of Octo-ber 1807 – basically an attempt to secure Napoleon's support for Ferdinand – backfired (Ferdinand being forced to make a humiliating retraction), it was the favourite and not the heir to the throne who became the focus of public ire. Thus, it was generally believed that the whole affair was a 'put-up' job designed to have Ferdinand replaced by Godoy as heir to the throne. Tension in the meantime mounted with the arrival of large numbers of French troops in accordance with the Treaty of Fontainebleau, which projected the Franco-Spanish occupation and partition of Portugal.[14]

Spain's crisis was being conditioned by the overbearing presence of Napoleon. *Fernandino* conspirators were accordingly fired up by a great sense of urgency, hoping to present the emperor with a *fait accompli*. In March 1808 they overthrew Godoy in the Mutiny of Aranjuez and forced Carlos IV to abdicate his throne in favour of Ferdinand. The Vizconde de Matarrosa, soon to become known to history as Count Toreno, asserted how Napoleon was popularly seen as the protector of Ferdinand's new reign, French encroachments on Spanish fortresses which the emperor had, in reality, ordered being blamed on the intrigues of Godoy.[15] The dissident diarist José María Blanco White thought that the invading French could have been 'welcomed as brothers' if they had only recognised Fernando after the March 1808 coup.[16]

The *fernandino* coup was launched on 19 March 1808 when the lead conspirator, Count Montijo, used money and propaganda to dispatch large numbers of peasantry to Aranjuez. Aranjuez was the seat of a royal palace where the insurgents made common cause with the embittered Spanish Royal Guard in attacking Godoy's residence. Carlos IV soon abdicated in a timely bid to save his wife's favourite, whilst news soon spread to Madrid, provoking attacks on Godoy's protégés.[17] Multiple sources attest that the property of *godoyista* elites was destroyed rather than pillaged. This was no mindless *jacquerie*, rather a mixture of 'moral economy' violence and political direction.[18] In fact, in punishing rather than robbing the rich, the rioters were foreshadowing the wider attacks on the elites which would unfold after the Second of May.

But Napoleon had his own plans for Spain. The new king accepted Napoleon's invitation to travel to Bayonne, close to France's border with Spain, hoping that an audience with the master of Europe would legitimise the Aranjuez coup. Yet the *fernandinos* had misjudged Napoleon's benevolence. Two French officers invaded a Madrid printing works and demanded that the owner print the protest made by Carlos IV at his forced abdication.[19] Tension mounted as Spain's French 'allies' treacherously occupied fortresses linking Madrid with the French frontier. When on 2 May, Marshal Murat's troops opened fire on a crowd in Madrid protesting their removal to France of remaining members of the royal family, the result was the famous uprising.

Second of May

Arguably few events have been more controversial or influential in shaping the political trajectory of Spain. Its fame, which emerged very quickly in the summer of 1808, gave rise to conflicting interpretations. For the moderate liberal Toreno, writing a generation later, both the Second of May in Madrid and the subsequent disorders in the provinces represented a spontaneous popular uprising in defence of *patria* (fatherland), an abducted king, and religion, all of which amounted to a violent assertion of national independence against what he saw as Napoleon's mendacious claim to regenerate Spain.[20] His radical-liberal contemporary, Alcalá Galiano, was more circumspect, undecided as he was whether it was 'enlightened patriotism' or 'blind fanaticism' which drove the disturbances.[21] Despite these liberal interpretations, the enduring legend of the May uprising actually had a decidedly conservative 'church and king' slant which conservative writers represented as a popular defence of king, tradition and religion (unsurprisingly this representation prevailed during the Franco dictatorship). Taking the ideology out of the Second of May has proved difficult. One of the most objective studies to have emerged is Arturo Pérez-Reverte's well-researched historical novel.[22]

Men who would soon be known as 'liberales' claimed the Second of May and subsequent risings that summer as evidence of Spaniards asserting their sovereignty. Juan Romero Alpuente declared that, as Spain had been abandoned by her grandees and generals, it was left to the 'nation' to resist Napoleon and Godoy: 'Spain today is what revolutionary France used to be'.[23] The first liberals were the first Romantics, and virtually all politicians versified. Many of these enlightened men featured in the juntas of Asturias and Galicia, the first to declare war on Napoleon.

Indeed, not just Spanish, but also international, opinion was ready to accept 1808 as a national uprising. The British government enthusiastically signed an alliance with Patriot envoys, Toreno and Argüelles. *Hispanophilia* rose along with the temperature in the fierce heatwave that struck Britain in July 1808. When Spanish forces under Patriot command in July inflicted a surprise defeat on the French at Bailén (Andalucía), the fame of the rising found resonance across the Atlantic in the United States, where newspapers waxed lyrical at the blow delivered by a 'free' people against the 'monster' of Europe.[24] The breathing space provided by Bailén allowed reform-minded Patriots to set the political agenda in the insurgent juntas. Radicalised by two generations or wars, disasters, news from France, Godoy, and a resurgent Inquisition, these Patriots would far surpass the enlightened reforms of Carlos III when they came to dominate the political agenda of Patriot Spain by 1810 by propelling the country through a series of radical economic and political reforms which would constitute Spain's first experience of Liberalism. And all this would be done in the name of the revolution of 1808.

The politicisation of the disorders of 1808 took place rapidly and enduringly, even though the events of 2–3 May seem closer to a mass panic than a national rising. With rumours flying around the capital, a crowd congregated outside the palace, whereupon the French troops panicked, opening fire as a means of heading off what threatened to turn into a stampede. Forced by the French into violence, ordinary people spontaneously took to arms against the thirty thousand French troops stationed in Madrid. This uprising would cost the lives of 413 civilians in combat, including about a hundred killed by Murat's draconian practice of executions after his troops re-established control. Almost half the Patriot casualties were ordinary wage earners, whilst between 15 and 17 per cent were women.[25]

The popular nature of this disorder is brought to life by eyewitnesses. The young Alcalá Galiano, whose anguished mother warned him 'it has begun', rushed out onto the streets of the capital looking to be a hero, only to be snubbed by the artisan and day-labouring insurgents who failed to see how they could use a nobleman in such times as these.[26] Blanco White remembered seeing the massacres unfold with an air of unreality before prudently rushing to the safety of his lodgings, only then realising the enormity of the situation.[27] The instinct of the Fernandine governing class was to side with their French 'allies' against the riots. Collaborators who would soon be called *afrancesados* believed in the contemporary Catholic-Thomist belief in the 'Common Weal' (*Bien Común*) and hoped that a reformist French regime might preserve the peace and their own positions of power and privilege.[28] Thus, the administrative apparatus of the regency left behind by Fernando had already been given strict instructions to avoid all confrontation with French soldiers, and to act swiftly against any popular 'effervescence'.[29] As dead civilians started littering the streets on 2 May, the bureaucracies of the Spanish *antiguo régimen* therefore wasted no time in siding with their killers. Spanish army units in Madrid were confined to barracks, the famous heroism displayed by the Patriot martyrs Pedro Velarde and Luís Daoíz, both army officers, notwithstanding. A truce was eventually brokered that day between Madrid's civilian authorities and the French military governor, Joachim Murat. In reality, many innocent artisans were added to the grim list of mass executions when scouring French troops loosely interpreted clasp-knives and tools in their possession to be offensive weapons whilst making sure that no notables were amongst the villains and nobodies about to be executed.[30] A complete breakdown of society thus seemed for the moment to have been avoided. But news of Ferdinand's humiliating abdication, extracted under duress at Bayonne, changed everything. Napoleon placed Ferdinand under house arrest at a chateau in Valençay while he arrogantly made his elder brother king of Spain (José I) and even rushed through an 'enlightened' constitution for his new satellite state (Constitution of Bayonne).

Chaos spread rapidly to the provinces where popular risings overwhelmed the Bourbon *godoyista* authorities, establishing in their place patriotic revolutionary juntas. As Charles Esdaile shows, this revolution manifested itself in three forms. The first (and probably most common) involved massive popular demonstrations which extinguished existing local authorities with little conspiratorial input; the second, and possibly least frequent, was enacted by conspiratorial cells which took the initiative and imposed their own solutions; and the third saw the legitimate authorities themselves manage to captain the revolution 'from above'.[31] Caught unawares, Spain's elites had to improvise accordingly or be overthrown. For the widespread disorders of the spring and summer of 1808 were directed at unpopular local elites rather than against the invading French, revolution only taking off in those parts of Spain free of Napoleon's troops. That said, French travellers and residents unfortunate enough to be in the wrong place at the wrong time could certainly find themselves served up as scapegoats. Most notoriously, some 330 wealthy French residents of Valencia were massacred in that city when a demagogue Franciscan friar exploited long-standing social tensions to rally a lynch mob.[32]

The Valencia victims were both unpopular and French. But countless other victims in Spain that summer were just unpopular. The 26–27 May revolution in Seville – directed by failed businessman Tap y Núñez – spread such propaganda as 'if there had not been rich people in Spain, then we would not have had to put up with the French either', and Tap's revolutionaries assassinated the local notable Conde del Águila, who had wanted to submit to Napoleon's authority. What really merited his assassination, according to the Tap propaganda, was that 'as a count, he could neither give his blessing to the disorders nor lower himself to mix with the revolutionaries'.[33] Even where no conspiracies took place, crowds might lynch unpopular or suspect individuals, or sometimes just intimidate the authorities with their vitriol. Blanco White, having fled Madrid after the massacre, was travelling through the Extremaduran *pueblo* of Almaráz where he found the magistrate straining every nerve to placate a crowd of armed peasants and labourers, which was radicalised by rumours of 'traitors' being executed in nearby Trujillo, Badajoz, and Mérida: 'Sir, we want to kill a traitor'.[34] Blanco White wrote that most killings were committed 'by Spaniards on Spaniards who, probably, owed their fate to private pique and revenge, and not to political opinions'.[35] Violence also enveloped the military. In Valencia, the Barón de Albalat was slain in revenge for his role in unpopular militia reforms and his part in suppressing the 1801 rising. In Galicia, meanwhile, a plea to the *fernandismo* of the crowd could not prevent Captain General Filanghieri from being lynched by a group of soldiers who were probably acting at the behest of disaffected junior officers.[36] Despite this obvious anarchy, generations of historians were convinced that patriotism was the real motivation for the violence.[37] Yet even when Frenchmen were targeted, the social mobilisation of their tormentors was very telling. Two thousand vigilantes cornered an unfortunate French army courier at an inn in Mérida.[38] Historians may never know the exact number of fatalities. Toreno would later write that the death toll of May and June, excepting the Valencia and Madrid massacres, did not exceed thirty.[39] But eyewitness evidence like Blanco White's would suggest that the actual figure was much higher.

Certainly, contemporary men of politics and letters would look back on the summer of 1808 as a watershed. As far as the twice future liberal prime minister Evaristo San Miguel was concerned, the daily experience of 1808 and the subsequent war changed men forever whilst ushering in a revolution in public opinion.[40] Alcalá Galiano meanwhile remembered how pre-1808 court and social conventions entailed much 'more respect and submission to all forms of authority'.[41] Their reflections mattered because the revolution of 1808, ensured that Spain would not endure as a French satellite kingdom. The Patriot victory of 18–22 July 1808, at Bailén (Andalucía), was, in large part, a result of Napoleon's complacent view that the march on Cádiz was a mere police action for which Marshal Dupont's inferior troops would be more than adequate. The victory galvanised the juntas into recognising that they needed a provisional government, and after hard bargaining, they therefore agreed to cede sovereignty to the Supreme Central Junta (Junta Suprema Central), established at Aranjuez on 25 September. Spain's chaos would now be reined in by the general establishment of local honorary militias controlled by pre-revolutionary elites, provincial juntas had been imposing conscription, but the Junta Central in 1809 turned it into a nationwide obligation. The Junta Central also tried to regulate society. Contemporary liberals like Count Toreno were disparaging of the Junta Central. But recent research is sympathetic towards the Junta Central's plight during the calamities of 1809. Even after Spain's last major field army was defeated at Ocaña in November 1809, the Junta Central never lost its sense of purpose. It issued orders for the election of deputies to a new parliament, or Cortes (last convened in 1789), a graduated income tax, a one-hundred-thousand-man levy, and removal of exemptions for military service.[42]

Despite the progressive manifestoes of such liberals as Quintana, the Junta Central mostly tried to turn the political clock back to before 1808.[43] Much of the pre-Godoy absolutist 'military monarchy' was resurrected for the sake of the war effort, even if at the same time neither the interests of traditionalists nor the provincial juntas were entirely neglected. The disentailment of ecclesiastical property was halted, Jesuits (expelled in 1767) were allowed to return to Spain, old press restrictions were reaffirmed whilst even an inquisitor-general was nominated (although the Junta Central stopped short of enacting any further anti-Jansenist measures).[44] And, finally, whilst the provincial juntas – in the eyes of some historians the institutional repositories of such revolutionary impulse as existed – were certainly not abolished, their powers were drastically reduced.[45] What was genuinely new was also unwelcome. The 1809 conscription law was the first-ever theoretically universal conscription in Spanish history. But it did not turn 'peasants into Spaniards', to paraphrase Eugene Weber's study of French nation building. Much more than was the case in Napoleonic France and the French satellite states, 'universal' conscription in Patriot Spain was inflicted on the poor rather than the rich. Even supposed revolutionaries in the provincial juntas turned a blind eye to this unfairness, happy as they were merely to get themselves out of the fighting.

Levies had never been popular throughout the eighteenth century, but at least the integrity of the Spanish Empire, the Bourbon alliance, and corporate privileges had managed to keep this burden comparatively low and infrequent. During the eighteenth-century levies were usually in four figures and usually took place once or twice per decade. Only in the war years of 1746,

1776, and 1794 did levies get into five figures. Yet the constant wars and revolutions of the early nineteenth century transformed the situation, with levies of five figures being enacted on average five times each decade, culminating in the unprecedented hundred-thousand-man levy at the height of the Carlist War in 1835.[46] Local notables and their protégés could avoid serving by offering up criminals, the insane and the unfit, whilst bribery or taking comfortable placements in socially exclusive militia units could also secure exemption from actual soldiering. As for the mass of the population, soldiering was equally disliked. Whenever the war arrived on their doorstep, as in Madrid on the 2 May, and later in two brutal sieges at Zaragoza, Spaniards responded belligerently. The second siege of Zaragoza lasted from 21 December 1808 until 21 February 1809, and half of the siege involved house-to-house fighting in the city centre. The siege turned Agustina Zaragoza Doménech (1786–1857) into Agustina de Aragón, a Spanish 'Joan of Arc' who avenged the killing of her sweetheart by firing cannon to repel a French onrush in a key part of the siege of Zaragoza.[47] Countless undocumented cases of civilian and military heroism in defence of hearth and home abounded besides.

The prospect, however, of being starved, drilled and killed far from home held no appeal for a population innocent of nationalism. Alas, Patriot propaganda often clouded the issue, as the Bailén victory gave room to suggest both that militarisation was unnecessary, and, in effect, that Spain had only to flex her muscles for the French to flee in terror. But reality soon came back to bite the Patriots, as the humiliation visited on French arms during the summer of 1808 (which forced the invader to pull back beyond the River Ebro) was answered by a winter campaign led by Napoleon himself. Now, conscription and mobilisation were precisely what the Junta Central was demanding with renewed vigour, whilst the grim war situation also dictated a series of crash military reforms. Meanwhile, emerging liberal elites, writing in an invigorated popular press browbeat unreconstructed Bourbon army commanders into proving their use on the field of battle against the superior French: with disastrous results. Seeing this tide of blood coming, lucky and the quick-witted men might dodge the draft by hasty marriage, flight, or self-mutilation. But for the majority there was no escape.

Elites managed to escape real soldiering, and the people noticed. In Don Benito (Extremadura) artisans and day labourers sabotaged a levy, demanding that it should be the rich, the only ones with something to lose, who should go to the war.[48] The Spanish Church was no help. It preached war as the sacred duty to expel the atheist invader, whilst at the same time, clerics retained their traditional exemption from military service. An anonymous complaint received at the end of 1808 asked, '[W]hy do none of the friars and priests under forty have to go to the army . . . so as to release back into agriculture and useful industries all those soldiers who have been called up?'[49] Perhaps the most egregious case of local elites' evasion was Cádiz, where the local militia had long been populated by the city's dominant merchant classes who in February 1809 strained every nerve to resist the Junta Central's order to mobilise. The 'Distinguished Volunteers' faked a riot which they then suppressed, thereby proving their indispensability and gaining a guarantee never to be ordered to serve outside the city.[50]

The reality of inchoate class conflict was hard to reconcile with the hopes of political regeneration spread by reformers and the burgeoning press. The Junta Central pledged to convene the Spanish parliament (Cortes), whilst promising that

> the basic rights of the citizen should be free from fresh attack, and that the fount of the common weal should have the blockage which has hitherto held it in check cleared away, and it should gush forth unimpeded, as soon as the war is done.

Meanwhile, 'means will be found of improving our laws, getting rid of the abuses which have crept in and making perfection of the laws possible'.[51] Read out in pulpits, squares and taverns, these words created popular expectations of change. But the already-dire social situation continued to worsen, thanks largely to the loss of farmhands to the war and the burden placed by requisitioning on systems of agriculture which even in peacetime afforded barely more than subsistence for the rural masses. A British officer passing through a Portuguese frontier village vividly described the poverty and war apathy which was symptomatic of any number of townships in Spain itself:

> The articles of life are all enormously dear, full three times as much as they were two years ago. . . . Men, women and children (alike) seem to have no occupation. . . . One of the great systems of this war is to eat up a country. The word itself sounds horrid, but the eating up is done to render it useless to an enemy. You can then advance or retire and find some other country to be devoured. This cannibal-like system may suit us, who are sure to find some other place when we have devoured the one we are in, but it does not suit the natives. . . . The little money they may have gained will not as in England purchase bread: that is all gone, and, if some little should remain, the owner will not part with it, not knowing where to get more. The people know that they must lose all their grain and cattle . . . and who can then wonder that they should be tired of war? After all, it makes not the slightest difference to them whether the house of Braganza or Bonaparte is upon the throne. The voice of the people would, if they were to open their mouths, call for peace upon any terms. It is the voices of the grandees you hear, who do not suffer the privations to the same extent and are influenced by different motives.[52]

The apparent vehicle for popular grievances was the guerrilla phenomenon which gripped Spain from the winter of 1808–09. There were as many as nine types of guerrilla: *partidas* (disciplined volunteers), *cuadrillas* (outlaws, usually smugglers), *somatenes* (Catalan volunteer militia), *migueletes* (Catalan militarised volunteers), *cruzadas* (holy warriors), *cuerpos francos* (post-1812 free corps police force), *corso terrestre* (mounted militia raiding French border and guarding coasts), *cazadores rurales* (landowners' militia), and various 'honorable' companies composed of local elites.[53]

For most of 1809 the guerrillas shared the field with regular Allied forces, both the Spanish army as well as two consecutive British expeditionary forces, the ill-fated army of Sir John Moore, and the more tenacious army of Arthur Wellesley (later Lord Wellington). But despite a tactical Anglo-Spanish victory at Talavera (New Castile) in July 1809, Wellington's forces were obliged to retreat into the safety of Portugal. Renewed efforts towards the end of 1809 exhausted the Allies, sending the Spanish reeling after Ocaña and the British back towards Portugal. For two-and-a-half years, the Anglo-Portuguese army had to limit itself to fighting battles along the Portuguese–Spanish border, decisively defeating a French invasion of Portugal in 1810. Without an effective Patriot army for the better part of that time, the Patriot guerrilla was the only armed force available to keep resistance alive. Without the guerrilla continuing to fight, the rearguard's resistance might well have crumbled into acceptance of the French occupation, making Wellington's later military victory more problematic. The guerrilla proved effective in its 'battle for food'. Their actions starved French soldiers' rations and increased their sickness rate to the highest amongst all imperial armies in Europe, as well as adding to their general demoralisation at their frequently futile pursuit of an 'invisible army'. In other words, tens of thousands of thousands of imperial troops which might have been used elsewhere were bogged down in Napoleon's 'Spanish ulcer'. Even Wellington, an Anglo-Irish Tory suspicious of his allies' bombastic claims, especially the *liberales*' obsession with 'popular' guerrillas, admitted the decisive role played by irregular warfare in the eventual Allied victory.[54]

That said, leading research by Charles Esdaile revises the popular resistance image of the Spanish guerrilla. Not only did the Patriot guerrilla bands fail to spark off popular resistance in French-occupied Spain; there was also a popular apathy towards the Patriot war effort in unoccupied Spain, as evidenced by draft riots, hoarding, and desertion.[55] The exception to this general rule was upland Navarra and the neighbouring Basque provinces, where popular religiosity, popular landownership inheritable by primogeniture, the pressures of overpopulation and wartime sales of common lands, and a local tradition of armed mobilisation, all combined to create the very sort of 'people's war' in this region which historians for a long time lazily ascribed to the rest of Spain besides. The 'patriotic' fight against the French occupier also tended to bring out the worst in people, involving a wide array of banditry, adventure, opportunism, and desertion from the appalling conditions of the regular army.[56] In November 1811 a local notable in San Climent de Llobregat (Catalonia) was arrested for recruiting 'patriotic volunteers' with the express incentive of exempting them from conscription.[57] Yet the guerrilla war was lionised by liberals all the same as it symbolised both national sovereignty and anti-militarism. As one liberal newspaper opined from the safety of Cádiz, 'the dignity of the Spanish nation is being upheld only by heroic guerrilla leaders', whilst the few scattered regular armies would perform better if more officers came from the wide ranks of talented countrymen.[58] The reality, however, was very different from the bombast of the Cádiz cafes. Pardo de Andrade was a liberal cleric from Galicia whose contemporary praise for the guerrilla proved appealing enough to be reprinted almost a century later as *Los guerrilleros gallegos de 1809*.[59] But in 1809 Andrade despaired at his countrymen's apathy. He appealed to them to redeem their 'cowardice', reminding them that it was their duty to sustain the fight, for it was they who had 'declared war in the first place'.[60]

The Patriot crisis peaked in the wake of the defeat in November 1809 of the last major Patriot field army at Ocaña. Ocaña cleared the path for a French blitzkrieg of Andalucía that winter, toppling the Junta Central from power. As the French swept all before them, the Junta Central made to evacuate its personnel from Seville, only to be hijacked by a popular riot whipped up by its provincial rival, the Junta of Seville.[61] A crowd was easily raised as *sevillanos* had had to endure more than a year of not just one but two mutually antagonistic juntas, both of which had provoked the populace to anger by awarding themselves hefty salaries and conscription exemptions. As the Junta Central abandoned the people to their fate, popular tensions boiled over. Thus, on 24 January, members of the Junta Central who set out to flee Seville for the safety of Cádiz were jeered, insulted, indeed everything but lynched, by the crowd.[62] Similar scenes were played out in other Andalucían provincial capitals (Granada), as crowds tried frantically to hold their elites, who had demanded sacrifices of the people whilst shielding themselves, to account. In Málaga a royalist army officer imprisoned the junta and led his rebels out to meet the French invasion. But General Sebastiani swept Vicente Abello's rebels aside, capturing Málaga, and imposing a punitive tribute on the town twice the size of that imposed on Granada.[63]

News of the Junta Central's collapse had a radical effect in Spanish America, where *criollo* elites were already bristling at such imperial measures as Godoy's extension to America of the 'Consolidation decree' which amortised the inflationary *vales reales*, squeezing New Spain's credit-based economy. For a while, Spanish America seemed to stand squarely behind the imperial motherland. News of the collapse of the Spanish monarchy in 1808 had provoked the rising of juntas in America just as in Spain, following the well-established Hispanic constitutional principle of sovereignty reverting to the people in the absence of kings. Novohispanos saw their kingdom as equal with those of the peninsula, despite resistance from several Peninsular authorities. What clinched the decision to autonomy was confusing news of the collapse of Spain, and crucially, news that the 'Supreme' Junta at Seville was not really supreme at all (i.e. other demands and representations arrived from Asturias and elsewhere).[64] Spanish America, which had needed no large coercive force for three hundred years, was subsumed in crisis. Its local militias, which were structured either on caste identities (Indians, free Afro-descendants, pardos, morenos) or on identities forged around recruitment origins – companies of 'Basques', 'Catalans' and 'locals' (*patricios*) – would fight autonomously, setting a precedent for independence.[65] Napoleon's seizure of the Crown of Castile married the 'how' (local militias) with the 'why' (the sudden, unexpected removal of unquestioned, legitimate authority across the Spanish dominions, including the Spanish motherland).

In Spain, meanwhile, temporary relief came during the retreat from Seville when a series of brutal forced marches and a brilliant rearguard action by the Patriot forces of the Duke of Albuquerque bought time to fortify Cádiz and, in effect, to save Andalucía from total conquest.[66] Cádiz would now become the Patriot's fateful refuge and a symbol of Free Europe. But 'King' Joseph was in high spirits. Public office holders swore allegiance to him in droves, including virtually all statesmen of the old regime apart from the elderly Floridablanca and the enlightened Jovellanos, and some 79 per cent of minor officials besides.[67] Joseph even dared tour his newly conquered Andalucían provinces. Landowners, weary of war and hopeful of French protection, turned out their dependents to offer the king a sumptuous welcome, Seville thereafter becoming a bulwark of collaboration where the *josefino* newspaper *Gaceta de Sevilla* launched a war of words against the Patriot authorities holed up in Cádiz.[68]

Great leap forward

The demised Junta Central was replaced by a Regency Council which convened the long-promised Cortes (parliament) in September 1810. Liberals soon came to dominate the reform agenda, especially in terms of pressing for the recognition of the sovereignty of the nation and private property rights. Feudal jurisdiction in the countryside was ruled 'incompatible with the nation' and abolished on 6 August 1811. Young aristocratic liberals in the Cortes (Toreno, Argüelles, Martínez de la Rosa) made an ostentatious show of renouncing their birthrights in a conscious imitation of the early days of the French Revolution (when noble after noble rose in the National Assembly to renounce their privileges). However, the abolition decree was implemented in such a way that essentially there was no change in landownership. Turning to its 'maximalist' flaws, its objective made sense only in those parts of Spain (parts of Andalucía, Extremadura, Castile) in which large estates worked by large numbers of landless labourers predominated. Elsewhere, landownership was marked by a complex array of emphyteusis, informal subletting, and informal freeholding, which defied legal 'proofs' of ownership, a particularly complex example being the clerical leasing of tiny plots ('*minifundia*') in rainy

Galicia. In short, little would have changed even had most of Spain not been under enemy occupation. As Spain began to undergo liberation from 1812, meanwhile, the decree was watered down still further. By 1812, the tribunal charged with interpreting it was doing so in such a conservative fashion that noble claims to ownership were being considered legitimate private property without the need to present title proofs unless villagers mounted a legal challenge. Feudal lords could outspend villagers, meaning disputes dragged on inconclusively for years and even decades.[69]

Young Cortes liberals like Count Toreno (1786–1843) and Agustín de Argüelles (1776–1844) were concerned with the rights of property rather than of people. Their economic philosophy was based on Jovellanos's 1795 *Informe de Ley Agraria* which argued for the transfer of entailed lands into the hands of private property holders, whose direct exploitation of their new properties would result in higher productivity than would be possible under illiberal systems of serfdom, sharecropping, leaseholding, or communal ownership. Nevertheless, the formal abolition of feudalism encouraged an emerging group of more radical elites who were convinced by the need for a social dimension to liberalism. The August 1811 abolition decree actually helped to fuel popular demands for landownership. There was no popular defence of the harsh feudal regime in the Valencian *huerta* during the French conquest of January 1812. Yet when the French were expelled, the result was a wave of rural activism as tenant farmers occupied the lands of unpopular grandees, withheld tithes and feudal dues, and made bonfires of noble insignia.[70] In the Serranía de Ronda (Andalucía), on the other hand, the decree gave communities the opportunity to assuage some of the severe economic burdens which marauding Patriot guerrilla bands imposed on them. Thus, the lands of local magnates were seized, the dispossessed nobles complaining that, having been mortally wounded by the French, they were now being finished off by the Patriots.[71]

The biggest political change during the Peninsular War was the Constitution of 1812. Whereas both contemporary and later conservatives exaggerated this constitution's French influences, liberals, in turn, championed its indigenous origins, just as the juntas claiming sovereignty in Spain (and in Spanish America) championed the legal precedent of the Seven-Part Code (Siete Partidas) of the thirteenth-century Crown of Castile. The 1812 constitution's proclamation of the sovereignty of the 'nation' also drew on the heroic demise of these medieval liberties in the doomed 1520s' 'Comuneros' revolt against a centralising Habsburg monarchy. Like all radicals, the liberals sought precedents in national history to legitimise their acts. Yet in the eyes of priests and reactionaries (dubbed '*serviles*' by the liberals), the liberals were at the very least guilty by association. *Serviles* were boosted in their charges by Napoleon himself, whose 1808 address to the Spaniards offered 'liberal' reforms, albeit in the eighteenth-century sense of the term, which influenced the Bayonne constitution for his conquered Spanish kingdom. By the end of the century the traditionalist historian, Menéndez y Pelayo, noted the 'small number of liberals who for whatever laudable reason did not become Frenchified (*afrancesado*)'.[72]

In fact, a great deal of the 1812 project was a continuation of the enlightened absolutism of Carlos III. The liberals' cherishing of the 1520s' Comuneros was no more of a stretch than the conservatives' defence of the early modern *Volksgeist* of Crown and church as inspiration for their nineteenth-century national model.[73] Certainly, the constitution's authors had all defied the Inquisition in their youth to read works of the French Enlightenment, and as liberals all had made the clear break with eighteenth-century enlightened thinkers by recognising Spain's political structure as the cause for its decadence and economic problems.[74] A clear break would be impeded, the liberals believed, if the Cortes acceded to the demands made by such older men as Gaspar Jovellanos, Martín de Garay, and *Generalísimo* Wellington to introduce an upper chamber to moderate the legislative supremacy of the Cortes.[75] Wellington witheringly noted that 'the Cortes have engendered a Constitution on the principle that an artist paints a portrait for it to be admired and yet no admirer has come forward for this role'.[76] In exile, Blanco White wrote in vain that an upper chamber would help the grandees 'to become citizens rather than the people slaves'.[77] But unlike the Thermidorians in Revolutionary France whose experience of the unbridled national will led them after 1795 to limit popular sovereignty by dividing it into two parliamentary chambers, Spanish liberals had not (yet) experienced political terrorism, and they refused all entreaties to shift from the unicameral system to bicameralism.[78]

The constitution's abstract radicalism, heavily criticised by Blanco White,[79] clashed with the reality of entrenched local power networks (called *cacicazgos*). Suffrage was proclaimed for all Spanish males who could prove they had property and a livelihood. The vote was denied to women, servants, foreigners (even naturalised ones), gypsies, cloistered monks and nuns, non-resident soldiers, non-whites, and anyone without known occupation. Voters chose electors in a fourfold parish–provincial–regional–national college which culminated in an unpaid Cortes deputy at the end. Unsurprisingly, widespread illiteracy and the filter of elites ensured that there was no mass irruption of new blood either in the Cortes or in the diputaciones provincials (county councils) established by the constitution. Moreover, the constitution offered little protection for voters with grievances against their local authorities. Voting districts were the same as existing parish boundaries and traditional loyalties outweighed the new language of political rights. Although the constitution empowered citizens to protest malpractice at election times, complaints had to be registered with the local authorities themselves, whose decision was final and who also had the power to punish 'slanderers' if they were 'proved wrong'.[80] Thus constitutional municipalities, which enjoyed huge powers over policing and gaols, became the fiefdoms of *caciques* (local power brokers), a byword of nineteenth-century Spanish liberalism. The *cacique* was not invented in 1812. Municipal leaders had grown in power since the mid-eighteenth century, partly because of the capitalisation of agriculture.[81] But after 1812 attempts at state building usually ended up strengthening the power of the *caciques*. Only in the expanding cities could their grip be challenged. In the meantime, as one Zaragoza historian observes, 'everything had changed in order to remain the same'.[82]

The liberals hoped that mass literacy coupled with sermons about the constitution would inculcate a love for 'liberty with moderation' ('libertad bien entendida'). Article 25 therefore pledged to exclude from citizenship all those Spaniards who remained unable to read or write by 1830, with municipalities being granted powers of supervision (*superintendencia*) over primary schools in order to achieve mass literacy.[83] But resources were lacking to establish schools. By 1830, the dissident Blanco White predicted that only the 'village priest and the escribano (scrivener) would be citizens'.[84] In fact, the only sustainable indoctrination fell to the priests, in a paradoxical situation in which modern Spanish political culture was 'born in the churchyard'.[85] Given the reputation of the nineteenth-century church as a bulwark of reaction, this attempted union between church and constitution may seem surprising. Yet there was a vocal minority of reformist clerics who believed that the Spanish Church needed to change, even if they were outnumbered by traditionalists who thought that wicked man, not Mother Church, needed to change. One of the leading 'liberal' clerics was Joaquín Villanueva (1757–1837), who thought that the division between politics and religion was artificial and that the work of the liberals could be reconciled with Thomist ideas.[86]

There were also overwhelming practical reasons for sacralising the constitution via the parish priest. Priests usually held sway amongst their flock and did not have to be paid; the church was typically the only building suitable for use as a classroom; the methodology of catechism enjoyed a traditional pedigree in Catholic moral teaching; all Spaniards were expected to go to church, article 12 of the constitution laying down that Roman Catholicism was the only religion of the Spanish nation and forbidding the practice of any other; and, finally, harnessing the church as an agent of the state in this fashion served both to legitimise the constitution and publicly to subordinate the church to the civil power.[87] Catholicism thus continued to be the qualification for Spanish identity, even amidst the crumbling post-1810 empire. The first of the three levels of indirect Cortes elections were carried out by parish priests, who were also charged with reading out the constitution to those who could not read. Thus, both the implementation and indoctrination of the constitution were sacralised.[88] Yet with many priests unhappy about the constitution, it is hard to imagine how effective the process was, and in some places, the authorities tried to hire special teachers to take the place of the clergy. The liberal press complained of the indifference or hostility of the pulpits and tried its best to report on isolated evidence of liberal enthusiasm, such as the prefect of Soria who early in 1814 was greeted by 180 children who parroted in unison key articles of the constitution.[89] But the children's fathers would have seen the efforts of their teachers belied by the machinations of the *caciques*. Unsurprisingly, the constitution would receive little public support on the return of Fernando VII in 1814.

Even so, the new politics ushered in an era of agitation. Some agitators used words, such as learned men in the cities who lectured on the constitution and whom the king would banish after May 1814. Others agitated with deeds, such as the Pablo López, popularly called the 'Lame Man of Málaga' (el Cojo de Málaga) who despite his humble and provincial origins in Coín (Granada) became the ringleader of the Cortes viewing galleries and of the pro-liberal mobs that haunted the streets surrounding the seats of power in Cádiz and Madrid.[90] Agitators were supported by a thriving café culture, some liberal, others absolutist. At the Apolo café in Cádiz, a mock trial theatrically sentenced Ferdinand VII to death in absentia.[91] The growing absolutist opposition liked to link the ideas and fate of the Spanish liberals with the French Revolutionaries, a calculated insult in a time of war which inflamed press and street agitation even more. The removal of the capital in October 1813 from Cádiz to liberated Madrid was key. Liberals had resisted this move as long as possible, and Joaquín Villanueva even organised a street demonstration against it.

Amidst the agitation real radical ideas were emerging which would focus on popular access to the land, a problem deeply rooted in Spanish history. As Moorish Spain was gradually 'reconquered' over the course of the Middle Ages, vast swathes of land were given as entail (which could be neither bought nor sold) in perpetuity to the nobility, the church, and other institutions. This complex mix of jurisdictions and rights (*fueros*) provoked the ire of eighteenth-century enlightened absolutist monarchs who wanted to establish uniform regal control, and whose ministers strove to achieve this end. In 1767 Campomanes began a project aimed at settling deserted land under regal jurisdiction. The following year Olavide proposed reforms designed to improve access to the land, whilst by the 1790s, Jovellanos was urging the proto-liberal need to introduce a free market in land.[92] Even if these reforms achieved little in practice, the intellectual argument for 'disentailment' (*desamortización*) had been largely won by the time the post-1808 liberals set about freeing up property in earnest. Liberals associated the feudal regime with the arbitrary rule of Habsburg kings who usurped the liberty of Spain's medieval *pueblos*, a romantic view which was inspired by the 1520s' Revolt of the Comuneros. Some of the more socially minded liberals demanded that the 'people's war' they believed was being waged in Spain should be rewarded with some element of social reform. If medieval nobles had won feudal estates from the defeated Moors, so must the people win their lands from the defeated French.[93]

Thus, the tenuous link started to emerge that the war against Napoleon should be rewarded with social justice. In his 1813 *Discurso sobre la*

Constitución, the radical priest Juan Antonio Posse attacked the 'slavery' of the *minifundia* in Galicia, singling out particular contempt for the ecclesiastical estates of the bishops, abbots, and monks who thrived parasitically on feudal dues without bothering to undertake pastoral care in return.[94] The lowly born Romero Alpuente (1762–1835) shared this indignation.[95] The most firebrand enemy of the seigniorial regime at this stage was the radical deputy for Soria, Manuel García Herreros, who during 1813 argued in vain with an increasingly *servil* Cortes that the onus should be on feudal landowners to present title deeds in order to prove their territorial possession of their lands. But such 'social liberal' elites were on the sidelines. Although they got a decree in January 1813 which provided for the distribution of small parcels of land to persons without property, this was watered down by a sort of municipal bankruptcy and inertia which would become a byword for nineteenth-century liberalism, and in any case came too late to win over a liberal constituency in the countryside.[96]

These ideas were still a minority, but they had greater resonance as the liberation of Spain after 1812 uncovered a population broken by famine and depredations. French troops generally and Anglo-Portuguese troops on occasions when storming cities were prone to commit atrocities against Spanish civilians. Spanish guerrillas and civilians often responded in kind, convincing both French and British veterans of the 'barbarity' of Spanish culture.[97] Most French atrocities were conditioned by material want, as unlike in central Europe, French armies in Spain could not live off the land. Logistics turned to pillage, starving civilians who also faced Patriot exactions. Even supplies from France were held up by guerrilla actions, poor roads, and ineffective blockade running by sea.[98] Madrid, which was first liberated by the Allies in August 1812, was evacuated thereafter, and definitively brought back under Patriot control the following June, witnessed popular disorders on both these occasions. An *afrancesado* diarist recorded how the entry of the Anglo-Portuguese army during the summer of 1812 provoked a 'revolutionary excess of the lower class of corrupted and bitter men', who set about stealing from the well-to-do. The wealthy, in turn, tried to hide their fears as best they could by turning out to applaud the parade of the allies, trying to reassert their position in the face of the anarchy which the liberation had provoked amongst the starving underclass.[99] When the capital was liberated for the last and definitive time during June 1813, the Holland circle diarist John Russell was on hand to report an even more impressive upsurge of vigilantism: 'the houses of the Grandees have all had their furniture pillaged and spoilt'.[100] In addition to being starved in the famine of 1812, the popular classes of the capital had under *josefino* rule been subjected to the full rigours of Enlightenment bureaucracy, with increased taxation, restrictions on taverns, gaming houses, prostitution, bullfights, and public meetings, all popular pastimes.[101]

By the time that elections for the first 'ordinary' Cortes were held in 1813, almost all of Spain had been liberated by *Generalísimo* Wellington's army in coordination with the Spanish regular army and their increasingly militarised guerrilla adjuncts. The Battle of Vitoria (21 June 1813) broke the back of the French army. But liberation during 1813 did not lead to order, as the political situation was so chaotic that the only authority which could be imposed was by force of arms. Thus, any sort of civilian administration, let alone elections, was frequently compromised by the activities of both guerrilla bands and troops. This chaos persisted despite Napoleon's release of Ferdinand back into Spain at the end of 1813: the Treaty of Valençay by which Napoleon hoped to extricate himself from Spain and persuade the Spanish to jettison their British allies.

As politics expanded beyond the liberal hothouse of Cádiz, the anti-liberal conservatives (pejoratively dubbed *serviles*) grew in influence both within and without the Cortes. One associate of the activist Pablo López complained that 'since the French have been thrown out of Castile, so many new deputies have entered the Cortes, and everything has been beset by contradictions to the effect that we've been losing much of the ground we had won'.[102] Many *serviles* wanted not absolutism in the eighteenth-century 'enlightened' sense; rather, many (or most, going by the signatories to the 1814 Manifesto) wanted to abolish not just the reforms of the liberals but also the eighteenth-century system of 'ministerial despotism' preceding it. In the words of the traditionalist historian Javier Herrero, in doing so they were 'denying the political conceptions of both Enlightenment and Liberalism'.[103] The bishop of Orense, who in 1810 resigned from the Regency Council in protest at the advance of liberal ideas, attacked the Constitution of 1812 for making the king and his successors 'vassals' of the Nation.[104]

The closing months of the constitutional regime would thus see a rise in *servil* agitation as placards were posted around Galicia which condemned liberal land reforms in the name of the king. *Serviles* also hired soldiers to sow division in the Cortes galleries, which had, of course, long been considered the bastion of the López radicals.[105] Indeed, the growing *servil* composition of the Cortes meant that the López radicals were regularly barred from entering the spectator galleries in the first place, as secret sessions, both at Cádiz and later at Madrid, became increasingly common. Although this prerogative was supposed to be granted only in matters of war or peace, alliances, subsidies, and special commercial treaties (articles 171 and 131 of the constitution), Romero Alpuente, for one, could see the writing on the wall. Attacking the secret sessions in the most populist manner, he claimed the two-hundred-odd deputies to be answerable to twenty thousand *Madrileños*, and beyond the capital millions of Spaniards who relied on the diffusion of Cortes debates in order to mould their opinions and celebrate their hard-fought liberty. Catechistically answering the charge that privacy allows more freedom for debate, Romero Alpuente betrayed the hostility to pluralism which remained a feature of Spanish radical liberalism: 'yes, there is more freedom; but it is freedom for fools and rogues'.[106]

As the Torenian liberals began to lose their command of the Cortes, all the more did they rely on the street to defend their programme. Thus, Madrid soon became the haunt of political gangs. In practice, this saw the Fontana de Oro, Lorencini, and Fonda de Malta become the headquarters of popular radicalism, whilst López himself commanded large daily crowds which assembled at a spot in the Puerta del Sol known as the Mayoral to hear his rousing oratory in defence of liberty and the constitution.[107] Furthermore, his radicals hired him a band of musicians who would punctuate his oratory with patriotic tunes whilst also accompanying him on patrols of the capital, including regular visits to the residence of the Duke of Medinaceli. Medinaceli was the greatest landowner in Spain, and his retainers resented this plebeian show of strength which recalled the sacking of property during the June 1813 liberation of the capital.[108] Even if the *serviles* were beginning to assert themselves in the Cortes, they still had to face the street outside: when in February 1814 the Seville deputy Juan López Reina made a speech defending the absolute kingship of Fernando VII, he moderated his tone not in response to the usual barracking from the gallery, but because he feared being lynched.[109] Thus, *serviles* were being terrorised in the streets, as any deputies who voiced strident opinions in the Cortes were being harassed when they left the building and followed home by underlings who would then disclose their new Madrid addresses to the López radicals.[110] The doors of hostile deputies would then soon ring to the cries of *mueras* just as surely as their liberal opponents would be serenaded by *vivas* courtesy of the oratory band. In response, and emboldened by the release of Fernando from French captivity, the *serviles* unleashed counter-mobs which roamed the streets of the capital shouting 'Long Live the King!' and 'Death to the *Cojo de Málaga*'.[111]

At least some of the liberal deputies themselves appear to have had forebodings that the crowd might seriously get out of control.[112] As signs grew during March and April that the king wanted to overthrow the constitutional régime, there was even an ephemeral stirring of explicitly republican agitation in the liberal press – including talk of civil war – as the deputy for Cuenca boasted that there were 'hundreds of daggers in Madrid' and 'ten thousand soldiers under arms in Cádiz' to defend the constitution.[113] But as the ten thousand soldiers under arms in Cádiz had no love for a liberal regime which had starved and belittled them, they therefore backed the coup. But they did so in the teeth of popular protests organised – according to one foreign observer – by a 'demagogue shoemaker' who rallied the audience at a *zarzuela* which, wistfully remembering the luxuries and power of their city when it was the bastion of free Europe, was 'outrageous' all night.[114] Fortunately, no blood was shed, although this tense spectacle of López radicals reaching out to the crowd was mirrored elsewhere. Thus, the *tertulias* of Valencia continued to thrive right under the king's nose as he lingered in that city with *servil* elites plotting the anti-constitutional coup. The radicals thereby made themselves conspicuous enough as to be marked out for easy arrest when the swoop on the cafés was ordered on 4 May. This *servil* act ended up making martyrs out of demagogues who had been a fixture of street life for several months.[115]

The years 1808–1814 had thus transformed Spain politically even more than they did militarily. Uniquely in Napoleonic Europe, Spain had been subjected to two concurrent processes of political reform. What made Spain unique was that both processes took place concurrently, as occupied Spain was subjected to Napoleonic reforms, on one hand, and Patriot Spain to liberal reforms, on the other.[116] The military failure of Napoleon's Spanish colony sent large numbers of 'Frenchfied' (*afrancesado*) collaborators into exile. Some 79 per cent of public officials and almost a quarter of army officers were *afrancesado* and accordingly went into exile in France from 1813.[117] But there were four kinds of collaborator in descending order of culpability. At the top were the *josefinos*, actively choosing to collaborate, as was the case with the intellectual and later *moderado* Alberto Lista (1775–1848) and the geographer, Sebastián de Miñano (1779–1845). Then came the 'sworn' (*'juramentado'*) collaborators who swore oaths of allegiance to the Josephine regime in order to continue exercising public offices. Then there were 'passive' collaborators who did not seek public office and, finally, the likes of shopkeepers and prostitutes trying to survive during temporary or long-standing French occupation.[118] Needless to say, the triumphant royalist press damned them all as 'traitors' and 'instruments of all horrors committed in Spain'.[119] To the human devastation, including perhaps as many as four hundred thousand soldiers and civilians killed,[120] was thus added the bitter memory of collaboration, and none of this legacy could be papered over by any popular peace dividend. Military victory for Patriot Spain came at a huge social, economic, and political cost. The king's coup of 4 May 1808 was an absolutist 'power grab without parallel in Europe'.[121] For all its initial popularity, the socioeconomic calamities facing his war-torn kingdom meant that Ferdinand's popularity would fade.

Notes

1 Laura Rodríguez, 'The Spanish Riots of 1766', *Past and Present*, No. 59 (May 1973), pp. 117–46.
2 Earl of Ilchester (ed.), *The Spanish Journal of Elizabeth Lady Holland (1791–1811)* (London: Longman, Greens and CO., 1909), pp. 85–124.
3 *Ibid.*, pp. 42–4, 134–5.
4 Charles Esdaile, 'The Spanish Army', in Frederick Schneid (ed.), *European Armies of the French Revolutionary Wars* (Norman, OK: University of Oklahoma Press, 2015), pp. 151–8.
5 César Herráiz de Miota, 'Los montepíos militares del siglo XVIII como origen del sistema de clases pasivas del estado', *Revista del Ministerio del Trabajo y Asuntos Sociales*, Vol. 56 (January 2005), pp. 107–208.
6 Esdaile, 'The Spanish Army', in Schneid (ed.), *European Armies*, pp. 159–62.
7 *Ibid.*, pp. 164–79; Linda Colley, *Britons: Forging the Nation, 1707–1837* (New Haven: Yale University Press, 1992); Alvarez-Junco, *Mater Dolorosa: la idea de España en el siglo XIX* (Madrid: Taurus, 2001).

8   Lluís Roura i Aulinas, 'Jacobinos y jacobinismo en los primeros momentos de la revolución liberal española', in Lluís Roura i Aulinas and Irene Castells (eds.), *Revolución y democracia: el jacobinismo europeo* (Madrid: Ediciones del Orto, 1995), pp. 55–84.

9   Antonio Moliner Prada, 'La conflictividad social en la Guerra de la Independencia', *Trienio: Ilustración y Liberalismo* (Madrid, May 2000), pp. 81–4.

10 Manuel Ardit Lucas, *Revolución liberal y revuelta campesina* (Barcelona: Ariel, 1977), pp. 98–102.

11 Ilchester (ed.), *Spanish Journal*, p. 28.

12 Antonio Moliner Prada, 'La conflicitividad social', *Trienio* (May 2000), p. 84; 'La España de finales del siglo XVIII y la crisis de 1808', in Antonio Moliner Prada (ed.), *La Guerra de la Inependencia en España (1808–1814)* (Barcelona: Nabla Ediciones, 2007), p. 46.

13 Cit. Moliner Prada, 'La España de finales del siglo XVIII', in Moliner Prada (ed.), *La Guerra de la Independencia*, p. 50.

14 José María Queipo de Llano (Conde de Toreno), *Historia del levantamiento, guerra y revolución de España* (Madrid: Imprenta de Berenguillo, 1953), pp. 23–9.

15 *Ibid.*, p. 27.

16 S.J.L., Joseph Blanco White, *Letters from Spain by D. Leucadio Doblado*, Spec B. W., VII, L65 (1822), Letter XII (Seville, 25 July 1808), pp. 389–420.

17 *Ibid.*, pp. 401–4.

18 E. P. Thompson, *Customs in Common* (London: Penguin, 1993).

19 Queipo de Llano (Conde de Toreno), *Historia del levantamiento*, pp. 40–41.

20 *Ibid.*, p. 56.

21 Antonio Alcalá Galiano, *Memorias de D. Antonio Alcalá Galiano*, Vol. I (Madrid: Imprenta de Enrique Rubiños, 1886), pp. 193–5.

22 Arturo Pérez-Reverte, *Un día de cólera* (Madrid: Debolsillo, 2007).

23 Juan Romero Alpuente, *El grito de la razón al español invencible* (Zaragoza, 1808), p. 19.

24 Manuel Moreno Alonso, *La revolución 'santa' de Sevilla (la revuelta popular de 1808)* (Sevilla: Caja San Fernando de Sevilla y Jerez, 1997), pp. 20–1.

25 Moliner Prada, 'La conflictividad social', p. 94.

26 Alcalá Galiano, *Memorias*, Vol. I, pp. 167–9.

27 White, *Letters from Spain*, pp. 411–12.

28 Francisco Javier Maestrojuán Catalán, *Ciudad de vasallos, Nación de heroes (Zaragoza: 1809–1814)* (Zaragoza: Institución 'Fernando el Católico', 2003), pp. 71, 300.

29 Moliner Prada, 'La conflictividad social', pp. 84–8.

30 Queipo de Llano (Conde de Toreno), *Historia del levantamiento*, pp. 44–5; White, *Letters from Spain*, pp. 414–15.

31 Charles J. Esdaile, *The Peninsular War: A New History* (London: Penguin, 2003), pp. 49–51.

32 Queipo de Llano (Conde de Toreno), *Historia del levantamiento*, pp. 72–3.

33 Moreno Alonso, *La revolución "santa"*, pp. 50–3.

34 White, *Letters from Spain*, p. 432.

35 *Ibid.*, p. 430; Barring Madrid and Valencia, Toreno estimated the death count in May and June not to have exceeded thirty (Queipo de Llano (Conde de Toreno), *Historia del levantamiento*, p. 79), although the "private pique and revenge" identified by Blanco White almost certainly meant that the deaths of undistinguished victims went unreported.

36 Queipo de Llano (Conde de Toreno), *Historia del levantamiento*, pp. 72–3; Charles Oman, *A History of the Peninsular War*, Vol. I (London, 1902, reprinted London: Greenhill Books, 2004), pp. 67–8.

37 Oman, *A History of the Peninsular War*, pp. 60–71; Gabriel Lovett held that "The Spanish people needed leadership, and leadership was not provided by the institutions which should have supplied it" (Gabriel Lovett, *Napoleon and the Birth of Modern Spain: The Challenge to the Old Order*, Vol. I (New York: New York University Press, 1965), p. 152.

38 White, *Letters from Spain*, p. 432.

39 Queipo de Llano (Conde de Toreno), *Historia del levantamiento*, p. 79.
40 Cit. Maestrojuán Catalán, *Ciudad de vasallos, Nación de heroes (Zaragoza: 1809–1814)*, pp. 12–16.
41 Alcalá Galiano, *Memorias*, Vol. I, p. 23.
42 Esdaile, *Peninsular War*, pp. 165–6, 215–21.
43 Cit. W. N. Hargreaves-Mawdsley (ed.), *Spain Under the Bourbons, 1700–1833: A Collection of Documents* (Palgrave Macmillan: London, 1973), pp. 217–25.
44 Queipo de Llano (Conde de Toreno), *Historia del levantamiento*, p. 135.
45 Moreno Alonso, *La Junta Suprema de Sevilla* (Sevilla: Ediciones Alfar, 2001), pp. 251–66, 293.
46 José Jiménez Guerrero, *El reclutamiento militar en el siglo XIX: las quintas de Málaga (1837–1868)* (Málaga: Fundación Unicaja, 2001), p. 3.
47 Valentina Fernández Vargas, *Las militares españolas: un nuevo grupo profesional* (Madrid: Biblioteca Nueva, 1997), pp. 37–40.
48 A.H.N., Estado 52-A, No. 85: 12 November 1808 anonymous complaint to Junta Central of popular disorders.
49 A.H.N., Estado 52-E, No. 256: 30 December 1808 complaint to Junta Central.
50 Alcalá Galiano, *Memorias*, Vol. I, pp. 226–32; Queipo de Llano (Conde de Toreno), *Historia del levantamiento*, pp. 176–8; Esdaile, *Peninsular War*, pp. 172–3.
51 Cit. Hargreaves-Mawdsley (ed.), *Spain Under the Bourbons*, pp. 229–30.
52 Ian Fletcher (ed.), *For King and Country: The Letters and Diaries of John Mills, Coldstream Guards. 1811–14* (Staplehurst: Spellmount Publishers, 1995), pp. 58, 63.
53 Antonio Moliner Prada, *La guerrilla en la Guerra de la Independencia* (Madrid: Colección Adalid, 2004), pp. 15–32.
54 Ronald Fraser, *La maldita guerra de España* (Barcelona: Crítica, 2006).
55 Charles J. Esdaile, *Fighting Napoleon: Guerrillas, Bandits and Adventurers in Spain 1808–1814* (London: Yale University Press, 2004).
56 Charles J. Esdaile, 'Patriots, Partisans and Land Pirates in Retrospect', in Esdaile (ed.), *Popular Resistance* (Basingstoke: Palgrave Macmillan, 2008), pp. 1–22.
57 Moliner Prada, *La guerrilla en la Guerra de la Independencia*, pp. 164–74.
58 *El Robespierre Español (Amigo de las Leyes ó Questiones Atrevidas sobre la España)*, 3 April 1811, pp. 25–7.
59 Cit. Ricardo García Cárcel, *El sueño de la nación indomable: los mitos de la Guerra de la Independencia* (Madrid: Temas de Hoy, 2007), p. 142.
60 *Semanario Político, Histórico y Literario de la Coruña* (henceforth *SPHLC*), No. 36, pp. 843–50, published in María Rosa Saurin de la Iglesia (ed.), *Manuel Pardo de Andrade: Semanario Político, Histórico y Literario de la Coruña (1809–1810)*, Vol. II (La Coruña: edición facsímile, Fundación Pedro Barrie de la Maza, 1996).
61 Ever since the 1 January 1809 regulations had curtailed its powers, the Junta of Seville had been involved in several conspiracies to overthrow the Central, even if success had to wait until the military collapse of January 1810 (Alonso, *Junta Suprema de Sevilla*, pp. 275–93).
62 Queipo de Llano (Conde de Toreno), *Historia del levantamiento*, p. 238; a conservative Junta member, Riquelme, was forced by an angry crowd to seek refuge on a Spanish frigate, only to meet his death when this ship came under French battery-fire en route to Cádiz.
63 Queipo de Llano (Conde de Toreno), *Historia del levantamiento*, p. 240; *El Robespierre Español*, 2 January 1812, pp. 337–52.
64 Rodríguez O., *"We are now the True Spaniards"*, pp. 38–60.
65 Natalia Sobrevilla, 'How (Not) to Make a Durable State', in Ginger and Lawless (eds.), *Spain in the Nineteenth Century*, pp. 20–1.
66 Charles J. Esdaile, *Outpost of Empire: The Napoleonic Occupation of Andalucíam, 1810–1812* (Oklahoma: Oklahoma University Press, 2012), pp. 30–1.
67 Miguel Artola, *Los afrancesados* (Madrid: Editorial Turner, 1976), p. 42; Irene Castells and Antonio Moliner, *Crisis del antiguo régimen y revolución liberal en España (1789–1845)* (Barcelona: Ariel, 2000), p. 73.

68 Queipo de Llano (Conde de Toreno), *Historia del levantamiento*, pp. 246–47; García Cárcel, *Sueño de la nación*, p. 190; Michael Ross, *The Reluctant King: Joseph Bonaparte, King of the Two Sicilies and Spain* (London: Sidgwick and Jackson, 1976), pp. 191–4; Michael Glover, *Legacy of Glory: The Bonaparte Kingdom of Spain* (New York: Leo Cooper, 1971), pp. 161–4.

69 Francisco J. Hernández Montalbán, *La abolición de los señoríos en España (1811–1837)* (Madrid: Biblioteca Nueva, 1999), pp. 95–155.

70 *Ibid.*; All but one of the Valencian Cortes deputies had voted for the abolition decree, the exception being the traditionalist, Francisco Javier Borrull (1745–1838) who objected to its liberal premise that sovereignty lay essentially in the nation (Ardit Lucas, *Revolución liberal*, pp. 70, 162–168).

71 Hernández Montalbán, *Abolición de los Señoríos*, pp. 178–81.

72 Marichal, *El secreto de España*, pp. 42–3.

73 Gregorio Alonso, 'The Crisis of the Old Regime, 1808–33', in Shubert and Alvarez-Junco (eds.), *The History of Modern Spain*, p. 18; Xosé M. Núñez Seixas, 'Nation and Nationalism', in Shubert and Álvarez-Junco (eds.), *The History of Modern Spain*, pp. 148–9.

74 Castells and Moliner, *Crisis del antiguo régimen y revolución liberal en España (1789–1845)*, p. 41.

75 Queipo de Llano (Conde de Toreno), *Historia del levantamiento*, pp. 282–4.

76 García Cárcel, *El sueño de la nación indomable*, p. 154.

77 Manuel Moreno Alonso, *Blanco White: la obsesión de España* (Sevilla: Ediciones Alfar, 1998), p. 474.

78 François Furet, *Revolutionary France, 1770–1880* (Oxford: Oxford University Press, 1992), p. 165.

79 Moreno Alonso, *Blanco White*, p. 470.

80 Pilar Chavarri Sidera, *Las elecciones de diputados a las Cortes Generales y Extraordinarias (1810–1813)* (Madrid: Centro de Estudios Constitucionales, 1988), p. 15.

81 Fernández, *El orígen del municipio constitucional*, pp. 155–8, 175–80.

82 Francisco Javier Maestrojuán, 'El período liberal y el regreso de Fernando VII', in *La Guerra de la Independencia en el Valle Medio del Ebro* (Segundo curso de verano de Tudela 9 al 13 de Julio de 2001, Ayuntamiento de Tudela, Universidad SEK de Segovia), p. 238.

83 Queipo de Llano (Conde de Toreno), *Historia del levantamiento*, pp. 386–93.

84 Cit., Antonio Viñao (ed.), *José María Blanco White sobre educación* (Madrid: Biblioteca Nueva, 2003), pp. 209–19.

85 Sobrevilla, 'How (Not) to Make a Durable State', in Ginger and Lawless (eds.), *Spain in the Nineteenth Century*, p. 23.

86 Gregorio Alonso, 'How to Be Religious Under Liberalism', in Ginger and Lawless (eds.), *Spain in the Nineteenth Century*, pp. 90–1; William J. Callahan, *Church, Politics and Society in Spain, 1750–1874* (Cambridge: Harvard University Press, 1984), p. 80.

87 Queipo de Llano (Conde de Toreno), *Historia del levantamiento*, pp. 385, 453.

88 Alonso, 'How to Be Religious Under Liberalism', in Ginger and Lawless (eds.), *Spain in the Nineteenth Century*, pp. 89–90.

89 *El Universal*, 25 February 1814.

90 Federico Suárez, *Las Cortes de Cádiz* (Madrid, 2002), pp. 195–6, f. 8; Alberto Gil Novales (ed.), *Juan Romero Alpuente: historia de la revolución española y otros escritos*, Vol. I (Madrid: Centro de Estudios Constitucionales, 1989), pp. 305, 453; *Manifiesto de la conducta y servicios hechos a la patria en el tiempo de nuestra gloriosa revolución, por Pablo López* (Madrid, 1814).

91 Mark Lawrence, 'Popular Radicalism in Spain, 1808–1844' (unpublished PhD thesis, University of Liverpool, 2008), pp. 55–6.

92 Castells and Moliner, *Crisis del antiguo régimen y revolución liberal en España (1789–1845)*, p. 25.

93 Hernández Montalbán, *Abolición de los señoríos*, p. 53.

94 Cit., Richard Herr (ed.), *Memorias del cura liberal don Juan Antonio Posse con su discurso sobre la Constitución de 1812* (Madrid: Centro de Investigaciones Sociológicas, 1984), pp. 260–1. The growth both in population and a market economy in agriculture in Galicia

during the second half of the eighteenth century had resulted in shrinking plots and higher rents. The nature of landownership in 'Spain's Ireland' was complicated by the fact that this process of subdivision was accompanied by purchases by the middle classes and wealthier peasants of rental properties nominally held by the aristocracy, and by speculation on ever-shrinking plots.

95 Gil Novales (ed.), *Juan Romero Alpuente.*
96 Lovett, *Napoleon and the Birth of Modern Spain*, Vol. II, pp. 442–3.478.
97 Gavin Daly, '"Barbarity More Suited to Savages": British Soldiers' Views of Spanish and Portuguese Violence During the Peninsular War, 1808–1814', *War and Society*, Vol. 35, No. 4 (October 2016), pp. 242–58; Philip G. Dwyer, 'It Still Makes Me Shudder: Memories of Massacres and Atrocities during the Revolutionary and Napoleonic Wars', *War in History*, Vol. 16, No.4 (2009).
98 John Morgan (2009), 'War Feeding War? The Impact of Logistics upon the Occupation of Catalonia', *Journal of Military History*, Vol. 73, No. 1 (2009).
99 B.U.Z., Faustino Casamayor, Años políticos e históricos de las cosas más particulares ocurridas en la Imperial Augusta y siempre heróica Ciudad de Zaragoza, Tomo XXIX, 1812: 28 August 1812 letter from R. N y N to Casamayor.
100 British Library, Ms Add. 51626: 16 July 1813 letter from John Russell to Lord Holland.
101 Esdaile, *Peninsular War*, pp. 240–2.
102 A.H.N., Consejos (*Causas de Estado*), leg. 6291–92: letter from Francisco Colombo to Angel Guzmán.
103 Javier Herrero, *Los orígenes del pensamiento reaccionario español* (Madrid: Alianza, 1973), p. 383.
104 Pedro Rújula, 'El mito contrarrevolucionario de la Restauración', *Pasado y Memoria*, Vol. 13 (2014), pp. 79–94, 84–5.
105 Cit., Queipo de Llano (Conde de Toreno), *Historia del levantamiento*, p. 504; *El Universal Observador Español*, 17 February 1814; 18 February 1814; *El Ciudadano por la Constitución*, 10 April 1814; 14 April 1814; 17 April 1814.
106 Romero Alpuente, *Pensamientos diversos sobre la conservación y felicidad de la patria* (Granada, 1814), pp. 8–10.
107 A.C., *Causas*, López: report of Relaño, in Escariche.
108 A.C., *Causas*, López: 29 May 1814 testimony of Antonio Abades, in Escariche.
109 Queipo de Llano (Conde de Toreno), *Historia del levantamiento*, p. 504.
110 A.C., *Causas*, López: Escariche.
111 A.C., *Causas*, López: 30 May-1 June 1814 testimony of Pablo López, in Escariche.
112 A.H.N., Consejos (*Causas de Estado*), leg. 6290/2, No. 128: 3 August 1815 testimony of Fadeo Ganate, López radical.
113 A.H.N., Consejos (*Causas de Estado*), leg. 6291–92, No. 118: 22 December 1814 testimony of former mayor, José Gervarco Escobar, in proceedings against Nicolás García Page.
114 C. Leslie, *Military Journal of Colonel Leslie of Balquhain* (Aberdeen: Aberdeen University Press, 1887), pp. 254–6.
115 A.H.N., Consejos (*Causas de Estado*), leg. 6295, No. 1: Case against Valencia deputy, Antonio Larrazábal (1815).
116 Charles Esdaile, 'Enlightened Absolutism Versus Theocracy in Spain, 1814–50', in David Laven and Lucy Riall (eds.), *Napoleon's Legacy* (Oxford: Berg, 2000), p. 66.
117 Castells and Moliner, *Crisis del antiguo régimen y revolución liberal en España (1789–1845)*, p. 73.
118 Claude Morange, 'Sebastián de Miñano durante la Guerra de la Independencia', *Trienio*, No. 35 (May 2000, Madrid), pp. 44–5.
119 Antonio Calvo Maturana, 'Como si no hubiesen pasado jamás tales actos', in Encarna García Monerris, Mónica Moreno Seco, and Juan I. Marcuello Benedicto (eds.), *Culturas políticas en la España liberal: discursos, representaciones y prácticas (1808–1902)* (Valencia: Universitat de València, 2013), p. 41.
120 Ronald Fraser, *Napoleon's Cursed War* (London: Verso, 2008), p. 624.
121 Rújula, 'El mito contrarrevolucionario de la Restauración', pp. 79–94, 80.

Chapter 2

1814–33: crisis of legitimacy

This chapter explains how and why the restoration of absolutism in 1814 failed to restore any consensus about the nature of legitimate power in Spain. The much-lionised King Ferdinand rejected both the recent 'Frenchified' and Patriot liberal projects for reform whilst also more subtly rejecting reactionary demands to reverse eighteenth-century enlightened absolutism. Post-war Spain faced a series of *pronunciamientos* – military interventions in politics – launched by officers mainly for careerist reasons but claiming to represent the Spanish 'nation'. Although most revolts failed, the Riego conspiracy at the end of 1819 was a success, with King Ferdinand being forced to restore the Constitution of 1812. The subsequent three years of liberal rule (the 'Triennium') brought into sharp focus all the strains of Spain's post-Napoleonic era. A profound liberal programme of reform clashed with a ruralised and regionalised traditionalist backlash, turning into outright civil war between 1821 and 1823. Spain's 'liberal imperialism' failed to reconcile the Americas to reformed Spanish rule, and Spanish affairs became once more centre stage in European diplomacy. The Holy Alliance invasion of Spain in 1823 ended Spain's liberal regime and restored the king to his absolute powers. What followed was the 'Ominous Decade', a crucial period during which the state tentatively modernised its political and economic structure amidst an ongoing economic depression while repressing the domestic and exiled challenge from liberalism, on one hand, and an ultra-royalist movement growing around the king's heir apparent, Prince Carlos (hence the term *Carlism*), on the other.

The absolutist Sexenio

Victory in 1814 exposed the weakness in Spain's international position. Spanish diplomacy floundered around the signing of the armistice with France on 23 April 1814. Spain's patent second-power status was compounded by political upheaval and by plenipotentiary Pedro Gómez Labrador's (1755–1852) subordination to the more capable Talleyrand over the sideshow issue of restoring the Bourbon 'legitimacy' in France, Italy, and Spain. Spain's lacklustre rearmament during the 'Hundred Days' marginalised Madrid even more. Once the full Congress met at Vienna in June 1815, Spain had been formally demoted from proceedings, as Europe's fate was decided by the well-connected Castelreagh, the conservative chancellor Metternich, and the victorious sword arm of reaction Tsar Alexander I.[1] Britain winked at Portugal–Brazil's occupation of Uruguay in 1816 and at the 1818 Congress of Aix-la-Chapelle (Aachen), Spain failed to get the Concert of Europe to agree to extend its protection of 'legitimacy' to the Americas.[2]

Prospects in 1814 appeared to be much better for Ferdinand's monarchy in Spain itself. Neither the army nor the people had risen to defend the constitutional regime. Indeed, the returning king was positively mobbed by ecstatic crowds which saw in him some palliative for all the suffering they had endured during the previous six years and before. The liberal leaders of the Cortes were imprisoned, banished, or condemned to death (Toreno, Argüelles) *in absentia*. A few López radicals who dared appeal to the streets quickly regretted their actions. Ángel Guzmán cried, 'Long Live the Constitution!' and 'Death to the king if he doesn't swear it!' His accomplice was arrested and Guzmán fled.[3] Wellington's brother, Henry Wellesley, was British ambassador in Madrid. He reported that royalist sentiment was so overwhelming that Ferdinand could not have accepted the constitution even if he had wanted.[4] Popular royalism swept Spain. A Zaragoza diarist recorded the festive atmosphere of May 1814: smashed constitution plaques, cheering at news of political detentions in Madrid, and three days of illuminated windows in deference to the king.[5]

For all the celebrations, only liberals and afrancesados felt the sharp end of restored absolutism. Most local elites could remain in their posts. Ferdinand's 30 July decree ordering the dissolution of the constitutional town halls and their replacement by those extant in 1808 was hedged around with enough qualifications and impracticalities as to ensure that no change of important personnel took place.[6] The *caciques* were relieved and a repeat of the chaos of 1808 seemed remote.

In theory, the re-imposition of absolutism cancelled all the acts of the Cortes, including, the August 1811 'abolition' of feudal jurisdictions. What in Restoration France would have been an impossibly provocative step was taken in Spain with the stroke of a quill. Yet all was not as it seemed. The judicial rights of the *señores* were never restored. In theory, villagers could seek to secure exemption from paying dues by presenting evidence of usurpation. In practice, much of the Cortes's agrarian reforms survived into absolutism. Even wartime buyers of church lands disentailed during the Cortes period tended to remain in possession of them. Ferdinand was loth to set a precedent which might embolden traditionalists to demand the reversal of Godoy's *desamortización*, too. Local oligarchs were therefore left in peace by the authorities. Peace was not on offer for the rural masses, however, who had to suffer acute poverty and often responded with banditry, tearing noble insignia from churches, refusing feudal dues, and making weapons out of tools.[7] In fact, in some ways, the situation was even worse. Spain underwent a renewed spate of diseases and famine, whilst the Justice Ministry was deluged with unsatisfied requests for land debt relief from small landowners, municipalities, and large feudal lords.[8] Property actions were eased by the actions of highly bribable scriveners (*escribanos*), a literate and unpopular figure in Spanish village life. French writer, Louis Viardot, discovered the proverb making the escribano the Spanish bogeyman: 'Go hide the cow, children! The escribano's coming!'[9]

Thus, for all the festivities of 1814, the coming of Fernando VII brought with it huge expectations of change which went unfulfilled. This feeling of popular entitlement was expressed by Quintana in a letter to Lord Holland:

> Less than 20 months after the King's arrival, enthusiasm for him had been replaced by despondency and anxiety. It was indeed bitter to reflect that nothing had changed for the better after such a bloody defence against Napoleon whilst Spaniards were bound to regret the loss of an order they had made no attempt to preserve, and subsequent plots showed a recognition of the need for change which could be felt in the air.[10]

Meanwhile, the social and cultural shocks of war drive the Spanish Church to adopt an unbending attitude towards political reform. The church, which chose to see in Spain's ills a legacy of the 'atheism' and 'Jacobinism' of the extinguished liberal order, launched sermons to combat this disorder which also contained thinly veiled condemnations of the growth in prostitution. Traditional attitudes bristled at the innumerable widows and girl orphans walking the streets unaccompanied by men. Women, who during the war had entered the public sphere in charitable activities, correspondence clubs with British admirers, and even in fighting, joined their mutilated menfolk as visible victims of war.[11] Royal decrees urged priests to proselytise in *pueblos* in order to 'correct the vices introduced during the war' and to 'moralise public customs'.[12] Thus, in Zaragoza a priest warned his flock against the 'perverse doctrines which, in the past, years have unfortunately degraded our customs, encouraged vice, and banished us from the love of God'.[13]

The post-war association of church authorities with policing awakened Spanish popular culture's normally dormant anti-clericalism. Thus, the hypocritical practices of Spanish Catholicism (such as the use of mistresses, or *barraganas*, by priests) which might have been overlooked by their flocks before now began to degrade the church in their eyes. Beyond this, anti-clericalism was also stirred by the activities of the Holy Inquisition (abolished in January 1813 and resurrected after the coup). Curiously, for all its 'black legend' infamy, the Inquisition was hardly a focus of popular ire before 1808. It was the enlightened elites, who, frustrated by decades of indiscriminate censorship of the works of the eighteenth-century *philosophes*, drove through its abolition in the Cortes of 1812–13.[14] But after 1814, the Inquisition, which had long ceased to attract the best and brightest clerics, became another arm of the police state. It maintained for this purpose, as one liberal fugitive discovered during his 1817 flight from Murcia to France, 'an active agent in every single village in the realm'.[15]

In fact, the Restoration police state was sustained by much more than the Inquisition. As befits an era in which elites were terrified by the prospect of losing control of public spaces, the captain generals used both spy networks and harsh police measures to maintain order in urban environments and forestall liberal conspiracies. Unpopular *Reglamentos de Policía* carved up towns and cities into easily watched suburbs.[16] The authorities frequently intervened to close taverns, restrict the sale of intoxicating liquors, establish curfews, and monitor the transit of outsiders. Thus Captain General Palafox was concerned enough by the movements in Zaragoza of 'persons hostile to order and disaffected with our sovereign' to tighten up the traditional passport system, whilst café owners were ordered on pain of imprisonment to report all 'secret meetings . . . and conversations hostile to order and the system of government'.[17] This move was followed up by a decision which had already been taken in other provinces, namely the creation of a secret police service of paid informants.[18]

The only hope of breaking the police state and the Inquisition lay with disaffected army officers launching *pronunciamientos*. Liberal historians have viewed these first *pronunciamientos* as evidence of generational and class conflict within the army.[19] Conservative historians, by contrast, stress the careerist motivations behind the *pronunciamientos*.[20] Elite conspiracies, such as the 1817 regicidal 'Richart plot' were penetrated with comparative ease. Espoz y Mina, the most successful guerrilla commander of the Peninsular War, hoped that he would be rewarded. But his hope of becoming Viceroy of Navarra was rebuffed by the king, and Espoz rebelled in the name of the Constitution of 1812. But his rising failed and he fled into exile. Juan Díaz Porlier in 1815 achieved some civilian support in his Galicia rising but was executed all the same.[21] Lacy's 1817 rising in Barcelona failed to gain support as the populace remembered his wartime role in a botched a mine explosion which killed several dozen civilians and as the church stepped in to pay the wages of loyal troops.[22] Frustrated veterans, for all their Masonic networks, could barely hope to command anything like the same sort of intelligence, nor instil the same degree of fear, as the absolutist state. Valencia's captain general, Francisco Javier de Elío, maintained spy networks that doomed Colonel Vidal's rising. Two of Vidal's accomplices who escaped the scene of his execution, wearing masks and on horseback, encountered a muleteer whose politics (liberal or absolutist) they demanded to know. The man replied, 'I'm whichever is the most convenient', before the masked riders left him in peace.[23]

The Fernandine state seemed secure. Pablo López, the ringleader of the Cortes viewing galleries, was publicly condemned to death by garrotting, immediately before his sentence was commuted to solitary confinement in a piece of political stagecraft which won over the public's pity.[24] The state was hardly threatened by such inchoate protests as peasants refusing to pay noble dues or students in Santiago rioting in February 1819 at the absolutist overtones surrounding the queen's funeral.[25]

Disaffection and disorders did, however, exacerbate the economic crisis facing the post-war Spanish monarchy. The burden of funding the army never ceased thanks to requirements to sustain the royalist counter-insurgency in Spanish America and to reinforce the Pyrenees during the 'Hundred Days' of Napoleon's 1815 return from Elba. The widows of army officers killed in action suffered as the cash-strapped military life insurance founded in the 1760s ('Monte Pío') could make only intermittent payments.[26] The regime found itself making the same excessive and unpopular demands as its predecessor, namely taxation and conscription. Most ominously, Martín de Garay introduced in 1817 a modern and unpopular fiscal reform targeting consumption, known as *derechos de puertas*. This reform turned provincial capitals into tax centres, and Garay's rational system was much harder to evade than the complex and baroque tributes that had pertained during the old regime.[27] Smugglers and bandits were lionised as a result. The government also decided to sell various commons and royal lands, which reduced the resources of the municipalities and the amount of land available for rent.[28]

Thus, army rebellions could often count on popular support which was far from negligible. But for support to be decisive, the army needed to profit from the other source of disaffection: conscription. The royalist counter-insurgency in America made this possible. For the regime, all depended on pacifying America so that bullion could flow to the treasury once more. Yet this task could only be achieved with the dispatch of sufficient troops, itself a task which was so costly as to be undertaken in circumstances which virtually guaranteed military rebellion (inadequate pay, troop concentrations caused by shipping bottlenecks). The king had, late in 1819, ordered ten army battalions to the province of Cádiz to await transport on festering hulks to Spanish America, and the stage was set for disgruntled commanders (Rafael de Riego, Quiroga) to rally their equally disgruntled men to overthrow the Restoration regime. Thus, the army in 1820, just as in 1814, was breaking a regime. The fact that Riego unveiled the Constitution of 1812 only at the last minute underlines how professional rather than political grievances drove his officers and how general support for the 1812 programme could not be taken for granted. The exiled essayist Blanco White, writing in 1820, witheringly observed, '[H]owever excellent it may be, the Constitution was not *popular*'.[29]

Riego's successful rising marked 1820 as the birthdate of the liberal *pronunciamiento*. Unhappy as the conscripts were, they could be manipulated by officers with political contacts and ambitions. The advent of the liberal *pronunciamiento* in 1820 set in train a tradition of often left-leaning, praetorian liberalism that was unique in Europe for its volatile mix of politicised officer corps, on one hand, and the aggravated conscript class, on the other. Conscripts were aggravated not just by the dire conditions of service but also by the yawning gulf between those who enjoyed the nation and those ordered to defend it. Even though Spanish liberals set great political store by the 'nation in arms' idea, best demonstrated in the guerrilla phenomenon of the 1808–14 war, in reality liberals rejected truly universal military service (service without exemptions would not be introduced until 1911). Propertied voters were empowered either to buy their way out of service or to join the gentler conditions of the liberals' paramilitary militia which was created whenever leftist liberals came to power in Madrid. Thus, the 'blood tax' of compulsory military service was paid by the poor, and the underdeveloped nature of the Spanish economy made the resulting popular anti-militarism more barbed than in most other European countries operating similar social filters. Whereas in 1789, 90 per cent of Spanish ranks comprised long-serving, professional soldiers, by 1868, 90 per cent of ranks were composed of draftees.[30] Calculations made by 'pronouncing' officers were increasingly dominated by decisions about how and when conscripts should be granted leave as incentives or rewards for a 'loyal' rebellion.

The Triennium

Riego's rising ushered in three-and-a-half years of constitutional government known as the Trieno liberal (1820–23). The works of two historians continue to shape our understanding of this period. Alberto Gil Novales, a left-wing historian, argued that the Triennium produced Spain's first modern political society which was on course for democracy had it not been betrayed by its own leaders.[31] The right-wing historian, José Luis Comellas, by contrast, argued that the masses in 1820 remained fervently royalist, essentially accepting liberalism only because the king himself made a display under duress of accepting the revolution.[32] The twentieth-century doyen of traditionalist history, Melchor Ferrer, wrote that 'outside of their lodges, salons and clubs, everyone was at odds with the liberals'.[33] Both Gil Novales and Comellas considered the Triennium to be the origin of Spain's radical politics, the former asserting the strong influence of the liberal clubs known as Patriotic Societies, the latter discounting these in favour of the wider and inarticulate agitation of cafés, secret societies, and National Militia as forms of 'parallel power' (*para-poder*). The governing elites of this era were distinguished by a generation divide. The men of 'order' who dominated the liberal governments from March 1820 until July 1822 were known as the 'men of 1812' (*doceañistas*). These figures, like Count Toreno and even the constitution's founding father, Agustín de Argüelles, were willing to accept limits to the liberal revolution and to seek to accommodate the king, perhaps by creating a senate to moderate the unbridled sovereignty of the unicameral Cortes. They were opposed by a younger generation of liberals known as the 'men of 1820' (*veinteañistas*), who had not made their reputation during the Peninsular War and who wanted to use full power of the constitution to drive liberal reforms, control the power of the king, and advance their own careers in the process. This tension opened up a divide in the liberal movement which would persist in various guises throughout the nineteenth century. The 'restrained' liberals or 'moderates' (*moderados*) were largely the men of 1812, whereas the 'hothead' liberals (*exaltados*) were largely the men of 1820.

The spring and summer of 1820 unleashed a popular frenzy of tax strikes. From the outset, the revolution of 1820 contained a certain populist social agenda. The port city of Algeciras, one of the first urban centres to be taken by Riego's army, saw its import duties on foreign goods abolished, the hated Garay tax system mothballed 'pending the design of a better system', and the tobacco monopoly broken up.[34] Similar crowd-pleasing measures were enacted as other cities fell to the constitutional rebellion in January, February, and March, whilst an open trade in grain imports was proclaimed as means of staving off recurrent famines.[35] These free-trade, liberal measures appeared to favour the interests of the urban minority population over the rural majority, who, in most provincial capitals, enjoyed a reprieve from the hated consumption taxes levied on produce as it passed the city limits. The *derechos de puertas*, abolished in most regional capitals, were replaced by a universal *contribución general*, a form of income tax which, though sharing similarities with the ephemeral *contribución única* of the 1813–14 Cortes, this time went on the whole uncollected.[36]

Yet even if Riego's revolt attracted urban consumers, it was viewed with suspicion by producers in the countryside. The prevailing 'moral crisis' had led the countrymen to fear soldiers both as thieves and ruffians and as harbingers of disease and conscription. Villagers were reluctant to supply the rebels who, in turn, resorted to pillage rather than risk their own poor logistics.[37] What saved the situation was, firstly, the 4 March rising by La Bisbal in Ocaña and, secondly, the opportunistic 'negative *pronunciamiento*' (refusal to obey orders) of General Ballesteros in Madrid. Crowds sacked the gaols of the Inquisition and invaded the palace, thus breaking the king's nerve enough for him to swear allegiance to the Constitution of 1812 on 7 March 1820.[38] Liberals were willing to forgive Ferdinand his recent felonies, not least because they needed a king to give legitimacy to their incoming regime.[39]

Therefore, politics had come to a full circle since 1814: a military coup once more drew hopeful crowds in its wake. The population, disillusioned by absolutism, might now be won over to the constitution. Yet again, however, such leadership was not forthcoming, for the rising had been launched essentially for professional reasons, Riego protesting the suffering of his troops in a manner which barely concealed his personal ambition. Even if there were manifestoes written by a handful of civilian conspirators, these were bland and non-committal (Alcalá Galiano, for example, wrote of the government's 'destruction of the nation and of happiness').[40] What interested the soldiers was not abstract politics but the promise that a successful rising would spare them the horrors of the American campaign. To be sure, they had also rallied to the promise of parcelled-out land (*reparto*). Soldiers elsewhere who had not been given such assurances refused to rally, and sometimes even briefly resisted the rebellion with arms, even in the case of garrisons in coastal cities with merchant populations sympathetic to liberalism. Once it became clear to the garrison at Cádiz that it would not be ordered to replace the rebels destined for the American expedition, its commanders ordered a brutal crackdown against revolutionaries in the city. The 10 March massacre, which claimed some 71 lives and 171 wounded,[41] was witnessed by a British traveller who sought refuge at the Portuguese vice-consulate:

> Taking post behind the trellis of one of the windows, I had an opportunity, without being observed, of seeing what was passing. Several of the inhabitants lay dead in the street beneath the window. These had been assassinated by a few struggling soldiers for the purpose of plunder, and the same armed party remained here at the junction of four streets, to rob all who passed. One word of remonstrance was sufficient to ensure the complainer's being bayoneted or shot.
>
> After three or four days, tranquillity was again restored, and the people began to appear on the streets. It was a corps of Guides and a Militia regiment that behaved the worst, the other corps only joined when they found the sack so profitable. The Constitution having afterwards been proclaimed, the corps of Guides was banished to Ayamonte, but the Government was too weak to punish even the ringleaders.[42]

Even port cities hostile to absolutism were at the mercy of the army. But events in March 1820 in Madrid were decisive. King Ferdinand's capitulation in March led to a provisional government of 'jailbird' liberals who were now being released from prison or liberated from internal exile. It was soon replaced by a Constituent Cortes, whilst those liberal politicians who had been exiled or imprisoned even claimed six years' worth of back pay in a self-serving bid to re-establish the continuity with 1814.[43] Amongst the deputies of the 1820 Cortes were fifty-four clerics, including their liberal minority represented by such men as Villanueva. For a while a moderate attitude prevailed between church and state, very much like the 1809–10 period of Patriot politics. But attitudes soon soured, starting in August 1820 when the Cortes decreed the dissolution of the Jesuit order.[44]

Cortes liberals tried to revive the memory of the first constitutional experiment. Pablo López was released from solitary confinement and granted a lavish pension rewarding 'his services to the nation'.[45] The restoration of the constitution had also encouraged a flurry of agitation in pamphlets and a few newspapers which addressed popular grievances. Thus, one pamphlet (*El Duende Extremeño*) stressed the need for schools, *reparto*, and the abolition of noble privileges whilst also reserving populist scorn for local elites, in particular the escribano: 'The *escribanos* do better than anyone else what Jesus Christ ordains. Jesus tells us to love others as we love ourselves. And the *escribanos* are so eager that they are not content with just loving their brothers: they have to swallow them whole!'[46]

The biggest financial burden was Riego's revolutionary army. The men of 1812 were grateful for Riego's restoration of liberty but were also mindful of the example of 1814, when the army had restored absolutism. As a safeguard, the 'people-in-arms' tenet of liberalism now dictated the creation of the National Militia, a part-time citizens' force which under the 1810–14 Cortes had barely left the drawing board. Zaragoza (population 36,000) for example was ordered to create six companies of 144 men each (873 in total, plus 9 officers), with daily active service pay ranging from 5 to 8 reales. Militia duties included 'patrols and the pursuit and arrest of deserters and wrongdoers'.[47] Militia enlistment was restricted to men possessing literacy and the uniform.[48] The militia was thus less 'national' and more well-to-do. The 'national' liability was conscription, whereas the well-to-do militia enjoyed the privileges of army service without the penalties of deployment. Militia officers enjoyed similar privileges to their army counterparts (the 'fuero militar') when on active service, entrenching inter-service rivalry. This rivalry was heightened when the parliamentary leader of the exaltados, Romero Alpuente, repeatedly called for the army to be replaced by the militia altogether.[49] But the army ultimately retained the upper hand, as it alone retained the power to declare states of siege (martial law), an option increasingly used in the face of armed counter-revolution, empowering the army to subject the militia to army regulations, stand it down, or even dissolved it altogether. The corporate exemptions from civilian law enjoyed directly by the army and indirectly by the militia undermined legislation passed in September 1820 and April 1821 instituting jury trials and 24-hour limits for pre-charge detentions.

The liberal state spent most of its budget on armies and policing, leaving very little for education or land reform. Liberal expansion of the state was not matched by expansion of the tax base. By October 1820, it became clear that only 12 per cent of the intake projected for the previous six months from the *contribución general* had been received.[50] Riego's revolutionary army remained under arms and drawing pay, and the re-establishment of the constitution had provoked a veritable scramble (*empleomanía*) for administrative sinecures. Spain received a 200-million *reales* loan from foreign bourses in return for a pledge to disband Riego's army. The government tried to sweeten the pill by passing a decree rewarding soldiers with bounties and small parcels of land in their parishes.[51] But Riego resisted dissolution. In September he entered Madrid amidst agitation stoked up by radical clubs known as 'Patriotic Societies'. Riego accepted an offer to become captain general of Galicia (later Zaragoza) and the crisis passed.[52] But the spectre of popular radicalism spooked the king. In the November 1820 'Carvajal affair', the king tried to block Interior Minister Argüelles's confiscation of monastic properties but backed down when the 'divine' author of the constitution threatened to stoke up riots in the capital. Even worse, the king had dared to leave Madrid to seek support at El Escorial palace, where a clerical circle around his brother, Don Carlos, held sway. Backing down meant returning to Madrid as a virtual prisoner, a predicament made worse when a few *exaltados* triumphantly joined the government.[53]

For all their political triumph, the liberals were hamstrung by money. Government economies fell hardest on the poor. The hated *derechos de puertas* were gradually re-established. The Argüellian confiscations of monastic property were followed by their auction to the highest bidder. Admittedly, the liberals also revived the legislation of 1811 abolishing feudal jurisdictions which, in theory, allowed villagers to challenge landowners' claims to receive rents and even to own the land itself. But the king used the suspensive veto permitted him by the constitution, blocking this legislation becoming law until May 1823 (when it would prove too late). Thus, the carrot was withheld from villagers even though the stick was applied. Early in 1821 the Cortes reduced tithes to the half-tithe. But the half-tithe was worse because it had to be paid in cash rather than in kind, a massive burden for a rural population still largely unaccustomed to a cash economy and which, most devastatingly, came at a time of a slump in prices for agricultural goods.[54] Moreover, the half-tithe encouraged landlords, themselves exasperated by the economic slump, to raise rents. Caught in a slump, liberal Spain was soon at the mercy of both foreign creditors and an increasingly clerical-royalist countryside.

Modern economic protests began. Alcoy (Valencia) had been the centre of some 40,000 textile outworkers whose employment practices were protected by their guilds before liberals abolished them in 1813 (and again in 1820). Factory owners seized their chance to introduce self-acting lathes (*selfactinas*) which took thousands of outworkers' jobs and provoked riots in which the workers overpowered the militia and seized control of Alcoy for four days. The workers returned home only when government reinforcements arrived and employers made a token pledge never to reintroduce the lathes. The Cortes liberals sided with the employers, condemning the workers as barbaric, even royalist. Romero Alpuente was a lone voice in siding with the textile workers.[55]

It was unlikely that the Alcoy Luddites were royalists. As Romero Alpuente explained to his disbelieving colleagues, rural landowners welcomed the lathes because they increased the supply of low-paid day labourers.[56] But counter-revolution certainly was stirring in the countryside, boosted in summer 1821 when the priest veteran of the Peninsular War Jeronimo Merino ('El Cura') took to the hills.[57] When reports arrived in May 1821 of the mass stoning of a plaque honouring the constitution in sleepy Maranchón (Guadalajara), the response of one liberal newspaper was both condign and patronising.[58] June 1820 saw inhabitants of Lorca use the restored freedom of the press to publicise the same sort of corruption and nepotism which had vexed them in 1813. Again to no avail: for two years later the situation had deteriorated enough to have been the cause of a riot against the authorities, the crowd lynching the local magistrate.[59] Elections and militia empowered local notables, leading to friction between as well as within communities. Thus, in the summer of 1821, long-standing animosity between the Málaga villages of Alhama de Granada and Zafarraya spiralled into open conflict. With the connivance of the prefect of Granada, and a provincial deputy infamous for raising and betraying Málaga in 1810, Vicente Abello, some five hundred men were dispatched by the town hall of Alhama to assault Zafarraya. The brutal fate of the *zafarrayano* refugees stayed in the press for weeks.[60] Abello, whom one correspondent called 'a man sent by God to punish Málaga', alerted Alhama's National Militia against any retaliation.[61] Abello's crimelord antics – along with the fluidity of Málaga's commerce, contraband, and clubs – shaped the city's political underground, as had been witnessed in May 1821 when four pardoned political prisoners were condemned for republican agitation.[62]

Málaga like other Mediterranean ports opened Spain to European radicals for whom Iberia, in the early 1820s, was a 'horizon of promise'.[63] Mary Shelley wrote in 1820 how she 'would very much like to be in Spain'.[64] Austria's 1821 suppression of Neapolitan liberalism turned Spain into a refuge for Italian *carbonari* refugees, the liberal nationalists whose secretive rituals were described by Lord Byron during his initiation in an Italian forest.[65] The Comunero clubs, which were already agitated by the king's dismissal of Prime Minister Argüelles in March, welcomed the émigrés and used their momentum in a press campaign against real and imagined absolutists in positions of power. The outstanding Italian leaders were Pacchiarotti and D'Atelly, who rallied Italian exiles in Barcelona, and the French ex-general, Guillaume Vandori, who agitated with somewhat less success in Valencia and Málaga, amidst an abortive republican plot in the latter city in November 1821.[66] The most famous Neapolitan fugitive 'General Pepé' was cold-shouldered by the *moderado* Masons of Barcelona but found a warmer reception in Lisbon. Riego himself is alleged to have been influenced enough to have had vague dealings with some exiled French and Italian republicans, a rumour which in any case was strong enough to persuade the *moderado* government of Feliú to dismiss him as captain general of Aragón in September 1821.[67]

The onset of internationalised civil war in Spain from 1821 also led to a Cold War between the two forces waging the counter-insurgency, the liberals' National Militia and Riego's army. On 21 September, the so-called Battle of las Platerías, named after the street in Madrid where the city hall was located, saw the National Militia and army riot over the symbol of the flawed *caudillo*. The Fontana de Oro organised a procession to carry Riego's portrait to the Puerta del Sol in the centre of the capital. Troops posted by the government along the streets allowed the protestors to pass, but no such sympathy was to found amongst the militiamen, who outside the city hall charged the protestors and seized the portrait, leading the city hall to convene an all-night emergency session to make arrests and clear the cafés and Patriotic Societies.[68] The radicals were unbowed. Even though *caciques* across Spain had engineered *moderado* victories in the October parish elections, the parish electors were then pressured by radical agitators to elect overwhelmingly *exaltado* provincial deputies the following month. These, in turn, created an *exaltado* parliamentary majority (albeit under an executive which was still *moderado*) which saw Riego – still an *exaltado* figure – elected president of the Cortes.[69]

Thus, the liberal revolution unleashed urban networks of activism which influenced politics at national levels. In Madrid, the cafés Fontana de Oro and Lorencini became what salons had been to the French Revolution. They also offered patronage. The Lorencini in Madrid offered free basic literacy classes so that patrons could learn to sign their names, thereby qualifying for service in the militia.[70] The pseudo-Masonic secret society, the Comuneros, was created by Romero Alpuente and colleagues early in 1821. It subsidised the membership of the lower orders, whom the *moderado* Marqués de Miraflores derided as the 'scum of the earth'.[71] The Comuneros were organised hierarchically, just like the *moderado* Masons who were known as *anilleros*. But the Comuneros differed by supporting a social agenda including the redistribution of land ('*reparto*') and in their confederal structure of activism. They met in provincial clubs known as 'towers' (*torres*), answering to a 'great junta' which was presided over an incognito leader known as 'The Great Castellan' who was probably Romero Alpuente. A snapshot of Comunero membership in Motril (Granada), a town of almost ten thousand souls, reveals twenty-six members in 1823, most of whom came from liberal professions, commerce and artisans.[72] Secret societies like the Comuneros maintained *exaltado* pressure on the central government. A failed counter-revolution on 7 July 1822 (revolt of the Royal Guard) transformed the national situation. King Ferdinand's attempt to break out of constitutional captivity was defeated in fighting in the capital between his Royal Guard and the victorious National Miltia.

Ferdinand's defeat in July 1822 was like Louis XVI's flight to Varennes in 1791. While the king remained a prisoner in his palace, being forced to appoint an outright *exaltado* government (under Evaristo San Miguel) for the first time, armed royalists took to the hills in Ferdinand's name, turning the hitherto fledgling insurgency into a full-scale revolt. The civil war in the countryside reached a brutal climax as Espoz y Mina and Torrijos enacted a veritable reign of terror against clerical-royalist villages and priests. In fact, much of this excess was triggered by the terror of the royalists themselves, thus inducing a sort of artificial 'popular liberalism', as soldiers, militiamen, and those constitutionalists who were in a sea of clerical-royalism found their ideals and indoctrination ennobled by blood.[73] The civil war also encouraged liberal newspapers to spread propaganda to show what allegedly lay in store for Spaniards if the reactionaries triumphed. Thus, a letter allegedly left behind by a royalist fleeing Espoz y Mina's army boasted that as soon as the liberals were crushed, the Inquisition would return, as would the *camarilla*, convents, and the full tithe.[74] Poor logistics and tactics led the government armies (and mobilised militia) to behave badly with real and imagined royalist civilians. Legislation in September 1822 formalised penalties to be faced by *pueblos* which supported the clerical-royalist *facciosos*, failed to resist them, or even failed to show 'due respect towards constitutional forces'. The sanctions amounted to the right for army officers on the spot to commandeer all horses and other movable chattels without compensation.[75] Meanwhile, anticlericalism became so rife that even religious in liberal bastions which had never fallen to the royalist bands were not safe.[76]

There now followed a kind of 'liberal dictatorship' which fought the royalist insurgency, while satisfying far too few social demands on the other. The San Miguel administration was slow to open up corporately owned land to private buyers. Even though the Comunero lodges had campaigned for land redistribution (*reparto*) for months, this was only carried out in a patchy fashion. Newspapers reported marginal land near Málaga being allocated to landless labourers, yet municipalities in the more fertile soils of Córdoba and Jaén dragged their feet.[77] The king's suspensive veto against the 1811 abolition of feudal jurisdiction finally expired in May 1823. Yet by then French troops were overrunning the country, and serious land reform became meaningless.

One foreign traveller found the political atmosphere now to be stifling in the extreme: 'in perhaps no capital of Europe was freedom of opinion less tolerated at this time than in Madrid'.[78] All the political clubs were ordered to close, even Romero Alpuente's Landaburiana, so named after a militiaman who fell in the 7 July Royal Guard revolt. Even though most of the *exaltado* clubs successfully defied this order, Spain smacked of Jacobin France, including 'revolutionary justice' that led to the execution of absolutist General Elío and the mass drownings in the Atlantic of absolutist conspirators who had been held by local authorities in La Coruña.[79]

In fact, Espoz y Mina's campaign managed to crush royalist bands by the end of 1822. Whether his men would resist a French invasion undertaken by a professional army, on the other hand, was a different matter. Firstly, the *exaltados* were obliged to reintroduce unpopular conscription, both to safeguard against the royalist threat and to meet the foreign invasion being sponsored by the Holy Alliance. They needed to raise recruits, yet even to attempt conscription was to drive the rural populace into the hills and thereby incur the risk that they would fall prone to banditry or even join the royalist bands. In fact, for once, the levy enacted in October 1822 was markedly successful: out of sixty-seven thousand men called up, some fifty thousand actually made it to the ranks.[80] What made this so successful was neither the popularity of the regime nor patriotism in the face of the threat of foreign invasion. Rather, the National Militia had ceased to be an attractive escape from army service ever since the San Miguel administration in declaring the state of emergency had made the former compulsory, thus spreading the appalling conditions of the army to the citizens' force and effectively closing it off as a means of advancement. Also a great deal of coercion had been applied by municipal oligarchs who now feared for much more than their posts.[81] But all this was to no avail: whatever leadership San Miguel might have imposed on this *levée en masse* was rendered abortive when a combination of foreign pressure and factionalism amongst the *exaltados* persuaded the king in February 1823 to dismiss him, notwithstanding a mob being raised to invade the palace grounds shouting, 'Death to the king!'[82] As the French army bore down on Madrid, the king defied his government again by refusing to accompany the evacuation of his government to Cádiz. The *exatlados* subjected Ferdinand to the infamous Article 187 of the constitution, declaring him 'temporarily bereft of sound mind', forcing him to join the evacuation all the same.

Ferdinand would not be rescued by royalist villagers on the road to Cádiz but by foreign invaders at his rear. The flagging royalist insurgency was rescued by the Concert of Europe (minus Britain) agreeing to dispatch a French invasion army to end Spain's revolution and restore Ferdinand to his absolute powers. In 1823, just like in 1814, Ferdinand would have the army to thank for his restoration, even if the army, ironically, was French (surviving royalist insurgents having become not much more than adjuncts to the main force). Unlike in 1808, there was little popular resistance to this French invasion. In effect there was no will to resist the invasion: the army melted away rather than resist the French, who were able to cross Spain and restore Fernando VII to his full powers without having to fire barely a shot, whilst civilian elites generally refused to rally. Several historians thus present 1823 as the abandonment of the revolution by its own leaders, Gil Novales writing of outright reaction whilst even the less ideological historian, Pedro Rújula, speaks of 'desierto liberal'.[83] But an army which refused to bow to royalist insurgents saw nothing dishonourable in surrendering to a professional army, albeit a foreign one. Even Espoz y Mina opted for French rather than Spanish captivity, ironically observing that 'although the Constitution of 1812 was made entirely for the people, they hated it'.[84]

On the heels of the French Army, the royalists unleashed a counter-revolution of their own. As the liberals retreated south with their captive king, taking up temporary residence in Seville in June 1823, a British adventurer called John Downie launched a plot to free Ferdinand. This miscarried, although not before the poor of the neighbourhoods of Triana, Humeros, San Roque and la Macarena, had invaded the wealthier parts of the city assaulting militiamen, sacking the Patriotic Society, and looting several luxury shops and the theatre.[85] Indeed the French advance was accompanied by a surge of *servil* agitation. A royalist officer operating in Córdoba damned the 'foul' constitution and unleashed his troops against villagers who had acquired church lands.[86] Speaking through his fictional figure, Salvador Monsalud, Benito Pérez Galdós blamed the collapse of 1823 on the failure of the Triennium liberals to have manipulated the people into following their lead.[87] Contemporary observers were convinced that the liberals' drive to a cash economy had been decisive. According to the French ambassador,

> taxes paid in kind are nothing at all here: what is a real burden is tax paid in cash. One of the greatest errors of the Cortes government was to have established this reform: one of the greatest sources of hatred felt by the nation towards the government.[88]

By November 1823, after a three-month siege of Cádiz, the liberals accepted defeat and released Ferdinand to the besieging French army.

The international impact of the collapse of Spanish liberalism was clear. It finalised the independence process in mainland Spanish America, where virtually everywhere beyond the slave-holding Viceroyalty of Peru had escaped peninsular control. Spanish state finances, so used to bullion flowing to Spain from the Americas, were reduced by 40 per cent. Although the Spanish state finances suffered, the loss of America did not much affect Spain's commercial activity. Only Cuba enjoyed strong commercial links to the Spanish motherland, and this island yet remained loyal.[89] For their part, pro-independence armies were forging independent states while the provincial deputations established by the Cádiz constitution in America converted themselves into state governments.[90] Yet international recognition of Spanish American independence was *de facto* before it became *de jure*. British Foreign Secretary Canning, responding to the 1823 French invasion of Spain, declared that although 'the Pyrenees had fallen' he would 'maintain the Atlantic'.[91] There certainly were French proposals to send a French fleet and army to assist in Spain's reconquest of the Americas, and it took considerable browbeating by Canning to secure a French guarantee of neutrality on the Latin American revolt, clearing the way for British recognition of the former Spanish empire in 1824, following the recognition proclaimed by the United States in 1822.[92]

By the end of 1824, even Peru had fallen from royalist control. On 9 December 1824, four thousand metres above sea level at Ayacucho (Peru), following a rousing speech by *criollo* General Antonio José de Sucre, the independence army defeated the last major royalist army on the American mainland. Defeated Spanish officers who returned to face bleak career prospects in Spain would become known as 'ayacuchos', even though most of them, including the famous Baldomero Espartero (1793–1879), were not present at the final battle which gave them their name.[93] With the consolidation of independence thereafter underway, French designs did not cross the Atlantic. Yet the French army would remain in Spain itself for another five years. Amidst the royalist vigilantism of 1823 the French army operated as a moderating force, countermanding some of the worst oppression demanded by the Spanish royalist regency and provoking a backlash in August 1823 from Navarrese Royalist Volunteers who protested that the French army was 'protecting liberals and absolving them of their crimes'.[94]

The 'Ominous Decade'

With Ferdinand restored to his full powers he enacted a far more ruthless repression than in 1814. The White Terror of 1823–24 was indeed severe. But in a manner often overlooked by liberal historians, for whom the 1823–33 period of restored absolutism was an 'Ominous Decade' and even a 'time without history',[95] the repression was less Ferdinand's doing and more a continuation of the vigilantism which had nurtured localised conflict since 1814. State-driven repression was not especially severe. By the time Ferdinand's 'Military Commissions' were dissolved in August 1825, only some 1,094 individuals had been brought before tribunals, and only a slight majority of these were charged with political (rather than common) crimes. Whilst about three-quarters were condemned to punishments of varying severity, including death (132), the rest were absolved. Although exact figures are lacking (except one source declaring that twenty-four thousand compromised families fled into exile[96]), rather more terror and repression appear to have been continuations of elements operating formally outside of the state. Such reactionary secret societies as the Ángel Exterminador, the Purísima and the Ancla had their roots in the clericalised violence of the previous three years. The self-proclaimed 'Royalist Volunteers' militia of the Triennium were maintained by Ferdinand in peacetime, partly out of a desire to channel radical royalism and partly to permit him to shrink his liberal-infested regular army. The odds were against officers regaining their commissions. The young veteran of the Spanish–American wars, Baldomero Espartero, managed this feat in 1826 only after proving his political reliability by denouncing some liberal officers involved in a fuzzy plot to replace Fernando VII with the emperor of Brazil.[97] Even the most reactionary policies of Ferdinand's post-1823 ministers, such as Tadeo Calomarde's 1824 university reforms, which suppressed 'liberal' natural sciences in favour of law, theology, and that reactionary sport *par excellence*, bullfighting, were more a continuation of traditional thought rather than a sudden break.[98]

Exaltado insurrections all ended in failure. Indeed, the most impressive popular mobilisation against the absolutist order came not from the *exaltados* but from the traditionalists in the form of the 1827 *apostólico* rising in Catalonia known as the War of the Aggrieved (Guerra de los Agraviados). The reaction of 1823 was undertaken with a more thorough degree of repression than had been the case in 1814. The absolutist police state was reimposed via the special Military Commissions and, from 1824, an internal passport system.[99] Royalist veterans of 1823 created 'faith juntas' (*juntas de la fé*) as a substitute for the Inquisition which the king felt obliged to tolerate, just as he tolerated the maintenance and expansion of the 'Royalist Volunteers'. These all combined to make life difficult for both *exaltado* leaders and followers, thus forcing those associated with the extinguished regime who had not fled or been imprisoned to impose a large degree of self-censorship.[100] Meanwhile, newspaper censorship was rigorously enacted, provincial readers generally being restricted to just one official gazette, whilst Madrid was comparatively privileged with its choice of two journals (the *Diario* and the *Gaceta*). Fernandine absolutism made sure to suppress inherently liberal print culture whilst imposing no constraints on such old regime pastimes as bullfighting.

The paranoid regime, whose police liberally estimated some half-a-million Spaniards to have been members of secret societies by the time of the French invasion, pathologised the people as a demagogue-prone mob which the chaos of the Triennium had confirmed could not be entrusted with any political responsibility.[101] Thus, the regime was lacklustre in capturing popular loyalty: the Royalist Volunteers soon proved a dead-end, as it proved impossible to sustain a virulent armed crowd on, say, the *Sanfedisti* model of 1799. Indeed, the Volunteers soon proved to be dominated by similar oligarchies as the militia before them. The motivations for creating what its first set of regulations outlined as a force for 'elements of order and monarchical subordination' were plausible enough, especially as the riotous example of the National Militia, 'which seemed set on turning each town into a state, and each town-hall into a government', was in recent memory.[102] The Volunteers were also impressive in number (rising from 70,000 in 1824 to a peak of 284,000 in 1832). But the conservative ideal of king and people failed to materialise, as the Royalist ranks were monopolised once more by the same local elites who had dominated previous militia forces. In 1831 Rentería and Oiartzun (San Sebastián) witnessed riots against venal municipal elites who, so the protestors complained, had seamlessly switched their political allegiances from José I, then to the Patriots, then to Ferdinand, then to the constitution, and now to absolutism, all with the exclusive aim of maintaining their oligarchy. Now they controlled the Volunteers as a sort of private army.[103]

For all the reactionary zeal of the Royalist Volunteers, many were former militiamen of the constitutional era and there was a great deal of continuity in the methods of policing. As Galdós would have said, many were the same dogs with different collars. Whether militia or Royalist Volunteers, the popular grievances amounted to the same. The Volunteers, just like the militia beforehand, ran their own municipal rackets in favour of their members (e.g. their being first in line for such jobs as town criers and public lightsmen). Meanwhile, the hated *fuero militar* likewise applied to them when 'on active duty', with the result that innumerable petty scores were settled whenever a Royalist rushed home to change into his uniform before returning to arrest his tormentor.[104] The late-1823 nationwide call for the arms of the disbanded National Militia to be handed in at town halls made for particular mercenariness, as – in going largely unheeded – the *Voluntarios* often blackmailed their predecessors, or denounced them in the knowledge that half of the hefty fine (50 *ducados*) imposed on those concealing weapons was shared with the informer.[105]

To be sure there were ultra-conservative forces coalescing around the king's restive younger brother and heir apparent, Don Carlos. Of these *ultramontane* secret societies, the most notorious was the Exterminating Angel (El Ángel Exterminador), which had as its members clerics from all stages of the church hierarchy and maintained networks of lay informers whose denunciations were enough to secure the arrest of any number of suspected *exaltados*.[106] The clericalisation of terror was answered by a popular ani-clericalism boosted by Ferdinand's decision in 1823 to dispose, without compensation, purchasers of clerical property during the Triennium. Thus, the spring of 1826 saw an organised wave of robberies and defamations of churches in Barcelona which were 'almost as bad as the worst outrages of the constitutional system' and which anguished authorities attributed to underground networks of *carbonarios* and Comuneros. These outrages might be forestalled, the bishop of Barcelona suggested, by the closure of cafés and a programme of public works to employ the 'idle mob'.[107] The church hierarchy still thought it was under siege. Confiscations and even killings of the Triennium had reduced the cloistered clergy in 1823 to the unprecedented low figure of eight thousand. Within ten years of the 'Ominous Decade', this figure would revive to 61,272.[108] The king's younger brother, Don Carlos, was being identified as the chief royal champion of clericalism. Unwisely embarking upon an unguarded transit through Madrid in the summer of 1826, the future Pretender and his princess, María Teresa, were mobbed only two hundred yards from the palace by several men who surrounded the carriage offering insults and *mueras*.[109]

Meanwhile, with the Spanish army was purged and reduced to a skeleton force in 1824, the *Voluntarios* had to face less competition from this natural rival, as the French garrisons stood aloof everywhere except in Barcelona.[110] Secondly, revised regulations passed in June 1826 implicitly cleared the way for day labourers to join the Royalist ranks, a move which Triennium liberals had contemplated only at the hour of direst need (1822–23). With a daily pay which compared with the lowest ranks of the erstwhile militia (4 *reales* for the first day of service, 5 *reales* for each subsequent day), the only vague proviso was for volunteers to have 'an honourable and identifiable occupation'.[111] On one hand, the prospect of a steady wage, which, of course, went further at a time of low agricultural prices, usually dissuaded the Volunteers from backing *exaltado* conspiracies (as the liberal invaders – see the following discussion – discovered to their cost). But on the other hand, the effective absence of a 'bottom limit' on enrolment to the Volunteers meant that local elites could pick and choose their hirelings. The watchwords of 'king and people' amounted to raw municipal favouritism, as the 'ins' flaunted their powers, whilst the 'outs' had to suffer the same depredations as under constitutional régimes. Ubeda (Granada), for example, in 1826 was rocked by riots provoked by an overbearing municipal racket run by the alderman (*regidor*). Alderman Santiago Manrique turned the Volunteers under his command into a posse which drew heavily on the municipal treasury and caused 'abuses in the nomination of prosecutors to the local law court'.[112] But effectively there were no remedies short of violence: the church condemned the people even more virulently than between 1814 and 1820 as authors of their own misfortune, whilst the popular goodwill shown towards Ferdinand VII in 1814 had entirely evaporated.

Attacks from the right

The first substantial armed insurrection against Absolutism came from the Right. The counter-revolution of 1823 had shrunk the liberal minority amongst the clergy still further, basically making them a group of ageing exiles. In their place reactionary clerics used violence and propaganda against not just the vanquished liberals but also against what they saw as the temporising acts of the Fernandine regime. The post-1823 church placed its faith in the countryside instead of the 'Babylons' of the liberal towns, which in itself marked a shift from the eighteenth century when the clericalism was generally greater in the towns and anti-clericalism generally a rural phenomenon.[113] Unlike in 1814, Ferdinand VII, in 1823, had no clerical honeymoon to look forward to. On 1 November 1826, three months after the last ever judicial execution for heresy had taken place in Spain,[114] the 'Manifesto of Pure Royalists' was launched in Madrid. This manifesto called for a 'legitimist' revolt against the 'legitimate' king, and indeed rural Catalonia soon erupted in a royalist insurgency of the 'Aggrieved' aiming to replace King Ferdinand with his more clerical younger brother and heir apparent, Don Carlos. The sort of innovation which reactionaries had attributed to their liberal enemies had now infected them. As historian Carlos Seco Serrano explained, 'for the first time in Spanish history, the legitimacy of the *exercise* of power eclipsed the legitimacy of the *origin* of that power'.[115]

The 1827 rising of the *Agraviados* was not the first 'Carlist' revolt. The 1824 Capapé affair and the Brihuega rising of Royalist Volunteers in 1825 showed the insurgent potential of the traditionalist right. Ferdinand's technocratic reforms, and the begrudging amnesty he offered to some exiled *moderados* in 1826, annoyed clerical circles at court. Ultra priests added to the apocalyptic atmosphere, condemning such enlightened practices as burying the dead in new-fangled cemeteries instead of churches. But the 1827 rising was of a different order.[116] As Jaime Torras explained, the leaders of the rebellion, from Agustín Saperes and José Bosoms down to 'limitless' numbers of army officers suffering cashierment or, at best, half-pay, were motivated by career frustration and ambition. Money to support the rising came from both well-connected *ultras* in Madrid and several clerics, whilst the 'Aggrieved' also had two accomplished *caudillos*, Saperes and Bosoms. Apolitical and adventurous, both these men shared similar personalities and backgrounds with their liberal opposite numbers who had attempted *pronunciamientos* before them: both groups having been passed over for prizes (in the case of Saperes and Bosoms, neither felt sufficiently rewarded for having fought the liberals during the 1821–23 civil war). Just like Riego, these *caudillos* were rebelling objectively on behalf of a political cause but subjectively on behalf of their careers.[117] The *Agraviados* also tapped into a rural unease at the unfettered advance of the cash economy and such measures as a decree which, in 1827, imposed a free internal market throughout Spain in wine, vinegar, oil, and meat.[118]

Unlike the liberal exiles, however, Saperes and Bosoms had a reasonably well-organised support base, for the interior of Catalonia had been rallied by *ultra* priests, whilst arms came from the *somatén* (the traditional Catalan militia), and later even some Royalist Volunteers who changed sides. The reasons for this large support-base have less to do with the godly fervour of the population and more to do with the chronic economic crisis of the 1820s, the nadir of prices for agricultural produce actually coming in 1827. Thus, when rebel priests offered a one-and-a-half *peseta* daily wage for underemployed farmhands, it was not long until a force of almost thirty thousand was formed that summer. Insurgents capturing villages conveniently discovered 'liberals' amongst the notables whose property they could loot and lives they could ransom.[119] A rebel capital was made of Manresa, whence a royalist newspaper briefly appeared, allowing the insurgents to explain their aims of the king's government those ministers deemed 'dovish' (*aperturistas*) towards the liberals. The heir apparent, Don Carlos, secretly supported the rising without actually captaining it (unlike in 1833). Determined to quash the legitimist threat to his rule, Ferdinand marched an army on Catalonia which pacified the region during September 1827. Dozens of rebel *cabecillas* were executed, whilst about three hundred combatants who were slow in taking the king's pardon were deported to the notorious garrison prisons of Ceuta. Saperes and Bosoms managed to flee to France, although the latter was lured back to the frontier in February 1828, where government agents briefly violated French territory in order to kidnap him and bring him to a swift execution.[120]

Attacks from the left

The absolutist police state likewise proved to be the nemesis of the *exaltado* invasions of Restoration Spain. All these foundered thanks to the failure to offer either sufficient force (Bazán) or a sufficient social-liberal agenda (Torrijos) to rally the popular classes. The exiles also divided themselves with an interminable shift towards the right and adventurism by many of the leaders. The exiles after 1823 set up two juntas, in London and Paris apiece. Of these the former was in the ascendant until the Wellington administration scrapped its subsidy in July 1829, whereupon the latter took over and was in consequence well placed to monopolise all operations in the wake of the July 1830 revolution. Historian, Irene Castells, divided the insurrectionary 'utopia' into two phases: the 1823–26 period of 'spontaneous agitation' and the 1826–31 period of 'organised agitation'.[121] Thus, 1824 was witness to two abortive incursions near Gibraltar, the August expedition of cashiered liberal General Valdés even captured the town of Tarifa. Nonetheless, this town was eventually retaken by Royalist Volunteers aided by French troops, despite a rising by agitators in the Serranía de Ronda (where an irregular bandit force was paid to proclaim the constitution in Benahavís).[122] The punishments were uniformly severe, several dozen men being executed and their bodies interred in makeshift unmarked graves away from consecrated ground. The government spy network proved repeatedly able to forestall other conspiracies hatched within Spain. Incursions from without set off a veritable paranoia about phantom ships, with the result that Royalist Volunteers were invariably ready at the beaches on those occasions when *exaltado* invaders really were disembarked.

Frustrated by the power of the régime, the London junta began to flirt with social radicalism (*reparto*) as a means of undermining absolutism from below. The exiles' leader, Espoz y Mina, saw tactical advantages in playing to popular grievances, observing that 'the common people, wishing to escape from their desperate condition, would be ready to follow anyone they believed might raise them out of their misery'.[123] In February 1826, Bazán's expedition to Valencia promised that future liberal disentailment of noble and clerical lands would see the plots shared out fairly. Bazán and his sixty men were executed soon after making landfall.[124] But the Madrid regime was rattled enough to answer Bazán's promises in the official *Gaceta de Madrid* which reported that the aims of the Bazán invasion were to 'defend the Garay tax system, establish a republic, banish our venerated customs, foster secret societies, and deliver honourable Spaniards to the fury of demagogues'. For good measure this false *précis* was circulated to the British and French embassies as part of the regime's campaign to convince these foreign governments to deny shelter to Spanish liberals.[125] Thus, the famous martyrdom of liberals, such as the *granadina* Mariana de Pineda, and of Torrijos obscured an uncertain number of humbler victims who either invaded in expeditions, rallied at the beachheads, or were simply condemned as members of *exaltado* networks. Thus, illicit Sunday political meetings were held at a secluded beach near Málaga by 'several constitutionalists looking to form a band'. In February 1830, the authorities closed in, arresting seven of the conspirators whilst the rest managed to flee. Similar meetings continued: three *exaltados* in June 1832 were sentenced to death, including Juan José Rumi, professor of the Colegio de Santiago in Granada; one Juan Mateo; and one Antonio Román Álvarez. Román Álvarez refused his last rites, so his body was interred in an unmarked grave.[126]

As for the exiles, the misery of the London skies was matched by their penury, which saw Mendizábal spend a brief spell in a London debtors' prison, and probably saw the elderly doyen of Spanish radicalism, Romero Alpuente, maintain a Madrid government spy as manservant in his service.[127] Other liberal elites were impressed enough by the régime's tenacity to suggest a more moderate liberal programme. It was during this decade that Espoz y Mina maintained a notoriously tight control over both internal and external revolutionary networks, with the effective aim, so he claimed, of keeping them in being until 'high politics' took a more favourable turn – as they certainly would between 1832 and 1834 – but which in fact was predicated by his desire that no one else should rival his position.[128] Just as younger liberals were starting to rebel against the old man's grip by rallying to the symbolic Constitution of 1812, Espoz y Mina reacted by formally disowning the document, conveniently reminding fellow exiles how it was 'hated by the people'. As for those *exaltado* exiles who kept the faith, their position nonetheless became increasingly desperate. José María Torrijos (1791–1831) managed, after 1827, to gain a certain say in the London exiles' agenda, aided by his well-connected 'Apostle' friends at the University of Cambridge. But he could not offset the frustration and despair felt by underground *exaltado* networks within Spain.

This drift towards the right even affected the author of the constitution himself, the 'divine' Agustín de Argüelles, who during his exile first became convinced by the need for a bicameral Cortes. Both Espoz's and Argüelles's rightward shift took place against what until 1830 was an unpromising diplomatic environment. In July 1829, the Spanish government successfully pressured the Wellington administration into scrapping Torrijos's subsidy.[129] Certainly, the Duke of Wellington's experiences in Spain had given him a pronounced distaste for revolutionaries. But if the *exaltados* were hoping for more solidarity from the liberal July Monarchy in France, they were to be disabused. For the following year showed how the 1830 revolution – though hailed by Pyrenean exiles as evidence of the progressive march of liberty – ultimately proved no bar to relations with Spain. The new Orleanist régime supported the Spanish liberals as a mere bargaining counter to be exchanged for Madrid's recognition of the dynasty. Once diplomatic relations were normalised, the exiles were cut off.[130]

In fact, it appears that the inconsiderate disclosure made by expeditionaries of the names of *exaltado* agents was beginning to drive a wedge between London and the peninsula.[131] It was unclear for how long Espoz could maintain his shaky grip on the exiles. In 1830 a certain José Osca creating a revolutionary junta in Madrid which answered only to conspirators within Spain.[132] Angered by this 'declaration of independence', Espoz y Mina dispatched a hasty expedition to Cádiz and San Fernando which, in being badly botched, persuaded Torrijos to steal a march on the old adventurer. In December 1831, Torrijos led an international expedition to the Costa del Sol, including some of his 'Apostle' friends from the University of Cambridge. The expedition was betrayed soon after it made landfall, and Torrijos and his fifty-two comrades were executed on the beach near Málaga. Torrijos thus joined the pantheon of liberal martyrs, at the right hand of Riego. In reality, Torrijos's heroic gesture had been a desperate grab for leadership by a young man.

As Ferdinand advanced into old age, he combined sensible policies, such as the creation of the modern public Bank of San Fernando in 1829 with backward policies, such as the last major attempt to reconquer Mexico in

1829. In 1829, an ominous policy was also produced, his marriage to his beautiful niece, María Cristina of Naples. Ferdinand's terminally declining health did not prevent him from rediscovering his virility and producing two children who, unlike in the case of his previous marriages, would survive infancy. But, ominously, the sex of both children was female. What in other circumstances might prove a commentary on dynastic sexism in the polarised politics of Spain would produce a civil war. Ferdinand, who, for all his timidity and vindictiveness, never lost his common touch or his common sense, aptly described himself as a 'cork in a bottle of beer'. Once the cork was removed, all the ills of the kingdom would surge forth. Ferdinand's death on 29 September 1833 left debate about the sexist 'Salic Law' unresolved.

In 1832, the dying king had seemed set to pass to his younger brother (and vehement 'throne and altar' reactionary), Don Carlos, in accordance with the Salic Law, which excluded female heirs from the succession and which had governed the Bourbon dynasty since the War of Succession. The Salic Law was not unique to Spain. The British monarch ended its personal union with Hannover in 1837 on Victoria's ascent to the throne and the Schleswig-Holstein question was also complicated by the Salic Law. But uniquely in Spain, this question sparked a civil war, when the king's brief recovery and effective surrender of authority to a moderately reformist regency under his last wife, María Cristina, dashed Carlos's hopes of a smooth transition. This regency revoked the Salic Law in favour of the succession of the royal daughter, Isabel, whose minority reign would be exercised by her mother's regency when the king's death finally came in September 1833. Yet this transition did not take place in a context of mere court politics, for proto-Carlist agitation had not entirely died down since the defeat of the *Agraviados* in 1827. An abortive rising launched at the end of 1832 in Don Carlos's name forced the prince to flee to Portugal, after which news of his exclusion from the succession finally provoked him into openly raising his standard. Exasperated by the news that Carlos would not recognise the Isabelline succession, the dying king ordered his younger brother into a permanent Italian exile as the most expedient means of guaranteeing Isabel's throne. Carlos prevaricated and reopened the *miguelista-agraviado* conspiratorial network which had been dormant since 1827 whilst at the same time making sure not to risk re-entering Spain until Fernando was dead and enough armed Carlist support was forthcoming.[133]

Notes

1 Pedro Rújula, 'Pedro Gómez Labrador en el Congreso de Viena', in Xosé M. Núñez Seixas (ed.), *Historia Mundial de España* (Barcelona: Destino, 2018), pp. 519–25.
2 Ivana Frasquet, '1824: Ayacucho, el fin del Imperio', in Seixas (ed.), *Historia mundial de España*, pp. 535–6.
3 A.H.N., Consejos (*Causas de Estado*), leg. 6291–92: 17 May 1814 police report into 'republican' disorders.

4 Cit. Charles Wentz Fehrenbach, 'Moderados and Exaltados: The Liberal Opposition to Ferdinand VII, 1814–1823', *The Hispanic American Historical Review*, Vol. 50, No. 1 (February 1970), p. 53.
5 B.U.Z., Casamayor, XXXI (1814): May diary entries.
6 García Fernández, *El origen del municipio constitucional* (Madrid: IEAL), pp. 304–5.
7 Miguel Artola, *La España de Fernando VII* (Madrid: Espasa, 1999), pp. 425–30.
8 A.H.N., Consejos, leg. 6120, No. 126: 22 July 1817 petition by Menéndez Valdés family to Consejo en Sala de Justicia); No. 88, 3 June 1817 plea from Parque to Consejo de Sala de Justicia.
9 *Eco del Comercio*, 20 January 1842.
10 Cit. Hargreaves-Mawdsley, *Spain under the Bourbons*, pp. 273–4.
11 Valentina Fernández Vargas, 'Las españolas durante la Guerra de la Independencia', in *La Guerra de la Independencia (1808–1814): el pueblo español, su ejército y sus aliados frente a la ocupación napoleónica* (Madrid: Ministerio de Defensa, 2007), pp. 127–49.
12 Cit. Juan Francisco Fuentes and Lluís Roura i Aulinas (eds.), *Sociabilidad y liberalismo en la España del siglo XIX* (Lleida: Editorial Milenio, 2001), p. 81.
13 B.U.Z., Casamayor, XXXIV (1817): 21 April 1817 diary entry.
14 *La abolición de la Inquisición Española*: Discurso leído el día 2 de diciembre de 1991, en su recepción pública, por el Excmo. Señor D. José Antonio Escudero y contestación del Excmo. Señor D. Alfonso García Gallo de Diego (Madrid, 1991), pp. 10–18.
15 Jules Renouard, *Narración de D. Juan Van Halen, Gefe de Estado Mayor de una de las divisiones de Mina en 1822 y 1823, ó relación circunstanciada de su cautividad en los calabozos de la Inquisición, su evasión y su emigración*, Vol. II (Paris, 1828), p. 58.
16 This practice often hampered the petty (and popular) activities of smugglers, particularly in such port cities as Málaga (Andrés Sarría Muñoz, *Breve historia de Málaga* (Málaga: Editorial Sarría, 1995), pp. 74–81).
17 B.U.Z., Casamayor, XXXIV (1817):11 February 1817 proclamation by Marqués de Lazán (Palafox).
18 Maestrojuán Catalán, *Ciudad de vasallos, Nación de heroes (Zaragoza: 1809–1814)*, p. 510.
19 For example, José Cepeda Gómez, *El ejército español en la política española (1789–1843): conspiraciones y pronunciamientos en los comienzos de la España liberal* (Madrid: Fundación Universitaria Española, 1990), pp. 304–5; María del Pilar Ramos Rodríguez, *Conspiración del Triángulo* (Sevilla: Universidad de Sevilla, 1970), pp. 9–10.
20 José Luis Comellas, *Los primeros pronunciamientos en España, 1814–1820* (Madrid: Consejo Superior de Investigaciones Científicas, 1958), pp. 355–68.
21 Artola, *La España de Fernando VII*, pp. 492–5.
22 Jordi Maluquer de Motes, *El socialismo en España, 1833–1868* (Barcelona: Crítica, 1977), pp. 122–3; Callahan, *Church, Politics and Society in Spain*, p. 113.
23 A.H.N., Estado, leg. 3128, Prisión de Cayetano Iluminati y estado de la masonería en Italia: (unnumbered document) 'Apuntes sobre la conspiración abortada el 2 de enero de 1819'.
24 Carlos le Brun, *Retratos políticos de la revolución de España* (Philadeplhia, 1826), pp. 210–12; *The Times*, 4 December 1815.
25 Lawrence, 'Popular Radicalism in Spain', p. 77.
26 Herráiz de Miota, 'Los montepíos militares del siglo XVIII como origen del sistema de clases pasivas del estado', p. 199.
27 A.H.N., Consejos, leg. 3781, tomo I, No. 2: 7 October 1826 recirculation of Garay's 30 May 1817 tax reforms.
28 Earlier attempts by Escoiquiz in 1815 to disentail some ecclesiastical and military estates met with the trenchant and successful opposition of the church and the Ordenes Militares (Fernández, *El origen del municipio constitucional*, pp. 304–5).
29 Moreno Alonso, *Blanco White*, p. 470.

30 Geoffrey Jensen, 'War and the Military', in Shubert and Junco (eds.), *The History of Modern Spain*, pp. 329–34.
31 Alberto Gil Novales, *Las sociedades patrióticas (1820–1823)* (Madrid: Editorial Tecnos, 1975), p. 127.
32 José Luis Comellas García-Llera, *El trienio constitucional* (Madrid: Editoriales Rialp, 1963), p. 43.
33 Cit. Ramos Rodríguez, *La conspiración del Triángulo*, pp. 7–8.
34 Gil Novales, Alberto (ed.), *Rafael del Riego, La revolución de 1820, día a día: cartas, escritos y discursos* (Prólogo, biografía sucinta, notas y recopilación de documentos por Alberto Gil Novales) (Madrid: Editorial Tecnos, 1976), pp. 45–6.
35 Nicolás Sánchez-Albornoz, *Las crisis de subsistencias de España en el siglo XIX* (Rosario: Universidad Nacional del Litoral, 1963), pp. 16–17.
36 Jaime Torras, *Liberalismo y rebeldía campesina (1820–1823)* (Barcelona: Ariel, 1976), pp. 149–64.
37 Gil Novales (ed.), *Riego, Revolución de 1820, día a día*, p. 38.
38 The Inquisition had become hated for its zeal for the police state. That said, as with the storming of the Bastille in 1789, only a handful of political prisoners was found, none of whom bore signs of torture (*La abolición de la Inquisición Española*, pp. 85–6.).
39 Víctor Sánchez Martín, 'Creación, construcción y dudas sobre la imagen del héroe', in Encarna García Monerris, Mónica Moreno Seco, and Juan I. Marcuello Benedicto (eds.), *Culturas políticas en la España liberal*, p. 64.
40 Cit. Artola, *La España de Fernando VII*, p. 507.
41 Antonio Moliner Prada, *Revolución burguesa y movimiento juntero en España* (Lleida: Milenio, 1997), pp. 109–10.
42 Thomas Bunbury, *Reminiscences of a Veteran Being Personal and Military Adventures in Portugal, Spain, France, Malta, New South Wales, Norfolk Island, New Zealand, Andaman Islands and India*, Vol. II (London: C J Skeet, 1861), pp. 48–54.
43 Comellas, *Trienio constitucional*, p. 51.
44 Callahan, *Church, Politics and Society*, pp. 120–1.
45 *Diario de Sesiones de Cortes* (henceforth *DSC*), No. 126, 7 November 1820, 2143; *The Times*, 29 September 1820).
46 Cit. Alberto Gil Novales, *Textos exaltados del Trienio Liberal* (Madrid: Ediciones Júcar, 1978), pp. 33–47.
47 B.U.Z., Casamayor, XXXVII (1820): 21 April 1820 transcription of Junta Gubernativa resolution to establish National Militia.
48 Juan Sisinio Pérez Garzón, *Milicia Nacional y revolución burguesa: el prototipo madrileño 1808–1874* (Madrid: Consejo Superior de Investigaciones Científicas, 1978), pp. 97–109.
49 *DSC*, No. 69, 11 September 1820, 931; No. 68, 26 April 1821, 1278–9; No.30, 24 October 1821, 369–70.
50 Torras, *Liberalismo y rebeldía campesina*, pp. 149–64.
51 Isidoro Lara Martín-Portugues, *Jaén: la lucha por la libertad durante el trienio constitucional (1820–1823)* (Jaén: Ayuntamiento de Jaén, 1996), pp. 204–5.
52 Comellas, *Trienio constitucional*, p. 83.
53 Gil Novales, *Sociedades Patrióticas*, pp. 574–7.
54 Torras, *Liberalismo y rebeldía campesina*, pp. 49–50.
55 *El Universal Observador Español*, 10 March 1821; Maunel Tuñón de Lara, *El movimiento obrero en la historia de España*, Vol. I (Madrid: Sarpe, 1985), pp. 54–5; Julio Berenguer Barceló, *Historia de Alcoy*, Vol. II (Alcoy: Llorens Distribuidor, 1977), pp. 90–6.
56 *DSC*, No. 12, 9 March 1821, 382.
57 Callahan, *Church, Politics and Society*, p. 124.
58 *El Espectador*, 9 June 1821.
59 Gil Novales, *Sociedades Patrióticas*, pp. 373–91; *El Espectador*, 11 May 1822.

60 *El Espectador*, 4 September 1821; 5 September 1821; 26 September 1821.

61 *El Espectador*, 5 September 1821.

62 *El Universal Observador Español*, 25 May 1821; Sarría Muñoz, *Historia de Málaga*, pp. 74–81.

63 Joanna Innes and Mark Philp, *Re-Imagining Democracy in the Mediterranean, 1780–1860* (Oxford: Oxford University Press, 2018).

64 Marichal, *El secreto de España*, p. 239.

65 Antonio Eiras Roel, *Sociedades secretas republicanas en el reinado de Isabel II* (Madrid: Instituto Jerónimo Zurita, 1962), pp. 15–16; Peter Quennell, *Byron: The Years of Fame, Byron in Italy* (London: Harper Collins, 1974), pp. 368–71.

66 *El Espectador*, 30 November 1821.

67 *El Espectador*, 8 September 1821; Comellas, *Trienio constitucional*, pp. 238–45.

68 A.H.N., Estado, leg. 3141, no. 3: post-1823 summary of the deeds of the Ayuntamiento Constitucional de Madrid; Gil Novales, *Sociedades Patrióticas*, pp. 652–60.

69 María Cruz Romeo Mateo, *Entre el orden y la revolución* (Alicante: Instituto de Cultura, 1993), pp. 162–3.

70 Pérez Garzón, *Milicia Nacional*, p. 109.

71 Marqués de Miraflorres, *Apuntes histórico-críticos para escribir la historia de la revolución de España desde el año 1820 hasta 1823* (London: Oficina de Ricardo Taylor, 1834), p. 102.

72 A.G.P., Papeles Reservados de Fernando VII, 67, Palacio, folios 216, 338: post-1823 details of organisational structure of the *Comuneros* and records of its membership in Motril.

73 *El Espectador*, 1 July 1822.

74 *Ibid.*, 3 July 1822.

75 A.H.N., Estado, 125, no. 31: 22 September 1822 resolution published by Council of State addressing collaboration between *campesinos* and *facciosos*.

76 Thus, the Zaragoza priest Pascual Ruiz was brutally murdered by some National Militia in that city after he appeared to have made a particularly strident sermon (B.U.Z., Casamayor (1822), XXXIX: 28 July 1822 entry).

77 *El Espectador*, 24 December 1822; 9 January 1823; 14 January 1823; 13 February 1823.

78 Cit. Fehrenbach, 'Moderados and Exaltados', p. 68.

79 Josep Fontana, *De en medio del tiempo: la segunda restauración española, 1823–1834* (Barcelona: Crítica, 2006), pp. 48–9; Gil Novales, *Sociedades Patrióticas*, pp. 401–2.

80 Comellas, *Trienio constitucional*, p. 216.

81 In fact, the 1822–23 dictatorship of the left gave conservative liberals an enduring opportunity to depict the *exaltados* as the "real absolutists" (*El Mundo: Diario del Pueblo*, 20 April 1838).

82 Pérez Garzón, *Milicia nacional*, p. 338; Eiras Roel, *Sociedades secretas*, p. 10.

83 Thus, the former presents as counter-revolution the refusal of the prefect of Granada to approve a June 1823 petition from the local Patriotic Society to arm the people (Gil Novales, *Sociedades Patrióticas*, pp. 500–1). Rújula, meanwhile, invokes the April 1823 decision of the constitutional authorities of Zaragoza to demobilise the National Militia, spike its artillery, and dump fifty thousand pounds of gunpowder into the Ebro, as acts of "liberal desertion" (Pedro Rújula, *Constitución o Muerte: el trienio liberal y los levantamientos realistas en Aragón (1820–1823)* (Zaragoza: Edizións de l'Astral, 2000), pp. 195–204).

84 Raymond Carr, *Spain (1808–1975)* (Oxford: Oxford University Press, 1982), p. 141.

85 Fontana, *De en medio del tiempo*, pp. 51–2; Esdaile, 'Prohombres, aventureros y oportunistas: la influencia del trayecto personal en los orígenes del liberalismo en España', in Alda Blanco and Guy Thomson (eds.), *Visiones del liberalismo: política, identidad y cultura en la España del siglo XIX* (Valencia: Universitat de València, 2008), pp. 65–87.

86 A.H.N., Diversos (*títulos y familia*), leg. 3353, doc. 6: 24 July 1823 proclamation by Antonio Salinas de Orellana, Comandante military of the province of Córdoba; *Eco del Comercio*, 14 September 1838.

87 Benito Pérez Galdós, *Un faccioso más . . . y algunos frailes menos* (Episodios Nacionales, 20, Segunda Serie) (Madrid: Alianza, 2005), p. 12.
88 Cit. Raul López López-Portillo, *España de Riego* (Madrid: Silex, 2005), p. 358.
89 Ringrose, *Spain, Europe and the 'Spanish Miracle', 1700–1900*, p. 118.
90 Rodríguez O., *"We are now the True Spaniards"*, p. 6.
91 Harold Temperley and Lillian M. Penson, *Foundations of British Foreign Policy, 1792–1902* (Abingdon: Routledge, 1966), p. 69.
92 Harold Temperley, *The Foreign Policy of Canning: 1822–1827* (Abingdon: Routledge, 2006), p. 109.
93 Natalia Sobrevilla, 'From Europe to the Andes and Back: Becoming "Los Ayacuchos'", *European History Quarterly*, Vol. 41, No. 3 (July 2011), pp. 472–88.
94 Maximiliano Barrio Gozao, 'La segunda restauración española a través de los despachos del nuncio Giustiniani (1823–1827)', *Pasado y Memoria. Revista de Historia Contemporánea*, Vol. 16 (2017), pp. 121–48, 123–4.
95 Gracia Gómez Urdáñez, *Salustiano de Olózaga: élites políticas en el liberalismo español 1805–1843* (Logroño: Universidad de La Rioja, 1999), p. 85; Even a monographical study of this decade by Josep Fontana was titled *In the middle of time* (Fontana, *De en medio del tiempo*).
96 Pedro Pegenaute, *Represión política en el reinado de Fernando VII: las comisiones militares* (Pamplona: Universidad de Navarra, 1974), pp. 84–7.
97 Manuel Espadas Burgos, *Baldomero Espartero: un candidato al trono de España* (Madrid: Biblioteca de Autores Manchegos, 1986), pp. 36–42.
98 Mark Lawrence, 'From Restoration to Indoctrination: Liberals, Reactionaries and the People in Spain, 1814–1823', in Michael Broers, Ambrogio Caiani, and Stephen Bann (eds.), *A History of the European Restorations: Culture, Society and Religion*, Vol. 2 (London: Bloomsbury, 2019); Fontana, *De en medio del tiempo*, pp. 140–55.
99 Alfonso García Tejero, *Historia politico-administrativa de Mendizábal*, Vol. 1 (Madrid: Ortigosa, 1858), p. 152.
100 When Catalonia's University of Cervera reopenedin May 1827, its opening address was 'far be it for us to indulge in the dangerous novelty of thinking' (cit. Fontana, *De en medio del tiempo*, pp. 152–53).
101 Fontana, *De en medio*, p. 98.
102 Cit. *Ibid.*, pp. 157–58.
103 Coro Rubio Pobes, *Revolución y tradición: el país vasco ante la revolución liberal y la construcción del estado liberal, 1808–1868* (Madrid: Siglo XXI de España Editores, 1996), p. 78.
104 Fontana, *De en medio*, pp. 114–17.
105 Pérez Garzón, *Milicia Nacional*, p. 352.
106 Fontana, *De en medio*, pp. 72–6, 140; Pío Baroja, *Siluetas Románticas (y otras historias de pillos y de extravagantes)* (Madrid: Espasa-Calpe, 1934), pp. 142–8.
107 A.H.N., Estado, leg. 217–2, No. 24: May 1826 complaint by Pablo, Bishop of Barcelona, to the Duque del Infantado, king's first minister.
108 *Eco del Comercio*, 9 March 1837; Fontana, *De en medio*, p. 102.
109 A.G.P., Reinados, FVII, Caja 27, No. 181: 24 July 1826 letter from Prince Carlos to the king.
110 A.G.P., Reinados, FVII, Caja 27, No. 146, 147: 25 and 26 July 1824 letters from Prince Carlos to the king.
111 Fontana, *De en medio*, pp. 159–60.
112 A.H.N., Estado, leg. 217–2, No. 48: 4 November 1826 investigation by Consejo de Gracia y Justicia into disturbances in Ubeda.
113 Callahan, *Church, Politics and Society*, pp. 128–36.
114 The victim was the teacher Cayetano Ripoll, found guilty of Deism by a 'faith council', or *junta de la fé* (unlike in 1814 Ferdinand in 1823 did not revive the Inquisition); *La abolición de la Inquisición Española*, pp. 92–3.

115 Cit. Jaime Elías Torras, *La guerra de los Agraviados* (Barcelona: Cátedra de Historia general de España, 1967), pp. XI–XII.

116 Fontana, *De en medio*, pp. 165–93.

117 Torras, *La guerra de los Agraviados*, pp. 1–40, 56, 95–109.

118 Fontana, *De en medio*, pp. 229–30.

119 Torras, *La guerra de los Agraviados*, p. 98.

120 *Ibid.*, pp. 66–94.

121 Irene Castells, *La Utopía insurreccional del liberalismo: Torrijos y las conspiraciones liberales de la década ominosa* (Barcelona: Crítica, 1989), pp. 26–7.

122 *Ibid.*, pp. 30–1; Fontana, *De en medio*, pp. 169–77.

123 Cit., Castells, *La Utopía insurreccional*, p. 62.

124 *Ibid.*, pp. 107–11.

125 A.H.N., Estado, leg. 217–2, No. 17: 9 March 1826 advice from *camarilla* to king on how to proceed with the manifesto of Antonio Fernández Bazán.

126 A.M.M., 3/183, *Anales*, pp. 18–22.

127 Baroja, *Siluetas románticas*, p. 78; Romero Alpuente pressurised the influential Hispanophile Lord Holland into interceding with Prime Minster Wellington on his behalf, but no subsidy was forthcoming (Moreno Alonso, *Forja de liberalismo*, pp. 394–6). Matters certainly could not have been helped by Wellington's memory of Romero Alpuente's pamphleteering during the 1808–14 war, when the radical condemned Britain as a "threat" to liberty and *Generalísimo* Wellington, in particular, for being a Tory willing to humiliate Spanish interests abroad and "encourage the *serviles*" to overthrow the revolution (Juan Romero Alpuente, *Wellington en España y Ballesteros en Ceuta* [Cádiz, 1813]).

128 José María Iribarren, *Espoz y Mina: el Liberal* (Madrid: Editorial Aguilar, 1967), pp. 370–5; Isabel Burdiel, Manuel Ledesma, and Manuel Pérez, *Liberales, agitadores y conspiradores: Biografías heterodoxas del siglo XIX* (Madrid: Espasa Calpe, 2000), p. 89; Castells, *La Utopía insurreccional*, p. 120.

129 Castells, *La Utopía insurreccional*, p. 153.

130 Artola, *La España de Fernando VII*, pp. 724–7.

131 A.H.N., Estado, leg. 217–2, No. 17: intercepted correspondence between Bazán and Fransico Milans and Antonio Salinas detailing the names of sympathetic and hostile residents in Guardamar (Alicante).

132 Castells, *La Utopía insurreccional*, pp. 148, 205.

133 A.G.P., Caja 28/3, Reinados, FVII, 27: series of letters between Fernando VII and Don Carlos.

Chapter 3

1833–44: Carlists, liberals, and *caudillos*

The First Carlist War (1833–40) is almost unknown outside of Spain, and yet it was the country's most decisive conflict in modern history. By some measurements it was bloodier than the Spanish Civil War, relative to population. The First Carlist War had an immense demographic and indirect political impact, even though the bloodshed was usually highly localised and economic damage limited. Because the physical manifestations of the war were localised and limited, historians often overlooked the immense bloodshed and suffering caused by hunger, disease, and desertion.[1] Contemporary observers at home and abroad saw in this war two Spains fighting as clerical-reactionary Carlists, on one hand, and the modernising Liberals on the other. The war would take twice as long to resolve as the civil war of the 1930s, and it would attract a similar degree of international partisanship. From 1834, thousands of European volunteers would enlist to fight with one of the two Spains locked in mortal combat. They did so independently in the case of Carlism, given Chancellor Metternich's refusal openly to challenge the diplomatic supremacy in Spain of the pro-Cristino liberal monarchies (Britain and France). Volunteering for the Cristino side, by contrast, became a more organised affair as Britain, France, and Portugal from 1834 raised 'auxiliary legions' for service in the Cristino army as part of a 'Quadruple Alliance' policy that could not have been more opposed to Carlism short of actually declaring war.

For all the diverse historiography concerning 1830s Carlism, the military historiography has been perhaps the least innovative. As Manuel Santirso remarked, students of history in Spain study their country's numerous nineteenth-century wars at best only in passing, and even academic and public military history 'follow the compass of commemorations'[2] Certainly, the First Carlist War (1833–40) abounds in the Spanish historiography more broadly. For a century, the war was presented in partisan terms, as traditionalists and liberals produced very learned if also tendentious histories.

The First Carlist War historiography may be divided into five broad categories. The first comprised nineteenth-century dynastic and classical diplomatic, biographical, and military histories. Antonio Pirala's six volumes are the outstanding example. The second comprised the panegyrics from Franco-era traditionalists who depicted Carlism as an organic Christian good resisting the onslaught of godless and artificial Spanish liberalism. The First Carlist War was but one protracted episode in the wider war between Christianity and the anti-Spain that was joined in 1808 and won by the crusaders only in 1939. The most impressive work in this vein was the thirty-volume history of traditionalism edited by Melchor Ferrer from the 1940s. The third category comprised the 'Navarra School' of Pamplona-based neo-traditionalists, led by Federico Suárez Verdeguer. These scholars sustained a far more sophisticated right-wing analysis based on modern empirical research. Their contention that Spain remained royalist, or apolitical, throughout this period viewed Carlism as an imperfect answer to a worse question posed by liberalism. As the best neo-traditionalist scholar of the First Carlist War, Alfonso Bullón de Mendoza, put it, the Cristino Liberals were waging war against their own people.

The neo-traditionalists were challenged from their own ranks by a heresy of 'neo-Carlists' writing from the 1970s who reinterpreted the nineteenth-century Carlist struggles as 'objectively revolutionary' and from the non-Carlist left by liberal and Marxist historians. Both the 'heretics' and the ideologues were interested in the socio-economic drivers of counter-revolution and much less in its military aspects. To a large degree this focus was justified by the complexity of 1830s Carlism. There were three major '*focos*' of armed Carlism: most of Navarra and the upland Basque provinces in the north, the Aragón-Valencia uplands centred on the Maestrazgo in the east, and, the smallest zone, the Catalan far west. The motives for armed counter-revolution have been shown to be complex, certainly more complex than the victorious Liberals allowed. A Barcelona newspaper in 1840 reflected on the recently extinguished civil war, attributing Basque Carlism to the defence of 'liberties' (especially the autonomous '*fueros*'), Catalan Carlism to 'religious fanaticism', and Aragonese Carlism to 'banditry'.[3]

In reality, the motivations for Basque Carlism were at least threefold: a 'foralist' wing driven by defence of the region's historical autonomy, a dynastic wing driven by 'Castilian' refugees from Cristino-held Spain who refused to accept María Cristina's 'usurpation' of the throne in the name of her daughter and an intransigent ultramontane wing with adherents from within the Carlist Basque country and from beyond. Catalan Carlism was driven, in part, by religiosity as well as by economic decline in the interior where the insurgency would take hold, as Carlist insurgents drew support from Catalan nobles under economic siege. Socio-economic motives also pertained in the Aragón-Valencia insurgency (where many villagers backed Ramón Cabrera's ruthless insurgency in defence of their use-ownership of lands which liberalism threatened to alienate with legal contracts).[4]

Paradoxically, even though Basque Carlism was more diverse in its motives and more developed in its political, economic, and military strategy, it was also the more 'solvable' from the Cristino point of view, as the application of Madrid's symmetrical warfare and timely concessions would show. Catalan and, especially, Aragonese Carlism, by contrast, baffled the Cristinos who usually ended up applying terror tactics to the usually even worse terror inflicted by such eastern warlords as Ramón Cabrera (1806–77) and Count España (1775–1839). When Evaristo San Miguel (1785–1862), Cristino captain general of Aragón during some of the worst fighting, wrote that 'agricultural improvements' in the Maestazgo might yet prize the population away from the grip of Cabrera's Carlists, his thoughts underlined the impossibility of waging a coherent counter-insurgency.[5] What united all insurgent regions was a popular tradition of armed insurrection, as witnessed in regional particularities in militia service which had been heavily bloodied in the national and civil wars of 1808–14, 1821–23, and 1827. In the Carlist Basque country formal militarisation would take place by 1835 at the latest, yet in the east, especially the Catalan far west, the irregular nature of warfare remained a major feature throughout.

Carlist insurgencies

The three months after the king's death in September 1833 witnessed the mobilisation of a substantial body of armed Carlist support, mostly comprising Royalist Volunteers and army officers cashiered for political unreliability. Thus, on 7 October 1833 in Vitoria, Royalist commander Valentín Verástegui, proclaimed Carlos V. Carlists also occupied Bilbao for 53 days at the outset of the war, imposing a regime of organised extortion until they retreated before the arrival of superior Cristino forces.[6] The geographical location of the first risings is significant. Conservative, ecclesiastical Álava and Vizcaya, set amidst a Basque countryside of stable peasant landownership, church–lay harmony, and powerful *fueros*, was natural Carlist territory, as landownership patterns were stable, prosperous, and without great disparities in wealth, whilst the church was popular enough to mobilise the countryside against the liberal towns (Bilbao). The same might be said of upland Navarra, but not the Ribera, where large estates and rural poverty resembled the Andalucían *latifundia* and where landowners remained Cristino throughout.

Over the course of 1834 Carlist territorial control increased over the rural Basque country thanks to the efforts of the greatest military genius of the Carlist War, Tomás de Zumalacárregui (1788–1835). Zumalacárregui implemented what turned out to be a three-stage strategy turning his insurgent '*foco*' into a regular 'Royal Army'. First, between the winter of 1833 and the following summer he employed his peasant soldiers in a guerrilla war of surprise and ambush. During this first stage his army lacked the strength to threaten urban centres, particularly the prized Vizcayan capital, Bilbao. Zumalacárregui's second phase ran from the summer of 1834 until the winter and involved controlling rural territory and communications. The ensuing third stage involved taking Cristino forts and fortified towns, which culminated in the failed first Carlist siege of Bilbao during the spring and summer of 1835. Even though Zumalacárregui was fatally wounded in this siege, his achievement of creating Carlist territorial control over almost all of Navarra and the Basque country, minus their provincial capitals, remained generally intact until 1839. Ramón Cabrera's eastern insurgency also underwent three incremental stages, although concerted Carlist rebellion here would not take off until 1835. During the first stage, from 1833 to 1835, the Carlist effort here was dispersed by the Cristinos and confined to rural guerrilla warfare. The second phase, from 1836 to 1837, produced a breakthrough as Cabrera expanded the rural boundaries of the Carlist control and turned it into a military state. During the third phase, from 1838 to 1839, in contrast to the stagnation in the Carlist Basque country, the Maestrazgo reached its apogee in terms of geography, military victories, and recruitment. The Carlist zone in rural Catalonia was more hemmed in by terrain and a particularly vigorous Cristino counter-insurgency during 1833–1834. It also had to wait longer for effective Carlist leadership to emerge, under, first, Juan Antonio Guergué (1789–1839) and, then, the Count España.[7]

If the above areas became the hotbeds of the Carlist insurgency, and the graveyards of angry young men serving in the *cristino* armies, the war also ebbed and flowed to include rural parts of northern Spain (and, to a lesser extent, New Castile and the south). These areas suffered invasions and counter-invasions which set off cycles of Carlist-liberal reprisal and counter-reprisal which amounted to brutal outbursts of the same sort of crowd grievances discussed in this thesis hitherto. Thus, even if pitched battles were fought (Amézcoas, Villafranca, Bilbao), and even if the militarily superior (though numerically smaller) Carlist armies managed to carry the fight far into the south in 1836, and again in 1837, the civil war was much more than a battle of armies, important though these were. Even the largest liberal towns contained Carlist sympathisers, whilst by the same token, liberals were found in those provinces north of the Ebro which for the most part had gone over to the insurgency. The climate of insecurity created by this political divide was exacerbated by banditry, a chronic problem now made acute thanks to desertion and the disintegration of Cristino armies deployed far from supply lines.

Liberalism returns

Even though Regent María Cristina was an absolutist at heart, the Carlist insurgency obliged her to seek political support from across the spectrum of Spanish elites. Thus, liberal exiles were pardoned and the Spanish state reformulated along liberal lines. Unlike in 1820 political reforms were gradual. Two laws in 1833 made municipalities more accountable via a restrictive franchise reserved to wealthier residents and guildsmen.[8] But unlike during the eighteenth century, when the monarch and the church hierarchy had agreed on enlightened reforms in order to strengthen the state, the Cristino transition decisively entrenched the pattern of the nineteenth century. Now the monarchy and church opposed enlightened reforms. Their hand was forced by such new forces as intellectuals, politicised army officers and civil servants, the latter including Javier de Burgos, who in 1833 modernised Spain's old regime territorial organisation into forty-nine provinces.[9] In February 1834, the liberals' militia was restored, albeit for the time being without the symbolic 'National' prefix and the 'Urban Militia' had more restrained powers of action than its 1820–23 predecessor. Finally, in April 1834, absolutism was broken when the Royal Statute (Estatuto Real) was 'granted' by the queen-regent, a charter which by establishing an appointed upper chamber, severely limiting franchise, and omitting all reference to the sovereignty of the nation, managed to be even more restrictive the French Chartre of 1814. Only such resolute radicals as Romero Alpuente and Flórez Estrada still wanted the Constitution of 1812, and the former died in 1835 whilst the latter focused more on social than political reform.[10] In late 1833, in response to the Carlist risings in rural northern Castile, Flórez Estrada convened a defence junta which defended Santander against a Carlist assault. The junta instituted universal suffrage for the election of its members, apparently repeating Flórez Estrada's youthful radicalism at the Oviedo junta of 1809. Yet the Cristino generals, whose political powers had been strengthened in the wake of the La Granja crisis of 1832, proved as hostile to the left as they were to the Carlists. In January 1834, General Quesada overthrew Estrada's junta at Santander, imposing military over civil power in an incident reminiscent of the Marqués de la Romana's action against the Oviedo junta of 1809.[11]

Similarly modest liberalisation was shown towards the press. Even if political newspapers were permitted for the first time since the Triennium, laws passed in January and June 1834 subjected them to previous censorship by prefect, whilst any journals which dared to print radical political opinions without notifying the censor ran the risk of incurring a harsh two-stage penalty of fines (2,000, then 4,000 *reales*), followed by outright suppression for the third infraction.[12] Journalists would quickly test the boundaries of these laws. The young Romantic, Mariano José de Larra, disguised his political criticism in literary and cultural journals. Early in 1835 he poked fun at the po-faced platitudes let through by the censors: 'Bad words are those that contain whole and determined meanings . . . anarchy, conspiracy, the press' . . . (whereas) 'good words are those that don't say anything at all . . . prosperity, enlightenment, justice, reform'.[13] The press laws were overhauled completely in 1836, not least because by then the press had become proxies for the two rival liberal parties. In part, this phenomenon reflects the premium placed on the written word at a time when there was no constitutional guarantee of freedom of speech (this did not come until the Constitution of 1869). But the civil war created an avid readership amongst the literate minority and their audiences in cafés and clubs, eager to know military and political developments, a curiosity which was satisfied by flourishing networks of provincial correspondents who reported the movements of armies and irregulars whilst also increasingly offering their own political opinions.

Newspapers also acted as semi-official organs of the political parties, becoming vectors of a recognisably bipartisan political system. The *progresistas* believed in 'municipal democracy', wider franchise for national elections, free trade and enterprise, whilst their *moderado* rivals favoured a centralised technocracy, restricted electoral franchise, economic protectionism and paternalism. As with the *exaltados* of the Triennium, it was the *progresistas* who embodied the *para-poder* by agitating in clubs and societies, and making 'balcony promises'.

Thus, the toll taken by the Ominous Decade combined with the ageing of erstwhile radical leaders dictated gradual rather than revolutionary reform. The bicameral legislature of the Royal Statute had no teeth to bring about radical change. In any case, only 27 *procuradores* of the 188-strong lower house had been deputies during the Triennium, whilst only half of this faction had been *exaltados*.[14] But radicals still had the streets, and as a consequence of the long civil war, they would soon have the army. In the summer of 1834, Romero Alpuente launched a secret society in Madrid, naming it impeccably after the infant queen, La Isabelina. This society aimed to overthrow the Royal Statute, replacing it with a modified bicameral version of the Constitution of 1812. La Isabelina mobilised multiple signatures to a petition to the queen-regent, which threatened street barricades and the convocation of a National Assembly if demands were not met. Yet the government penetrated this conspiracy, arresting leading figures. As these men were quickly released, it is difficult to judge whether a lengthier imprisonment might have resulted in the barricades springing to life and the Assembly being convoked.[15] What seems likely is that the government feared that to take condign measures against the conspirators would run the risk of making martyrs out of them (in fact, the continued imprisonment of a single member of the conspiracy and author of the abortive Isabelina constitution, Eugenio de Aviraneta, proved to be a lingering grievance which drove the Urban Militia revolt in Madrid during the August 1835 revolution of the juntas[16]). In any case, Romero Alpuente died of natural causes in January 1835, depriving radical liberalism of one of its ablest and most determined leaders.

Associations of Carlism with populist violence were quick to form in the minds of Cristino elites. As one *moderado* newspaper warned, Carlism could never be attractive to people who have something to lose 'because it is in fact a kind of pure democracy, demagoguery, and anarchy'.[17] Instead, Cristino liberals believed in 'liberty within the law' (*libertad bien entendida*). Yet this mantra, frequently repeated in the press, was belied by the unequal demands imposed by the civil war. The wealthy could still buy their way out of conscription whereas for those without funds or friends in authority the appeal of deserting to the Carlists was obvious. A year into the struggle, one Cristino commander reported that his men were demoralized, performing police actions in the Maestrazgo as their rations were unreliable whereas the rebels 'take and eat what they want'.[18] Luckier men might join the liberals' militia, where conditions of service were better. But the new Urban Militia, like its predecessor in 1820, required entrants to own property and their own uniform.[19] In some cases, new entrants were barred altogether as former Royalist Volunteers managed to switch their allegiance to the Urban Militia, protected by powerful patrons, as was the case with the Meoro y Sánchez family in Alborea (Albacete).[20]

Unsurprisingly popular disaffection grew against the *señoritos* strutting the streets in militia uniforms or, even worse, accompanying troops on missions against real and imagined Carlists. Communities resented being charged for their own 'liberation' and poor city dwellers resented the sight of exempted militiamen when their sons and lovers had been conscripted. The preponderance of rural insecurity, and the displacement of refugees, usually from countryside to town, localised the experience of daily survival. In many ways, the 1830s were experienced as a war between town and country. The British Carlist volunteer, Captain Henningsen, future artist and biographer of Zumalacárregui, thought that Spanish civil wars were essentially a conflict between liberal towns and royalist countryside.[21] The Carlist War also had both centrifugal and nationalising effects. Although the experience of mobilisation, violence, and *caudillos* tied Spaniards into a national awareness more than ever before, especially in the context of politics, the same experiences also mobilised the peripheries to assert provincial rights.[22] During the revolution of the juntas in 1835 (see the following discussion) elites in Aragón pledged to re-create the provincial rights that had been enjoyed by Aragón, Valencia and Catalonia before the Bourbon conquest of 1707. The 1830s witnessed the Renaixença, or Catalan cultural revival. For decades to come, however, regionalism was different from separatism. Rather, regionalist cultural figures and politicians like Víctor Balaguer would seek to reinforce and improve a wider vision of 'Spain'.[23]

Church, war, and revolution

Although only one of Spain's forty-two bishops declared allegiance to Carlos V in 1833, both the ascendant *ultramontane* current and memories of the anti-clericalism of the Triennium drove many, perhaps most, lower-ranking clergymen to support the Pretender both in sermon and sometimes even in combat.[24] Fines were imposed upon priests who refused to offer blessings to Isabel II during mass, and priests failing to secure certificates of loyalty from the local authorities were barred from practising.[25] Yet for all the invectives, the vast majority of parish priests outside of the Basque country stood aloof from the armed struggle, not least because even the most radical-liberal programmes never threatened their livelihoods. Cloistered clergy had much more at stake, but even they were often constrained, for example, by the bishop of Valencia's firm loyalism.[26] A capuchin of Valencia called Serafín de la Pena-guila was probably reprimanded by the bishop after news reached the liberal press of his fiery sermon condemning the anti-clerical massacres in Zaragoza: Serafín had promised that a plague of cholera would visit liberal Spain for its 'philosophical' wickedness.[27]

The priest's warning must have instilled the fear of God into his parishion-ers. Only months before a cholera epidemic had ravaged the population.[28] In fact, cholera provided the pretext for elites to indulge the growing anti-clericalism of Cristino Spain. Influenced by similar phenomena in central Europe and Russia (and the assaults on the Jesuits during the July 1830 revo-lution in Paris), liberal elites in July 1834 stage-managed a demonstration of power against the church by spreading a rumour in Madrid that the cholera was caused by Jesuits poisoning the wells. Mobs allied with radicalised ele-ments of the Urban Militia to attack monasteries in the capital, massacring dozens of their religious inmates. The authorities reported that for weeks after the massacre militiamen in the capital could be heard 'boasting of their crimes' and 'showing more pride and haughtiness than the French after Marengo'.[29] The connivance of the government in the massacre was clear, and the Span-ish Church developed a siege mentality that would persist for more than a decade.[30] In fact, this massacre was copied in both Barcelona and Zaragoza, when mobs attacked convents, burning most of them to the ground, whilst the militia stood by and watched before, a few hours later, most actually went over to the side of the assailants.[31] The militia stepped in to halt the riots only at the point when the crowd, having satiated itself on the church prop-erty, moved on to rob nearby shops.[32] Violent anti-clericalism amidst mortal combat with a clericalised enemy thus presented authorities with a quan-dary about when to intervene. Drawing this lesson, the military governor of Huesca forestalled similar riots in his provincial capital, by temporarily evacu-ating the nuns from their convents and placing them in asylums which were protected by militiamen he could trust.[33] Amidst violent anti-clericalism reli-gious also experienced such legislative restrictions as the abolition of the Jesuit order in 1835, the replacement of tithes in 1837 with a local tax organised by municipalities and payable exclusively priests who had sworn allegiance to future queen Isabella, and the abolition of the special clerical tax levied in Galicia known as the *Voto de Santiago*. Even though the church's fiscal grip on Galicia was loosened, the small plots which during the 1808–14 war had so vexed the social-liberal priest Juan Antonio Posse remained.[34]

The civil war's complication of church–state relations sharpened the growing savagery of the war. Cristino forces, untrained in mountain warfare and unin-terested, despite the example of the Peninsular War, in counter-insurgency, faced huge problems trying to arrest the spread of insurgent Carlism. Both Generals Valdés and Quesada failed as commander-in-chief of the Army of the North to stem the expansion of Carlist territorial control masterminded by the Carlist commander-in-chief, the brilliant Tomás de Zumalacárregui. General Rodil, who like Valdés had experience fighting Spanish American irregulars, from September 1834 squandered his resources by saturating the Basque hillsides with fortifications in a vain attempt to interdict the movements of the Carlist army.[35]

The war also produced a cycle of reprisals which influenced the way Europeans saw the conflict and the ways they intervened. For the first eighteen months, both sides treated the other as rebels with no right to quarter. The Carlists, feeling more affronted by their black legend spread in the re-emerging liberal press, codified brutal reprisals in their 11 March 1834 *Ley de Represalias*.[36] Some relief from this barbarism was provided in April 1835, when the Eliot Treaty was signed by both sides establishing the right for soldiers of both sides to quarter, prisoner status, and exchange with an equal number of captives held by the other side. It was the brainchild of the British doyen of Spanish affairs, the Duke of Wellington, who despite his avowed insistence that the factious Spaniards should be left to fight amongst themselves, dispatched Lord Eliot to Spain in order to broker a humanitarian agreement in a war whose brutality was alarming the whole of Europe. Yet the treaty protected only soldiers, not militiamen or guerrillas, and it applied only to the Basque–Navarra theatre of operations. A propagandist in besieged Bilbao condemned 'the Spanish Generals who ought to have spurned the mere idea of bargaining for their own safety at the cost of the families who fed, clothed, and paid them'.[37] In reality, however, this attitude was exaggerated as whenever Carlists chose to apply the Eliot Treaty to their captives, they often included Cristino militiamen in its provisions, for in being worse fighters than the regular troops, the militiamen made more attractive candidates for prisoner exchanges. The treaty also did not protect the British, French, and Portuguese auxiliaries who, from spring 1835, were in action as part of the Quadruple Alliance. More tragically, the Eliot Treaty was in any case frequently violated. Both soldiers and militiamen falling into Carlist hands might still be shot out of hand or executed in reprisal for some outrage committed by their own side. Likewise, captured *facciosos* were prone to being massacred whenever Cristino populations feared the prisoners might escape, conspire, or spread disease. For all its ramifications, the Eliot Treaty became a frequent sore point in the press as the war dragged on.

As the eastern front opened from 1835, the absence of any humanitarian treaty here divided opinion, as Madrid policymakers under the pressure of public opinion rejected dignifying Cabrera's '*caribes*' (hoodlums) as combatants worthy of quarter. Regional liberals were equivocal. Three Aragonese contemporaries wrote five years after the end of the war: 'not extending the Eliot Treaty to the *facciosos* of Aragón and Valencia was to consider as national the opinions of those who shouted slogans in cafés far from the dangers of the war'.[38] Even on the Basque–Navarra front the prisoner swaps regulated by the Eliot Treaty were controversial, as liberal newspapers commented how prisoner exchanges benefitted the smaller Carlist army relatively more than the larger government army.[39] Despite the treaty, combatants captured in the north could still be subjected to atrocities as part of the war's reprisal culture, while in the east the absence of any formal quarter gave combatants little incentive to care about the sufferings they inflicted on the civilian population and more incentive to attack 'soft' targets.

The burden of war politicised the armed forces on both sides, In January 1835, Lieutenant Cardero led a revolt of his infantry regiment against the *moderado* government of Martínez de la Rosa. After killing Madrid's captain general and barricading themselves into the capital's Royal Post Office, the rebels accepted amnesty from the government. The rank and file were dispatched to fight the Carlists in the north while Cardero was promoted and later even entered the Cortes as one of the most controversial deputies.[40] In March 1835 Málaga's Urban Militia mutinied when the military governor tried to purge the citizens' force of radicals and mobilise the remainder to fight under army command. After days of unrest military governor, Isidro resigned and fled. His successor suspended the state of siege and was forced to accompany the civil governor in a ceremony presiding over the laying of a plaque commemorating the Constitution of 1812.[41] Throughout the spring and summer, politicised insubordination mounted throughout the Cristino army and militia forces. Typically, rebellious commanders, including junior ones, demanded the restoration of the Constitution of 1812, edifying their hostility to army service with an abstract and vague political symbol.[42] Yet visceral motives were key. The liberal martyrdom of Riego and Torrijos inspired the army and militia very little when compared with unequal demands of the war itself.

War-weariness combined with Carlist military breakthroughs, militia agitation, and socio-economic grievances in creating a revolution during summer 1835 that, in September, would topple Count Toreno from power and bring the *exaltados* to power. The revolution began in Barcelona, where workers in Barcelona destroyed the state-of-the-art Bonaplata ironworks that had put them out of work. Ramón Xaudaró y Fabregas, author of the *Bases de una constitución política*, a blueprint for a federal republic, was the intellectual lead behind Barcelona radicalism. His text enjoyed a readership amongst that still tiny minority of parliamentarians who professed republican sympathies (Luis Pizarro, Manuel García Uzal and Patricio Olavarría).[43] But Xaudaró's real impact was as a commander of the Urban Militia and (1835–36) editor of the influential *El Catalán*. He managed to subvert the property qualifications for militia service by recruiting lower classes into its ranks. Joining the militia for the 5 *reales* daily wage, Barcelona workers triumphed under exaltado leadership, pledging manifestoes ranging from Xaudaró y Fabregas's republicanism to the Constitution of 1812. One pamphlet promised that 'the Constitution will offer plenty to those who are barely able to afford the shirt on their backs'.[44] Once the Barcelona workers revolted, they were at the forefront of the most radical episodes of the summer of 1835. *Moderado* Captain General Bassa was lynched, consumption taxes suspended, and the militia expanded to accommodate underemployed workers.[45] Similar, though less bloody, risings shook other cities as *exaltado* juntas until Prime Minister Toreno, on 14 September, finally lost his nerve and headed into his French exile[46]

The chaos unleashed by the 1835 revolution, combined with Carlist military advances, would have severely tested any leader. Even though Don Carlos had been disappointed in 1833 to find only a minority of the army rallying to his cause, he nonetheless gained a core of rural support in Navarre, the Basque provinces, and the Catalan interior, aided as he was in these regions by a clerical, popular anti-liberalism allied to a traditional culture of armed popular mobilisation. Accordingly, pitched battles during the first two years were fought in these regions north of the Ebro, whilst liberal forces were repeatedly held in check, and defeated (at Amézcoas and Villafranca), by Carlist forces serving under the command of the only military genius of the war, General Zumalacárregui. The June 1835 Cristino defeat at Villafranca gave Zumalacárregui the initiative to begin the siege of Bilbao. Although the Carlist hero was mortally wounded during this siege, and although the rising star of the liberal camp, General Espartero, managed to relieve the Biscayan capital, the Cristino forces thereafter could offer no more than a holding action. Chastened by their failure to take Bilbao, the Carlists, on the other hand, forged ahead with their plans.

The liberal leader who took power amidst this military crisis was the exaltado, Juan Álvarez Mendizábal, a Cádiz financier of Jewish ancestry. Mendizábal, who had been involved in liberal conspiracies since 1817, been exiled after 1823, and was, in 1835, in London negotiating the finances for the British auxiliaries, accepted an invitation to join a beleaguered *moderado* government. Mendizábal earned generally favourable treatment at the hands of nineteenth-century Spanish progressives. Antonio Pirala contrasted his bigheartedness, ambition and imagination with Toreno's cerebral, sceptical, and unambitious demeanour. Mendizábal certainly had more success mobilising the home front when he had inherited worse circumstances than Toreno.[47]

By the time he reached Madrid in September 1835, Mendizábal became Spain's first *exaltado* prime minister since 1823. Mendizábal managed to restrain the autonomy of the revolutionary juntas, including the juntas of Catalonia, Aragón, and Valencia which were inspired by the liberties which the victorious Bourbons had extinguished in the Crown of Aragón in the early eighteenth century.[48] Mendizábal also made war. Three rounds of conscription of twenty-five thousand men each had already been enacted since the start of the Carlist War. But in September 1835, Mendizábal enacted an unprecedented levy of one hundred thousand men. Only the disabled, only sons, the ordained and veterans were exempted: the rest must draw lots or exempt themselves paying a 'blood tax' beyond the reach of the vast majority of men aged between 18 and 40. Barely half of the hundred thousand sent to reinforce the Army of the North were actually available to serve, as desertion and sickness over the winter of 1835–36 exposed the reality behind Mendizábal's 'Liberal Union' propaganda, and relations between the *exaltado* prime minister and the commander-in-chief of the Army of the North, General Córdova, accordingly grew worse. Despite Cristino victories in July 1835 at Mendigorría and the first siege of Bilbao, the Cristino front thereafter was everywhere in retreat. Not much more than Bilbao, San Sebastián, Vitoria, and Pamplona, all provincial capitals, remained in Cristino hands, and the Carlists even dispatched guerrilla-style expeditions beyond the River Ebro. General Córdova demanded more men and supplies before committing to an offensive and Mendizábal demanded that the commander-in-chief show initiative in order to justify reinforcements.[49]

Mendizabalista radicalism was too much for the queen-regent, who, in May 1836, sided with her commander-in-chief and fired Mendizábal, replacing him with a *moderado* government. Mendizábal's firing unleashed a summer of riots, especially in Andalucía. The riots often pitted the army against the militia as well as sergeants and junior officers against their superiors. This unrest helped the Carlists immensely. In the summer of 1836, they would attract world attention by launching the 'Gómez Expedition', a raid across Spain which attracted deserters and isolated Carlists before returning to the safety of the Basque Country in December. In August 1836, sergeants stationed at the queen-regent's Summer Palace at La Granja forced her to swear allegiance to the Constitution of 1812 and to appoint a 'progressive' government (the new name for the *exaltado* party), including Mendizábal as finance minister. General Córdova, meanwhile, wisely fled into exile[50] Córdova had been worried by the radicalism sweeping his army. In April he had warned General Narváez about 'agents of extreme parties working our men with sinister aims, singling out sergeants who are most vulnerable to seduction and intrigue'.[51] In November 1836, during the campaign against the Gómez Expedition, Lieutenant Francisco Vázquez led a mutiny, crying '[N]ow is the time to march on Madrid!' General Narváez re-established order, retorting, '[N]o, we are here to destroy the rebels', and executed eleven of the mutineers, thus outdoing his rival, Espartero, by one.[52] The 'democratisation' of army politics unsettled elites with memories of the example of Napoleon. Whereas Riego had been a colonel, and Cardero a lieutenant, the revolt which sealed the success of the revolution of 1836 was made by sergeants. Unbelievably to foreign diplomats, these sergeants had been suffering months of pay arrears despite their proximity to the queen-regent.[53]

1836–40: praetorianism and the first Carlist war

None of this progress can be attributed to the military prowess of the Carlist armies alone. The Cristino ranks were constantly being thinned by desertion. Even though the medium-term finances of the Cristino government looked stable owing to Finance Minister Mendizábal's confiscation and auctioning from 1836 of monastic properties as national assets, the immediate needs of the expanded armies depended on private contractors whose supplies seldom reached the troops without having experienced pilfering or Carlist raids en route.[54] Soldiers thus faced interminable hunger, cold, and waiting in northern encampments and garrison towns, broken up only by the simple pleasures of smoking and music, the reading aloud of radical newspapers, or the mixed relief provided by engagement with the enemy. Seeing both the suffering and agitation of their men, the officers and sergeants could hardly remain impassive. A social history of the Cristino army during the Carlist War must focus on the tensions between soldiers and officers, as the dire conditions forced sergeants either to champion or discipline their men. A platoon of elite Basque volunteers on the Cristino side (known as *chappelgorris*) who looted a church in the fishing village of Guetaria were promptly subjected to courts-martial and the death sentence carried out.[55] General Espartero, the rising star of the Cristino camp, intervened directly to impose this sentence, and he did not take kindly to being criticised by civilians in the press controversies that followed. An officer of the British Auxiliary Legion later encountered the sister of one of the executed men, a market seller in San Sebastián, who 'swore to avenge her brother'.[56]

Yet soldiers could also strike back at unpopular and callous officers. Admittedly, much rank-and-file discontent was 'managed' by channelling it into mutinies launched either by ambitious officers seeking promotion (Madrid, January 1835; La Granja, August 1836; the Alaix division of November 1836) or by established political elites trying to gain revolutionary momentum. The consequences of this adventurism for popular army politics mirror those of civilian life, as soldiers frequently detested their officers. General Narváez, as commander of the Army of the Reserve, managed this crisis as best he could by ruthlessly securing supplies from villages for his troops in the south, and maintaining constant pressure on governments in Madrid for what he considered his fair share of contracted supplies (the cumbersome and expensive 'asentista' system of private military contractors). Narváez's assiduousness fed his growing rivalry with Baldomero Espartero, the hero of the second siege of Bilbao and commander-in-chief from 1836 of the most senior command in the Cristino military, the Army of the North. Espartero argued that Narváez's pacification of Carlist bands in La Mancha was glorified bandit hunting which drained supplies from the decisive northern front.[57]

But bandit hunting came into vogue when the Carlists in June 1836 launched their most audacious plan yet. The years of 1836–1837 have been identified as 'deep war', not just because of the intensified efforts at mobilisation carried out by both sides but also because of geographical range.[58] Don Carlos ('Carlos V' to his supporters) grew impatient at his failure to take Bilbao, which he correctly understood to have been a precondition for receiving serious military and financial aid from absolutist Europe. Failure to take Bilbao also prolonged the blockade of the Carlist Basque country. For all the Carlist genius in active defence, exploitation of terrain, and internal lines, Cristino fortresses around Bilbao, San Sebastián, and Miranda del Ebro hemmed in the Pretender's mini-state even while more asymmetrical Carlist zones of control flourished in the east and the Galician countryside. Don Carlos therefore agreed to launch an expedition led by Andalucían general Miguel Gómez to break through the Cristino front and reach the Carlists in Galicia. This raid penetrated west across northern Spain capturing Oviedo and Santiago before turning south, arriving outside the walls of Madrid only a few days after the La Granja rising, then marching south into Córdoba and beyond, even striking both the Mediterranean Sea and the Atlantic Ocean at various places.[59] It seemed that the Carlists had Cristino Spain entirely at their mercy, a state of affairs which would inspire them to mount a second, more decisive invasion, the following summer.

As neo-Carlist Josep Clemente has argued, the Gómez expedition frequently found that villagers throughout northern Castile welcomed the Carlists more than the pursuing Cristino counter-insurgency. Those who urged the people to fight had to flee when inhabitants welcomed the Carlists.[60] Staying put was dangerous, but so was flight on bandit-strewn roads. The perils of asymmetrical warfare were felt across the country wherever irregular Carlists operated. Thus, three-hundred-odd irregulars under the command of El Organista and El Serrador passing through the Maestrazgo township of Alcalá de la Selva dragged out of his home and executed 'the only liberal in the village'.[61] Nor could Cristino security forced be relied on. The press recounted Carlist raids on exposed villages, like Malpica del Tajo (Toledo), which produced a pattern of sacking, looting, targeting of wealthy 'liberals', and of outnumbered Cristino militia proving powerless to mount much of a defence.[62]

In fact, the invasions of both regular and irregular Carlist forces often brought out the worst in people, as long-running grievances which had festered both within and between communities could now be settled invoking the name of the Pretender. One of the greatest calamities to face Cristino Spain during the Gómez expedition was the fall of Córdoba, whose three-thousand-strong militia force surrendered to a Carlist force less than three times in number and which had to suffer a mere four fatal casualties.[63] This humiliation was arguably the final blow to the popular image of the militia, which was increasingly seen as a club for playboy revolutionaries and which even without the Córdoba fiasco was becoming notorious for its reluctance to match the sacrifices of the army. Complaints poured into newspapers about how government and municipal *empleados* were constantly finding excuses to shirk militia duty now that the need was dire, whereas humble artisans still found the time to down their tools and report for duty. The salaries of government and municipal employees, of course, were guaranteed, whereas a day's militia service could be quite a boon for an artisan underemployed or who had fallen on hard times.[64] The Carlists' fleeting occupation of Córdoba led to an upsurge of social violence which saw several militia prisoners executed to popular applause, along with their commander and the prefect.[65] Prisoners dragged along by the Carlists on their onward march fared even worse. The luckier hostages were merely robbed and locked up in the gaols of Andalucían villages through which the Carlists passed. Those who could not keep up with the march were killed by the wayside. Villages in the path of the expedition, these were generally pillaged (Gómez invoking the suffering of his men as justification), whilst liberal bastions, like Algeciras, were burnt to the ground.[66]

Authorities in Madrid panicked at their inability to capture Gómez, and the military crisis added to the woes faced by the 1836–37 Calatrava administration the Sergeants' Mutiny at La Granja had placed into office. In the end, Gómez by the end of 1836 managed to retire to the Basque country with more men than he had set out with. The Gómez crisis had edged Calatrava into enacting a virtual revolutionary dictatorship. Thus, a state of siege was imposed in Madrid, attempts were made at an extraordinary mobilisation for the war effort, and the draconian *infracción de Constitución* legislation of the Triennium was revived against suspected Carlist fifth columnists.[67] At the same time, Calatrava was concerned to limit political radicalism in the knowledge that necessary economic reforms must take precedence. In January 1837, the suspensive royal veto was amended to the constitution, which anticipated the bicameral legislature of Congress and Senate which *moderados* desired and which would be a feature of the Constitution of 1837.[68]

The second half of the Carlist War is significant for the liberal social, economic, and political reforms it witnessed in both the Mendizábal administration (September 1835–May 1836) which had been hoisted into power by the revolution of the juntas, and the 'revolutionary Cortes' of August 1836 to July 1837 – that is, firstly, the *mendizabalista* spoliation of church property and, secondly, the definitive abolition of feudalism under the revived Constitution of 1812. The *mendizabalista* assault on the church had already been pre-empted when anti-clerical riots provoked the Toreno administration into abolishing the Jesuit order on 7 July 1835, using its assets to pay down the ballooning national debt. Most dramatically, all monasteries and convents containing fewer than twelve inmates were suppressed and put up for sale. During the revolutionary Cortes, those citizens who had bought church property during the Triennium, only to see it confiscated in the 1823 crackdown, were now reunited with their purchases courtesy of a July 1837 decree.[69] Along with the ending of tithes the Spanish state's drive to replace entail with capitalist property rights seemed complete: the law passed on 25 August 1837 definitively abolished feudal jurisdictions. The eldest sons of noble families ceased to enjoy their special advantages, and it was often the second son who would now prosper.[70] But few *progresistas* showed any interest in expropriating families and redistributing lands to new owners. In Valladolid, as in most other localities, the vast majority of the buyers of disentailed property were *rentier* landlords who had friends and influence at the town hall.[71] Even though the revolutionary Cortes revived the 1811 decree, it was enacted in a conservative manner. The former noble (now capitalist) land-owners did not have to provide property deeds, placing the burden of proof on villages if they wished to assert their rights to land.[72] Now constitutional municipalities, especially those in *latifundia* districts, were effectively owned by landowners who were empowered to levy rents and charges on municipalities, thereby burdening the latter with a fiscal servitude which would last well into the twentieth century.[73]

Nonetheless, the monopolisation by local oligarchies of the liberal revolution in landownership did not go unchallenged. Popular demand grew for *reparto* to such a degree that by the early 1840s the countryside was steeped in agitation. That said, this movement, though admittedly hard to quantify, remains either absent or incidental in the existing historiography on land reform which has focused on the winners rather than the losers. The 'bourgeois revolution' historiography of the 1970s and 1980s stressed how pre-existing feudal landowners held the whip hand during disentailment by both retaining and expanding their properties, especially in Spain's more valuable soils (like lower Andalucía). Even though 'bourgeois' buyers also entered the market with a limited degree of success, they remained so weak as to be 'feudalised'. Comparisons were drawn with nineteenth-century Prussia, where *Junkers* retained economic hegemony even after they had to relinquish their jurisdictional authority. Any 'new' buyers therefore realigned themselves with the forces of reaction by being wholeheartedly complicit in the proletarianisation of erstwhile sharecroppers and smallholders.[74] 'Normalisation' historians in the 1990s presented a more optimistic analysis of the property revolution. Thus, areas of upper Andalucía witnessed peasants purchasing marginal lands, expanding their smallholdings, and even some day labourers (*jornaleros*) owning land for the first time. But the latter usually still had to make ends meet by doing odd jobs in urban centres and day labour on *latifundia*.[75]

In fairness to Mendizábal, as a classical liberal economist of the Jovellanos school, he genuinely hoped that the rural masses might benefit from disentailment and endowed his legislation with certain checks and balances to this end. Thus, as the Treasury functionaries of the central government, it was the *Intendentes* who were empowered to designate the lands to be offered for auction. Yet they were to be aided in this task by a staff of local 'experts' (*peritos*) who were usually the agents of local oligarchs and therefore tended to rig auctions in their favour. Moreover, the *Intendentes* themselves were frequently open to bribery. Even though the disentailment legislation provided for sanctions against bribery, including banning those involved in this dishonesty from holding public office, fines, and disqualification from participating in further auctions, these measures appear seldom, if ever, to have been applied.[76] Thus, existing elites (dubbed '*los de siempre*') tended to reap the benefit from the liberal revolution, and legal safeguards were usually toothless.

Not all political elites were blind to the derailing socio-economic reforms of 1836–1837. The deputy for Alicante, Joaquín Abarques, proclaimed that the only reason why the rural population in his province had not supported Carlism was because it expected the radical 1811–1823 decrees, which demanded that landlords either present property deeds or face confiscation, would be enforced.[77] Although Romero Alpuente was now dead, his intellectual contemporary, Álvaro Flórez Estrada, now distinguished himself as the parliamentary leader of social liberalism. The subsequent proclamation of the Royal Statute put paid to any further attempts by Flórez Estrada to enact his vision of municipal democracy. Yet the *mendizabalista* disentailment programmes of 1835–1836 inspired him to publish his social-liberal treatise, *La cuestión social, o sea, origen, latitud y efectos del derecho de propiedad*, which explained the need for smallholders and *jornaleros* to gain access to the land. In February 1836, Estrada introduced his proposals in *El Español*, the most important being fifty-year renewable leases for landless labourers in return for affordable rent.[78] Flórez Estrada's plan attracted support from such Romantic intellectuals as Espronceda and Larra. The Cortes's rejection of the fifty-year lease plan led Larra to charge that the liberals were an elite directing the people without having the latter's interests at heart.[79] Mendizábal later acknowledged the disaster of his *desamortización*. But when in the 1846 Cortes elections Mendizábal campaigned offering *reparto* to Carlist War veterans, by then it was too late, as the *moderado* administration was bringing the process of disentailment to a halt.[80] As for the other 'high political' attempt at social liberalism, this too had failed miserably. A 1839 Cortes motion to reward Carlist War veterans with plots of land was voted down in its third reading.[81]

To be sure, *reparto* was frequently ventured as an issue of local politics, although when offered as an electoral pledge, it often backfired. Thus, in Bornos (Cádiz), a certain Antonio Trambet González, himself having made good out of the land auctions, stood for election to the local constitutional municipality promising to distribute nearby pastures (*dehesas*) to landless *jornaleros*. But he was outvoted by the *moderado* candidate who, thanks to having done even better out of the disentailment, accordingly mobilised his larger number of dependents for the municipal election.[82] The radicalism provoked by the land racket was often expressed in *charivari*. In October 1839, the villages of Carataunas and Cañar (Granada) held rough music during which figurines of the local mayors of the preceding three years were symbolically executed, their fake corpses then being paraded about in ridicule.[83] Meanwhile, municipalities and provincial deputations were swamped by demands for *reparto*. Occasionally the authorities granted these petitions as a desperate means of solving the law-and-order problem, such as during the spring of 1839 when the civil governor of Granada authorised the parcelling-out to *jornaleros* of remaining municipal lands in the province. His hand had been forced by lawlessness in the area around Guadix, where the exasperated local mayor complained of deserters and 'criminals' robbing and killing local farmers and overwhelming the militia.[84]

Carlism and the Royal Expedition

The population found no relief during the 'deep war' of 1837 either, as the Carlist 'Royal Expedition' and ongoing banditry turned communities into islands. In May 1837, in response to revolutionary crisis and diplomatic feelers to the queen-regent about a compromise peace, the Carlists launched the 'Royal Expedition'. This large-scale raid towards Madrid also served the logistical problem of Carlist Spain's embattled redoubts in the Basque country and Maestrazgo. Both the Carlist Basque country and Maestrazgo were straining under the demands of the war economy and militarisation. Hence the paradox of the strategic need to revert to the raiding and insurgency styles of warfare that characterised the first 18 months of Zumalacárregui's command. The difference during the 'deep war' of 1836–37 is that the raids would be long range and strategic in aims. The 1836 Carlist Gómez Expedition had successfully traversed Spain and fascinated the world. In May 1837, a new raid was planned, this time with greater strategic aims as betrayed in its 'Royal' title (the Royal Expedition). Don Carlos's advisers were acutely aware of the blockaded facing the Basque country. In March 1837, mutinies over pay affected the Carlist Royal Army, and the king was told that the Basque country could sustain only fifteen days more of operations.[85] Other calculations were diplomatic: feelers between Madrid and pro-Carlist Naples had revealed that Spain's queen-regent was willing to strike a peace involving her exile and her daughter's future marriage to a Carlist prince. Metternich's Europe pledged no more financial support for the Carlists unless they established themselves beyond the Ebro, and King Louis-Philippe of France (privately pro-Carlist) hinted that he might liberate France from the pro-Cristino 'Quadruple Alliance' if Don Carlos could clear the French frontier of Cristino control. Thus, when the Royal Expedition was launched from the Carlist capital of Estella on 15 May 1837, it looked in some ways more like a regime on the run than an invasion. It had no artillery arm and was overburdened by Carlist bureaucrats and their dependents who were already sizing up the furnishings they were expecting in Madrid.

The debilitation of the Cristino Army, caused by a year of liberal revolutions and mutinies, could not disabuse the Carlists of their notions. The Carlists also had a moral firepower to compensate for artillery: religion. Two years of legislative and violent anti-clericalism in Cristino Spain had plunged ordinations to the priesthood, alienated monastic properties, and disturbed the religious practice surrounding parish priests (who, for example, were barred from practising if they did not swear allegiance to the queen). The Carlist press had trailed stories of abandoned parishes in the wake of the schism with Rome, the powerlessness of the bishops, the expulsion or imprisonment of priests by Cristino soldiers and militia, and, above all, the *mendizabalista* disentailment: indeed, some four hundred parishes closed due to lack of ministers during the first half of 1836 alone.[86]

Despite the mobilisation of some twelve thousand National Militia from Huesca and Zaragoza and the pursuit of General Espartero's Army of the North, the first Expedition victory went to the Carlists. At the battle of Huesca on 24 May 1837, some one thousand Cristino soldiers and militia were either killed or captured as the Carlist invaders were skilled at pinning General Iribarren's troops against the sticky mud of adjoining the swollen river Cinca, forcing him to retreat. Virtually all Cristino authorities fled Huesca minus the bishop who remained, protesting his 'ill health'. Perhaps the religious strategy was working. Don Carlos remained for three days in the city before moving on to take Barbastro, which surrendered without a shot being fired. En route the hungry Carlists resorted to routine excesses against villages, especially Angués. Don Carlos again heard Mass in this ancient city's cathedral whilst the Cristinos tried to regroup. General Oráa, respected by the Carlists as the 'grey fox', rushed forward with 12,400 infantry, 1,400 cavalry and artillery towards the Carlist forces which were now fortifying Barbastro. The Carlists during this battle on 2 June 1837 were in roughly equal numbers to the Cristinos, though vastly inferior in artillery. But despite this disadvantage, the Carlists proved to be expert in active defence, defeating the Cristinos advance in detail by again using the geographical contours of the river bank to their advantage. The Carlist victory was marked by a 'civil war within a civil war', as the Carlists' 'foreign legion' (some 850 defectors from the foreign auxiliaries) exchanged fire with their former comrades, and the killing zone echoed with cries in French and German.[87] Barbastro was a Carlist defensive victory, even though the Carlist foreign legion bore the brunt of the combined 1,200 casualties shared both sides; in fact, their numbers were so diminished to fewer than 130 sick and wounded that Don Carlos dissolved them.[88]

The Carlists' onward march into Catalonia was conditioned more by environmental than military factors. Particular tragedies, like the loss of three hundred men drowned crossing the swollen Cinca, mixed with the general war for food. Wilhelm von Rahden's fond memory of Don Carlos subsisting on a pan of fried potatoes per day obscures the calamity facing villagers in the invaders' path.[89] Meanwhile, the entourage of favourites, place seekers, priests, wives, and other dependants gave a desperate quality to invaders whose momentum soon ended up being governed by their stomachs.[90] When the invaders reached Estopiñan (Huesca) on 6 June, the villagers did their best to hide their foodstuffs until some Carlists came across telltale eggshells in a pantry which drove them to break in the chicken pens and slaughter the poultry before moving on.[91] Other inhabitants staved off the worst by ostentatiously welcoming the Expedition, in reality to keep the Carlists as much at arm's length as possible. As a visiting Polish aristocrat reported,

> [v]illages are so exhausted that they make their own solutions for the invasion of armed bands. When news arrives of the approach of a Carlist column, the Cristino authorities hide in the church. The priest then steps in to receive the Carlists. Once they have left the real authorities re-emerge who remain ready to restore the priest the moment danger returns.[92]

In return, the Carlists held public masses, sanctifying the confiscation of food and other supplies before invariably moving on.

Proximity and clerical militancy made the Catalan far west the first destination for the Expedition. But northern Aragón had first to be traversed and the king's subalterns complained that agriculture in the Huesca area was too poor to support a sudden human influx. Thus, the Expedition had to keep advancing on a nutritional shoestring. They also complained that the region was thickly garrisoned by Cristinos whose strength threatened to turn the merest defeat into a rout. In reality, the revolutionary crisis affecting the cities during 1836–1837 paralysed the government counter-insurgency, as captains general, like Baron Meer in Barcelona, feared the radicals in the clubs and militia as much as the invading Carlists. Meer's victory over the Carlists at Gra on 12 June could have been decisive, even leading to the capture of Don Carlos, the radicals complained, had Meer not held back his cavalry.[93] In the event the Carlists 'escaped forwards' raiding deeper into Cristino territory, into Catalonia, raiding as far as Santpedor before retiring to Súria on 23 June. With Cristino counter-insurgency forces once more at their heels, the Carlists moved the following day towards the southwest, aiming for the next Carlist safe zone in the Maestrazgo.[94] Linking up with Cabrera's vanguard at Xerta (Catalonia) on 29 June, the whole Expedition managed to cross the River Ebro, frustrating the Catalan counter-insurgency. The Expedition remained one day in Xerta, following the same patterns of pillage sanctified by Mass, the latter more symbolic than usual given the theatre of the personal encounter between the king and Cabrera. The fusion of the Expedition with Cabrera's seasoned troops emboldened the Carlists to seize a large town. Castellón de la Plana (Valencia) offered such a prospect, being a wealthy target close to the Mediterranean. But the large militia forces in Castellón were waiting with hastily reinforced defences boosted by the disembarkation of regular troops from Admiral Parker's Royal Navy squadron. Thus, the Carlists broke off the siege, escaping the approach of counter-insurgency forces again, marching southwest in the direction of the Maestrazgo.

Fatigue, hunger, and desertions weakened the Expedition by the time of its next battle at Chiva (Valencia) on 15 July. Cristino General Oráa's force, despite being outnumbered by two to three in both infantry and cavalry, surprised the Carlist flank (which was busy cleaning its weapons), forcing the whole Expedition to retreat northwards. Only a rearguard action led by Cabrera himself and the hunger and thirst of Oráa's troops prevented the flight from turning into a rout.[95] The retreat northwards through the Maestrazgo inflicted the direst suffering on soldiers and civilians alike of the whole 1837 campaign. The starvation facing civilians in the path of the Carlists was made worse by *Generalísimo* Espartero's policy of seizing harvests and storing them in safe warehouses against receipts which would be honoured. Starved Carlist invaders accordingly gorged themselves on whatever remained in the villages. The hypocrisy of official welcomes and masses broke down entirely as villages in the armies' path were unceremoniously pillaged by one army and then occupied by the pursuing army whose men, as starving and fatigued as the first, ended up taking out their frustration violently on the civilians. But the ingrained Carlism of the devastated Teruel region, aided by the insurgents' 'first-mover advantage', alienated the Cristinos more than the Carlists, and General Oráa's effectiveness was being diluted besides by a careerist dispute with *Generalísimo* Espartero. Thus, when Don Carlos halted his retreat at Villar de los Navarros (Aragón) in order to give battle on 24 August 1837,[96] the Carlists secured a major defensive victory including a booty of prisoners and badly needed guns and supplies.[97] The fate that befell the Cristino prisoners who were moved around the starved countryside performing forced labour was horrific in the extreme. Most would die of hunger and typhus over the next months, as starvation rations forced them to scavenge for unripe root crops and, eventually, to commit cannibalism against their demised comrades. Cabrera condemned to execution some cannibals caught *in flagrante*, yet the emaciated men could not even stand to receive the bullets. Thus, they were tied together to the ground in a seated position, and the execution squad, in an apparent aim to dissuade the other prisoners from committing cannibalism, spent hours using the condemned men's heads as target practice until all were killed.[98] Six months later, after an outcry from both sides, the surviving minority of captives were exchanged.

Meanwhile, the Carlist victory at Villar de los Navarros was supported by another expedition of five battalions and 280 cavalry, launched from Navarra in July under the command of Juan Antonio Zaratiegui. This raid, which had begun as a feint for the Royal Expedition, soon ended up developing a momentum of its own, not least because from August, it penetrated areas of Old Castile which had not been scarred by fighting and, accordingly, offered more food. Early in August Zaratiegui conquered Segovia on the approaches to Madrid around the same time as the Royal Expedition approached the capital from the east.[99] News in the capital of Zaratiegui's approach caused panic. On the 6 August, the government imposed a state of siege in Madrid, decreeing a wide range of pro-Carlist activities and opinions to be punishable by councils of war. The capital's militia came out in a show of force and was supplemented by the formation of some companies of distinguished citizens (*compañías de ciudadanos honrados*) which patrolled suspect districts of the capital.[100] Key military institutions in the Carlists' path, the Military College at Segovia, the Artillery College at Alcalá, and the Engineers School at Guadalajara, were evacuated to the capital.[101]

Old Castile fell neatly into Carlist hands. Garrisons surrendered after a few potshots and Zaratiegui got new recruits, both volunteers and conscripts. Some communities, like those on the Ribera del Duero, showed the same degree of public enthusiasm for the Carlists as they had previously for the Liberals, for whom they would again show renewed enthusiasm. Partisan ideology was negligible in this. Rather communities were so terrified by the prospect of violent occupations and counter-occupations that they resolved to 'manage' their occupiers by staging public welcomes which in reality kept the soldiers at as much arms' length as possible.[102] Local authorities across Old Castile discovered their Carlist sympathies. Or, rather, perhaps, they rediscovered them: the Pretender's ideas of theocratic monarchy were far from being alien to men who under Cristino occupation would opt for *moderantismo* (conservative liberalism) but who would also without much difficulty move from one camp to another. Valladolid was occupied in a gentlemanly manner. Its war-weary municipal delegation rode out to meet Zaratiegui, Liberal members of the local government resigned and departed whilst pro-Carlist administrators took their place and awaited Zaratiegui's instructions. This accommodation spared the city from pillage and atrocities.[103] But good manners ceased once a Cristino counter-thrust obliged Zaratiegui to abandon Valladolid and join Don Carlos's Expedition. The Cristino effort in Castile was in such disarray that Zaratiegui was unmolested. Despite *Generalísimo* Espartero's personal reassurances to the queen-regent, the Cristino front appeared to be collapsing. Espartero prudently spared the rod as a spate of Cristino military mutinies affected Aravaca outside Madrid. Evaristo San Miguel, Madrid's military governor, admitted that the gravity of the Carlist invasion outweighed the need to punish indiscipline.[104]

Eventually the Carlists occupied Arganda and stood in front of Madrid's city walls on 10 September 1837. The capital, which had already been placed under a state of siege, was now in a state of suspended animation. Contemporaries poignantly associated this crisis with dust being settled: quite literally, as Madrid, which was already known as the 'city of dust', was choked by the dust thrown up by the demolition of nationalised church property underway since the revolution of 1836.[105] As the Carlists neared the walls, the capital fell deathly quiet with its shops and industry paralysed and the streets emptied of people apart from the patrols of the National Militia. Isolated attempts by Carlist agents to whip up a fifth column failed, even though one foreign journalist, who had visited the capital the previous year reckoned that some 'three-fourths of the respectable portion of the population are in favour of Don Carlos'.[106] San Miguel judiciously sent one general whose sympathies were suspect to the centre of the capital. Now the radicals demanded defence *à la outrance*, but nothing could have been further from the minds of the well-to-do militia commanders who were happy to preside over glittering street patrols by day – especially when the *infante* Don Francisco and the queen-regent came to inspect – but shirked the more dangerous night watches.[107] Meanwhile, the capital's underground Carlist junta made a clever ploy by circulating a promise not to reintroduce the Inquisition or despotism, whilst also promising an honourable Italian exile for María Cristina (as widow of Ferdinand VII) and the marriage of the child Isabel to the Carlist crown prince. María Cristina, for whom the civil war almost exclusively a dynastic question, seemed ready to exit her Spanish trauma.

In the midst of this crisis, on the 15 September 1837, Captain General Quiroga gave a show of strength, condemning the Carlists as vainglorious and murderers. This was a brave stand given that many on both sides suspected that a compromise peace (*transacción*) would now take place, the Carlist troops, in particular, believing that their halt order in front of Madrid was due to negotiations taking place. Even the session of the Cortes in the capital when the Carlists were only a few miles away was remembered for being quiet and sombre rather than inflamed and belligerent. Admittedly, a Carlist takeover was not the only threat on the deputies' minds. Espartero had been drawn into a standoff with the capital's revolutionary dictatorship of General Seoane over the political leadership of the revolution, which since 18 July 1837 had seen its Constitution of 1812 moderated by a bicameral legislature and other brakes on radicalism that were part of the Constitution of 1837.[108] A *moderado* army insurrection in Pozuelo de Aravaca, just to the west of the capital had Espartero's blessing and so the left-liberal Calatrava administration fell. Now Seoane's 'revolutionary dictatorship' had lost its political support. Espartero's mobile forces overawed Seoane's garrison largely thanks to the Carlists' decision to withdraw in the face of Espartero's march. This series of events allowed Espartero – and the army as opposed to Seoane's militia – to be seen as the saviour of the capital and the Liberal fatherland (*patria*).[109] Both men were veterans of Spain's lost wars against Spanish American independence ('*Ayacuchos*'), but Espartero's victory outmanoeuvred his comrade all the same. Key to the image of Espartero and 'saviour' was that his approach to the capital impressed the queen-regent to suspend her unofficial channels to the Carlists. Don Carlos, for his part, finally lost his nerve, and withdrew from the capital, even though the king's belligerent nephew, Prince Sebastián, had wanted to fall on Espartero's flank.[110]

Redeploying to Alcalá in a bid to fall on Espartero's flank, the Carlist army then received an order to retreat further still, causing outrage in the ranks. Rumours ran that Don Carlos had ordered the retreat to a more salubrious location in order to hear Mass. Others asserted that he wanted to avoid bloodshed. But the shifting diplomatic situation was the main cause. When the Calatrava administration expelled the queen-regent's intermediary, the Marqués de la Grúa, the Carlist agent carried a letter from the queen-regent to her brother, Ferdinand II of Naples, proposing a compromise peace based on Don Carlos's accession in return for a general amnesty and the marriage of the infant Isabella to the Pretender's son. All depended, including Metternich's vital approval, on Don Carlos's occupation of Madrid. But the downfall in August of the radical Calatrava ministry and the accession of the *moderado* Eusebio Bardají Azara meant that when the Carlists were at the gates of the capital on 12 September, the queen-regent no longer felt like a prisoner of the revolution. Hedging her bets even more, María Cristina sent Espartero a letter begging him urgently to rescue the capital, a letter that the Carlists intercepted, which sowed even more confusion amongst their ranks.[111] Never a decisive commander, Don Carlos thus began an initial retreat which turned into one of general proportions, whilst luck made Espartero appear the saviour of the capital and the liberal revolution. Carlist historians condemned the queen-regent's spite and duplicity and regretted that Don Carlos did not force the issue.[112] Madrid was now free of external threats. Antonio Quiroga made a triumphalist victory declaration couched in terms of popular defence and remarking the queen-regent's constitutional patriotism by having inspected the capital's militia in person.[113]

The Carlists, meanwhile, saw their retreat open a chapter of misfortunes. Espartero, having at first prudently remained outside the capital to ascertain the enemy's intentions, caught up with and defeated their rearguard at Aranzueque, taking some two hundred prisoner. In desperation, the king invited Cabrera to replace Moreno as the Carlist commander-in-chief, but Cabrera – who had also reached Madrid was poised to storm the capital as part of a pincer action – refused in thinly disguised disgust at the failure of the king's leadership. Cabrera, after all, had wanted a lightning descent on Madrid lasting only two weeks as opposed to the leisurely 'throne-and-altar' carnival march which the army's supreme commander, Prince Sebastián, had undertaken under the king's influence.[114] German auxiliaries – anticipating the frustration of their great-grandchildren with Franco's slow offensive one hundred years later – were exasperated with the absence of the strategic vision worthy of Cabrera. Lichnowsky was baffled: 'It was as if no-one had given any thought to descending on Madrid'.[115] The artillery expert Wilhelm von Rahden did not understand why Carlist victories were squandered with decorations and festivals of grace rather instead of a purposeful thrust.[116] Meanwhile, the Carlist retreat ploughed north to the safety of the Basque provinces, Espartero hard on its heels. Although the Cristinos could not prevent the Carlist forces of Zaratiegui and the king regrouping in their retreat, Espartero was ruthless in his pace, and in the way, he treated civilian populations in his path (not least because an unusually high number of Castillians had defected to the Carlists), sometimes promising the death penalty against hoarders of food and drink. But Espartero was slowed down by the desperate hunger and neglect faced by his own men, as even the shoes which the hated *asentistas* (private contractors) supplied often had wooden or even cardboard heels which fell apart soon into campaigning.[117] Despite, this Espartero still managed to work wonders for the Cristino cause. On 4 October he gained a close victory at Retuerta after committing his reserves at the most opportune moment.[118] The tired remains of the Royal Expedition thereafter escaped back across the River Ebro and into their safe zone.

From late 1837, Carlism in the Basque country lapsed into terminal crisis. Popular enthusiasm for the war evaporated, and factionalism within the Carlist high command led to the rise of a commander-in-chief with the vision to end the war with a compromise peace (known as *transacción*). Early in 1839 General Maroto executed several diehard Carlist generals and presented his dumbfounded king with a coup for peace. By August 1839, after a complicated series of negotiations with *Generalísimo* Espartero, Maroto secured honourable terms. The Convention of Vergara evicted Don Carlos and his diehards from Spanish territory and allowed Carlist officers to join the national army. Espartero even agreed to speak for the defence of the Basque *fueros* in the Cortes. Cabrera, who denounced Maroto's 'treason', held out in the east until the following summer, inflicting some of the worst acts of terror of the war, as Cabrera's forces found 'soft' targets more appealing. But by the summer of 1840, Cabrera, too, interned himself and thousands of diehard followers in France.

The legacy of praetorianism

The outbreak of peace in 1840 should have opened up an era of liberal unity and peace. But even though the 1839 Convention of Vergara allowed Carlist officers to keep their swords, ranks, and pay, the bulk of their rank and file were either sent home penniless or allowed to share the appalling conditions of the victorious army. Certainly, the victory year birthed a flurry of public festivities. Given the controversy of civil war, the peace of 1840 actually spawned celebrations of the unimpeachably 'national' revolt of 1808. The *Eco del Comercio* garlanded the header of its 2 May edition in patriotic commemoration of the 1808 rising. In 1840, the Paseo del Prado was adorned with a monument commemorating the dead of the Second of May. As early as 1835 the *moderado* intellectual Ramón Mesonero Romanos drew up a plan to regenerate Madrid. *Moderado* Ramón Mesonero Romanos's regeneration plans included the construction of a 'Pantheon of Illustrious Spaniards', which, despite much pomp, was not ready for peace (and indeed would not be finished until as late as 1926). All these projects were possible in Madrid, which had unlike Barcelona lacked industry and the same competition for space.[119] Yet Barcelona made up for its lack of space with a surfeit of patriotic and revolutionary enthusiasm in 1840, General Espartero being literally dragged off his horse and carried aloft by adoring crowds during his victory procession through that city.

Between 1836 and 1841, Spain abolished the entire legal and political structure of the old regime, a radical process ahead of developments in more 'advanced' European countries.[120] The Constitution of 1837 restricted suffrage for national elections whilst still leaving *progresistas* the powerbase of munici-palities elected by wide-ranging suffrage. While not as radical as the 1812 charter, the 1837 constitution still empowered active citizens at local levels. That said, high politics were now dominated by the *moderado* faction which, in its zeal both to end the war and smother popular radicalism, allowed pseudo-dictatorial powers to pass both to the Reserve and Northern armies (led by the embittered rivals, Generals Narváez and Espartero, respectively) and to the captain generals of the provinces who imposed states of siege (martial law) in order to subordinate, or even disband altogether, the riotous militia, and to suppress various radical clubs. The 1837–40 military ascendancy has thus been shown to be the advent of praetorian politics in liberal Spain.

As yet this was no twentieth-century phenomenon: the army did not impose itself as a corporate body on civil society. Rather, generals merely used their armies as a springboard for political power and were faithful there-after to the interests of their chosen political parties, but army command was the key revolving-door in the politics of the liberal state.[121] At a popular level, this military hegemony meant soldiers being both hired and ordered by *moderado* placemen to determine the outcome of elections in their favour. The phenomenon of soldiers making and breaking elections which Romero Alpuente denounced during the Triennium was now repeated.[122] Such mal-practice undermined the 'municipal democracy' beloved of the *progresistas*, which was the cornerstone of the Constitution of 1837. In fact, as is discussed the following, the supposed 'golden age' of municipal democracy was flawed in more serious ways.[123]

For the last three years of war, however, the 'golden age' was elusive as the *moderados* won the 1837 Cortes elections and implemented a policy of 'order'. Thus, a growing number of provinces, by no means all of them close to areas of fighting, were subjected to states of siege which subordinated or disbanded the National Militia and overruled local municipal democracy, the very power base of the *progresista* party beloved of *Generalísimo* Espartero. The *progresista* press, now liberalised by the 1836–1837 laws, turned the states of siege into a focus for mobilisation.[124] Worse was afoot. The *Ley de Ayun-tamientos* dictated that constitutional mayors would be replaced by mayors appointed by the prefects, whilst the competence of the municipalities would be purely functional. As the municipality was the lifeblood of *progresista* poli-tics, this liberal party turned to General Espartero as its champion. When the *moderado* government received royal assent for this reform, the response was the famous revolution of September 1840. But Esaprtero's position was not unambiguous until late in the crisis. But once the *moderado* government of Pérez de Castro got María Cristina's eager approval to demolish the autonomy of the troublesome town halls, the *progresistas*, backed by Espartero, sprung into action. The Castro ministry fell, and an anguished queen-regent threw herself on the mercy of the man who might still be her protector, *Generalísmo* Espartero.

Rise and fall of regent Espartero

Espartero, whose politics were basically *progresista*, refused María Cristina's offer to lead a government implementing the municipal law, so the regent herself was forced into exile. Her parting refrain to her former ally was 'I have made you a count. I have made you a duke. But I cannot make you a gentleman'.[125] News of Espartero's negative *pronunciamiento* of 29 July 1840 provoked crowds of several hundred in Seville to take to the street, led by a group of disbanded militiamen illegally sporting their uniforms. When a local *moderado* newspaper dared ridicule Espartero's resignation, its offices were burned to the ground by a mob of five hundred people. Three weeks of barricades led the provincial deputation to cave in, and on 16 August Seville's National Militia was formally reconstituted.[126] The militiamen drew salaries afresh from the municipal budget in recognition of their service during the civil war. Yet the plight of workers at Seville's state-of-the-art artillery foundry, who had been dismissed with pay arrears in October 1839, suggested that some wartime service was more equal than others.[127]

During the summer of 1840, the *moderado* elites were swept from office thanks to this revolution. No sooner had the revolution of 1840 been launched, however, than the rot began to set in. For a start, *progresista* elites turned to mobs in order to overawe their opponents, thereby placing into perspective the 'popular' impression afforded by much of the existing historiography.[128] Córdoba, for example, had long been notorious for extortion and mob behaviour as *reparto* failed to materialise.[129] Thus, *moderado* opponents in Córdoba during the revolution were attacked by mobs which sometimes let their real socio-economic grievances emerge (in this case, the preponderance of cheaper Galician migrant labour at harvest time). Local oligarchs were forced to rein in their mobs, reminding them 'not to hit the Galicians' but to attack 'the fat people'.[130] Otherwise, the revolution provided the chance merely for *progresista* 'outs' to be rewarded with office. A deluge of correspondence from Valladolid in October complained of how the revolution was supposed to reduce the financial burden of *empleos* but had actually ended up increasing it.[131] Nonetheless, social-liberal voices were finally beginning to speak out in protest. The more civic-minded National Militia sometimes protested against these abuses. In September 1840, amidst the post-war revolution of the municipalities, eleven militiamen published a manifesto against their own officer and against the inclusion of public office holders in revolutionary juntas. Above all, the demanded that the revolution should 'represent the people' and exclude officers, officials, and ecclesiastics. Eleven members of Segovia's National Militia, who issued a manifesto calling for their local revolutionary junta to be purged of cronies, were denounced by the authorities as 'anarchists' and banished from the province.[132]

Meanwhile, the property revolution accelerated, albeit not always to the advantage of the popular classes and their mutilated civil war veterans. The *latifundia* region of Jérez de la Frontera had been the centre of both peaceful (petitions) and violent (tax strikes) agitation throughout the autumn of 1840 as peasants and *jornaleros* demanded to be reinstated with lands they had been awarded in 1823.[133] During the summer of 1841, the provincial deputation obligingly decreed the parcelling-out of former clerical property. But the provincial decree rewarded only those militiamen who during 1823 had remained at their posts. These were now to be given land as a reward for their 'distinguished service in the sacred cause of liberty, a double share being granted to those wounded in service and the sons of those killed'. Yet the abiding grievance in 1841 was not the symbolic skirmishes of 1823 but the Carlist War, which had littered both town and country with maimed and hungry soldiers turned to begging and banditry. In any case, as this measure was so clearly municipal nepotism, the response was a wave of riots stretching from Jerez to Benaocaz, in which the subversive anti-government taunts of 'Long Live Cristina' and 'Death to the *Negros*' mingled with the radical cries of 'Long Live the Republic'.[134] In fact, the iniquity of land redistribution in Jérez had the effect of providing substance to the popular republican movement in this province which hitherto had been ridiculed by the press for its reliance on demagogues offering free sherry to rally support.[135]

For all the episodes of political violence, the September 1840 revolution was less of a revolution and more of a restoration of the *progresista* gains of 1836–1837: the right to insurrection and the protection of town-hall democracy.[136] After scenes in Madrid of violence and a few killings between *moderado* and *progresista* vigilantes, local elites came off the fence and established a 'revolutionary' junta whose first act was to ban public meetings.[137] The leaders of the Madrid junta were the same men who, two weeks earlier, had counselled resistance to the revolution.[138] In Granada prefect, Joaquín de Alba proclaimed loyalty to the queen-regent and two weeks later disowned her by leading the city's junta.[139] In Jaén, local *progresista* landowners tried to stall demands from veterans for land by raising a mob which chased the prefect out of town.[140] In Salamanca, the *moderado* prefect waited too long to jump ship and had to flee ahead of a lynch mob.[141]

Yet this merry-go-round of local worthies could not conceal the groundswell of popular radicalism that had surged out of the military and socio-economic upheaval of the civil war. The Republican newspaper *El Huracán* published the names of radicals pledging their names to regional manifestoes demanding land redistribution and universal suffrage, showing a self-confidence lacking in the radical press hitherto. The Patriotic Constitutional Association in Madrid offered its members 'mutual protection against attacks and persecutions' and made plans to dig trenches and erect barricades in the Calle de Alcalá in anticipation of a crackdown being ordered by the government. The association was led by the well-travelled poet Jacinto de Salas y Quiroga, who championed a petition to the provisional government which demanded that 'this time the revolution should not be made by the many for the benefit of the few'.[142] Salas y Quiroga's leadership inspired a sister Patriotic Constitutional Association in Barcelona, which from the outset had far greater success at attracting a solidly working class following in the Catalan industrial capital. Amongst the 199 members registered at the inauguration of 1 October 1840 were twenty-five weavers, forty-one unskilled labourers, and ninety-two assorted artisans.[143] This association proved the prototype for subsequent working-class mutualism and militancy.

The republican businessman (and Cortes deputy during 1843–44) Lorenzo Calvo y Mateo signed a manifesto on behalf of the 'Spanish nation' demanding an end to the 'illegal' sale of *bienes nacionales* which 'have been alienated without any public benefit' and should instead be handed over to 'the worthy defenders of liberty, both veterans and militiamen, as reward for their heroic community spirit (*civismo heróico*)'.[144] The charge of illegality was based on *desamortización* owing its origins to Mendizábal's emergency decree of 1835. As far as the republicans were concerned, even if the decree was formally legalised under the Constituent Cortes, this body was still monarchical, and thus violated the sovereignty of the people. In any case, the land question buoyed up republican agitation. The junta of Andújar (Andalucía), scene of republican agitation in 1836, launched a manifesto demanding a halt to land sales. Two weeks after the reaction of the Madrid junta, *El Huracán* defiantly headlined with the demand for sales of disentailed lands to be halted.[145]

The moderation of the Madrid junta, however, set for tone for General Espartero's provisional government. The war hero appointed mainstream *progresistas* to the crucial Madrid junta, excluding radicals like the editor of the *Eco del Comercio*, Fermín Caballero, who demanded land for war veterans and the integration of the September juntas into a new government.[146] Whereas the *progresista* press championed Espartero as a 'son of the people' whom the revolution elevated to a provisional tripartite regency before making him sole Regent in May 1841, demonstrated much of what was wrong with liberal elites. As with Riego, Espoz y Mina, and Cardero, personal ambition drove army men to bend with the political wind, no matter what the cost to the rank and file or crowd politics at large. During the Carlist War, however, Espartero's ambition at least appeared well served. For his relief of Bilbao in 1835, he was rewarded the following year with the command of the Northern Army, the most powerful position in the *cristino* military which, combined with his election to the Cortes, gave Espartero a growing king-making role in Spanish politics. As he took the credit for arranging the negotiated peace of Vergara in August 1839, thereby ending the war in the north to popular acclaim, the Duke of Victory was the best placed to champion the *progresista* rise to power the following year. Yet Espartero's politics, like those of Riego before him, were decidedly mediocre. 'Let the National Will be fulfilled!' (*¡cúmplase la voluntad nacional!*) was Espartero's rhetorical response to the gulf of 1840 between the queen-regent and the nation. In practice, this did not amount to much, for whilst the Regent left *progresista* oligarchs to manage their politics, he had ears only for his inner clique of fellow *ayacuchos*, several of whom he rewarded with high office and lucrative monopolies whilst the rank and file of the army were left hungry and penniless.[147]

During the summer of 1840, however, it was only a minority of far-sighted commentators, like the Olavarría republicans of *El Huracán*, who rightly feared Espartero's ambition to become regent. Meanwhile, Espartero enjoyed a popular honeymoon, as his symbol of the humble-born war hero leant itself to ready portrayal by the ascendant Romantic movement.[148] Eulogies were let loose comparing the 'son of the people' with George Washington.[149] Indeed, such was the popularity of Espartero the pacifier that the well-oiled machine of *progresista* crowd politics for once seemed surplus to requirements. Five hundred people in Barcelona were paid three *pesetas* each to give Espartero a rapturous welcome into the Catalan capital, but these hired agitators were quickly drowned out by some eighty thousand who spontaneously turned out, the crowd proving so thick that the war hero had to abandon his horse and let himself be carried by the people.[150] So had Napoleon been welcomed back into Paris during the Hundred Days, an ominous portent perhaps, for over the course of the next three years, Espartero would steadily acquire a new title, that of the 'Spanish Napoleon', or a pale imitation of the French arch-adventurer who betrayed the revolution.[151]

Economic unrest

Espartero's regime was marked by a post-war wave of economic mobilisation caused by the Regent's own policies, post-war demobilisation and the liberal property revolution. Autonomous town halls discovered just how autonomous their neighbours were, and local understanding of age-old boundary and water disputes could become violent once mayors had National Militia units at their command. A dam that widened the breach of friendship between Ohanes and Canjáyar (Almería) was destroyed by force and a document-waving *escribano* beaten up for his insolence. The editor of the powerful *Eco del Comercio* weighed into a dispute in his native Cuenca province about a mayor evicting foragers from 'common' land which had now become private.[152] The sleepy village of Alhama de Granada (Málaga) made the national press when a local councillor conspired with the *escribano* to rob a local miller of his life savings the night after he had signed the documents certifying the sale of his mill.[153] There was no redress, for, being members of the militia, they all enjoyed the *fuero militar* and were therefore untouchable anyway. In fact, the Málaga authorities, responding to this and subsequent abuses, repeated the canard that criminals masquerading as militiamen were to blame.[154] Such arbitrary *caciquismo* might not have been so unbearable had municipalities adopted a popular, social-liberal agenda, but unfortunately this was seldom the case. June 1842 saw a rising in Chiclana de la Frontera (Cádiz) in protest at the levying of higher taxes to fund the militia.[155] Constitutional municipalities also proved a byword for corruption and profligacy. Meanwhile, the British traveller T. M. Hughes was struck by the largesse of municipal oligarchs:

> In the last year's municipal account of Cádiz appears an item of eight hundred *reales*, or eight pounds sterling, for cigars, for one member only of the Provincial Deputation during a journey to Madrid. The journey is charged at 6,000 *reales*, or £60, for travelling and hotel expenses; and the item for cigars amounts to one-seventh of the entire. Even this, perhaps, is as legitimate as the turtle-soup and venison of the municipal men in London; yet it is impossible to defend the outlay of a large sum, without the slightest authority, in providing a fine funeral for a deceased member of the Deputation, and the squandering of 7,000 *reales*, or £70 sterling, out of the sacred municipal funds, upon a portrait of Espartero.[156]

Economic insecurity also followed the demobilisation of the National Militia which had stood at some half-a-million at the time of the 1840 revolution. Unsurprisingly, this policy meant reducing the citizens' force to a cadre of local elites and municipal favourites. For the other militiamen, on the other hand, disbandment was often brutal. As early as October 1840, *El Huracán* complained of militiamen being demobilised across Spain as if they were mere lackeys.[157] Favourites retained for militia service were often used as political pawns. In Córdoba, for example, the December *progresista* victory in the municipal elections relied on half-a-dozen ringleaders who were kept in the militia to launch attacks on local *moderados*. Thanks to this street violence, these elections were secured. Yet the *progresista* victory was achieved only by violence between rival gangs which, like in Madrid during the summer, spared the elites. Thus, *cordobense* hatters were employed by *moderado* masters who forbade their employees to enter the militia. Not that these masters could afford their charges any protection, however, as the hatters were singled out for violence and intimidation by the *progresista* mob that December. Even worse, *progresista* elites proved equally callous to their own mobs: far from being rewarded for making the election, the six ringleaders were arrested on fabricated charges of 'Carlism'.[158] Meanwhile, the Córdoba militia was stood down all the same, from a peak of eleven thousand in December 1840 it had declined to fewer than a thousand by the following April.[159]

The Carlist War left soldiers seething with discontent. Spain was still awash with arms as the *esparterista* regime dared not demobilise the army fully, whilst even those soldiers and militia who were disbanded often concealed their muskets. Yet the retention of so many men under arms also encouraged unrest. One *progresista* who turned against Espartero wrote that '60,000 well-paid troops would be better than 140,000 in rags'.[160] But a large army also offered the regime leverage against unwelcome radicalism, especially when this so often involved the militia. The republican Abdón Terradas was dismissed from his post as commander of a battalion of militia in Catalonia, an act which sparked altercations between militia and army officers and provoked journalists to condemn the Carlist War legacy of praetorianism.[161]

But the plight of demobilised veterans in a war-torn economy had no obvious answer. In the defeated Basque country veterans faced the double burden of demobilisation without pay and liberal economic reforms which were concentrating wealth in the wrong hands. Whilst most of the *fueros* were left intact, the definitive removal of the Spanish customs frontier to the Pyrenees privileged the liberal, commercial oligarchies of San Sebastián and Bilbao at the expense of the paternalistic Carlist heartland of Vitoria.[162] The Basque armaments industry was prevented from supplying the Cristino army because Espartero feared that their finished products might get diverted into Carlist hands once more. Workers made redundant, along with demobilised Carlist soldiers, were thus driven to emigrate to Cuba and the River Plate (Montevideo). The winter and spring of 1841 witnessed a surge in emigration from Spain's northern ports, whilst newspapers related depressing coverage of the haemorrhage of youth, many of the latter ending up shipwrecked, indentured, or exploited on arrival in Cuba and Spain's former colonies.[163] Carlists who accepted the offer to serve in Espartero's newly reunified national army fared little better. Pay arrears in July 1841 provoked Carlist and Cristino veterans alike at the North African garrison colony of Alhucemas to mutiny.[164] After having committed several killings and rapes and defied government police actions for a month, the mutineers were drugged into submission after the authorities had arranged for supplies to reach the garrison of barrels of wine laced with opium.[165]

The general discontent plaguing Espartero's regime was manipulated by the *moderado* opposition at home and abroad. As conditions in the army were so miserable, the Espartero régime was thus made chronically vulnerable to subversion. Conspiracy turned into revolt in the autumn of 1841. Conspiratorially backed by the exiled María Cristina, in October 1841 *moderado* military risings shook Pamplona, Vitoria, and even the Royal Palace in Madrid. When, in 1841, war hero Diego de León and his *moderado* conspirator, Manuel Concha, raided the Royal Palace in an attempt to kidnap Princess Isabella, one late nineteenth-century foreign commentator called this incident a Romantic throwback to the days of Bothwell and Mary Queen of Scots.[166] The *moderado* plot was thwarted by both *progresistas* and republicans mobilising the National Militia and a number of self-defence juntas. But this modern mobilisation was balanced by the Romantic. Espartero tearfully rejected appeals for clemency on behalf of the condemned Diego de León, who met his death after giving his cigars to his firing squad and appealing to them not to shake and to shoot straight. But in 1841, the modern was getting the better of the Romantic. As soon as Espartero was sure of having decapitated the conspiracy, he rapidly demobilised the leftist juntas and militia which had risen in defence of his regime, an action which various leftists and even some of Espartero's political allies condemned as rank ingratitude.[167]

A Madrid radical expressed outrage at Espartero's actions: 'the government shows itself ridiculous and arrogant to gloat in the victory of October 1841: victory belongs to the people'.[168] Spain's 'son of the people' became ever more autocratic in his behaviour, suspending elections won by radicals, like Abdón Terradas and driving republican newspapers like *El Huracán* underground.

Most juntas were quickly dissolved under pressure from the regent's army. But in Barcelona, the junta members had too many interests to let themselves be overwhelmed by the Spanish state. Barcelona had been seething at Espartero's free-trade policy with Britain, which, though solving the notorious contraband problem across Spain's huge and unpoliceable coastline, also threatened to swamp Spain with cheaper Lancashire cotton goods.[169] Espartero began his sole Regency in May 1841 with a manifesto liberalising imports. In essence, the Regent proposed to abolish the hated *derechos de puertas*, disband the notoriously corrupt carabineers, hand over their customs collection duties to the army, and replace all import restrictions on cotton products by a single tariff levied at the port of entry.[170] The implications of this policy favoured pro-free trade Andalucía but horrified protectionist Catalonia. A radical secret society called the 'Confederation of Spanish Regenerators' placed the 'protection of national industry' at the heart of its programme, warning that the British wanted to 'turn Iberia into a new India, have no principles beyond their own egotism, and want to keep us poor and ignorant so that we might work for them as slaves'.[171] Given this economic context, the October 1841 junta in Barcelona employed workers to begin demolishing the hated Montjuic fortress, which was a symbol of Bourbon oppression and recent gaol for victims of the Barón de Meer's martial law. But the junta soon ran out of money and resistance to Espartero's dissolution order finally crumbled a month after the failed *moderado* rising. The leaders of the October junta took ship for Marseilles, leaving population to face General Van Halen's state of siege.[172] Subsequently, Van Halen disbanded the militia at the point of his army bayonets, depriving artisans of their service wages.

Given this context, it is hardly surprising that new radical forces were emerging, first and foremost, republicanism. Popular acclaim of Espartero's *progresista* regency in 1840 was short-lived when the regent dissolved all Patriotic Societies in 1841 and misinterpreted economic grievance in Barcelona against free trade as a threat to 'public order'.[173] Republicanism was organised both formally through electioneering and clandestinely through secret societies. Regarding the former, republicans triumphed in December 1841 municipal elections at Seville, Huelva, Valencia, San Sebastián, Teruel, Cádiz, and, especially, Barcelona.[174] Adopting the 'social republic' model of *El Huracán* as a loose manifesto, republican mayors often adopted 'pork-barrel' policies of reducing taxes for their electors, exempting them from the perennial burden of conscription, and squeezing those who voted against them.[175] Yet republicanism violated the Constitution of 1837 and was therefore illegal. *El Huracán* was banned and survived only as a flysheet (*hoja volante*) after the

October 1841 crackdown. Thus, republican candidates were rarely able to mobilise beyond the 'direct action' of the cafe. For articulate republicanism, Spain was thrown back onto the well-trodden path of secret societies, which, frustratingly for historians, by their very nature leave few details of their rank-and-file membership.

But if a full picture remains patchy, Barcelona certainly offers a clear example of post-war radicalism. Workers in its cotton industries formed mutualist societies which set their own socio-economic agenda. Much of Barcelona's mutualist success was due to industrial elites who found themselves not only sponsoring their workers' mutualist societies but also, crucially, reaching out to them as allies to thwart Espartero's free-trade policy. February 1839 had seen the creation of the Society of Weavers (Sociedad de Tejedores) which, formally bowing to the strict *moderado* Law of Associations, eschewed politics and concentrated on providing sickness and unemployment insurance.[176] By May 1840, this workers' organisation had exhorted factory owners to engage it in bilateral arbitration over pay and conditions.[177] The following May, the first anniversary of this bilateralism brought out some fifteen to twenty thousand workers onto the streets of Barcelona. Even though the festivities were carried off with religious ceremony and the participation of elites, thereby making a public display of class harmony, this mobilisation could not but demonstrate the physical strength of labour in Spain's first industrial city.[178] But in 1842, workers and owners made common cause against Espartero, the former as much agitated by a rise in tax on foodstuffs (*consumos*) as the latter were at free trade.

Bullangas in Barcelona

Barcelona during the Carlist War had been infamous for its *bullangues*, or political riots. The Catalan term *bullangue* even entered the Castilian language ('*bullanga*') as a consequence. The risings of 1842–43 showed the greatest social mobilisation yet witnessed. The *esparterista* state of siege in force since October 1841 had made a martyr of Abdón Terradas, who was imprisoned after winning municipal elections as a republican. Having refused to flee into exile like the rest of his allies of the October junta, Terradas was imprisoned early in 1842.[179] Amid the repression, the government in January 1842 revived the edict which suppressed the Society of Textile Workers.[180] Yet again, however, the workers continued to organise and exert pressure on employers, and the skeleton militia, which Van Halen dared keep in uniform, could not be trusted to police unrest.[181]

The spark that lit the Barcelona tinderbox came on the night of 13 November 1842, when a member of the *Tejedores* defied soldiers posted at Barcelona's city gates who had wanted to search him. His arrest provoked some republicans to take to the streets, whereupon they too were arrested. Now hundreds of armed militiamen and youths took to streets to demand their release.

Even though the army temporised by moving the prisoners to a militia barracks, this concession came too late: the city government felt constrained to side with the militia against the government, Terradas was released from prison, and the army was forced to pull out of the city. Barcelona was now in open rebellion for twenty days.[182] It is likely that María Cristina, who was already lavish in her support for conspiracies against Espartero, also financed the republican risings in Barcelona in some way.[183] The first two days of the rising saw the militia ally with the republicans. They erected barricades all over the city and some five hundred soldiers were killed in protracted skirmishes, insurgent casualties being considerably less. Even though troops in Montjuich at first held out, they had no supplies and were forced by sheer hunger to quit the city. However, with 'order' now restored by the revolutionary authorities, things started to go wrong. For the insurgent junta hoisted into power as president one Juan Manuel Carsy, an adventurous embezzler who had escaped prison in 1835, made for exile and then returned to Catalonia after 1840 in order to ingratiate himself with a republican rank and file eager to accept his credentials (Carsy probably reinvented himself as a political, rather than criminal, fugitive). If the movement thus seemed contaminated from the start, the junta nonetheless produced a popular programme demanding that Espartero share his regency, convene a Constituent Cortes, and, most important, protect national industry.[184]

Even if the streets of Barcelona were now in insurgent hands, only fraternal risings elsewhere in Spain could impose this programme on the government. Yet ongoing censorship of republican newspapers in Spain prevented any risings, whilst even if some towns elsewhere in Catalonia pronounced, these proved too weak to withstand the government onslaught which Van Halen would now orchestrate. In the meantime, for two weeks Barcelona was steeped in a 'pork-barrel' revolution as the junta revived the militia, thereby providing wages for workers laid off by the free trade crisis. Yet the relentless motto of the junta, 'union and constancy', proved ephemeral, as the wealthy classes, fearing that social revolution was afoot, dispatched *agents provocateurs* in an attempt to incite to mutiny the troops who had joined the rebellion. In fact, open class war was forestalled, as Van Halen marched a government army on the city, retook Montjuich, and subjected the city to a bombardment which lasted thirty-six hours. Whilst several militiamen stood their ground, the French Consulate brokered a deal which allowed for Carsy's escape to France in return for power being handed over to a conservative junta comprising the bishop of Barcelona and several wealthy merchants and industrialists. This new junta formally invited government troops to re-enter the city, whereupon an onerous tribute was imposed on the municipality, thereby exacerbating the condition of the poor, whilst even more starkly, some 239 militiamen who had idealistically remained at the barricades were arrested and subjected to the full rigours of courts martial. Whilst the Carsy junta was safely in exile, the rank and file were thus abandoned to their fate. The luckier ones were conscripted into carrying out reconstruction work on the hated Montjuich fortress. Thirteen of the insurgents were executed. About half of these were former Carlist regulars who were thus shot for being treacherous twice over.[185] Carsy's betrayal sold out a revolution inspired by genuine social grievances. That said, the revolution of 1842 had also fatally undermined *progresismo*. When Barcelona erupted again the following year, *progresista* élites would turn on the regent.

The events of Barcelona turned many erstwhile *progresista* supporters of Espartero against him, and the exiled court of María Cristina noticed. May 1843 was a crucial month when a broad alliance of *progresistas*, *moderados*, and even some republican elites, all of whom feared that social revolution was afoot, rose in juntas against Espartero. This nationwide movement was obscured by the return of the *bullanga* in Barcelona. This erupted again in the summer of 1843, but this time without the support of the employers who instead saw the exiled General Narváez as their saviour. For this reason, the so-called Jamancia of 1843 was more radical than in 1842. The Jamancia produced a class-based form of popular radicalism with an unequivocally social agenda: a social republic shored up by lower taxes and protection of workers from the vagaries of depression and liberal capitalism. Between June and October 1843, some 1,200 armed workers controlled the streets of Barcelona, as some 20,000 wealthy commercial and industrial elites fled to the countryside, whilst the army garrison proved so infiltrated by radicals that it, first, stood aside from the revolution and, later, even went over to the side of the crowd.[186] But as during December 1842, brute government force, including the terrifying bombardment, eventually overpowered this revolution. But in 1843 Espartero's regime faced not just Barcelona but also a dizzying combination of the juntas and army revolt being masterminded from María Cristina's court in Paris.

The insurgent juntas organised their militia units to face Espartero's increasingly outnumbered army. Their first policy enacted was to demand the surrender of all weapons not in the possession of the militia. They also declared all males of fighting age liable to being conscripted into security columns that were to be sent out of towns to fight the *esparterista* armies.[187] In fact, such was the malaise that there was little fighting to be done. General Narváez re-entered Spain supplied with copious funds supplied by María Cristina's exiled court and confident of army loyalty dating back to his time commanding the Army of the Reserve. The money flowed via the juntas in order to bribe Espartero's troops – not that these needed much persuasion. Rather the troops of all ranks generally accepted the juntas' offer of promotion to the next rank.[188] Whilst Narváez thus indulged the juntas, he also fulfilled a better promise to the ranks. After ousting Espartero from power, those soldiers who had been conscripted during the emergency of 1836, and kept by Espartero in the ranks ever since, were now finally given *licencia absoluta* and allowed to go home.[189] The Battle of Torrejón fought between *esparteristas* and *moderados* near Madrid on 22 July was really a skirmish. But the battle was decisive in sending Espartero's dwindling troops reeling south into Andalucía. During Espartero's disastrous retreat south into Andalucía that summer, which included an abortive bombardment of Seville, he told his men that he was so satisfied with their loyalty and conduct that he would decorate each of them with a special Cross of Isabel II. Yet his exasperated men broke ranks and proclaimed that they 'would happily swap their crosses for a glass of wine'. Only the prompt encirclement by cavalry stopped the men from deserting.[190] Ultimately, however, there was little to be done. Town after town pronounced against the regime whilst soldiers drifted away into desertion or went over to Narváez's Junta de Salvación. On 30 July 1843, Espartero took ship at Cádiz for a British exile, thereby leaving Narváez and, ultimately, the *Moderado* party, the master of Spanish politics.

Moderado counter-revolution

The more sophisticated newspaper-reading public reeled in disgust at hearing how *progresistas*, who, years earlier, talked of nothing but liberty and revolution, now sold their services to the new 'man of the moment'. One of Espartero's last desperate acts had been to convene a government led by the radical *progresista*, Joaquín María López. López bowed to army pressure by declaring states of siege against insurgent juntas. But he was eased out of office by the bulk of his own party which cynically tried to curry favour with Narváez.[191] López's replacement was the erstwhile street radical of the Triennium, Salustiano de Olózaga, who, though now shorn of his youthful idealism, yet maintained a modicum of decency which made him vulnerable in these cynical times. In brief Olózaga was forced to resign amid a fallacious scandal that he had forced the hand of the young queen for the dissolution of the Cortes.[192] This story had been fabricated by a former radical, González Bravo, who had sold his services to General Narváez as a cat's paw for the General's own assumption of the premiership. Bravo, who in 1839 had edited a satirical, democratic newspaper called *El Guirigay*, now carried out the *moderado* 'dirty work' by sanctioning the brutal suppression of diehard radical juntas, only for himself to be outmanoeuvred in May 1844 by Narváez. Narváez now took the prime ministerial office for himself and hurriedly arranged for Princess Isabella to become queen in her own right as a figleaf of legitimacy. The juntas that had risen against Espartero now faced the triumphant *moderado* army alone. Some of the bloodiest resistance to the *moderado* takeover was offered at Alicante, where General Roncali's bombardment of the city was described in the foreign press:[193]

> According to a despatch from General Roncali, he opened his fire against Alicant on 17th March, and had thrown a great number of shells into the town. The insurgents made a sortie, but were driven back. The horrible

butcheries on both sides continued unabated, and scenes of a still more horrid description are anticipated on the fall of Alicant, which cannot hold out long.

After Roncali had brutally pacified Alicante, his bellicose bulletin tried to bury the radicalism of the past years: 'Woe to those of you who do not believe that the hour of revolution has passed. You have closed it in all of Spain with the keys of this conquered city'.[194] A British journalist, who published under the pseudonym 'Poco Más', wrote that 'Spain is apparently retrograding under a military despotism towards the darkest periods of her history'.[195] Narváez's brutal crackdown of 1843–44 showed how the bourgeois winners of the 1836–41 property revolution were siding with 'order' against the workers and against further revolution. For the *moderados*, the brutality did not affect their electoral chances at all, helped as these would be by a highly restrictive franchise. Yet for *progresismo* the events surrounding the fall of Espartero were disastrous. The popular appeal nature of *progresismo* had proved to suffer from a limited shelf-life once the property revolution began to reshape social relations. The post-war 1840s began to loosen the grip of *progresismo* on the allegiance of the lower-middle classes, in ways which threw up such anomalies as the absence in Spain of great revolutionary upheaval in 1848, and failure to resist the blatant authoritarianism of the *moderados* after 1844.

The *moderados* were now free to impose their programme which had been derailed in 1840, and more besides. Narváez's policies won the approval of the anguished propertied classes. In June 1844, Barcelona's local government presented him with gifts in gratitude for his restoration of 'order', whilst Madrid's authorities wrote that 'with the Militia dissolved, born in the fire of the Spanish revolution, the throne may arise upon solid foundations'.[196]

Notes

1 Antonio Caridad Salvador, 'Las consecuencias socioeconómicas directas de la Primera Guerra Carlista', *Cuadernos de Historia Contemporanea*, Vol. 40 (2017).
2 Manuel Santirso, 'Prólogo', in Antonio Caridad Salvador (ed.), *El ejército y las partidas carlistas en Valencia y Aragón (1833–1840)* (Valencia: Universitat de València, 2013).
3 Núria Sauch Cruz, 'Un retrat del general carlista Ramon Cabrera', in Daniel Montaña i Josep Rafart (eds.), *El carlisme ahir i avui* (I Simposi d'Història del Carlisme, 11 de maig de 2013), p. 102.
4 Carlos Marichal, *Spain (1834–1844): A New Society* (London: Támesis, 1977), pp. 118–23. Marichal suggests that the hostility of the peasantry in the Maestrazgo towards change was the main cause of popular Carlism here. Such contemporary liberals as Evaristo San Miguel, on the other hand, thought that "agricultural improvements" in this bleak, sparsely populated, zone, could win over the population to liberalism (Pedro Rújula (ed.), *Historia de la guerra última en Aragón y Valencia (escrita por F. Cabello, F. Santa Cruz y R. M. Temprado)* (Zaragoza: Institución 'Fernando el Católico', 2006), pp. LXXXVI–LXXXIX).
5 Rújula (ed.), *Historia de la guerra última en Aragón y Valencia*, pp. LXXXVI–LXXXIX.
6 *Eco del Comercio*, 28 October 1834.

7 Mark Lawrence, 'Poachers Turned Gamekeepers', *Small Wars and Insurgencies*, Vol. 25, No. 4 (2014), pp. 843–57.

8 Fernández, *El orígen del municipio constitucional*, p. 311.

9 José Alvarez-Junco, 'The Debate Over the Nation', in Nigel Townson (ed.), *Is Spain Different? A Comparative Look at the 19th and 20th Centuries* (Sussex: Sussex Academic Press, 2015), p. 27.

10 Isabel Burdiel, *La política de los notables: moderados y avanzados durante el régimen del Estatuto Real (1834–36)* (Valencia: Edicions Alfons el Magnànim, 1987), pp. 92–264.

11 Vicente Fernández Benítez, *Burguesía y revolución liberal: Santander, 1812–1840* (Santander: Estudio Librería, 1989), Ch. 4.

12 Juan J. Trías and Antonio Elorza, *Federalismo y reforma social en España (1840–1870)* (Madrid: Seminarios y Ediciones, 1975), pp. 95–104.

13 *La Revista Española*, 10 February 1835.

14 Burdiel, *Política de los notables*, pp. 94, 164.

15 *Eco del Comercio*, 5 August 1834; Romero Alpuente, *Historia de la revolución*, Vol. I (ed. Gil Novales) (Madrid: Centro de Estudios Constitucionales), pp. LXIX–LXXVIII; Miguel Artola-Gallego, *Partidos y programas políticos, 1808–1936* (Barcelona: Aguilar, 1979), p. 220.

16 Pirala, *Historia de la Guerra civil civil y de los partidos liberal y carlista*, 6 vols., Vol. II (Madrid: Turner/Historia, 1984), pp. 151–8.

17 *El Castellano*, 4 March 1837.

18 Mark Lawrence, *Spain's First Carlist War, 1833–1840* (Basingstoke: Palgrave Macmillan, 2014), p. 60.

19 Pérez Garzón, *Milicia Nacional*, pp. 556–94.

20 *Eco del Comercio*, 5 November 1834; 14 April 1841; 8 September 1841.

21 Comellas, *Trienio constitucional*, p. 312.

22 Josep-Ramón Segarra Estarelles, 'El reverso de la nación. "Provincialismo" e "independencia" durante la revolución liberal', in Javier Moreno Luzón (ed.), *Construir España: Nacionalismo español y procesos de nacionalización* (Madrid: Centro de Estudios Políticos y Constitucionales, 2007), pp. 40–5.

23 Smith, *Origins of Catalan Nationalism*, p. 86.

24 Julio Aróstegui, Jordi Canal, and Eduardo G. Calleja, *Las guerras carlistas: hechos, hombres e ideas* (Madrid: La Esfera de los Libros, 2003), pp. 61–3.

25 Callahan, *Church, Politics and Society*, pp. 189–90.

26 Antonio Caridad Salvador, 'Los carlistas de Valencia. La reacción en una ciudad liberal (1833–40)', *BROCAR*, Vol. 36 (2012), pp. 161–83, 180.

27 *Eco del Comercio*, 6 February 1835; 25 October 1834; 18 July 1835. *Filosofía* in the Spanish context dates from the Cortes of Cádiz when it was used pejoratively by *serviles* to describe the liberals.

28 *Eco del Comercio*, 8 July 1834; Juan Antonio La Comba, *Sociedad y política en Málaga en la primera mitad del siglo XIX* (Málaga: Librería Ágora, 1989), pp. 37–42.

29 Mark Lawrence, *Spain's First Carlist War*, p. 62.

30 José Manuel Cuenca Toribio, *La iglesia espanola ante la revolucion liberal* (Madrid: Ediciojnes Rialp, 1971), pp. 105–7, 118.

31 A.H.N., Diversos (*títulos y familias*), leg. 3601: 8 April 1835 letter from Captain-General of Aragón to Ministerio de la Guerra; Pirala, *Guerra civil*, Vol. II, pp. 123–30.

32 Cuenca, *Iglesia española*, pp. 19–21.

33 A.H.N., Diversos (*gobierno y política*), leg. 167/106: 13 August 1835 letter from interim military governor, José del Arenal, to Captain-General in Zaragoza.

34 Maluquer de Motes, *Socialismo*, pp. 32–3.

35 Alberto P. Risco, *Zumalacárregui en campaña* (Madrid: Imprenta de José Murillo, 1935), p. 74; Admittedly, the 'blockhouse' strategy of counter-insurgency warfare had been successfully pioneered by the French during the 1808–14 war.

36 Risco, *Zumalacárregui*, p. 29.
37 Cit. Eric Christiansen, *Origins of Military Power in Spain, 1800–1854* (Oxford: Oxford University Press, 1967), p. 57.
38 Cit. Pedro Rújula (ed.), *Historia de la guerra última en Aragón y Valencia*, Vol. I, p. 108.
39 *Eco del Comercio*, 20 August 1837; 26 September 1837; 17 April 1838; 2 May 1838; 5 September 1838.
40 *Eco del Comercio*, 26 January 1835; Christiansen, *Origins of Military Power*, p. 54; Pirala, *Guerra civil*, Vol. II, pp. 88–108.
41 A.M.M., 3/183, Anales de Málaga: 1821–1881 (Recortes de la prensa de la Unión Mercantíl), January–March 1835; *Eco del Comercio*, 17 February 1835; A.H.N., Diversos (*gobierno y política*), leg. 167. Doc. 60: account given by Fernando Córdova, civil governor of Málaga, to the Minsterio de lo Interior on the events of 22, 23, and 24 March 1835.
42 Pirala, *Guerra civil*, Vol. II, pp. 123–30; Lawrence, 'Popular Radicalism in Spain'.
43 Miguel Ángel Esteban Navarro, *La formación del pensamiento político y social del radicalismo español (1834–1874)* (Zaragoza: Universidad de Zaragoza, 1995), pp. 103–5; Trías and Elorza, *Federalismo*, pp. 80–2.
44 Pirala, *Guerra civil*, Vol. II, pp. 134–42.
45 Burdiel, *La política en el reinado de Isabel II* (Madrid: Marcial Pons, 1998), p. 70.
46 Burdiel, *Política de los notables*, pp. 177–180; *Eco del Comercio*, 22 September 1835.
47 Pirala, *Guerra civil*, Vol. II, pp. 360–2.
48 Burdiel, *Política de los notables*, pp. 200–11.
49 Lawrence, *Spain's First Carlist War*, pp. 117–18.
50 Mark Lawrence, 'Juan Álvarez Mendizábal', in J. álvarez-Junco and A. Shubert (eds.), *Nueva historia de la España contemporánea (1808–2018)* (Barcelona: Galaxia Gutenberg), pp. 632–43.
51 Lawrence, *Spain's First Carlist War*, p. 117.
52 R.A.H., Archivo Narváez, 9/7809, Caja 1: 30 November 1836 account of mutiny from General Narváez to War Ministry; 9/7811, Doc. 32: 21 March 1850 recollection by Lt. Sebastián Banuchi of events of November 1836.
53 Christiansen, *Origin of Military Power*, pp. 159–61.
54 *Ibid.*, p. 72.
55 *Eco del Comercio*, 2 January 1836.
56 Edward Brett, *British Auxiliary Legion in the First Carlist War, 1835–38* (Dublin: Four Courts Press, 2005), p. 109.
57 Andrés Révesz, *Narváez: un dictador liberal* (Madrid: Aguilar, 1953).
58 Aróstegui, Canal and Calleja, *Las guerras carlistas*, pp. 50–1.
59 Josep Carles Clemente, *Las guerras carlistas* (Barcelona: Península, 1982), pp. 98–109.
60 *Ibid.*, pp. 98–101.
61 *Eco del Comercio*, 21 January 1836. The humdrum titles *Organista* and *Serrador* ('Organist' and 'Sawyer') were typical of Spanish *nomes de guerre*.
62 *Eco del Comercio*, 1 April 1837.
63 *El Español*, 13 October 1836; 14 October 1836.
64 *Eco del Comercio*, 16 October 1836; 24 September 1837.
65 *Eco del Comercio*, 12 October 1836.
66 R.A.H., Archivo Narváez, 9/7810, Caja 2, Doc. 15: November 1836 account offered by General Rivero in his operations against Gómez in the Campo de Gibraltar.
67 Christiansen, *Origins of Military Power*, pp. 71–3; *Eco del Comercio*, 28 October 1836; 3 April 1837.
68 Mguel Artola-Gallego, *Partidos y programas políticos, 1808–1936* (Madrid: Aguilar, 1974), pp. 228–9.
69 Anes and Castrillón (eds.), *Economía, sociedad, política y cultura en la España de Isabel II*, pp. 61–3; Cuenca, *Iglesia española*, pp. 29–65.

70   Thomson, *Birth of Modern Politics*, p. 249.
71   Jorge Luengo Sánchez, *El nacimiento de una ciudad progresista: Valladolid durante la regencia de Espartero (1840–1843)* (Valladolid: Ayuntamiento de Valladolid, 2005), pp. 63–4.
72   Marichal, *Spain (1834–1844)*, pp. 108–9.
73   Fernández, *El origen del municipio constitucional*, pp. 315–17.
74   Antonio Miguel Bernal, *La lucha por la tierra en la crisis del antiguo régimen* (Madrid: Taurus, 1979), pp. 66–7, 111–15; Miguel Gómez Oliver, *La desamortización de Mendizábal en Granada* (Granada: Excma. Diputación Provincial de Granada, 1983), pp. 24, 56, 172–74; Marichal, *Spain (1834–1844)*, pp. 108–9.
75   Manuel Martínez Martín, *Revolución liberal y cambio agrario en la alta Andalucía* (Granada: Universidad de Granada, 1995), pp. 9–26, 140–3, 243–4.
76   For example, in his study of disentailment in Granada, Miguel Gómez admits to finding not a single such case (Gómez Oliver, *Desamortización de Mendizábal*, p. 42).
77   Marichal, *Spain (1834–1844)*, pp. 108–9.
78   *El Español*, 28 February 1836.
79   Juan Marichal, *El secreto de Espana*, pp. 95–7.
80   Maluquer de Motes, *Socialismo*, pp. 94–6.
81   Marichal, *Spain (1834–1844)*, pp. 139–40.
82   Bernal, *Lucha por la tierra*, pp. 111–15.
83   A.H.N., Consejos, leg. 12232, Doc. 5: 15 November 1839 report by Juez de primera instancia de Orgiva.
84   A.H.N., Diversos (*gobierno y política*), leg. 167, Doc. 82: 1 April 1839 letter from mayor of Guadix to Civil Governor; Martínez Martín, *Revolución liberal y cambio agrario*, pp. 172–81.
85   Mark Lawrence, *Spain's First Carlist War*, p. 167.
86   *Gaceta Oficial*, 9 August 1836.
87   Felix Lichnowsky, *Erinnerungen aus den Jahren 1837, 1838 und 1839*, Vol. I (Frankfurt-am-Main: Johann David Sauerländer, 1841), p. 137; Pirala, *Guerra civil*, Vol. IV, pp. 107; Román Oyarzun, *Historia del carlismo* (Madrid: Maxtor, 1965), pp. 78–9.
88   Pirala, *Guerra civil*, Vol. IV, pp. 94–107; Alfonso Bullón de Mendoza, *La Primera guerra carlista* (Madrid: Actas, 1992), p. 636.
89   Rahden, *Cabrera: Erinnerungen aus den Jahren 1837, 1838 und 1839*, Vol. I (Frankfurt-am-Main: Johann David Sauerländer, 1841), p. 220.
90   Pirala, *Guerra civil*, Vol. IV, pp. 108–15. Rahden, *Cabrera: Erinnerungen aus den Jahren 1837, 1838 und 1839*, Vol. I (Frankfurt-am-Main: Johann David Sauerländer, 1841).
91   Felix Lichnowsky, *Erinnerungen* (Paris: J. Dumaine, 1844), Vol II, pp. 238–45.
92   Carlos Dembowski, *Dos años en España durante la guerra civil, 1838–40* (Madrid: Crítica, 2008), p. 40.
93   Pirala, *Guerra civil*, Vol. IV, pp. 115–22.
94   *Ibid.*, pp. 127–32.
95   Pirala, *Guerra civil*, Vol. IV, pp. 144–54; Oyarzun, *Historia del carlismo*, p. 81.
96   The battle of Villar de los Navarros is also known as the Battle of Herrera.
97   Pirala, *Guerra civil*, Vol. IV, pp. 154–60.
98   *Ibid.*, pp. 161–6, 662–72.
99   Jaime del Burgo, *Para la Historia de la primera guerra carlista: Comentarios y acotaciones a un manuscrito de la época 1834–1839* (Pamplona: Institución Príncipe de Viana, 1981), p. 247; Pirala, *Guerra civil*, Vol. IV, pp. 177–83.
100 Pirala, *Guerra civil*, Vol. IV, pp. 214–15.
101 Bullón de Mendoza, *La Primera guerra carlista*, p. 191.
102 Pirala, *Guerra civil*, Vol. IV, pp. 193–9.
103 Oyarzun, *Historia del carlismo*, pp. 79, 82–3. Pirala, *Guerra civil*, Vol. IV, pp. 206–7.
104 Pirala, *Guerra civil*, Vol. IV, pp. 215–18.

105 Peter Janke, *Mendizábal y la instaración de la monarquía constitucional en España, 1790–1853* (Madrid: Siglo Veintiuno, 1974), pp. 250–2.
106 Michael Burke Honan, *The Court and Camp of Don Carlos: Being the Results of a Late Tour in the Basque Provinces, and Parts of Catalonia, Aragón, Castile, and Estramadura* (London: John Macrone, 1836), p. 389.
107 *El Castellano*, 16 September 1837.
108 This charter provided one Cortes representative per fifty thousand inhabitants, enfranchised all men paying at least 200 *reales* in annual taxes or receiving an annual private income of at least 1,500 *reales*, which amounted to one inhabitant in forty-eight enjoying full citizenship (whereas under the 1834 Royal Statute this figure had been 1 in 213) (Vicente Palacio Atard, *La España del siglo XIX* (Madrid: Espasa-Calpe, 1978), pp. 200–2).
109 Espadas Burgos, *Baldomero Espartero*, p. 61; Pirala, *Guerra civil*, Vol. IV, pp. 431–9.
110 Aróstegui, Canal, Calleja, *Las guerras carlistas*, p. 61; Clemente, *Las guerras carlistas*, p. 111; Pirala, *Guerra civil*, Vol. IV, pp. 227–8.
111 del Burgo, *Historia de la primera guerra carlista*, pp. 186–7, 235–7, 240–1.
112 Francisco Melgar, *Pequeña historia de las guerras carlistas* (Madrid: Gómez, 1958), pp. 69–72.
113 Pirala, *Guerra civil*, Vol. IV, pp. 230–1.
114 Holt, *Carlist Wars*, p. 172.
115 Lichnowsky, *Erinnerungen*, p. 134.
116 del Burgo, *Historia de la primera guerra carlista*, pp. 212–13.
117 Pirala, *Guerra civil*, Vol. IV, pp. 232–7.
118 *Ibid.*, pp. 237–9.
119 Jesús Cruz, *Rise of Middle-Class Culture in Nineteenth-Century Spain* (Shreveport: Louisana State University Press, 2011), pp. 154–8.
120 María Cruz Romeo Mateo, 'The Civil Wars of the Nineteenth Century', in Nigel Townson (ed.), *Is Spain Different? A Comparative Look at the 19th and 20th Centuries* (Sussex: Sussex Academic Press, 2015) p. 57.
121 Christiansen, *Origins of Military Power*, pp. 67–98; Diego López Garrido, *La Guardia Civil y los orígenes del estado centralista* (Madrid: Crítica, 1982), p. 44.
122 *DSC*, No. 69, 11 September 1820, 931, 942. Examples of soldiers intervening in elections are legion. January 1840 elections in Cartagena saw both sailors and soldiers hired to vote, whilst in Córdoba, meanwhile, a cavalry regiment distributed proclamations heaping insults on *progresistas* (*Eco del Comercio*, 17 January 1840).
123 Javier García Fernández calls the 1836–1843 era of local democracy a "golden age" (Fernández, *El orígen del municipio constitucional*, pp. 315–17).
124 The 16 August 1836 proclamation of the Constitution of 1812 revived the press regulations of the Triennium (i.e. no previous censorship, infractions to be judged by juries). Whilst a law of 22 March 1837 required editors to pay hefty deposits in order to secure publication licences, thereby driving radical pamphlets and manifestoes underground, the rest of the Triennium legislation was left untouched (Trías and Alorza, *Federalismo y reforma social*, pp. 95–104).
125 Holt, *Carlist Wars*, p. 200.
126 *El Huracán*, 6 August 1840; *Eco del Comercio*, 3 August 1840; 24 August 1840.
127 *Eco del Comercio*, 11 January 1841.
128 Fernández, *Origen del municipio constitucional*, pp. 312–22; Pirala, *Guerra civil*, Vol. VI, pp. 147–212; Marichal, *Spain (1834–1844)*, pp. 144–50; Moliner, *Revolución burguesa*, pp. 223–5.
129 *El Mundo*, 28 August 1838; *Eco del Comercio*, 14 September 1838.
130 Lawrence, *Spain's First Carlist War*.
131 *Eco del Comercio*, 16 October 1840.
132 *Ibid.*, 1 October 1840.

133 Antonio Cabral Chamorro, *Socialismo utópico y revolución burguesa: el fourierismo gaditano, 1834–1848* (Cádiz: Diputación Provincial de Cádiz, 1990), pp. 103–4.

134 *Eco del Comercio*, 6 September 1841; 19 November 1841; 25 November 1841. The term *negro* was the Carlist pejorative for liberal.

135 *Eco del Comercio*, 1 April 1841; 4 April 1841. Democrat Party historian, Antonio Eiras Roel, by contrast, judged this *jerezano* republicanism to have been purely ideological in its motivation (Antonio Eiras Roel, *El partido demócrata español (1849–1868)* (Madrid: Rialp, 1961), p. 97).

136 Javier Pérez Núñez, 'La revolución de 1840: la culminación del Madrid progresista', *Cuadernos de Historia Contemporánea*, Vol. 36 (2014), pp. 141–64.

137 *El Huracán*, 18 July 1840.

138 *Eco del Comercio*, 25 August 1840; 5 September 1840; 7 September 1840.

139 Cepeda Gómez, *El ejército español*, p. 243.

140 A.H.N., Diversos (*Gobierno y Política*), leg. 167, Docs. 32, 40: 8 September 1840 account by *jefe politico* of Jaén, Muñoz, of events of 7 September 1840; 11 September 1840 account by José Manuel Arenas, commander of 2nd battalion of Volunteers of Granada, of *prounciamiento* of previous day.

141 *El Huracán*, 8 September 1840.

142 *Eco del Comercio*, 25 August 1840; 5 September 1840; 7 September 1840.

143 Trías and Elorza, *Federalismo*, pp. 167–75.

144 *El Huracán*, 5 September 1840.

145 *Ibid.*, 23 September 1840.

146 Marichal, *Spain (1834–1844)*, pp. 91–4.

147 Nemesio de Pombo, *Situación de España a fines del año 1842* (Madrid: Imprenta Hernández, 1843), p. 25.

148 Raúl Martín Arranz, 'Espartero: figuras de legitimidad', in José Álvarez-Junco (ed.), *Populismo, caudillaje y discurso demagógico* (Madrid: Siglo XXI de España, 1987), pp. 101–20.

149 *El Huracán*, 23 July 1840.

150 Maluquer de Motes, *Socialismo*, pp. 275–84; *El Huracán*, 21 June 1840.

151 Cepeda Gómez, *El ejército español*, pp. 214–16.

152 Mark Lawrence, *The Spanish Civil Wars* (London: Bloomsbury, 2017), pp. 112–16.

153 *Eco del Comercio*, 1 April 1841.

154 *Ibid.*, 13 May 1841.

155 Clara Lida, *Anarquismo y revolución en la España del siglo XIX* (Madrid: Siglo XXI, 1972), p. 35.

156 Terence McMahon Hughes, *Revelations of Spain in 1845* (London: Henry Colburn, 1845), Vol. II, pp. 19–23.

157 *El Huracán*, 27 October 1840.

158 *El Correo Nacional*, 12 December 1840; 15 December 1840; *Eco del Comercio*, 28 December 1840.

159 *Eco del Comercio*, 8 April 1841.

160 de Pombo, *Situación de España a fines del año 1842*, p. 25.

161 *Eco del Comercio*, 22 July 1841.

162 Coro Rubio, *Revolución y tradición*, pp. 93–126.

163 *Eco del Comercio*, 12 February 1841; 3 March 1841; 12 March 1841; 17 March 1841; 26 March 1841.

164 Christiansen, *Origins of Military Power*, p. 111.

165 *Eco del Comercio*, 1 July 1841; 2 July 1841; 10 July 1841; 20 July 1841; 16 July 1841; 24 July 1841; 2 September 1841.

166 David Hannay, *Don Emilio Castelar* (London: Bliss, Sands and Foster, 1896), p. 19.

167 Marichal, *Spain (1834–1844)*, p. 167; Espadas Burgos, *Baldomero Espartero*, p. 78; Cepeda Gómez, *El ejército español*, pp. 222–36; Eiras Roel, *El Partido demócrata*, pp. 102–6.

168 de Pombo, *Situación de España a fines del año 1842*, pp. 8–9.

169 Marichal, *Spain (1834–1844)*, p. 175.

170 *Eco del Comercio*, 30 May 1841.
171 A.G.P., Caja 28/32, No. 1, Reinados, FVII, 27: undated (1842?) police transcription of the manifesto of the Sociedad de Regeneradores Españoles.
172 Pirala, *Guerra civil*, Vol. VI, pp. 318–23.
173 Florencia Peyrou, *El republicanismo popular en España 1840–1843* (Cádiz: Universidad de Cádiz, 2002), pp. 60–95.
174 Eiras Roel, *El Partido demócrata*, pp. 102–6.
175 José A. Piqueras and Manuel Chust (eds.), *Republicanos y repúblicas en España* (Madrid: Siglo XXI, 1996), pp. 100–5; Peyrou, *Republicanismo popular*, pp. 77–8; Marichal, *Spain (1834–1844)*, pp. 169–72.
176 Lida, *Anarquismo y revolución*, pp. 33–4.
177 Thus, the first bilateral agreement was struck in January 1841 concerning wholesale prices for handkerchiefs (*Eco del Comercio*, 2 February 1841).
178 Pirala estimated the strength of the *Tejedores* at some six thousand in Barcelona and twenty thousand in the rest of Catalonia (Pirala, *Guerra civil*, Vol. VI, p. 323).
179 Trías and Elorza, *Federalismo*, pp. 168–75.
180 *Eco del Comercio*, 11 January 1842.
181 Eiras Roel, *El Partido demócrata*, pp. 102–12.
182 *Ibid.*, pp. 117–18.
183 E. Jones Parry, *The Spanish Marriages, 1841–1846* (London: Palgrave Macmillan, 1936), p. 65.
184 *The Times*, 25 November 1842; 28 November 1842; 3 December 1842.
185 *Ibid.*, 3 December 1842; 22 December 1842; 17 October 1843; Maluquer de Motes thought that Carsy escaped the city on the pretext of rallying armed émigrés, who, of course, did not exist (Maluquer de Motes, *Socialismo*, pp. 275–84).
186 Moliner, *Revolución burguesa*, pp. 229–55; *The Times*, 22 August 1843; 24 August 1843; 5 September 1843 11 September 1843; 12 September 1843; 15 September 1843; 18 September 1843; 30 September 1843; 2 October 1843; 13 October 1843; 17 October 1843.
187 Moliner, *Revolución burguesa*, pp. 229–54.
188 Hughes, *Revelations of Spain in 1845*, Vol. II, p. 64.
189 *The Times*, 5 August 1843.
190 R.A.H., Archivo Narváez, 9/7812, Caja 4, Doc. 3: Comunicaciones de la Junta Provincial de Salvación y de la Capitanía General de Valencia (July, 1843).
191 Moliner, *Revolución burguesa*, p. 255.
192 Gracia Gómez, *Salustiano de Olózaga*, pp. 155–65.
193 *Illustrated London News*, 2 March 1844.
194 Isabel Burdiel, 'The liberal revolution, 1808–1843', in José Alvarez-Junco and Shubert, Adrian (eds.), *Spanish History since 1808* (London: Arnold, 2000), p. 32.
195 Poco Mas, *Scenes and Adevntures in Spain, 1835 to 1840*, 2 vols., Vol. II (London: Richard Bentley, 1845), p. 345.
196 R.A.H., Colección Narváez, Caja 9, 9/7817, I-D-d (29): 7 June 1844 letter to Narváez from Ayuntamiento de Barcelona detailing gifts and remarks from Madrid.

Chapter 4

1844–68: search for security

This chapter shows how the civil war legacy of eroded obedience to the state, combined with army officers' political pretensions, meant that Princess Isabella, declared of age as queen in 1844, faced an impossible reign. She was the first constitutional monarch in Spanish history and a woman in a context of prevailing gender attitudes and military strongmen. The cause of Isabella and her mother in the First Carlist War had opened a period of praetorianism in Spanish history that culminated in the civil war one hundred years later. Victory over Carlism in 1840 undermined civilian supremacy in the liberal state. Just like her father during the Peninsular War, Isabella could not live up her propaganda image forged during the Carlist War. The 'innocent' princess turned worldly soon after coming of age in 1843. Her crown was the lynch-pin of a dysfunctional party system which rendered both 'restrained' liberals (*moderados*) and, to an even greater extent, 'advanced' liberals (*progresistas*) beholden to military champions to get them into power. The veteran generals of the Carlist War dominated ministerial politics. 'Pronouncing' in favour of political change could yield promotions to officers and leave for men, if executed successfully. Failure did not have to mean the ultimate penalty. The army retained a 'gentlemanly' attitude towards its politics and the queen herself felt no particular duty to honour civil supremacy. Even though the civil war against the Carlists had been waged in the name of liberalism, the victors, beginning with the queen herself, retained remarkably illiberal political and social values. A British obituary of the queen, coming from the foreign country which had done the most to ensure her victory in the 1830s, captured this situation perfectly, as the leading generals of her day: 'whatever their mutual dissensions . . . were always interested in keeping her on the throne as an instrument of their own power'.[1]

Women had not been entirely excluded from the liberal public sphere before the young queen came to symbolise it. Women had participated in the Patriotic Societies of the Triennium (1820–23) and in a number of phil-anthropic initiatives during the Carlist War, while the defence of hearth and home inherent in the Patriot propaganda and (to some extent) the reality of the Peninsular War placed women at the centre of the war effort.[2] Unlike

Queen Victoria in Britain, Isabella failed to master the symbolic trappings pertaining to Spain's new constitutional monarchy and could not channel her barely concealed absolutist and religious instincts in strategic directions. The queen's discomfort symbolised a wider insecurity in the new liberal society. 'Respectable' politics remained the preserve of a small number of wealthy men and their patronage networks, wives and daughters remaining outside the political nation and within the realm of family, religion, and morality. The right-liberal *Moderado* party set the tone for this era, centralising politics and public order and staying in power except during the *progresista* 1854–56 Biennium and the 1858–63 centrist 'Liberal Union'. General Espartero's *progresistas* sought to expand the political nation, but their greater appeal to the lower-middle classes was also volatile due to the very mixed impact of the liberal economic reforms they promoted when in power.

The *moderados'* dominance between 1844 and 1854 has been called the 'Moderate Decade'. *Progresistas*, who, barring the 1854–56 period, were out of power, saw their political aims quashed. They could never establish a single parliamentary chamber, a decentralised state based on historic provinces with sovereignty vested in town councils guaranteed by locally controlled National Militia, and still less could they establish a decorative monarchy on the British model. Instead, between 1845 and 1868, Spain was ruled in the *moderado* image: a Cortes which shared sovereignty with the monarch, an appointed second chamber (Senate), a centralised state on the Bourbon model, larger provinces under appointed civil and military governors, cities and larger towns governed not by elected mayors but by appointed prefects (sub-governors), no National Militia but, instead, a Civil Guard (established in 1844), and a monarch vested with powers to veto legislation, dismiss governments and call elections. These ideals were enshrined in the constitution of 1845 which would remain in force until June 1869. The only successful (and fleeting) challenge to moderantismo came with the alliance of *progresistas* and army in 1854 which forced the Crown to accept a left-liberal administration. More radical challenges were frustrated by extremely limited representation, constraints on freedom of association and conscience, and the limitations of the subsequent culture of clandestinity and conspiracy.

The power of the town halls and *diputaciones* (county councils) was reduced, the freedom of the press suppressed, and suffrage was cut to a tiny percentage of major taxpayers. The town halls and councils were the main powerbase of the radicals. So important was it that Espartero, in 1840, exiled the regent rather than submit to *moderado* manoeuvres to have town halls appointed rather than elected. Local mayors were now to be appointed by the Crown's prefects in all settlements of more than two thousand inhabitants. Direct election in all but the smallest municipalities was abolished.[3] The strife-torn National Militia was replaced with the paramilitary, centrally controlled Civil Guard (Guardia Civil), whose effectives were expressly not hired from the communities to which they were posted. Parts of the political press such as the socialist *La Reforma Económica* and *El Eco de la Juventud* were now obliged to become clandestine. Voting now became the preserve of a tiny minority. Even these votes were diluted by the upper chamber which was appointed by the monarch and could counterbalance the elected lower house.

Thus, in 1845, there was a major leap towards French-style centralised nation building, and efforts were symbolically helped by the institution of the first-ever national flag for Spain in 1843.[4] As the economy recovered, wealth rather than wartime sacrifice now became the qualification for political representation. During the inaugural session of the Cortes in November 1844, the *moderado* deputy Calderón Collantes proclaimed that 'poverty, gentlemen, is a sign of stupidity'. Two years later a newspaper article decried the phenomenon of noisy stagecoaches running over the poor in Madrid.[5]

Contemporaries sensed that political and cultural change had been gathering speed since the liberal revolution opened by the Carlist War. The liberal poet and pessimist, Larra infamously took his young life in 1837, having been unable to withstand 'the pace of life'.[6] The same year as Larra's suicide, the young clerical intellectual Jaime Balmes decried the 'licence' of Sunday trading and moneylending, commenting that Spaniards would end up being 'as barbarous and slavish as the English'.[7] Balmes was aghast at the social cost exacted by the industrial growth of his native Catalonia. Amidst this sense of crisis, Isabelline high politics seemed remarkably predictable. It was an era dominated by the 'broadsword' politician (*espadón*), by generals who discarded their sashes and donned prime ministerial frock coats (and performed this transformation in reverse) in a symbol of a weak political society. 'It's a pity I'm not ruling the Swiss' was the complaint of the mastermind of the 1843–44 reaction, General Narváez, who found himself responsible for the riotous Spaniards instead.[8] Whereas Narváez, after 1844, ensured regular pay for officers and soldiers in an effort to remove the penury of the Carlist War, the structural problem of a politicised officer corps remained. In the early nineteenth century, there was one officer for every twenty soldiers; by 1868, this ratio had reached one for every five.[9] The top-heavy nature of the Spanish army was dictated by the political promotions system entrenched during the Carlist War. From 1845, it became clearer that the army was part of a triarchy of power including the Crown and dynastic political parties. Any two of those three elements in this triarchy were powerful enough to force the hand of the third, and this system remained intact until army and parties united against the crown in 1868.[10] Yet despite the counter-revolution of 1843–44, the *moderado* regime remained vulnerable to revolts by disaffected officers, Carlists, and leftists. Between 1844 and 1849 there was, on average, one attempt every sixteen days to overthrow the regime.[11]

But at least until 1847, the *moderados* could rely on the young queen to do their bidding. The Olózaga controversy also gave María Cristina, now assembling a court in exile in Paris, a motive to apply to return to Spain and reclaim the regency. She returned in March 1844 but was denied regency status to her royal daughter. This snub was cloaked by a sumptuous official welcome, while the enraged *progresista* leadership found itself too distracted by the simultaneous funeral of the author of the 1812 constitution and recent tutor to Isabella, Agustín de Argüelles.[12] The demise of the royal tutor represented another victory for María Cristina, who from exile had shown her displeasure at the political education of her daughter. The Romantic poet Manuel Quintana, now a senator and director of Spain's National Library, had wanted the 11-year-old Isabella to 'show gratitude to the Spanish people who have made so many sacrifices for her . . . and respect the political institutions the nation has created, when it shed rivers of blood in defence of her throne'.[13] Olózaga's sleight of hand with the 14-year-old Isabella merely widened the gulf between hectoring *progresista* statesmen and a teenage girl in her formative years. Spanish and European opinion was reminded of the vulnerability of a woman on the Spanish throne, the very *casus belli* of the recent civil war, and the courts of Europe matched the elites of Spain in fretting over the vexed question of Isabella's future marriage.

The electoral dominance of the *moderados* after 1845 allowed them to use the stick of economic penalty against the radicals. One of the most significant hindrances to diffusing opinion to a public radicalised by the Carlist War was the press laws. Initially, the radicalised politics between 1833 and 1843 had led to a reasonable degree of freedom of expression, involving laws which were liberalised from a harsh two-stage penalty of newspaper fines and third-stage suppression under the 1834–36 Estatuto Real, followed by a revival of the liberal regulations of the Triennium and a new law in March 1837 which guaranteed jury trials to judge press infractions. Yet despite such an ostensibly tolerant press environment, newspapers were often suppressed by governments just the same, as was the case when a government circular responded to republican gains in the municipal elections of 1841 by demanding the suppression of any publication advocating a different political system. Such arbitrariness was usually overturned by juries but not before financial damage had been done. It required either a brave or a very rich newspaper owner who would risk confiscation of the editorial deposit which ranged from 40,000 *reales* in Madrid to 10,000 in smaller cities. This forbidding press environment would, in any case, be made worse by the post-1844 Moderate amendments to the press laws which abolished jury trial, empowering instead the politicised office of the captain general to decree fines and suppression. Criminal proceedings against editors were sometimes quashed thanks to skilful defence by such radical lawyer-politicians as Nicolás Rivero, born an orphan in 1815 and later leader of the '*cimbrio*' wing of pro-monarchy Democrats. But the fining out of existence of many radical newspapers combined with a ruthless and often dictatorial political will to make diffusion of propaganda dangerous and costly.[14] The best aspiring politicians could aim for was, in the words of José Luis Comellas, 'to rise once from the ranks' (*subir una vez*). Men who 'made it' into elite ranks could then be assured of some protection against the authoritarian state and weigh contending offers for public office by the different liberal factions.[15]

Press controls and post-revolutionary fatigue meant that in 1848 Spain did not undergo significant revolutionary turmoil. Not only did the Year of Revolutions fail to make much of an impact south of the Pyrenees, but successive *progresista* attempts beforehand to break the post-1843 *moderado* grip on power (the Zurbano *pronunciamiento* of 1845, the Galician risings of 1846) all failed for lack of popular support, even though their programmes were modest by wartime standards (the failed Galician risings, for example, aimed to reinstate the 1837 constitution, not that of 1812).[16] The mutualist societies of Catalonia continued to flourish clandestinely, agrarian unrest continued to simmer, especially during the famine year of 1847, whilst a radical leadership had emerged which realised the need for a serious social agenda. In 1849 the Democrat Party would answer this call, motivated by the absence of revolution in 1848 and the failure of left-leaning *progresistas* to raise much support in the Galicia revolt of 1846. As the leader of the most reactionary wing of the *moderados*, the Marqués de Viluma, wrote, 'Spain in 1846 is very different from 1836. The country is tired of revolts, abhors revolutions, and has suffered harsh disappointments'.[17]

Monarchy and gender

Aristocratic women in the last third of Spain's eighteenth century had occupied the public sphere via the growth of ladies' salons and the *cortejo* tradition of married women being escorted by young bachelors. Yet in many ways, the political, property, and legal revolution ushered in by nineteenth-century liberalism confirmed in law what had already been reality in fact: that women were subordinate to men, and exceptions proved the rule. The Peninsular War (1808–14) offered examples of female agency. During the Peninsular War, the heroine of Zaragoza, Agustina de Aragón, became hallowed in Spain's collective memory as a woman who, during the brutal French siege of that city, stepped into the masculine domain for feminine reasons, namely to defend her hearth and home and, as the story was routinely extrapolated, her religion.[18] Even though Agustina survived and thrived to tell her tale, several other women died as martyrs, such as the 15-year-old heroine of the Madrid *Dos de Mayo*, Manuela Malasaña, or the volunteer at a skirmish in Valdepeñas, Juana Galán. In the Peninsular War, it was largely the conservative, 'Church and King', 'hearth-and-home' legend of women fighters that prevailed. The idea of the female soldier rather than the reality of her experiences that was held up as 'unnatural' exceptions that prove the rule of war being the masculine preserve.[19] Even though Spanish women offered some famous examples of military courage against Napoleon, thereafter they were airbrushed from nineteenth-century history. Unlike their Protestant sisters in northern Europe, Spanish women were considered traditional beings who minimised their engagement with the public sphere.[20] Even republican ideals gathering momentum in the 1840s considered 'the people' to consist of honest male heads of household.[21]

The subordination of women in liberal society faced an obvious paradox once Spain's first-ever properly constitutional sovereign happened to be a woman and a marriageable one at that. Spain in 1846, so tired of revolts, was the year of Queen Isabella's contested marriage, a matter which exposed the faultlines of domestic and European politics. Chancellor Metternich pressed the marriage of Don Carlos's son with Isabella as the best solution, General Narváez quickly vetoed it, even though, arguably, the victorious Liberals, in so doing, overestimated the dynastic threat to the victory of 1839.[22] Abroad, the problem was that Britain and France, Europe's Liberal superpowers, supported suitors who logically promised to do most for their respective national interests. Suitors proved to be too French, too Carlist, or too stupid. Therefore, in September at 1845 at Eu (France), the two Liberal powers agreed that neither of their preferred candidates should be proposed.[23] Thus, Britain voiced protest when in August 1846, in the wake of a failed (Anglophile) *progresista* rising in Galicia, it was announced that the (Francophile) *moderado* candidate, Francisco de Asís, Isabella's cousin, was put forward as the match.[24] On 10 October 1846, Isabella's sixteenth birthday, the young queen married her cousin, Francisco de Asís, thus heading off a potential disaster as the marriage obscured the fact that Asís had written to the new Pretender, Don Carlos's son, Conde de Montemolín, a grovelling letter, advising that he marry Isabella and promising to recognise his crown.[25] Montemolín's Carlist revolt in 1846 was, in large part, caused by the dynastic path to power being denied to the Carlists yet again. The fact that the *moderados* forced Isabella to marry Asís proved both the subordination of Spain to French foreign policy and, more important, the duplicitous relationship of the *moderados* with the monarchy. Far from restoring the monarchy to extensive constitutional prerogatives, the *moderado* faction relegated Isabella to a directly instrumental role, negating the notion that the monarchy should be erected as an institution with power of its own.[26] The neo-absolutist priest Jaime Balmes thought that an instrumentalised young queen made a mockery of monarchy: 'Spain needs a purely Spanish monarch who can reclaim truly sovereign powers'.[27] Balmes regretted that Isabella had not married the Carlist Pretender, Count Montemolín. He thought that there could be no question of Isabella marrying a prince consort as Queen Victoria would do, as this would be 'an aberration ill-fitting in a well-organised brain'.[28]

By all accounts, Isabella hated her husband Francisco, and the latter was the butt of popular ditties alluding to his impotence brought about by Bourbon inbreeding. The several children Isabella bore either tragically died in infancy or were tainted with rumours of their illegitimacy. It was not long before the queen took a lover, General Serrano. Serrano was connected to the *puritano* (left-leaning *moderado*) and *progresista* factions of liberalism.

When challenged by her *moderado* cabinet to give up her general, Isabella responded by using her first exercise of regal prerogative under the authoritarian Constitution of 1845, namely forcing the cabinet to resign and calling on the *puritano* administration of Pacheco instead. Pacheco did the queen's bidding, restoring Serrano to favour, and Pacheco offered rewards and royal patronage to his financier friend, José de Salamanca, the property speculator after whom an entire nineteenth-century district of Madrid was soon named. Isabella's 27 March 1847 coup de main appeared to open possibilities for *progresismo* which had been brutally absent since 1843. Espartero was pardoned and returned from exile to sit in the Senate, whilst Olózaga was also recalled in a symbolic recognition of his innocence concerning the infamous 'sleight of hand' incident of 1843. Ironically, it was the *progresistas* who would have been the real friends of the monarchy, as they would have been content to leave the private sphere to the queen and dominate the public sphere in such a way as would have diffused scandal. Thus, as Isabel Burdiel has argued, the commonly held belief that Isabella was a '*moderado* monarch' is ironic.[29]

Contemporaries and most historians saw nothing ironic in Isabella's predicament. Her name initially gave contemporaries hope. The American Hispanist William Prescott, in 1837, hoped that the child-heroine might live up to her famous medieval namesake:

> Clouds and darkness around the throne of the youthful Isabella are no deeper darkness than that which covered the land in the first years of her illustrious namesake. We may humbly trust, that the same Providence, which guided her reign to so prosperous a termination, may carry the nation safely through its present perils, and secure to it the greatest of earthly blessings. . .[30]

The writer José Güell y Renté had secretly married Isabella's cousin in 1848 and tried his best to flatter his in-laws by comparing the queen to Isabel I of Castile. Thus, both queens had undergone tumultuous childhoods, and both were great in uniting their realms, Isabel I in terms of marriage and Isabella II in terms of progress, uniting a country 'separated by customs and immense distance' through political and cultural initiatives.[31] Güell was wise to leave out marriage. Her frequent affairs cuckolded the morganatic king, turning the child-heroine of Isabella the Innocent into what one French liberal called the 'devil made into flesh'.[32] Behaviour which would have gone unremarked in a man was an affront in a woman, Spain being governed by laws which criminalised adultery outright for wives but only in cases of 'public scandal' for husbands. Despite the efforts of hagiographers like Güell y Renté, the prevailing image of the queen was very much in the sexist vein familiar to the writings of the contemporary French historian Jules Michelet. One British biographer blamed Isabella's mother, attributing Isabella's 'nymphomania' to her lack of moral upbringing, which meant that 'she did not invent it for herself as an adult'.[33] The twentieth-century dictator Francisco Franco used Isabella's example to fend off calls to restore the exiled Bourbons: 'the last man to sleep with Doña Isabel cannot be the father of the King and what comes out of the belly of the Queen must be examined to see if it is suitable'.[34]

Isabella's reign witnessed a veritable avalanche of books, essays, and pamphlets debating the proper role of woman in liberal society, given the contemporary assumptions that the private sphere of womanhood could not be reconciled with the masculine public sphere of politics. The vast majority of works on the woman question perhaps predictably revered the default feminine values of tradition, religion, morality, self-abnegation, and self-control, only the first two of which were evident in the queen's conduct.[35] Isabella's reign witnessed concerns not just about women but also about gender more broadly. Liberal politics were masculine, even excepting extraordinary cases, usually in wartime, like 18-year-old Luisa Casiñol (called 'Luis' by her comrades), who, in 1837, distinguished herself fighting in the 'Riumbau' battalion of the Army of the Centre.[36] The political upheaval of the nineteenth century created anxieties about what constituted 'correct' masculinity. Military veterans, strongmen like Narváez with access to the Crown, could perform their own rites of masculinity on Carlist or imperial battlefields or in the queen's bedchamber. Officers from the rank of captain upwards who were killed in action died knowing that their female next of kin would gain a pension from the military 'Monte Pío' funded out of officers' salaries since the 1760s. Repeated wars and state penury since 1808 had curtailed regular payments and eligibility. But few officers would have quibbled with the paternalistic ordinance of 1829 which stopped the payment of military pensions to male orphans once they reached the age of 18 (and therefore became men in their own right) but which guaranteed lifelong payments to officers' widows and their female orphans unless they (re)married or became nuns (and therefore became wards of man or Christ).[37]

But for civilians, correct 'masculinity' was more elusive. Newspaper evidence suggests that male suicide became more common during the accelerated pace of life in the 1840s and 1850s, perhaps inspired by Mariano de Larra's Romantic example in 1837.[38] Whereas working-class uncouthness (demonstrated in bullfighting) was considered too violent, the effeteness of the refined classes – the cultural afrancesados who were the butt of jokes before 1808 – was considered foppish and unmanly. Thus, it is unsurprising that cultural works tried to produce a 'middle ground' of middle-class masculinity for the liberal age, of fondness for beards, and of the sort of civilised violence offered by fencing in an age when duelling was fast disappearing. A foreign visitor quipped how republicans were a class of men distinguished by their 'intensity of political feeling and great length of beard'.[39] Above all, liberal masculinity exaggerated care for appearances which was strangely fitting in an era when so many political changes remained superficial.[40]

Middle-class masculinity marginalised or objectified whatever did not conform to the liberal ideal. Homosexuality had always been a 'problem', if the early nineteenth-century 'moral degradation' facing teenage sailors which Alcalá Galiano commented on in passing can be taken as an example, or the complaints about 'the corruption of conscripts of a youthful or gentle disposition' during the First Carlist War.[41] But it was considered an unwelcome side effect of military life, often buried in innuendo such as in the case of the homosexual General José de Canterac (1786–1835), who signed the surrender of Ayacucho (1824) and was killed in a Carlist War mutiny in Madrid in 1835.[42] But from the mid-nineteenth century, homosexuality was seen as an endemic problem to be 'solved' by the growing forces of state and medicine.[43] While liberal society marginalised homosexuals, it also objectified women. Women who refused to remain corseted in the private sphere were objectified in salacious ways. Prosper Mérimée's 1845 novella *Carmen* was allegedly based on the real life of a gypsy woman and tobacco-factory worker in Seville. The racy heroine seduces a young Navarrese army officer, driving him into a sex-crazed frenzy in which he obeys Carmen's every demand, even murdering her bandit husband until madness and revenge lead him to murder Carmen. The Romantic fascination with *Carmen* grew over the century. Foreigners indulged their fantasies of Romantic Spain and lawless Andalucía, Spaniards objectified the gypsies as 'outs' beyond polite society in ways which would even influence scientific racism later in the century and its hostility to 'miscegenation', and readers everywhere relished their sexist notions of the *femme fatale*.[44]

Prominent women active in the liberal public sphere usually ended up merely extending rather than subverting the masculine order. Countess Espoz y Mina, widow of the famous guerrilla captain of the Peninsular War, from the early 1840s, edited the bulletin of the *esparterista* 'Instituto Español'. Widowhood both tied womanhood to patriarchy and allowed unprecedented agency at the same time. Later, the free-thinking pioneer of Spanish feminism Concepción Arenal (1820–93) rose to prominence as an abolitionist who also dressed as a man in order to be able to attend law school (women being barred from higher education until the 1880s). Arenal was easily Spain's most prominent female intellectual in the nineteenth century. Her ideas shared common ground with Jaime Balmes, whom she greatly admired. Arenal understood humans as fundamentally social beings preoccupied with morality and that 'thinking the Spanish nation' was an essentially Catholic exercise. Arenal had even supported the idea of Queen Isabella marrying her uncle and nemesis in order to conciliate the Carlists.[45]

Hungry Forties

Spain along with Britain and Russia experienced no revolution in 1848, despite its shaky international position. Isabella's throne was still not recognised by the three great absolutist powers in Europe, nor by the Holy See. But over the course of 1848–1849, General Narváez would pursue a policy of rapprochement, sending an expedition to protect Rome from revolutionaries and overseeing the reconciliation amongst Spain, Holy See, and the pope.[46] The strongman of Spain's Moderate Party, General Narváez, became the toast of reactionary Europe. Whereas revolutionary upheaval in Paris and Vienna led Louis Philippe to abdicate and Metternich to resign, Prime Minister Narváez famously appeared in the Spanish Cortes on the 28 February 1848 in full-dress uniform demanding dictatorial powers, the suspension of constitutional guarantees, the authority to raise both a forced loan of some 2 million pounds, and a *quinta*, or levy, of twenty-five thousand men into the army. Such bold moved suggested that Narváez was confident that revolution could be constrained. This demand rode roughshod over a divided *progresista* opposition, and as of 22 March, Spain became a virtual dictatorship for the next nine months.[47] Narváez, now known as the 'the broadsword of Loja', deployed the same terror as he had during his 1836 counter-insurgency campaign in New Castile: mass arrests, summary executions, and mass deportations to overseas presidios, but this time in respect of bread rioters in Castile in 1847 and radical movements in Madrid and the provinces in 1848, in addition to the shaky Carlist revolt in the east.

Indeed, on the surface the Spanish state seemed to emerge stronger from its experience. Relations with the Vatican were resumed, opening the way for a Concordat in 1851, whilst the reactionary powers of Prussia, Piedmont, Tuscany, and Austria recognised the legitimate throne of Isabel II and reopened diplomatic relations with Liberal Spain. Moreover, whilst elsewhere in Europe learned men looked to such radicals as Mazzini, Kossuth, or Garibaldi, the Spaniard who dominated Spain's intellectual 1848 was the 'neo-Catholic' social conservative Donoso Cortés. Cortes was to the 1848 Revolution what Joseph de Maistre had been to the French Revolution of 1789.[48] The February revolution in Paris convinced Donoso of the perils of socialism, materialism, and nationalism. Donoso mobilised his formidable oratorical power to declare that 'liberty was dead' and that a demagogic and socialist world state must be warded off, starting in Spain via an alliance between Church and State. Donoso judged Narváez's dictatorship a necessary evil, and his oratory and writings, especially his 1850 'Speech on Europe', won him the respect of aged ex-chancellor Metternich and the future emperor Napoleon III. Madrid even made him ambassador to the prestigious Paris embassy. Alas, congenital syphilis killed Donoso in 1853, depriving the neo-absolutist right of another great thinker (Balmes had died even earlier in 1848).

Whilst it is the reactionary side to Spain's 1848 which is perhaps most remembered by Europeans (personified on the one hand by a ruthless man of action and on the other a formidable man of thought), the revolutionary side has been shown to be weak, divided, cut off from revolutionary France, and insignificant in the context of a wider Spanish century dominated by civil war, military risings, revolutions, and upheaval. Benito Pérez Galdós's historical novel of 1848 (*Las Tormentas del 48*) emphasised the childish and unsophisticated behaviour of the street radicals, who decorated their barricades with images of the radical demagogue, General Espartero, and religious iconography.[49] The actual revolutionary risings in Spain during 1848 can be counted on one hand, and only one of them, the 26 March rising in Madrid, involved a civilian strength of more than a thousand. On this occasion the Marquess Albaida, José María Orense, who was called 'mad' because he was both a peer and a Democrat, planned the rising with a Lieutenant Colonel Joaquín de la Gándara. Gándara had enlisted the support of some six hundred discharged officers suffering pay arrears, as well as some members of revolutionary secret societies, former officers of the disbanded National Militia, and a youthful following of some thousand civilians from the poorer quarters of Madrid. Although a wide-ranging social base, they were few in number and were easily crushed by the next day by troops who had stayed loyal to the government.[50] Later purely military risings at Madrid and Seville were repressed harshly. Barcelona, Spain's industrial capital and hotbed of the popular radical revolution in 1842–1843, is assumed to have stayed generally quiet thanks to an effective expulsion of unemployed migrants and troublemakers as well as a proactive programme of public works which helped to mitigate the effects of the economic downturn.

Yet Narváez's regime was not complacent about the prospect of revolution in Spain. The Ministry of War was so horrified by Narváez's cavalier bravado on the 26 March 1848 that it placed constant armed protection around his residence in the Calle de María Cristina.[51] Foreign observers were terrified of the power of the Madrid mob, and Spanish elites were wary of the progressive power of 'youth' in its Romantic form. Former radicals like Alcalá Galiano baulked at the radicalism displayed by youngsters during 1848.[52] Popular plays such as *William Tell* were censored or banned and reading clubs placed under vigilance. In 1845 a centralised university system on the French model had been introduced, turning rectors into civil servants required to craft their teaching in the government image.[53] Student awareness of events in France combined with the introduction of a reactionary university curriculum provoked a wave of disturbances. Students in Barcelona on the 28 March 1848 mounted a lock-in, and the authorities cordoned off land routes to the city and unleashed the Civil Guard. Two students were shot and killed, whilst the guardsmen killed a greengrocer, allegedly for shouting, 'Long Live the Republic!'[54] The students had protested in solidarity with a student who had been expelled for resisting the new curriculum, and the political dimension grew as other protestors joined the disturbances.[55] Similar disturbances at Madrid, Seville, and Granada led to arrests and the closure of educational establishments. Government anxiety also spread to the newspaper clubs which has spread across Spain during the 1840s. On 10 March, four young men were arrested outside the Seville Newspaper Society (Sociedad de lectura periodística) for singing the 'Marseillaise' and offering 'vivas' to the republic.[56] This club, along with others across Spain, was closed down days afterwards.

Although these disturbances were insignificant compared to what was happening in Paris, Vienna, and Berlin, the hospital records of the wounded and the dead from the March disturbances in Madrid reveal a popular radicalism whose social base was proletarian and artisan rather than bourgeois. Of the thirteen patients being treated for sabre and bullet wounds, all bar one came from working and artisanal backgrounds. Fifteen unharmed protestors now in prison were of similar walks of life, as were the seven confirmed killed, and there is no reason to assume that the uncounted other wounded who were now being treated with new-fangled chloroform in taverns and houses were any different. The instigator of the civilian part of the March uprising in Madrid, one Francisco García, who was later arrested by the Civil Guard in Ciudad Real,[57] was probably of a similar occupational background. What was peculiar to Spain was a surfeit of veterans, especially of the disbanded and politically conscious National Militia, whose cultural claims to leadership (as witnessed in Barcelona 1842–43) now fostered a subculture given to agitating economic discontent. Newspapers during the economic crisis years of 1846–1848 reported on the unhappy lots of disbanded militia veterans who in demands for work and respect tragically invoked their sacrifices to no avail. In July 1848, dictator Narváez accepted an invitation from Madrid's Philanthropic Society of National Militia Veterans to attend a July 1822 anniversary event raising money for militia veterans and their orphans and widows.[58] But societal charity in the capital could not obscure the sufferings of the countryside as the subsistence crisis affected veterans and civilians alike.

The severity of the economic and subsistence crisis raging in Spain since early 1847 was the Iberian version of Europe's 'Hungry Forties'. The government banned the export of grain yet retained high tariffs on grain imports, compounding a crisis which sent the Madrid stock exchange plummeting during April.[59] The poor grain harvest resulted in price increases which were exacerbated still further by the iniquitous taxation of foodstuffs which penalised the poor, a tax which led to widespread starvation in Andalusia during the spring. On the 28 April 1847, angry villagers seized control of Ubeda (Andalucía), blocking the movement of grain, and demanding the banishment of 'outsiders' who were considered hoarders and speculators. When authorities dared arrest a ringleader, the villagers liberated him all the same and forced the local mayor to champion their cause.[60] A week later, vigilantes looted a granary in Granada which they believed hoarded twenty thousand bushels in speculation for higher prices. This time the Civil Guard acted ruthlessly, opening fire and killing women and children. The events gripped the national press when the mentally ill son of the master-hatter Pedro Ponce was included in the list of fatalities. Ponce reacted to the commotion in the streets by setting fire to his father's workshop and climbing onto the roof in a bid to attract attention, only to be shot down by a group of soldiers and guardsmen.[61] Others tried radical ways out from hunger. 'Icarian' communism, influenced by the philosophy of Étienne Cabet, had taken hold of part of Catalonia's clandestine workers' associations, and during 1846–1847, it sponsored emigration for 'communists' to the United States.[62]

Opposition from the right

In addition to such raw protest at the lack of items of basic necessity, the subsistence crisis also helps us to explain why government troops took so much time bringing to an end the guerrilla war known in Catalan as the 'Guerra dels Matiners', or in English as the 'War of the Early Risers', which ranged from 1846 to 1848. This renewed Carlist revolt, sometimes called a Second Carlist War, was triggered by the refusal in 1846 of Isabella's government to let the young queen marry the Carlist Pretender Carlos Luis de Borbón, Count of Montemolín.[63] Montemolín enjoyed a steady stream of recruits to his bands in Catalonia thanks to his proximity to thousands of hungry and laid-off industrial workers who in any case were often seasonal labourers from a countryside with an active tradition of banditry and revolt. The Early Risers were so named because so many of them were farmhands who rose early in order to tend to farmwork and animal husbandry.

One of the strangest features of the 1846 rising in Catalonia were its allies. Exiled *progresistas* and Democrats entered into an alliance with the clerical rebels against the common *moderado* enemy, with Montemolín, and even Cabrera, sent to lead the insurgency, recognising in their proclamations the justice of liberals' grievances alongside their own Carlist programme.[64] The Carlist rising, often referred to as a Second Carlist War in its own right, centred on rural Catalonia which contained some of the most defiant clerics who were unbowed by the defeat of 1840 and by subsequent government attempts to cut clerical funding and enforce clerical recognition of the victorious constitutional system.[65] The revolt also spread outside their Catalan heartland, attracting irregulars in the bandit country Serranía de Ronda, The misery provoked by a price rise in Málaga in March 1847, for example, persuaded the Pretender to establish outside this city a permanent junta tasked with offering incentives to young men to join his offensive in the Serranía de Ronda.[66] But the Carlist message to the poor was more than just bread and regular pay; it was also a message of planting a neo-feudal social order on the ruins of liberal land reform. Carlist guerrillas who occupied fresh towns made a point of burning land-sale registers and often treated the population with respect. Moreover, although Carlist propaganda centred on 'throne and altar' absolutism as during the civil war of the 1830s, it also encroached on the patriotic ground which liberal governments had, in part, conceded due to their free-trade deals and unpatriotic dealings with competing French and British agents. The overbearing behaviour of the British ambassador, Bulwer, confirmed popular perceptions of Perfidious Albion which had been in revival since Espartero's discussion on a free-trade deal with Britain in 1842.[67]

But the Montemolinista revolt failed to gain significant support in the Basque country, cradle of 1830s' Carlism. Cabrera's opportunistic alliances with Republicans were decried in more purist quarters of Carlism, and the ebbing of support more generally obliged Cabrera towards the end of the war to resort to his familiar tactics of terror. The Spanish government, which at first had been distracted by its Quadruple Alliance intervention in Portugal in 1847 protecting María de la Gloria from an absolutist rising, managed to suppress the Carlists by 1849.[68] Thus, the Narváez regime in 1849 had seen off both extremist challenges, and even though Jaime Balmes's last prophecy was that 'Spain contained more socialists than Paris',[69] the regime seemed secure. Matters were helped by the ending of the food crisis, as the price of grain fell by almost a third between May 1847 and April 1848.[70]

Opposition from the left

Meanwhile, the dynastic liberal parties faced the defiance of populist forces outside the mainstream political spectrum. To the right was the weakened but unbowed Carlist movement with its strong regional appeal, along with, from the 1850s, more modern and patrician forces of traditionalism. To the left, the Spanish Democrat Party, formed in Madrid in April 1849 in the wake of failed attempts at revolution in 1846–1848, offered a hybrid legal and insurrectionary challenge to the constitutional order. In many ways, this new party was a child of 1812: it upheld the principles of the rights of man, a single parliamentary chamber, universal suffrage, elected *ayuntamientos*, and mass education. But the Democract Party, responding to the pressures brought about by the expansion of capitalism and the coercive power of the state, also had an advanced social programme concerning property and conscription. While Democrats were divided on the issue of capitalism, the cash exemptions codified in Spanish conscription law between 1837 and 1912 were an obvious source of grievance for poor and middling families who could not afford to pay the 'blood tax'.[71]

The centre of gravity in its seventeen-point programme was political democracy and individual political rights. Its social agenda of land redistribution (*reparto*), freedom from conscription, and lower taxes all certainly advanced beyond the expansion of representation for the propertied classes advocated by the *progresistas*. But the new party was always a mix of former *progresistas*, republicans, and 'utopian' socialists. Thus, the most radical ideas were sidelined by the phenomenon of moderate Democrats participating in the Isabelline political spoils system which turned its party leader, Nicolás Rivero, into a 'monarchical' Democrat and governor of Seville.[72] The bulk of the party would be effectively barred from participating in 'respectable' politics owing to restrictions on association, the high property qualification for the vote and tight policing. Thus, the party faced two options. It could either force a revolution through the 'spontaneous revolution' model of Giuseppe Mazzini, or it could forge alliances with the *progresistas*. The former option always ended in failure, yet the latter required Democrats to water down their programme to universal suffrage and to the popular, but not socialist, abolition of conscription and of consumption taxes. Even this minimalist programme would be a hostage to events whenever Democrats influenced such revolutions as 1854 and, especially, 1868. *Progresista* leaders just like *moderados* were military men, more concerned with discipline than popular representation. Thus, much of the impact of democracy throughout the 1850s and 1860s was felt in terms of local mobilisation, education, and patronage. The emphasis on popular education through establishing night schools and reading rooms, the distribution of democratic newspapers, and the adoption of the Italian Carbonari model of conspiracy, combined to extend the Democrats' organisation beyond provincial capitals to smaller towns and rural settlements. The response of the historic liberal parties to this new actor on the political stage was at first to ignore it, certain that restricted suffrage would continue for the foreseeable future to keep Democrats on the fringe of parliamentary representation.[73]

The rise of the Democrats influenced the revolutionary momentum originating in Spain's Hungry Forties and culminating in Spain's own '1848', the revolution of July 1854. Centralising administrative reforms angered municipalities, as did the state's détente with the church and the promotion of labour-saving devices in industry. The Concordat agreed in 1851 between Spain and the Holy See gave the church an important stake in education, banishing theology from the state-controlled universities and restoring it to the seminaries and merging the liberal Ministry of Public Instruction into the conservative Ministry of Grace and Justice.[74] The Concordat dismayed *progresistas* who were already recoiling at the clerical influence in the queen's inner circle, and Democrats who were seeking a laic state. Labour-saving devices in manufacturing in Catalonia produced a more organised and assertive working class and increased popular scorn for well-connected capitalists (called '*polacos*') enriching themselves in the early railway mania. In turn, the construction of the national railway network (the first line was completed in 1849 linking Barcelona with nearby Mataró) concentrated organised labour and thus increased labour mobility and militancy.

From 1851 to 1854, María Cristina's favourites governed Spain, from the technocratic Juan Bravo Murillo to Luis José Sartorius. Bravo Murillo, the most right-wing of the *moderados*, had been inspired by Louis-Napoleon in governing with a firm counter-revolutionary grip from 1850.[75] But unlike Louis-Napoleon Murillo showed no interest in educating the masses. In language revealing *moderado* agrarianism, Murillo rejected a proposal in 1850 to introduce universal primary education: 'What use are schools? What we need are oxen for ploughing'.[76] Murillo had alienated both *progresistas* and most *moderados* in his own party by launching a plan to strengthen the powers of the monarchy. Bravo Murillo was a slow talker, which annoyed his sonorous colleagues from Andalucía; he was also a civilian, which annoyed army

officers who referred to him using Narváez's favoured term of abuse for med-
dling civilians: '*el abogado*' (the lawyer).[77] The generals disliked Bravo Murillo's civilian attempts to curtail a constitutional system that allowed officers
to make and break regimes. Both dynastic parties recoiled at his attempts
to professionalise the civil service which would have removed the bureau-
cratic reserve army of '*cesantes*' (redundant or half-pay public officials seeking
patronage). His adversaries in December 1852 managed to oust him in Spain's
first-ever personal 'veto' by implicating him in a court corruption scandal.[78]
Bravo Murrillo prorogued the Cortes but was replaced by Luis José Sartorius,
a flamboyant journalist ennobled as Count of San Luis, whose network of
nouveaux riches political friends (*polacos*) personified the crony capitalism of
the *moderado* era. Trigger-happy forces of order treated the poor with contempt. In August 1852, troops opened fire on farm labourers working on
a Catalan estate, mistaking them for thieves. When the local Civil Guard
commander sought to calm tensions by denouncing the army's actions in the
press, the captain general reacted furiously that the upstart Civil Guard had
no business denigrating the name of the army.[79] The following year legislation
was passed banning '*derrotas*', the age-old custom of poor cattle owners graz-
ing their animals on the useless stubble on the fallow lands of large estates.[80]

Amidst episodes like these Sartorius reopened the Cortes and offered to
drop Bravo Murillo's authoritarian plan of 1852 in return for parliamentary
ratification of shady railway concessions for his cronies. But Sartorius was
outvoted, the Cortes prorogued again, and the course set for a revolutionary
solution for Spain's impasse.[81] More than fifty journalists from across the political spectrum petitioned against the regime's violation of already-draconian
press laws, and a Democrat carpenter from Málaga became a celebrity when
he slapped Sartorius in public.[82] The political implosion of Sartorius's regime
did for the *moderados* what 1843 had done for the *progresistas*.[83]

1854 revolution

In July 1854, an army revolt accompanied by a popular insurrection in
Madrid, led by advanced *Progresistas* and Democrats, toppled the government
of Sartorius and heralded the return of the Progresistas to power after ten
years in the political cold. The 1854 revolution peaked at the end of June with
the famous revolutionary victory at a skirmish at Vicálvaro outside Madrid
(known as the *Vicalvarada*). This was the culmination of several months of
unrest unleashed by Sartorius's dissolution of the Cortes and a police actions
against the opposition. After Leopoldo O'Donnell narrowly escaped arrest in
February, he spent months in hiding in the capital, bribing and evading the
police, before finally slipping out of the city in June in order to take command of rebellious troops.[84] Revolutionary soldiers who had triumphed at
Vicálvaro outside Madrid were rewarded with reduced terms of service, and
their sergeants were promoted to lieutenant. Their gruelling terms of service

certainly gave soldiers more reasons to revolt than their officers, but equally rebellious officers promising parole or promotion often succeeded in commanding a 'loyal' insurrection from their men.[85]

Over several confused days in July, juntas sprang up throughout Spain, including ones with distinctly working-class aspects, like those of Barcelona, Málaga, Valencia, and Madrid's Junta del Sur. The urban geography of Madrid dictated the radicalism of the July revolution just as had been the case in Paris in 1848. Central Madrid was vertically segregated. Wealthy inhabitants lived in larger ground-floor accommodation whereas poorer dwellers lived on the floors above, the poorest usually occupying the smallest rooms at the top. Thus, wealthy patrons tended to exert moral pressure upstairs, turning a building *progresista, moderado*, or 'apolitical', with the odd eccentrics (Carlists and Republicans) as well. Thus, intimate networks of coercion tended to moderate the political climate of the central Madrid, as recalcitrance upstairs could lead to such reprisals from downstairs as sackings and evictions. By contrast, the popular neighbourhoods to the south of the city centre tended to be horizontally integrated, with fewer wealthy patrons and more generalised poverty on all levels, especially in the notorious slums (*'infraviviendas'*).[86] The south thus developed a spatial working-class consciousness, leading to the erection of barricades in the already–poorly accessible streets. The symbol of the Sur was the flamboyant bullfighter ('Pucheta'), a *costumbrista* symbol of Madrid's popular classes and leader of the three-thousand-strong vigilantes in southern Madrid.[87] The mainstream revolutionary leadership of Leopoldo O'Donnell clashed with the obvious radicalism of the barricades which was leading to restrained but targeted violence (such as the lynching of Madrid's hated chief of police and attacks on the house of the unpopular financier José de Salamanca).

In the end, once Sartorius's resignation and flight on 17 July forced her hand, the queen sent for Baldomero Espartero, who was now 62 years old and semi-retired as a gentleman-farmer in Logroño. Unlike O'Donnell, Espartero was a man of order who could also appeal to the barricades. Even though a crestfallen O'Donnell toyed with the idea of a coup, and even though Isabella had had to allow a former regent to overawe her own discredited position, Espartero became prime minister and O'Donnell minister of war. Isabella was at the mercy of the revolution once more, now as a 23-year-old woman instead of the 5-year-old held hostage by the sergeants of 1836 or the 11-year-old being lectured by Espartero's palace *progresistas*. In the end, Isabella weathered the storm, making a public appearance at an opera after a discreet few weeks of self-imposed house arrest at the palace. Her mother, by contrast, was not as fortunate. María Cristina's immense wealth, her corrupt *camarilla*, and rumours of her slush fund (*bolsillo secreto*) had made her a hate figure. Prime Minister Fernando Fernández de Córdova survived in his post as Sartorious's replacement for two days after his 'grapeshot ministry' had gunned down a crowd that was looting María Cristina's residence in the Calle Mayor.[88] When the new Cortes eventually decided to expel her from Spain and confiscate all her property, Madrid Democrats on 28 August 1854 rioted, demanding that the former regent at least be put on trial.[89]

The revolution was marked by an urban and revolutionary character that justly gave it its reputation as 'Spain's 1848'. Benito Pérez Galdós reproduced this atmosphere in the half-starved artisan Gamoneda, who was central to his novel *La revolución de julio*. In some ways the pattern was decidedly Spanish, a revolution, as one historian remarked, of *cesantes*, or 'half-pay civil servants wanting to be back on full pay'.[90] The revolutionaries accordingly reinstated the councillors and National Militia deposed in 1843 and kept the barricades at arm's length. But Democrat Party gains in the Cortes elections of November 1854 laid bare the divide between patrician *progresistas* in power and the 'Circle of Union' society of Democrats forged out of the barricades of July. Most of the political divide was evident in the Democrat newspapers launched by Fernando Garrido and the utopian socialist Sixto Cámara. The Catalan journalist and radical Francisco Pi y Margall (1824–1901) promoted Cuban autonomy, the abolition of slavery, and his as-yet-little-noticed plans for a federal Spanish republic.[91] His 1854 *La reacción y la revolución* treatise criticised his fellow Democrats for their failure to impose their programme.[92]

Much of the popular radicalism was at odds with the capitalism of the *Bienio* policymakers, who were mostly *progresista* but also included some Democrats. They legislated furiously to modernise infrastructure, investments, and property rights. They either left social justice as an afterthought or believed like the 'mad' Democrat José María Orense, Count Albaida, that small government and big capitalism in themselves promoted individual rights and therefore democracy. The *progresistas* also showed political restraint. Although they revived electoral legislation from 1837 giving the vote to 5 per cent of men (as opposed to a mere 1 per cent of the 1845 constitution), they refused to introduce the universal suffrage demanded by the Democrats.[93] Such 'progress' gave no representation to the workers militating in Barcelona and elsewhere against poor conditions and the high price of bread in 1855. The classical liberal *progresistas*, in bed with landowners, refused to ban grain exports, despite the wheat shortages caused by the Crimean War.[94] British consul Brackenbury said that the Castilian landowners wanted 'water and sun, and war in Sebastopol'.[95] Cholera and floods exacerbated the misery of hunger. Amongst the most important reforms of the Biennium was the 1855 disentailment law which placed an unprecedented amount of corporate lands – that of the secular clergy and village commons – up for public auction. Virtually all lands except those physical buildings and gardens occupied by clerics were subjected to auction. Prime Minster Espartero dealt with clerical opposition to this reform in ways reminiscent of his regency years. His government expelled the bishops of Barcelona and Osma, removed suspect parish priests, and his justice minister defiantly restored a faculty of theology to Madrid University in June 1855. Relations between Spain and the Holy See cooled to a degree not witnessed since 1841.[96]

The spring of 1855 witnessed reports of religious apparitions, a sure sign of a revolt. Fernando Garrido was rattled by the opening in Barcelona of 'school of virtue' for workers, which he thought was a Jesuit plot.[97] Cabrera met with fellow Carlist exiles in Paris, fuelled by the enormous wealth of his English wife, and in the summer of 1855, an insurrection began. Yet the revolt was confined almost entirely to the former conflict zone of Aragón, where the rebels managed to turn a few Cristino soldiers and bring some guerrilla veterans out of their slumber. Even here the civilian population showed little enthusiasm to repeat the horrors of civil war, not least because agricultural prices had been rising since 1845, removing one of the major grievances that had caused Carlism to grow in the 1820s. The bishop of Zaragoza's condemnation of the rising, repeated in altars across the countryside, sealed the matter. Even though the nineteen-day rising in Aragón was accompanied by sporadic Carlist risings also in Catalonia and northern Spain, the government turned its army and National Militia against the Carlists with ease.[98] Carlist diplomatic back-channels about marrying the unhappy queen into Carlism got nowhere. In many ways, the Madrid government had deliberately exaggerated the scale of the threat. Armed Carlism was used as a pretext to impose a politically useful suspension of constitutional guarantees.[99] The ensuing martial law targeted both rural Carlists and urban radicals.

Even though radicalism flourished to the left of the ministerial *progresistas*, the radicals, just like during the European revolutions six years earlier, failed to achieve any constitutional breakthrough. Cortes debates on a new constitution more in accord with the principles of 1812 were indefinitely postponed, leaving the *moderado* Constitution of 1845 in force, pending the approval of a new charter which never left the drawing board. Democrats, who expected some reward for their contribution at the barricades in July 1854, were sidelined and their supporters excluded from the National Militia. Barcelona's 1855 working-class revolt, a strike by fifty thousand textile workers whom authorities believed must have been agents either of foreign revolutionaries or Carlists, was answered in the same way as in 1843.[100] Protests demanding the socialist aspects of the Democrat Party programme also gripped Zaragoza, Valencia, and even normally conservative provincial capitals in Old Castile. Democrat attempts in parliament to censure *ayacucho* General Zavala's repression of these protests got nowhere, as did their attempts to replace O'Donnell as war minister.[101] The government kept the state of siege in place, citing the ongoing threat of Carlism. Captain General Juan Zapatero bombarded the city like Espartero before him, refusing to entertain Barcelona workers' demands for the right to collective bargaining any more than a *moderado* captain general would have done. Zapatero was dubbed 'General Four Shots', on account of his preference for using four-man firing squads against strikers.[102] No relief came from the bishop of Barcelona, who sided with 'law and order' (the employers) in short order.[103] The execution of Barcelona strikers, summarily sentenced in a Castillian language many of the condemned Catalans could not even understand, widened the gulf between patrician politics and popular radicalism, and pushed Catalanism from a cultural phenomenon towards a political direction.

One of the biggest causes of popular disaffection was conscription. Despite Democrat agitation, War Minister O'Donnell jealously kept conscription in place along with the 'blood tax' for exemption which remained beyond the reach of the popular classes. In the autumn of 1855, O'Donnell used the pretext of Carlism to increase the standing army from sixty thousand to ninety thousand, stripping National Militia units of weapons, so the radical press charged. During an unpopular drawing of lots for conscription being held in Valencia in April 1856, local militia units exchanged fire with the army, reopening the inter-rivalry wounds of the Carlist War.[104] In Zaragoza, National Militia which been ordered to protect grain shipments ended up going over to the side of the angry crowd. [105] As food riots spread that summer even into normally prosperous Old Castile, pressure mounted on Espartero's regime. Finally, on 14 July 1856, Espartero resigned the premiership in the hope of safeguarding whatever progressive fame remained attached to his name. His departure meant that a thirty-three-thousand-signature petition from workers (mostly in Catalonia) in favour of collective bargaining could not be motioned by the Cortes.[106]

Espartero was replaced by O'Donnell who marched into Madrid ahead of an army ordered to suppress the barricades of the infamous Sur. After engaging with esparterista militiamen in skirmishes claiming some thirty-eight killed, including the bullfighter Pucheta, O'Donnell managed to pacify the capital while Espartero slipped away to the coast and into exile, just like in 1843, on a British ship. Radical juntas elsewhere were suppressed by the end of July and the National Militia disbanded.[107] The previous two years had exposed the party of progress as an intellectual void in all areas of policy except classical liberal capitalism. As Isabel Burdiel has argued, the 'Progressive Biennium' is really a misnomer, as the *progresistas* never really enjoyed hegemony to begin with, given their lack of cohesion in the face of republicanism and democracy on the left and liberal 'order' on the right.[108]

Towards Unión Liberal

With the radicals suppressed O'Donnell also dispersed remaining Carlist bands in Catalonia. No more threat came from the dynastic opposition until 1860 when the Carlist convert and captain general of Mallorca launched an expedition against San Carlos de la Rapita (Catalonia). It failed as soon as the troops were told at the last moment before landfall that they were engaging in a Carlist revolt.[109] The following year, the Carlist Pretender Count Montemolín died of cholera in Trieste. Once the *moderados* recovered power in

1856, they, in any case, re-established a détente with the Catholic Church which went further than during the 1844–54 Moderate Decade. O'Donnell had refused to halt disentailment altogether, so in October 1856, the queen replaced him with the more conservative Narváez. The railway investment bubble remained as corrupt as ever, the only difference being that it was a *moderado* rather than *progresista* political caste now handing out the best contracts. Narváez presided over a reactionary government which restored María Cristina's confiscated estates, all the restrictive electoral legislation of 1845, and indirect taxation. The cabinet even included a former Carlist general and recent pacifier of the Philippines, Juan Antonio de Urbiztondo, as war minister, and the future parliamentary Carlist Cándido Nocedal as interior minister. New auctions of clerical property were halted and in 1857 the church was guaranteed its religious monopoly in primary education via the 1857 Moyano law. Challenges to clericalism no longer being posed by establishment politicians were instead posed by intellectuals. The same year that the Moyano law was passed, Sanz del Río gave his inaugural and Krausist lecture at Madrid's university, enraging clerical opinion which recoiled at how a university system placed under state control in the 1840s could permit a heretical 'pantheist' address by its rector.[110]

The stifling atmosphere of Narváez's conservatism was relieved by the victory in the September 1858 Cortes elections of Leopoldo O'Donnell's coalition of left-leaning *moderados* and right-leaning *progresistas* that was known as the Liberal Union. The Liberal Union, first coined by Mendizábal in 1835, was finally launched as a party by O'Donnell in June 1858. O'Donnell's ideas had formed during his year spent as Cuba's Captain General. Comprising reformist elements from both historic liberal parties, the Liberal Union promised moderately to extend suffrage, to increase provincial and municipal autonomy, to relax repressive press laws and to reduce executive intervention in the electoral system. Although O'Donnell failed to deliver on any of these pledges the Liberal Union secured five years of relative domestic peace, helped by economic growth spurred by railway construction and bolstered by patriotic euphoria accompanying neo-colonial ventures, especially a much-hyped victory in the Moroccan War in 1859.

The world's third-biggest empire

The torment around the throne obscured some remarkable successes in Spanish foreign policy. The dogma of Spain's Isabelline foreign policy may be summarised as 'joining France and Britain whenever they are united, abstaining whenever they are at odds'.[111] This policy sometimes left considerable opportunity for Spain's own imperial expansion. Contrary to many studies which are interested in nineteenth-century Spanish imperialism only in terms of the losses of the 1810s and 1898, more recent studies have underlined the importance of Spain's surviving post-Ayachucho empire. The O'Donnell era of expansionist foreign policy led to a strange era when the Spanish army finally performed its proper role of fighting abroad. In a series of conflicts which historian Stephen Jacobson has defined as 'micromilitarism', of 'quick wars and easy victories with few domestic casualties', O'Donnell not only quashed appearances of imperial decline but also raised Spain's status as a serious European colonial power.[112] By the mid-nineteenth century, Spaniards did not perceive themselves as living in an era of imperial decline. In the mid-nineteenth century, Spain had the third-most populous overseas empire (behind Britain and the Netherlands), and by 1860, Cuba produced 40 per cent of the world's demand for cane sugar.[113] Spain's imperial prominence contradicts the prevailing view of historians who wrote in the twentieth century and saw a comparative weakness of a Spanish colonial identity. Spain after 1821 was largely considered an 'ex-empire', even before the shock of 1898. Even though the islands of Cuba and Puerto Rico (but never the Philippines) were invited to send delegates to Spain in several of the earlier constitutional regimes, 'special laws' governed these Caribbean islands from the 1830s.

But the importance of empire was obvious even in Spain itself. The development of empire, especially in Cuba, allowed Spain to make sense of the geopolitical shock of its 'children' on the American mainland declaring independence. Even intellectuals were constrained to look outwards, to universal ideas and values, and held the example of empire as proof that Spain could rank highly in world affairs, even if it remained in second-power status. As Andrew Ginger has observed, '[m]any nineteenth century Spanish subjects longed to be universal. It was a way for a people – fallen from its perch and shoved to the margins – to participate in humanity's grand design'.[114] In all sorts of subtle yet telling ways, intellectuals and opinion-formers continued to cling to Spain's imperial identity. The 1846 Mexican–American War dominated press headlines in Spain, where the menace of the 'Anglo-American' empire led to calls for solidarity with Spain's Mexican 'brothers'. Fernando Garrido's 1867 universal history, *La humanidad y sus progresos*, argued that nations can progress to modernity in a time scale of their own choosing between the natural life cycle of a human and the unfathomable life cycle of the stars and planets. The inference, according to Geraldine Lawless, was that 'Spain's irreversible decline could be waved aside'.[115]

Beyond the world of ideas, the empire played a growing role in economics, demography, and foreign policy. The O'Donnell government legislated for Spain's first Overseas Ministry in 1861. When it opened for use in 1863, visitors entering the building were directly greeted by a statue of Christopher Columbus[116] Returning Spaniards who had enriched themselves in the colonies, the so-called *Indianos*, were a recognisable link to the empire. They flaunted their wealth in mansion building and investing in Catalan industry. Spanish imperialism also remained a going concern from the perspective of the colonised themselves. The Philippines were brought largely under Spanish military control from the 1840s with often violent counter-insurgencies. Yet the Hispanicising agents on these islands remained predominantly the religious orders, along with indentured convicts from the homeland. There was no slavery in the Philippines, unlike Cuba and Puerto Rico, where the industry continued to thrive right up until the end of the slave trade in 1867 and the final abolition of slavery in the Spanish empire in 1886. Spanish slavers were creative in getting around British-led anti-slavery missions. The African island of Fernando Po, for example, saw slavery abolished in order to pose as an entrepot for indentured labour instead (to be exported to the Caribbean where they would be slaves all the same). Colonials had no feeling that Spanish colonialism was in decline. Until the 1880s, Cuba and, to a lesser extent, Puerto Rico were prime destinations for Spanish emigrants. Thereafter, the Southern Cone became more attractive in response to the abolition of slavery plantations. Even before slavery was finally ended in 1886, manumission was more common in Cuba than in the United States, hence the lack of a sudden backlash of 'Jim Crow' laws in Cuba after abolition.

As the late Christopher Schmidt-Nowara explained, empire shaped the 'contours of nineteenth-century Spain's imagined community'.[117] Yet, as Nowara explained, this imagined community never convinced Spanish Americans:

> The Spanish liberal regime was hindered in its nation-building project by endemic political conflict, but in this case, between colonies and metropolis. Spaniards sought to construct a national identity that folded the colonies into metropolitan historical narrative. But patriotic creoles, despite frequent collaboration with the colonial regime, always resisted those efforts, either by countering with their own version of Spain's history in the Caribbean and Pacific or by crafting their own national histories and spaces that excluded Spain altogether.[118]

Importance of Cuba

This discord persisted after the 1820s as Cuba's slave economy expanded. The Cuban sugar boom of the 1830s, as well as a boost in transatlantic trade, prompted massive economic and urban development, especially in Catalonia.[119] The upward trend in prosperity from the mid-1840s led on the whole to an absolute increase in the standard of living, whilst the opening of new agricultural export markets was boosted by the Crimean War. This slow increase in wealth was, however, truncated by regular subsistence crises and economic downturns.

From the late 1830s, Cuba's sugar and coffee plantations brought fiscal salvation to a struggling Spain bankrupted by the Carlist War and Cuba became one of the most productive colonies in the world.[120] The first railway was laid down in Cuba in the 1830s, a decade before the first line was constructed in Spain. Sugar barons like Francisco Arrango y Parreño saw slavery as a form of 'progress' that was key to developing the Cuban economy inside the Spanish empire.[121] The *criollo* plantocracy tried to justify the growth of the slavery economy on moral as well as economic grounds. Carefully selecting extreme case studies for contrast, the plantocracy pointed out that Spanish slavery was more humane than the French system that led to the slave revolt on Saint-Domingue (later Haiti) or the American slavery system that replaced the Spanish system in Florida after 1819.

Yet ultimately such delusions rested on fragile foundations. The Cuban plantocracy ultimately relied on Spanish protection of inhumane slavery which was being attacked by abolitionism within and without Spain. Spain, in turn, could never treat its colonies as equals. Growing fears of regional nationalism and federalism in Spain itself stopped Spain from instituting 'Dominion' status as the British had done with respect of Canada in 1867. Developments in the remaining colonial territories, particularly the expansion of slavery in Cuba, further reinforced the arbitrary and martial character of the Spanish state. Hence, the *progresista* Constitution of 1837 was not applied to colonial territories for fear of encouraging abolitionist and republican movements. This only inflamed sentiments amongst abolitionist and reformist groups in Cuba who rebelled during the 1840s and mounted a fully fledged insurrection in September 1868 coinciding with the revolution known as the Gloriosa in the mother country.

Splendid little wars

The war in Morocco, also called la Guerra de África, was of particular significance to mid-nineteenth-century Spanish culture. Lasting only six months, from October 1859 to April 1860, the conflict in Morocco was fought with the Moroccan tribesmen and armies of the sultan for infringing on Spanish territories in northern Morocco. After a rare unanimous call for a declaration of war from the Cortes O'Donnell put his campaign in action. Even though the Moroccans were poorly equipped, Spanish military performance was slow and unimaginative. As Friedrich Engels, war correspondent for the *New York Daily Tribune* reported, Spanish logistics were slow, troops ravaged by disease, always the worst enemy during colonial campaigns, and tactics were ill suited to the intrinsically guerrilla character of Moroccan resistance and topography. Few lessons appeared to have been learnt from the Carlist War, guerrilla warfare still being treated as 'cowardly' in Spanish military academies. Yet eventually overwhelming Spanish force and improved tactics (including the use of skirmishers) forced the Moroccans to sue for peace. Spanish territories around the cities of Ceuta and Melilla were expanded, although under British diplomatic pressure Spain had to evacuate Tangier and Tetuán.[122] This six-month conflict in Morocco and subsequent victory were heavily capitalised on by the Isabelline government. The state used the wave of national sentiment following the victory in Morocco as a platform to promote the reinvigorated military prowess of the nation and colonial expansion through elements of state-sponsored culture. The 1859–60 'Tetouan War' was a rare overseas victory against a foreign opponent, and it combined with another rarity, a concerted attempt at an independent and expansionist foreign policy. Thereafter, Spain embraced the 'new imperialism' like other European countries.

Leopoldo O'Donnell's tenacious ability to remain in office for five uninterrupted years was in many ways linked to his colonial adventures, especially his masterminding of the 1859–60 war in Morocco. O'Donnell was made the Duke of Tetuán by royal decree from the queen in order to 'perpetuate the memory of the glorious campaign of Africa'.[123] O'Donnell entered Madrid at the head of his troops returned to Madrid in a garlanded procession. In 1860, two bronze lions were commissioned to be cast from the cannons captured from enemy troops and were then placed on either side of the Spanish parliament building's main entrance.[124] Furthermore, this military campaign became the common theme of contemporary literature and theatrical productions in the mid-nineteenth century. Romantic writer and orientalist Gustavo Adolfo Bécquer (1836–70) was inspired by Morocco to publish in 1863 *La cueva de la mora* (*Moorish Woman's Cave*) and the following year *La rosa de la pasión* (*Rose of Passion*). Set in early modern Spain amidst the conclusion of the Reconqusita, Bécquer's Moor sacrificed her faith and family in order to convert to Christianity and marry a Catholic knight who had been her father's prisoner of war. Bécquer's *Rose of Passion* revealed his traditionalist anti-Semitism by portraying Sara as a victim of her fellow Jews' grudges, vindictiveness, and hypocrisy as she is driven to embrace her lover's faith by converting to Catholicism.[125] The patriotic flurry of victory in Morocco also inspired such theatrical productions as *Los moros del Rif*, *¡Españoles, A Marruecos!* and *El pabellón español en África*.[126] In 1887, the Battle of Tetuán was the first destination of Enrique Gaspar y Riumbau's science fiction novel about time travel, *El Anacronópete*.

In 1861, Spain dared defy the United States, now embroiled in civil war, in its own backyard by joining a French-led punitive expedition to Mexico, and Spain defied late-imperial China with token participation in the French expedition to Cochin-China. The outbreak of civil war in the United States appeared to open further imperial opportunities. Spain's lucrative slave colony of Cuba gave the nearby Confederates hope of strategic depth and logistical base to break the Yankee blockade. Cuba was usually a sore point in US–Spanish relations, especially during the Pierce presidency (1853–57) and the repeated filibusters, but the rebel Confederates appreciated how Spain's neo-imperial political establishment was broadly sympathetic to Confederate principles and hostile to 'Anglo-Saxon' imperialism.[127] Spain even managed to divide and rule politics in Santo Domingo, where local fears of invasion from neighbouring Black Haiti led to a political faction voluntarily accepting the annexation of this former colony to the Spanish Crown in 1861. The ensuing conflict in Hispaniola and the end of American Civil War obliged

Spain to relinquish its 'voluntary' colony in 1865, but the symbolism of pan-Hispanism heartened nationalists in Spain.[128] Spain also fought a guano war with its former colonies of Peru and Chile between 1862 and 1867. In addition to regaining former territories like Santo Domingo, Isabelline imperialists also extended control over territories which were nominally Spanish to begin with. After 1857, the captain general of the Philippines colonised remote parts of the archipelago in order to police piracy.[129]

The campaign in Morocco and O'Donnell's victory brought with it a kind of popular nationalism.[130] It helped the anti-liberal Spanish right accept nation building and cast aside their outdated notions of throne and tradition. Both Balmes and Donoso Cortés were now dead, but their neo-Catholic ideas helped reconcile traditionalism with the 'nation'. The War of Africa thus appealed to Spaniards from varying political backgrounds by invoking the historic military campaigns of the Reconquista which appealed to the more religious and conservative parties as well as the liberal ideals.[131] Victory made a national figure out of General Prim, just like Espartero before him. The decisive role played by some four hundred Catalan Volunteers from Barcelona gave Prim's native Catalonia a privileged role in the 1860 victory celebrations, even if the volunteers comprised only some 1 per cent of the Spanish expedition.[132]

Pandering to nationalism, on one hand, O'Donnell's 'Liberal Union' also pandered to internationalism, on the other. The Risorgimento – the Italian movement for national unification under a republic or a modern constitutional monarchy – had emerged with renewed energy since 1856, outflanking the Liberal Union on the left by rekindling the conspiratorial politics of the insurgent wing of the Spanish Democrats. O'Donnell, reaching for a symbolic gesture, moved to recognise the new state of Italy proclaimed in 1860. However, Queen Isabel, who had come under the influence of her confessor, Catalan cleric Antonio María Claret, forbade O'Donnell from recognising a regime which sought to remove the temporal powers of the papacy and to establish its capital in Rome. Claret was a more astute influence than the discredited stigmatic nun, Sor Patricinio, had been, and the breach widened between the queen and more liberal elements in the Liberal Union, for whom Italian unification held great symbolic power. When, in 1861, the liberal leader Práxedes Sagasta told the Cortes that Isabella 'owed her position as queen to the concept of national sovereignty', he caused a scandal by exposing the queen and her *moderado* ministers' indulgence of her mysticism.[133] As a consequence, Spain delayed recognition of the new state of Italy for a further six years (until 1865). In the meantime, abandoned by prominent Progresistas, the five-year Liberal Union would collapse in January 1863, returning the country once more to the firm but diminishingly safe hands of Narváez and the *moderados*. Inexorably the queen's political isolation by 1868 would be complete.[134]

Instability at home

All the hubris of colonial warfare could not remedy the structural problems in the Spanish Army: a top-heavy and politicised officer corps, resentful conscripts unable to buy their way out of army service, and, in between, the peculiar role played by the sergeants, dedicated professionals who rose to their rank through merit (and in isolated cases could even get promoted to major). The sergeants, as the events of 1836 had demonstrated, had a politically powerful role in representing army discontent. Yet the army was not (yet) a praetorian force and so could not effect change without an alliance with civilian politicians. As during the Biennium, O'Donnell maintained officers' salaries and conditions at a better level than during the Carlst War, and overseas campaigning improved career prospects. Thus, even though officers' political allegiance could be secured by *progresista* or *moderado* politicians excluded from the Liberal Union, there was little chance of 'outs' securing a broadsword. Carlist converts in the military were still isolated eccentrics, except for the exiles, and by 1867, the Democrat Party managed to secure the allegiance of only one general, Blas Pierrard, a deaf former military governor of Madrid and veteran of Moroccan and Philippine campaigns who discovered his democratic soul in his mid-50s after failing to ignite a *pronunciamiento* from across the Pyrenees.[135]

Thus, opposition to the O'Donnell regime was increasingly civilian in nature. The Democrat Party adopted a Janus-faced strategy of participating in Isabelline politics via its moderate 'monarchical' wing (centred on Nicolás Rivero), on one hand, and insurrection via its carbonario cells, on the other. Whereas the regime ignored establishment Democrats, often censoring their press, it turned the army and Civil Guard against insurgents. Democrat resistance, in turn, was often weakened by doctrinal strife. When Sixto Cámara in July 1857 launched a republican rising in Seville and Jaén, his manifesto reached out to impoverished day labourers by offering land redistribution. But Nicolás Rivero's newspaper *La Discusión* disowned Cámara's 'socialism', marginalising the party's radical wing for the sake of hierarchical cohesion and legality.[136] But legal niceties did not prevent General Narváez from imposing a state of siege and ordering the execution of hundreds of Democrat militants in the Sierra de Cádiz.[137] The judicial murder of a Democrat candidate for the 1858 elections provoked a press subscription for the benefit of his next of kin, a form of protest against a legal system unwilling to investigate electoral intimidation.[138] Certainly, O'Donnell's 1858–63 regime proved relatively more tolerant towards the Rivero wing of Democrats, exposing itself to recriminations from the *moderados* that it was allowing democracy to enter via the back door. But the Democrats were still refused recognition as a party in the December 1858 Cortes elections, and they were also banned from holding electoral meetings in Madrid and several provinces.[139]

The party's insurgent wing thus retained credibility with militants. Renewed risings in the summer of 1859 in Andalucía and Alicante sharpened the tension between Rivero and the insurgents. All risings were failures, entering a canon of heroism in the Democrat subculture. Authorities briefly detained Fernando Garrido in Seville, and Sixto Cámara died of thirst, failing to reach the Portuguese border after having fled his failed insurrection at Badajoz. Rivero, ever anxious about the party's legal position, had dissolved the party's 'Central Circle' at a crucial moment in the insurrection, depriving the movement of coordination and exposing himself to recriminations of treachery. More than ever, Rivero needed to demonstrate his leadership and, in 1861, successfully defended Eduardo Ruiz Pons, a democrat intellectual, who faced trial having enraged the authorities for publishing an inflammatory newssheet titled 'The Decrees of Democracy'. Ruiz Pons later republished a similar article and was condemned. Only hasty flight to Oporto spared him the twelve-year prison sentence.[140] The greatest insurgent efforts came at Loja (Granada) in the summer of 1861. Despite fierce odds, not least the proximity of General Narváez's family estate, a physical neighbour of the local Democrat leader, veterinarian Pérez del Alamo, Democrats had managed to control Loja's town council. Pérez del Alamo plotted a rising for the summer of 1861, prepared by his clandestine organising and the preparation of forged money to pay day labourers whom local militants were about to drag from the harvest. When the militants seized control of Loja, their feat shocked O'Donnell's regime, as the rising had worked without the usual requirement of military support. They kept control of Loja for a week before authorities sent troops and Civil Guard to clear the town. The Liberal Union repression was milder than the *moderados*, and Pérez received a royal pardon in 1862, along with homilies from the queen that Loja should be pacified 'not with soldiers, but with missions'.[141] Tighter gun controls and watchfulness against Protestant troublemakers from Gibraltar summed up official responses to the Loja crisis, along with Catholic missionary work in a region which the liberal property revolution had released from the grip of the church but not from the grip of grinding poverty.

The collapse in 1863 of O'Donnell's Liberal Union opened up scope for disaffected *progresistas* and Democrats to seek an alliance with officers. When the *moderados* in 1863 introduced a law excluding from electoral meetings all non-voters (those paying less than 400 *reales* per year in direct taxation), the *progresistas* joined Democrats in urging voters to boycott elections (a policy known as *retraimiento*). The boycott boosted the insurrectionary wing of the Democrat Party which had been clandestinely organised by a *carbonario* society founded in 1858 by the Catalan republican, Ceferino Tressera. Fernando Garrido estimated that Tressera gained more than eighty thousand members, disproportionately concentrated in Andalucía and Catalonia.[142] Workers' schools teaching democracy and federalism flourished in Madrid, Catalonia, Valencia, and Catalonia, and Democrat insurrection at Loja and elsewhere certainly showed that Carlism was no longer the default insurrectionary movement in the countryside.[143] Worried by the leftist sacralisation of the Second of May uprising against the French of 1808, the *moderado* government under the Marques de Miraflores in 1864 refused to recognise the customary annual commemoration of this national event out of fear that it might provide a focus for insurrection. Miraflores's government wisely refused to suppress the several thousands of Democrats and *progresistas* who descended on the centre of Madrid anyway, some of them dressed as peasant insurgents in commemoration of 1808.[144]

Moderados were wise to fear the mobilising potential of left-wing politics. *Retraimiento* turned some *progresistas* into allies of the Democrat insurgents. For the time being, Spanish Democrats found the path to 'respectable' politics resolutely blocked by the centralised state, its politicised judiciary, restrictive franchise, and ultimately the guns of the Civil Guard and the army. Recent history showed that even whenever ministerial *progresistas* were in office (as during 1854–56) the basic problem remained the same. Barred from open politics, Democrats used newspapers in order to engage ever more people in an expanding public sphere which linked readers with the accelerated democratic and anti-slavery struggles overseas. Garibaldi, the Polish revolt, Irish nationalism, emancipation in the American Civil War, and Benito Juárez were all celebrated. Until research by such historians as Guy Thomson and Florencia Peyrou, it was unclear exactly how international events were received by a largely illiterate Democrat rank and file meeting clandestinely in small towns and villages. Certainly, Spanish republicanism developed its own international ambitions, favouring a 'progressive' imperial expansion in Africa, 'pan-Iberian' union with Portugal, and a 'motherly' relationship to progressive currents in the independent republics of Spanish America.[145]

But Spanish republicanism could only reflect international events and would not be in a position to shape them until the early 1870s. The 1860s, meanwhile, bestowed Spanish politics with a greater degree of liberation in terms of ideas and proselytisation. The Spanish Royal Academy in 1863 passed a motion condemning the old dynastic parties as stuck in outmoded worldviews and endorsing Democracy and Neo-Catholicism as modern and 'European'.[146] In 1865, the Krausist Democrat Nicolás Salmerón was elected leader of the Madrid section of the Democrats, and the following year opened up the Krausist 'International College' (Colegio Internacional) in the capital.[147] In April 1866, students were shot down in the 'Night of Saint Daniel', a protest against the government's sacking of Madrid University's directors who had refused to silence Professor Emilio Castelar's fiery rhetoric. The student deaths shocked Alcalá Galiano (1789–1865), *moderado* minister for development but also an old Romantic, to an early grave.[148]

The *moderado* political system concentrated voting rights in the hands of a small oligarchy, and all but the smallest municipalities were led by centrally appointed mayors. Thus, it was hard for popular economic grievances to be represented legally. Around mid-century, the average daily wage for an agricultural labourer in Andalucía was four-and-a-half *reales*, half of what a water seller earned in Madrid. Often, patrician networks survived, either via charity from the diminished Catholic Church or via landowners in the form of free or subsidised food and the provision of shelter (*alojamiento*) during seasonal times of dearth.[149] As a distinguished economic historian explained, 'the master had a feudal relationship to his business: he gave workers their daily bread and expected obedience and reverence in return'.[150] Migration and emigration were other options. In 1853, the last legal restrictions on emigration had been removed from Spanish law, allowing the departure to Latin America of a trickle of the rural dispossessed that would become a flood by the end of the century.[151]

But, for all the safeguards, the mid-century railway boom distorted Spain's economic modernisation, leaving it vulnerable to the recessions that were becoming a cyclical feature of advancing capitalism. Railway investment soaked up most Spanish capital in the 1850s and 1860s, helped by the liberalisation of banking and credit regulations during 1855–1856. Although almost 5,000 kilometres of railway track were laid between 1848 and 1856, this effort did not stimulate industrial development, which remained patchy. The railway mania also diverted capital away from improving structural deficiencies in the economy, especially agriculture, which was dominated by low-capital and labour-intensive methods leading to low productivity and vulnerability to harvest failures and to the sort of geopolitical shocks to wheat and cotton offered respectively by the Crimean and American civil wars.[152]

Matters came to a head in 1866 with the economic crisis which, apart from spectacularly bursting the railway investment bubble, breaking the banks, also bankrupted the numerous conscription insurance companies which had been advertising their services in the press since the 1840s. Tens of thousands of policyholders thus found themselves suddenly vulnerable to the draft.[153] The ranks of the conscript class were swelled in 1866 by nationwide poor harvests and droughts. The price of grain increased by 45 per cent between 1863 and 1867.[154] During the nationwide industrial unrest of 1866, the newspaper *La Asociación* reacted bitterly to the suspension of civil liberties and banning of strikes by despairing that there had been no progress as far as the working class was concerned since 1840: 'what have we advanced since 1840? Absolutely nothing!'[155] Rivero's control of the Democrat Party waned as allies deserted him for more radical options. Pi y Margall, as editor of *La Discusión* from 1864, radicalised the newspaper's stance, starting with his seconding of the London-based First International's call for a right to work and property as a stepping stone to socialism.[156] Pi opposed time-serving Democrat colleagues who were either bent on union with the Progresistas (like Castelar and Orense) or on working within the existing political spoils system (like Rivero). Much of the party's history after 1865 was characterised by Rivero using political theatre to safeguard his position. In 1865, he led a mass resignation from the party's committee, ostensibly in protest at the party's *retraimiento* but really in order to distract attention from the party's rising star, Emilio Castelar (1832–99), whose rousing attack in 1865 on the queen in his 'El Rasgo' article got him dismissed from his chair in history at the University of Madrid.[157]

The financial crisis, which was exacerbated by Spain's unsuccessful Santo Domingo adventure, also radicalised the dynastic opposition to Isabella's regime. When the queen offered to donate to the nation a 75 per cent stake in royal real estate, she was condemned by the *progresistas* for wanting to keep the proceeds from the remaining 25 per cent. Little could be done to avert the strong recession. In 1866, O'Donnell hiked land taxes by 10 per cent in a bid to fund the half-baked war effort against Peru and Chile. The tax remained in place even after Spanish involvement ended in 1866, while the regime also cancelled a large naval construction order, exacerbating the recession in Catalan industry.[158] Amidst this economic plunge, the *retraimiento* of the main opposition parties (Democrats and Progresistas), ongoing since 1863, continued to dramatise the diminishing support enjoyed by *moderados* and the Crown.

In 1866 two *pronunciamientos* rocked the regime. The first was launched at Villarejo near Madrid by the colonial war hero General Prim, who failed to achieve popular support and fled incognito towards the Portuguese frontier and exile in order to await better times. The second *pronunciamiento* alarmed the government for its radical and plebeian character. The failure of the San Gil barracks uprising in July 1866 prevented the Democrats from gaining a Madrid stronghold to counterbalance *progresista* General Prim's revolutionary leadership from exile. On 22 June 1866, sergeants under Democrat leadership rebelled at the barracks of San Gil in Madrid. Its brutal suppression, including the execution of sixty-six mutineers, was considered too soft by a beleaguered queen, who showed her displeasure with Leopoldo O'Donnell by rejecting his list of senators for her approval, forcing him to resign. The fact that most of the sixty-six executed men were sergeants and corporals revealed an obviously class-based aspect of the *pronunciamiento* for the first time.[159] The failure of the *sargentada* underlined the weakness of the radical opposition. The opposition was growing more constrained with the draconian press law passed in 1865, and the advent of General Narvaez's last ministry in 1866. Despite his claims that he would be 'more liberal than Riego', Narváez ruled as a dictator, and his replacement, the former radical, González Bravo, performed a shift to the right which was the most egregious example of a pattern of politicians' behaviour that dated back to 1835 when the 'divine' Agustín Argüelles renounced his magnm opus, the Constitution of 1812. The pattern continued when Mendizábal, in the 1850s, denounced the National Militia, splitting the *progresista*, and when Salustiano de Olózaga became a reactionary in the Liberal Union of the 1860s, denouncing socialism especially harshly.[160]

The Isabelline state now switched to panic mode. The ageing Narváez was recalled to the premiership. Despite his promise to be 'more liberal than Riego', Narváez imposed an authoritarian regime, arresting dissidents, censoring the press, purging suspect local authorities and army officers, all amidst a brutal recession and debt crisis. Narváez's natural death from pneumonia 'broke of the spine of *moderantismo*' in the words of Donoso Cortes, and as Narváez's demise had followed that of O'Donnell from typhus five months earlier, the queen was left as a political orphan. Years of *moderado* and Liberal Union collusion in the queen's diabolical reputation as a convenient cover for usurping the Crown's prerogatives would now recoil on the establishment politicians. Owing in large part to their own ruthlessness, the fall of the queen would now also mean the fall of the Bourbon monarchy itself.[161] The death of O'Donnell removed the last block preventing such disaffected Liberal Unionists as General Serrano from joining the exile-based conspiracy of *progresistas* and Democrats, and the death of Narváez removed the last figure who might remotely have been able to head off the coming revolution. The appointment to the premiership of Luis González Bravo, the former radical long since sold out to the reaction increased the repression even more. Prominent revolutionaries, like Pi y Margall, wisely went into exile. But the government crackdown did not affect the clandestine circle of revolutionaries in Madrid who were known as the 'Centre' and who communicated with different cells using only assumed names.[162] González Bravo commanded Narváez's authoritarianism but very little of his respect.[163] In September 1868, the revolution began.

Notes

1 Lawrence, *Spanish Civil Wars*, p. 10.
2 Mónica Burguera, 'Mujeres y Revolución Liberal en perspectiva, esfera pública y ciudadanía femenina en la primera mitad del siglo XIX en España', in Moerris, Frasquet, and Monerris (eds.), *Cuando todo era posible*, pp. 262, 270.
3 López Garrido, *Guardia Civil*, pp. 55–140; Artola-Gallego, *Burguesía revolucionaria*, p. 212.
4 Fox, *La invención de España*, p. 55.
5 José Luis Comellas García-Llera, *Los Moderados en el poder, 1844–54* (Madrid: CSIC, 1970), pp. 60–3.
6 Burdiel María Sierra, 'The Time of Liberalism, 1833–1874', in Shubert and Alvarez-Junco (eds.), *The History of Modern Spain*, p. 31.
7 Cit. Callahan, *Church, Politics and Society*, p. 184.
8 Révész, *Un dictador liberal*.
9 Jensen, 'War and the Military', in Shubert and Álvarez-Junco (eds.), *The History of Modern Spain*, p. 335.
10 Raymond Carr first elaborated the triarchy interpretation (Carr, *Spain, 1808–1975*, pp. 210–14).
11 Comellas García-Llera, *Los Moderados en el poder*, p. 140.
12 Isabel Burdiel, *Isabel II: no se puede reinar inocentemente* (Madrid: Espasa Calpe Mexicana, 2004), pp. 245–7.
13 Richard Meyer Forsting, *Raising Heirs to the Throne on Nineteenth-century Spain* (Palgrave: Basingstoke, 2018), p. 47.

14 Trías and Antonio, *Federalismo y Reforma Social en España (1840–1870)*, pp. 95–104.
15 Comellas García-Llera, *Los moderados en el poder, 1844–1854*, pp. 158–60.
16 Burdiel, Ledesma, and Pérez (eds.), *Liberales, agitadores y conspiradores*, p. 225.
17 Comellas García-Llera, *Los Moderados en el poder*, pp. 51–2.
18 Ignacio Peiró Martín, 'Los sitios de Zaragoza y la Guerra de la Independencia en 1958: las conferencias de la cátedra "General Palafox"', in *VI Congreso de Historia Militar (Zaragoza, marzo-abril 1808)*, Vol. I (Madrid: Ministerio de Defensa), pp. 53–68.
19 David Hopkin, 'The World Turned Upside Down', in Alan Forrest, Karen Hagemann, and Jane Rendall (eds.), *Soldiers, Citizens and Civilians: Experiences and Perceptions of the Revolutionary and Napoleonic Wars, 1790–1820* (London: Palgrave Macmillan, 2009), pp. 77–92.
20 Susan C. Karant-Nunn, 'The Reformation of Women', in Renate Bridenthal, Susan Mosher Stuard, and Merry E. Wiesner (eds.), *Becoming Visible: Women in European History* (New York: Houghton Mifflin, 1988), pp. 182–3.
21 Florencia Peyrou, 'A Great Family of Sovereign Men: Democratic Discourse in Nineteenth-century Spain', *European History Quarterly*, Vol. 43, No. 2 (2013), pp. 235–56, 241.
22 Burdiel, *Isabel II*, pp. 268–70.
23 Jones Parry, *Spanish Marriages*, pp. 116–23.
24 Burdiel, *Isabel II*, p. 278.
25 *Ibid.*, pp. 289–91.
26 Isabel Burdiel, "The Queen, the Woman and the Middle Class. The Symbolic Failure of Isabel II in Spain", *Social History*, Vol. 29, No. 3, Spain (August 2004), pp. 301–19, 311.
27 Cit. Diego Sevilla Andrés, *Antonio Maura: la revolución desde arriba* (Barcelona: Aedos, 1954), pp. 36–7.
28 Isabel Burdiel, '1846: El matrimonio de Isabel II: un asunto europeo', in Seixas (ed.), *Historia mundial de España*, p. 577.
29 Burdiel, *Isabel II*, pp. 303–13.
30 William H. Prescott, *History of the Reign of Ferdinand and Isabella, the Catholic*, Vol. 1 (New York: A. L. Burt Publisher, 1837), p. 10.
31 José Güell y Renté, *Paralelo entre las reinas catolicas Doña Isabel Iª y Doña Isabel II* (Paris: Imprenta de Jules Claye, 1858), pp. 48–50.
32 Burdiel, *Isabel II*, pp. 18–19.
33 Francis Gribble, *The Tragedy of Isabella II* (London: Chapman and Hall, 1913), p. 174.
34 Paul Preston, *Juan Carlos: A People's King* (London: Harper Collins, 2004), pp. 25–7.
35 Burdiel, *Isabel II*, p. 25.
36 *Eco del Comercio*, 23 September 1837.
37 Herráiz de Miota, 'Los montepíos militares del siglo XVIII como origen del sistema de clases pasivas del estado', p. 192.
38 Comellas García-Llera, *Los Moderados en el poder*, p. 120.
39 Hughes, *Revelations of Spain in 1845*, Vol I, p. 258.
40 Colin McKinney, 'How to Be a Man', in Ginger and Lawless (eds.), *Spain in the Nineteenth Century*, pp. 147–67.
41 Alcalá Galiano, *Memorias*, Vol. I, pp. 54–7; Lawrence, *Spain's First Carlist War*, p. 106.
42 Bullón de Mendoza, 'La primera guerra carlista' (PhD thesis, Universisad Complutense de Madrid, 1991), p. 145.
43 Richard Cleminson and Francisco Vázquez García, *'Los Invisibles': A History of Male Homosexuality in Spain, 1850–1940* (Cardiff: Universiy of Wales Press, 2007), pp. 29–94.
44 María Sierra, '1845: Carmen, la gitana imaginada', in Seixas (ed.), *Historia mundial de España*.
45 Anna Caballé, *Concepción Arenal: la caminante y su sombra* (Barcelona: Taurus, 2018), p. 147.
46 Juan B. Vilar, 'España en la Europa de los nacionalismos: entre pequeña acción y potencia media (1834–1874)', in Juan Carlos Pereira (ed.), *La política exterior de España (1800–2003)* (Madrid: Ariel, 2003), pp. 404–5.

47 Daniel Headrick, 'Spain and the Revolutions of 1848', *European Studies Review*, Vol. 6 (1976), pp. 197–223, 199.
48 John Graham, *Donoso Cortes: Utopian Romanticist and Political Realist* (Columbia, MO: University of Missouri Press, 1974), p. 3.
49 Sonsoles Cabeza Sánchez-Albornoz, *Los sucesos de 1848 en España* (Madrid: Fundación Universitaria Española, 1981), pp. 8–9.
50 Lida, *Anarquismo y revolución*, p. 42; Headrick, 'Spain and 1848', p. 201.
51 R.A.H., Colección Narváez Caja 7, 9/7815.
52 Victor Kiernan, *The Revolution of 1854 in Spanish History* (Oxford: Oxford University Press, 1966), pp. 30–1, 67.
53 Vicente Cacho Viu, *La Institución Libre de Enseñanza* (Madrid: Rialp, 1962), pp. 42–4.
54 *Eco del Comercio*, 5 April 1848.
55 *El Observador*, 3 April 1848.
56 *Ibid.*, 17 March.1848.
57 R.A.H., Colección Narváez Caja 7, 9/7815.
58 *Ibid.*, 9/7815: I-D-d (4), 5 July 1848 reply from General Narváez to 'la Sociedad Filantrópica de Milicianos Nacionales Veteranos'.
59 Sánchez-Albornoz, *Los sucesos de 1848*, pp. 40–1.
60 *Eco del Comercio*, 1 May 1847.
61 *Ibid.*, 9 May 1847.
62 Esteban Navarro, *La formación del Pensamiento radical*, pp. 42–4; Maluquer de Motes, *Socialismo*, pp. 236–74.
63 Jorge Luengo Sánchez, 'Representar la monarquía: festividades en torno a la reina niña', in Encarna García Monerris, Mónica Moreno Seco, and Juan I. Marcuello Benedicto (eds.), *Culturas políticas en la España liberal*, p. 125.
64 Josep Carles Clemente, 'La riqueza ideológica del carlismo en torno a la guerra de los "matiners"', in Daniel Montañà and Josep Rafart (eds.), *Estat carlista: tradició i furs* (II Simposi d'Història del carlisme, 10 maig de 2014), pp. 107–14.
65 Gregorio Alonso, *La nación en capilla* (Madrid: Editorial Comares, 2014), pp. 155–7.
66 *Eco del Comercio*, 16 March 1847.
67 Palacio Atard, *La España del siglo XIX*, p. 268.
68 Francisco Barado y Font, *Literatura militar española en el siglo XIX* (Madrid: Administración, Florida 14, 1889), pp. 154–5.
69 Comellas García-Llera, *Los Moderados en el poder*, p. 82.
70 Sánchez-Albornoz, *Crisis de subsistencias*, p. 24.
71 Artola-Gallego, *Burguesía revolucionaria*, pp. 170–3.
72 Eiras Roel, *El Partido Demócrata*, pp. 164–5, 250–1, 283.
73 Guy Thomson, '*Democracia*: The Cult of Heroic Self-Sacrifice and Popular Mobilization in Southern Spain, 1849–1869', *Bulletin of Spanish Studies*, Vol. 94, No. 6 (2017), pp. 927–53.
74 Cacho Viu, *Institución Libre de Enseñanza*, pp. 50–2.
75 Francesc A. Martínez-Gallego, *Conservar progresando: la Unión Liberal, 1856–1868* (Valencia: Centro Francoscio Tomás Valiente, 2001), pp. 14–15.
76 Walther L. Bernecker, *España entre tradición y modernidad: política, economía y sociedad (siglos XIX y XX)* (Madrid: Siglo XXI, 1999), p. 107.
77 Comellas García-Llera, *Los Moderados en el poder*, pp. 76, 118.
78 Sevilla Andrés, *Antonio Maura*, p. 37.
79 López Garrido, *Guardia civil*, pp. 108–13.
80 Brenan, *Spanish Labyrinth*, p. 109.
81 Victor Kiernan, *The Revolution of 1854*, pp. 37–9.
82 Eiras Roel, *El Partido Demócrata*, pp. 186–91.
83 Burdiel, *Isabel II*, pp. 381–95.

84 Kiernan, *Revolution of 1854*, pp. 46–52.
85 Hannay, *Don Emilio Castelar*, pp. 56–60.
86 Inbal Ofer, 'Class, Space and Urban Development: Madrid, 1860–1936', *Cuadernos de Historia Contemporánea*, Vol. 39 (2017), pp. 339–44.
87 Comellas García-Llera, *Los Moderados en el poder*, pp. 350–51; Kiernan, *Revolution of 1854*, p. 84.
88 Kiernan, *Revolution of 1854*, pp. 60–100.
89 Encarna García Monerris and Carmen García Monerris, '¿Interés de familia u objeto político?' in Encarna García Monerris, Mónica Moreno Seco, and Juan I. Marcuello Benedicto (eds.), *Culturas políticas en la España liberal*, pp. 204–8; Eiras Roel, *El Partido demócrata*, pp. 210–12.
90 Kiernan, *Revolution of 1854*, p. 86.
91 Eiras Roel, *El Partido demócrata*, pp. 202–18.
92 Charles Hennessy, *The Federal Republic in Spain: Pi y Margall and the Federal Republican Movement 1868–1874* (Oxford: Oxford University Press, 1962), pp. 7–8.
93 Kiernan, *Revolution of 1854*, pp. 86–100.
94 *Ibid.*, pp. 136, 177.
95 Sánchez-Albornoz, *Crisis de subsistencias*, p. 59.
96 Vicente Cárcel Ortí, 'Un siglo de relaciones diplomáticas entre España y la Santa Sede (1834–1931)', *Anales de História Contemporánea* (febrero 2009), pp. 313–31, 324–5; Cacho Viu, *Institución Libre de Enseñanza*, p. 63.
97 Palacio Atard, *España del siglo XIX*, pp. 477–8.
98 Antonio Caridad Salvador, 'El carlismo aragonés en armas. La revuelta de 1855', *Cuadernos de Historia Contemporánea*, Vol. 36 (2014), pp. 165–88.
99 Kiernan, *Revolution of 1854*, pp. 147–53.
100 *Ibid.*, pp. 160–61.
101 Eiras Roel, *El Partido demócrata*, p. 222.
102 Álvarez del Vayo, *The Last Optimist* (London: Putnam, 1950), p. 179.
103 Callahan, *Church, Politics and Society*, pp. 227–8.
104 Kiernan, *Revolution of 1854*, pp. 170–2, 199–200.
105 Sánchez-Albornoz, *Crisis de subsistencias*, pp. 92–3.
106 Palacio Atard, *España del siglo XIX*, p. 480.
107 Kiernan, *Revolution of 1854*, pp. 224–38.
108 Isabel Burdiel, 'Monarquía y nación en la cultura política progresista', in Encarna García Monerris, Mónica Moreno Seco, and Juan I. Marcuello Benedicto (eds.), *Culturas políticas en la España liberal*, p. 220.
109 Holt, *Carlist Wars*, pp. 220–1.
110 Callahan, *Church, Politics and Society*, pp. 199–208.
111 José María Jover Zamora, *España en la política internacional* (Madrid: Marcial Pons, 1999), p. 136.
112 Stephen Jacobson, 'Imperial Ambitions in an Era of Decline: Micromilitarism and the Eclipse of the Spanish Empire, 1858–1923', in Alfred W. McCoy, Josep M. Fradera, and Stephen Jacobson (eds.), *Endless Empire: Spain's retreat, Europe's eclipse, America's decline* (Madison, WI: University of Wisconsin Press, 2012), p. 75.
113 Stephen Jacobson, 'Empire and Colonies', in Shubert and Álvarez-Junco (eds.), *History of Modern Spain*, p. 195.
114 Andrew Ginger, 'How to Be Universal', in Ginger and Lawless (eds.), *Spain in the Nineteenth Century*, p. 54.
115 Geraldine Lawless, 'How to Tell Time', in Ginger and Lawless (eds.), *Spain in the Nineteenth Century*, p. 71.
116 Christopher Schmidt-Nowara, *The Conquest of History* (Pittsburgh: Uinversity of Pittsburgh Press, 2006), pp. 55–6.

117   Schmidt-Nowara, 'La España ultramarina: Colonialism and Nation-Building in Nineteenth-century Spain', *European History Quarterly*, Vol. 33, No. 191 (2004), pp. 204–5.
118   Schmidt-Nowara, *The Conquest of History*, p. 55.
119   Jacobson, 'Imperial Ambitions in an Era of Decline', in McCoy, Fradera, and Jacobson (eds.), *Endless Empire*, pp. 77–8.
120   Josep M. Fradera, 'Empires in Retreat: Spain and Portugal After the Napoleonic Wars', in McCoy, Fradera, and Jacobson (eds.), *Endless Empire*, p. 66.
121   Vicent Sanz Rozalén, 'Francisco Arrango y Parreño', in Shubert and Álvarez-Junco (eds.), *The History of Modern Spain*, pp. 381–5.
122   Geoffrey Jensen, 'The Spanish Army at War in the Nineteenth century', in Wayne Bowen and José E Alvarez (eds.), *A Military History of Modern Spain* (Westport: Praeger, 2007), pp. 27–9; Adolfo Campoy-Cubillo, *Memories of the Maghreb: Transnational Identities in Spanish Cultural Production* (New York: Palgrave Macmillan, 2012), pp. 1–3.
123   *La Gaceta de Madrid*, n. 39, 8 February 1860, p. 1.
124   Álvarez-Junco, *Spanish Identity in the Age of Nations*, pp. 339–40.
125   Begoña Regueiro Salgado, 'Una nueva forma de orientalismo romántico: presencia y valores de lo oriental en la obra de Gustavo Adolfo Bécquer', *Bulletin of Spanish Studies*, Vol. 90, No. 2 (2013), pp. 177–94, 186–8.
126   Blanco, 'España en la encrucijada: ¿Nostalgia imperial o colonialismo moderno?' in Blanco and Thomson (eds.), *Visiones del liberalismo*, p. 224.
127   Wayne H. Bowen, *Spain and the American Civil War* (Columbia: University of Missouri Press, 2011), pp. 1–20.
128   Emilio C. Conde Fernández-Oliva, 'Sobre el pensamiento en relación a las fuerzas armadas de Cánovas del Castillo', in Alfonso Bullón de Mendoza and Luis E. Togores (eds.), *Cánovas y su época*, 2 vols., Vol. I (Madrid: Siglo XXI, 1999), p. 143.
129   Juan Antonio Inarejos Muñoz, *Intervenciones coloniales y nacionalismo español* (Madrid: Sílex, 2010), pp. 45–6, 99–134.
130   Josep M. Fradera, 'La importancia de tenir colonias', in *Catalunya i ultramar: poder i negoci a les colònies espanyoles* (Barcelona: Ambit Serveis, 1995), pp. 22–52.
131   Jensen, 'War and the Military', in Shubert and Álvarez-Junco (eds.), *The History of Modern Spain*, p. 336.
132   Fernando García Sánchez, *Las campañas militares del general Prim en el exterior (1853–1862)* (Granada: Universidad de Granada, 2018), p. 72.
133   José R. Milán, *Sagasta, o el arte de hacer política* (Madrid: Biblioteca Nueva, 2001), pp. 96–7.
134   Callahan, *Church, Politics and Society*, pp. 199–208.
135   Hennessy, *The Federal Republic in Spain*, p. 36.
136   Eiras Roel, *El Partido Demócrata*, p. 235.
137   Guy Thomson, 'Garibaldi and the Legacy of the Revolutions of 1848 in Southern Spain', *European History Quarterly*, Vol. 31, No. 3 (2001), p. 363.
138   Thomson, *Birth of Modern Politics*, pp. 75–6.
139   Eiras Roel, *El Partido demócrata*, pp. 242–3.
140   *Ibid.*, pp. 263–7.
141   Thomson, 'Garibaldi and the Legacy', pp. 375–9; Callahan, *Church, Politics and Society*, p. 239.
142   Eiras Roel, *El Partido demócrata*, pp. 237–9, 270–4.
143   Juan José Gil Cremades, *Krausistas y liberales* (Madrid: Seminarios y Ediciones, 1975), p. 62; Thomson, *Birth of Modern Politics*, pp. 295–8.
144   Thomson, *Birth of Modern Politics*, pp. 203–5, 212.
145   Peyrou, 'Great Family of Sovereign Men', pp. 235–56, 243.
146   Gil Cremades, *Krausistas y liberales*, p. 69.
147   Carlos Dardé, 'Biografía política de Nicolás Salmerón (c. 1860–1890)', in José A. Piqueras and Manuel Chust (eds.), *Republicanos y repúblicas en España* (Madrid: Siglo XXI, 1997), pp. 136–9.

148 Cacho Viu, *Institución Libre de Enseñanza*, pp. 142–4.
149 Comellas García-Llera, *Los Moderados en el poder*, p. 86; Thomson, *Birth of Modern Politics*.
150 Jaime Vicens Vives, *Historia de España y América*, Vol. 5 (Madrid: Editorial Vicens Vives, 1971), p. 214.
151 Antonio Eiras Roel (ed.), *La emigración española a ultramar, 1492–1914* (Madrid: Tabapress, 1991), p. 18.
152 Juan Bautista Vilar, *El despegue de la revolución industrial en España, 1827–1869* (Madrid: Istmo., 1990), pp. 192–200.
153 Jensen, 'War and the Military', in Shubert and Álvarez-Junco (eds.), *The History of Modern Spain*, pp. 335–6.
154 Sánchez-Albornoz, *Crisis de subsistencias*, p. 34.
155 Trías and Elorza, *Federalismo y Reforma*, pp. 299–327, citing (p. 324) *La Asociación*, 13 May 1866.
156 Eiras Roel, *El Partido demócrata*, pp. 288–9.
157 *Ibid.*, pp. 308–11.
158 Bernecker, *España entre tradición y modernidad*, pp. 126–8.
159 Cepeda Gómez, *Los pronunciamientos en la España del siglo XIX*, p. 82.
160 Moreno Alonso, *Blanco White*, p. 501; Artola-Gallego, *Burguesía revolucionaria*, pp. 209–11.
161 Burdiel María Sierra, 'The Time of Liberalism, 1833–1874', in Shubert and Alvarez-Junco (eds.), *The History of Modern Spain*, pp. 34–5.
162 Gregorio de la Fuente Monge, *Los revolucionarios de 1868* (Madrid: Marcial Pons, 2000), p. 23.
163 José Luis Comellas, 'Narváez', in Francesc Martínez Gallego Comellas, Trinidad Ortuzar, Angee Ramón Poveda, and Germán Rueda (eds.), *Los generales de Isabel II* (Madrid: Ediciones 19, 2016), pp. 126–7; Josep Fontana, 'La época del liberalismo: volume 6', in Josep Fontana and Ramón Villares (eds.), *Historia general de España* (Barcelona: Crítica, 2007), pp. 315–50.

Chapter 5

1868–76: republicanism, Carlism, cantonalism, and Cuba

This chapter explains how the collapse of the Isabelline system in the revolution of 1868 led to a brief but diverse experimentation in politics, society, and culture known as the 'Revolutionary Sexennium' (1868–74). Over eight years, the Spanish government changed its forms from constitutional monarchy to federal republican to unitary republican and then to conservative monarchy, all under the strains of three wars against Carlists, cantonalists, and Cuban autonomists, as well as an intensely felt new international order. The Second Carlist War is explained in terms of its 'modern' politics and its traditional military and cultural appeal (morale, terrain, religiosity, and regional claim), especially in the northern Carlist heartlands. Republicanism will be analysed in terms of its doctrines (especially Pi y Margall) as well as its expressions of sectarianism, internationalism, and anti-militarism. The chapter also explains the growth in the intellectual current known as *krausismo* and of the new radical politics of anarchism.

Isabelline liberalism came to an end in the 'Glorious Revolution' of 1868, which opened up six years of disintegration and reintegration amidst cantonalist revolts, another Carlist War, and the reassertion of the army's role in political life from 1874, now as the spearhead of counter-revolution and adopting an insular, corporate ideology. The post-war Canovine Restoration of 1876 would entrench the socio-economic power of the large landowners (*latifundistas*), bestowing Spain with a dangerous and long-term social crisis. Carlists were quick to see the advent in 1869 of religious freedom in apocalyptic terms, and the international context of the Paris Commune increased their alarm.[1] Such long-lasting Carlist traditions as the humanitarian 'margaritas' (named after the Pretender's wife, Doña Margarita) were begun in the 1870s' war, as was the precedent of international Red Cross intervention. The regional republican risings known as cantonalism were the radical response, conditioned by conscription, morale, livelihoods, and war aims.

The Pact of Ostend of August 1866 united Democrats and Progresistas in their determination to remove Isabel II, and the exiles were joined by Liberal Unionists driven by Narváez's repressive policies into the revolutionary fold. Once the revolutionaries were ready to act in September 1868, their efforts witnessed a series of risings hatched from within and without which culminated on 17 September with the meeting off the coast of Cádiz of General Prim, recently arrived from exile in London, and Admiral Topete's fleet. The navy had recently become alienated by budget cuts during the 1867–68 economic crisis, and the floating *pronunciamiento* was an innovation in Spanish history. That said, the army remained key. The leader of the conspiracy and effective leader was the *progresista* Juan Prim y Prats (1814–70). Prim was a rare example of a Catalan career officer, and he had fought against Carlists in the 1830s and had thereafter lived a life of intrigue and exile that typified military politics in the Romantic era. Prim's revolutionary triumph was called 'Gloriosa', in conscious copying of Britain's 'Glorious' Revolution of 1688. But artistic licence revealed relatively little glory. Galdós's novel, *España sin rey*, was scathing of the revolutionaries' motivations: 'Sick of receiving honours from Isabel II, they rudely dethroned her, before begging for a king from foreign nations'.[2] The pragmatic struggles to implant the regime and then to defend it would likewise reveal much chaos, but very little glory.

Topete issued a manifesto blending *progresista* and Democrat ideals which *gaditanos* at first received coolly. Yet the rising two days later of a Cantabria regiment in the city, supported by a new militia called the 'Volunteers for Liberty', composed of paid agricultural labourers from nearby Jérez, swung the cradle of liberalism decisively behind the revolution. The year 1868 was another bad harvest year, and many unemployed across Spain leapt at the offer of a wage to join the Volunteers. Four republicans in Cádiz who led the Volunteers were hastily rewarded with seats on the city's revolutionary junta. Elsewhere fortunes were mixed. Nicolás Rivero's hasty attempt to preempt other risings failed at Zaragoza on 18 September, whereas the rising at Santander not only succeeded but also produced a republican junta which anguished nearby army units suppressed a week later. In other places, little-known and opportunistic elements took advantage of the confusion. Revolution in the capital freed from prison Brigadier Escalante, who immediately set up a junta with cronies which created enough attention for Escalante to form a joint presidency of Nicolás Rivero's Madrid junta. The defeat of the final army units loyal to Isabella at Alcolea on 28 September 1868 sealed the success of the revolution and opened up what would be six years of radical political experimentation.[3]

The revolutionary leaders' moderation was matched by the local elites in the juntas who, far from being 'bourgeois revolutionaries' as studies used to claim, were generally indistinguishable from the moderate and professional middle classes of the Isabelline era: lawyers, professors, and journalists. Popular participation was generally scarce and usually lacked autonomy.[4] The historian and Democrat Fernando Garrido wrote that mainstream liberals gave the revolution its leaders but republicans its ideas, principles, and doctrines.[5] Emilio Castelar thought that the 1868 revolution triumphed on two forces: military and ideas.[6] On 30 September 1868, Madrid's revolutionary junta proclaimed universal male suffrage for men from the age of 25. But majority illiterate voters were vulnerable when casting ballots, the result being that established elites were elected, even if they were also popular (such as the monarchical Democrat Manuel Bravo, who, in 1865, had led a welfare initiative for victims of Madrid's cholera outbreak). Turnout was generally lower in poorer neighbourhoods, owing both to illiteracy and to the notorious precarity of residential lettings in poor areas of a city where more than 90 per cent of the population rented their homes. Usually, elites recognised the need to do something to ameliorate the economic crisis of the past two years, and in the case of Madrid, the new authorities unleashed public spending to restart infrastructure projects suspended since 1866 (usually demolishing old convents), five thousand labourers being hired on 9 October 1868.[7]

The swift and enthusiastic response to Prim's landing at Cádiz from armed volunteers – Voluntarios de la Libertad – organised by the Democrat Party in cities and towns throughout Andalucía, convinced the Progresista and Liberal Unionist leaders of the revolution to embrace key parts the Democrat programme: universal suffrage, freedom of conscience, and the abolition of *consumos* and *quintas*. However, although the new constitution in June 1869 extended suffrage to include males over the age of 25 and guaranteed freedom of religious belief and practice, attempts to abolish *consumos* and to replace the *quintas* with voluntary recruitment were shelved in the face of the financial and personnel demands of the Cuban insurrection. Democrats, their party now renamed the Partido Republicano Democrático Federal, were also dismayed by the new constitution's declaration that Spain's form of government should be a constitutional monarchy. Fearing electoral extinction, sixty thousand Federal Republicans launched an unsuccessful armed rebellion in October 1868. For the moment the leader of the provisional government, General Prim, was safe. He soon betrayed his promise to abolish the unpopular '*quinta*' system of military recruitment (which fell on the poor) which was the cornerstone of Democrat Party radicalism. After the election was safely won, Prim issued a demand for twenty-five thousand men to help suppress the Cuban autonomy revolt raging since 1868. Other backtracking was evident in Prim's refusal to lower the new universal suffrage age younger than 25 years of age, thereby excluding from active citizenship those young men who were most affected by the hated '*quinta*'.[8]

General Prim, a humble-born careerist whose decades of experience in foreign wars and Catalan and national politics had made him the object of admiration and suspicion alike, was finally hoisted by his own petard. On 27 December 1870, the same day that Amadeo I set sail from Italy to Cartagena, Prim was mortally wounded by gunshots fired at his coach travelling in Madrid's Calle del Turco. His assassination was probably instigated by the federal-republican newspaper editor Paul y Angulo, who had felt slighted by Prim ever since 1868 and who promptly fled overseas after the shots were fired.[9] The Catalanist Victor Balaguer, who had accompanied Amadeo on his voyage, wrote in his diary of the 'immense responsibility' facing the new king being taken to 'an unknown country, agitated by the tempest of political passions . . . what great sadness, what eternal regret, if political tempests, evil passions, or our own madness prevent us from realising the end aim of our efforts!'[10] One of the first official acts of the new king was to visit the body of his biggest supporter. Prim was considered to be a large part of the 'soul' of the Spanish Revolutionary government, and his death was a shock to the newly elected king.[11]

The world of ideas

The international aspect of Spain's 1868–74 upheaval impressed contemporaries in Spain and abroad, creating a freer atmosphere for radical political ideas. The Cuban-born lawyer Rafael María de Labra graced world and Spanish intellectual circles promoting his ideas to abolish slavery. A prolific author, Labra centred his prolific career on three main objectives: the abolition of slavery, individual rights, and colonial autonomy.[12] Throughout his career, Labra constantly strove for a closer, better-functioning relationship between the Spain and *las colonias ultramarinas*. He argued that there was a 'great intimacy' between Spain and the Antilles but that his contemporaries sought only to exploit rather than develop into an equal relationship.[13] Labra criticised Spain's hitherto tight grip on its colonies as 'restrictive' and 'absurd', and his testimony influenced Sexennium governments' policy to increase autonomy for Cuba.[14] Labra published numerous arguments in favour of the phased abolition of slavery in the Spanish Empire as a way of balancing the demands of common humanity whilst also safeguarding the essential 'Spanishness' of Cuba. The integrity of the Spanish nation, exalted in 1868, was directly tied to the abolition of slavery, even though it was impractical to have an abrupt end to slavery.[15] 'Disasters' that had happened elsewhere in the Caribbean would be averted by gradual abolition.[16] Labra's campaigning bore fruit. The Spanish Abolitionist Society, which had been founded in 1865 demanding the immediate emancipation of four hundred thousand slaves in Cuba and Puerto Rico, agitated in the freedom of the Sexennium and won official support from leading politicians. Anti-slavery figures like Pi y Margall, Nicolás Salmerón, and Manuel Becerra, all leading lights of the left, pressed for abolition as part of a wider process of colonial reform, which mostly took effect during the Democratic Sexennium.[17]

Writing thirty years later, the Krausist intellectual Giner de los Ríos recalled 1870 as an international revolution in which Spain, for once, was not on the margins: 'a heroic enterprise to live through the deepest and most radical transition that Europe has contemplated hitherto'.[18] From 1870, Krausists welcomed American Protestant missionaries who attempted to offer progressive education to women.[19] At the other political extreme, the young Emilia Pardo Bazán (1851–1921) was inspired to tour France and Italy, where she formulated her conservative worldview and even dabbled in Carlism. Emilia would later become Spain's first self-declared feminist and (unlike Countess Espoz y Mina) an unabashed celebrity comfortable in the 'masculine' public sphere.[20] The intensely felt new international order of the early 1870s was one to which the Spanish revolution of 1868 significantly contributed. The revolt in Spanish Cuba, the appeal of the Paris Commune to Spanish revolutionaries and of the 1871 French counter-revolution to the Spanish government side, as well as the mutual appeal between militant Spanish Carlism and international legitimist movements, all testified to this new climate. The new anarchist doctrine of Bakunin found greater headway in Spain than almost anywhere else, soon rivalling Pi y Margall's federalism to the extent that later anarchists claimed the Catalan intellectual as one of their own.

It was also an era in which a homespun blend of republicanism and anarchism made a serious impact. Francisco Pi y Margall was already well known in political circles. Like Prim and Espartero, Pi was an outsider to the boisterous world of liberal politics and its Castillian and Andalucían generals with noble titles. Pi was a literary journalist from a working-class background and a Catalan to boot.[21] He was also remarkably consistent and unbribable in his political principles to a degree remarkable in a Spanish politician. One contemporary compared Pi to a chef who insisted on persuading oysters to open their own shells rather than forcing them open with a knife.[22] Certainly Pi's gradualism was much more threatening to the establishment than the bombastic superficiality of his rival, Castelar. Pi's radicalism was premised on the sovereignty of the individual, which would be reconciled with the state via a contract doctrine of pacts amongst cities, provinces, and central government. Pactist theory was, in many ways, inspired by Joseph Proudhon's anarchism, which Pi had read avidly. This radicalism, Pi hoped, would overcome Spain's traditional problems of the political spoils system and political backwardness.[23] Pi's radicalism lay in his understanding of the Spanish nation as the product of the will of the people. His subjective understanding contrasted with the orthodox radicalism of Castelar and *progresista* converts to republicanism who understood the Spanish nation as an object to be constructed by an expanding state unable and unwilling to rely solely on the will of the people.[24]

Pi's exile in France had been quieter than most and he took months to re-enter Spain after the 1868 revolution. Nonetheless, his persistent and increasingly prestigious theory of pactist republicanism (often shortened to 'abajo-arriba', or 'from below upwards') was enough to win over such fair-weather ideologues as Castelar. Republicanism was boosted by the lack of an obvious king to replace Isabella and by radical subcultures which had flourished especially in the south since the 1850s. Thus, while monarchical Democrats in Madrid throughout 1869 failed to agree on a replacement monarch, with Fernando of Portugal, Olózaga's favoured 'pan-Iberian' candidate apparently in the lead, provincial radicals made their own plans.

Long-standing radical networks meant that provincial republicanism in such port cities as Málaga was more strident and millenarian than the 'respectable' republicanism of Madrid, hence the reluctance of the Democrat Party to back state intervention lest it be accused of 'socialism'. This stance persisted despite the disastrous 1866–68 harvest and cholera outbreaks and associated general economic crisis. The risk of alienating potential middle-class support for the Democrat Party seemed too great to pander to 'socialism'.

The world of politics

The 1868 revolution opened up a fast-evolving spectrum of political parties. It soon became evident that a democratic Spain was no more easily governed than Bourbon Spain. A sequence of political initiatives saw the country shift from a provisional government under Juan Prim and Francisco Serrano (1868–71) to an elected monarch chosen from the house of Savoy (1871–73) to the First Republic, following Amadeo's abdication in February 1873, to the restoration of the Bourbons following General Arsenio Martínez Campos's *pronunciamiento* at Sagunto of December 1874. Politics during this period involved the participation of four principal political blocs: Liberal Unionists under General Serrano; Progresistas led at first by General Prim and after his assassination in December 1870 by Práxedes Mateo Sagasta and Manuel Ruiz Zorrilla; Monarchical Democrats, known as '*cimbrios*', led by Cristino Martos and Nicolás María Rivero (Democrat deputy for Seville since 1858); and Federal Republicans led by Estanislao Figueras, Francisco Pi y Margall, Nicolás Salmerón, and Emilio Castelar. Beyond these blocs, other political groups emerged, or re-emerged: in October 1868, the First International arrived in Spain, with the Neapolitan Giuseppi Fanelli drawing working-class support away from the Democrats; with the arrival of Amadeo in 1872, Carlists launched their third and final campaign; the old Moderado Party, defeated in September 1868, regrouped around a younger generation of conservative liberal '*alfonsinos*' led by Antonio Cánovas del Castillo.

Meanwhile, the traditional legitimist Right was energised by the freer political environment following the 1868 revolution. Carlism, as we have seen, was in some ways the rural equivalent of urban federalism in its desire for local devolution. But the Carlists had Catholicism as their unifying factor whereas Pi y Margall had his ideal of philosophy and science as unifying forces in this 'age of doubt'.[25] In 1869, Pi anticipated President Azaña a half-century later when he said 'Catholicism has perished in the consciousness of humanity and in the consciousness of the Spanish people'.[26] His 1854 manifesto, which demanded a constitution to 'respect the consent of each sovereign individual', was widely read.[27] The Spanish Federalists were increasingly moulded by Pi's ideas, especially by his idea of international republicanism. The attractions of this were obvious: international solidarity might be compensation for internal weakness.[28] But despite Pi's appreciation of Proudhon's anarchism and other international currents, his federalism was mainly Spanish in emphasis. Pi thought that if the state should have any role, it should be to offer cheap credit. The *progresista* disentailment laws, Pi thought, should not be the last word on land reform. His colleague and devotee of cooperativism, Fernando Garrido, estimated that fewer than half the lands auctioned since 1855 had been sold to modest middle classes and almost none to the poor.[29] Thus, Pi argued, the Democrat panacea of universal suffrage would mean nothing in the current backward political environment of Spain as it would merely expand the powers of the *caciques*. So Pi proposed wider peasant landowner-ship as a first step, helped by cooperatives and then universal suffrage. These steps would translate into real democracy.[30]

The revolution sharpened the formulation and argumentation of federal-republican ideology in a context which set Pi against Castelar. Whereas Pi was rational, Castelar was bombastic and emotional, distinguished by an exceptional verbosity that was exceptional even by Spanish standards. The emotional propaganda of the federalists was more characteristic, which pre-vented it from engaging the masses and from accepting that class struggle had become the most important issue for the left. Instead, most federalists remained wedded to the now-outdated notion of 'spontaneous revolution' sustained by popular enthusiasm, even though this model had failed in 1848. Hence, Castelar and other leaders were annoyed when the illiterate masses followed the new and rapidly growing creed of Bakuninist anarchism brought to Spain in 1869. Historians during the first half of the twentieth century tended to view Spanish anarchism in millenarian terms, as a form of secu-lar faith popular in areas of southern Spain desacralised by liberal disentail-ment policies and then abandoned by Catholic missionaries.[31] Even leading Cold War Marxist historians deemed anarchism a 'primitive' expression of an inchoate political consciousness.[32] Yet from the 1970s, more sophisticated social histories of Spanish anarchism emerged, partly as a consequence of the era's affinity for libertarianism and social history. This research explained anarchism as a logical rather than millenarian response to an oppressive Spanish state. Much of this new focus contrasted the ideas and practices of anarchism, including its bifurcated geography. It contrasted anarchist propa-ganda 'by word' (diffusion) with propaganda 'by deed' (terrorism); libertarian anarchism in non-industrial Andalucía, with growing anarcho-syndicalism in industrial Catalonia; and the theory of libertarian philosophy with the reality of entrenched gender and cultural relations.[33]

Spain certainly acquired an early and enduring reputation for Anarchism, with the result that the 'International' continued to be synonymous with Anarchism even after the 1889 Second International expelled the libertar-ian Marxists. The rapid diffusion of anarchism in Spain after Fanelli's 1869 mission alarmed the Cortes. In October 1871, with tempers still frayed in the wake of the suppression of the Paris Commune, Cortes moderates and conservatives outvoted the Democrats and Republicans in declaring the

International 'unconstitutional', setting the course for decades of state criminalisation of anarchism.[34]

Most republicans showed little desire to advance the politically revolutionary process opened in 1868 in radical social directions, and they showed little tolerance for the unwelcome invasion of the International. Castelar, like most federalists and Democrats, clung to the stubborn, elitist belief in class harmony (e.g. most federalists disapproved of strike action), whilst they continued to reproduce the abuses of the political spoils system and time-serving of other parties. On repeated occasions, ambitious federalist journalists exploited the new guarantees of free speech in order to get noticed and promoted. An angry young editor of a radical newspaper was transformed overnight into a moderate when he was promoted to become the civil governor of Cáceres. Serious and complex issues like the Cuban revolt were distorted by this politicking. As the contemporary Mesonero Romanos observed, revolution was always a godsend to men trapped between youth and maturity, retired officers, journalists without an audience, doctors without patients, lawyers without cases, and, above all, 'cesantes' of the previous regime.[35] *Gloriosa* politicians with more abstract plans tended to be neutered by European and Spanish opposition. The pro–Iberian Union sympathies of many of the revolutionary leaders, including of Prim but especially of the Krausists, had to be retracted due to negligible Portuguese support and of British and French refusal to countenance such a move. Meanwhile, most of the federalist party stubbornly rejected Pi's emphasis on propaganda to reach the masses by instead meeting and conspiring in secret clubs. This merely reproduced an elitist mode of politics in the dawning age of the masses.[36]

In 1869 there were a series of failed federalist risings and divisions between 'unitarian' and 'pactist' factions. The risings were particularly marked in Andalucía, owing to the stagnation in the rural economy along with the decline of Málaga's uncompetitive iron and steel industry.[37] Castelar had increasingly to cede to Pi, still seen as the 'right' of the federal party, because of his insistence on legal opposition and propaganda rather than on armed revolt. Meanwhile, the *caudillo* of the revolution, General Prim, wanted to keep as many lines of action open as possible and did not want the federalists to retreat into *retraimiento* (which would have been even more dangerous). Práxedes Sagasta, by contrast, wanted to confront the federalists. The Unitarian federalist newspaper *El Pueblo* vigorously attacked Pi's pactism as much as it did the monarchists. Nevertheless, during the first half of 1870, Pi reorganised the Federalist Party, and by the end of May 1870, he was accepted as its official leader.[38]

Yet while republicans debated the monarchists had already got their way. As a consequence of republican disunity during 1869 the form of regime which divided Spaniards the least turned out to be a constitutional monarchy. The 1869 constitution, Nicolás Rivero's brainchild, established a monarchy with fewer powers of royal prerogative than in the 1812–1837 charters, and the stage was set for the regent, General Serrano, and the real power broker in Spain, General Prim, to search the courts of Europe for a suitable king. This was no easy task. The peculiar Spanish feuds of royalism, especially Duke Montpensier's killing in a duel of the exiled queen's cousin, Enrique de Borbón, witnessed a revival in Carlism. Moreover, the Spanish question became a European one as Prussian Chancellor Bismarck manipulated a French rejection of his disingenuous Hohenzollern candidate for the Spanish throne into the *casus belli* for the Franco-Prussian War (1870–71).[39]

Amidst the Franco-Prussian contest simmering in 1870, Pi's leadership was challenged from the right of the Federalist Party, the Unitarian faction, which tried to persuade the leadership to be opportunistic rather than doctrinaire. The Krausist Unitarian intellectual Revilla claimed that Pi's pactist theory of independent cities, regions, and central government consenting to cooperate and respect each other's respective competencies, was the only stumbling block preventing unity between Federalists and Unitarians, and a coordinated press declaration on 7 May 1870 challenged Pi to this end. Krausist intellectuals rejected the revolutionaries' politics of compromise (*pactismo*) because it contradicted their conception of the state as solely the legal interpretation of a free Spanish society, with all its regional, cultural, and linguistic nuances.[40] In particular, the Krausists wanted to integrate the workers (whom they called the 'fourth estate') into a free Spanish society in order to harmonise conflicting interests.[41] Pi, who was Hegelian in his world view, found the Krausists too abstract and faced down their criticism, and the key federalist newspaper, *La Igualdad*, announced its adhesion to Pi's governing Directory. Pi was still attacked for not showing the 'flexibility' (which was code for opportunism) that was characteristic of Spanish politicians and even of promoting his native Catalan interests at the expense of the rest of Spain. This last charge was not credible as Pi was actually out of touch with the mainstream feeling of Catalan republicans, and his theory of pactism would have meant equality for all Spanish regions, not just Catalonia. The Federalists also had to fight to gain working-class support after the competing Socialist International convened in Barcelona. Spain's foreign policy, meanwhile, continued to be dominated by Cuba and the question of a dynastic replacement for Isabella II. On 26 June 1870, in Paris, Isabella formally abdicated her throne. The Unionists wanted Montpensier as her replacement; the pro-Iberian Union Prim wanted Fernando of Portugal. Ominously for Franco-Prussian relations, Leopold of Hohenzollern was also a candidate. This candidacy was the trigger for the Franco-Prussian War and Napoleon III's defeat which led to the French Republic. The proclamation of a republic in France immediately won the Spanish Federalists support and even the promise to Gambetta of a Spanish legion to fight the Prussians.

In the event, Amadeo of Savoy accepted the offer of the Spanish throne on 30 October 1870, after the Cortes had narrowly voted for him. Now Pi faced challenged from the left. Before the Cortes vote on Amadeo, the Directory had called for peace and order; after Amadeo's acceptance, it did not budge in these instructions, which unsurprisingly led to demands from leftist federalists for more radical action. They found a leader in Paul y Angulo, who launched a newspaper called *El Combate* which argued for armed revolution. The revolutionary mood grew in Catalonia where Federalists and Carlists – opposing sides of the political spectrum – even planned a joint rising. But Pi's leadership was saved by the assassination of Prim at the end of December 1870. Paul y Angulo's *El Combate* closed on the day of Prim's shooting, and its editor mysteriously vanished. Prim's Progresista-Democrat coalition was now leaderless. The right (*progresistas*) looked to Sagasta whereas the left (Democrats) looked to Ruiz Zorrilla as their respective leaders. Ruiz Zorrilla wanted to advance the revolution of 1868 in new reformist directions whereas Sagasta merely wanted to preserve it. Meanwhile, the Directory knew that a Federal rising would draw these two forces together to crush it.[42] The assassination of Prim was significant because he was the last of a triarchy of liberal army leaders whose very person seemed to symbolise the hopes of the masses, hopes which logically were dashed as no single man could solve Spain's contradictions.[43] The previous symbols, Riego and Espartero, after all, had been executed and withered by age and exile respectively.

Amadeo's throne was a formally democratic monarchy, but he was a lonely king. His plain tastes and respect for democracy were misread by Spaniards as simple-mindedness, and the Democrat leader Castelar was convinced that no Spaniard could ever feel satisfied with a foreigner as king.[44] Rejected by the Alphonsists, Carlists, and Republicans, he was forced to rely on the slender majority of Cortes deputies who had voted for him: even most Spanish grandees refused to attend his court. Thus, for Amadeo to work as a constitutional monarch, he would need unity from the Progresista and Democrat deputies who voted for him, but this was not forthcoming. Amadeo's short reign was punctuated by as many as seven governments, led directly or indirectly by the men of the moment, Serrano, Sagasta or Ruiz Zorrilla. Whereas Sagasta was instinctively conservative and would have welcomed a politically stabilising role for the king, Ruiz Zorrilla wanted 'as little king as possible'. Meanwhile, Serrano was inflated in his ego for having been Regent and kept a stranglehold on army loyalty amongst the older officers. Serrano also bore a constant chip on his soldier for being snubbed by the Alfonsine aristocracy which never forgave him his ungallant betrayal of the queen he had once loved. Thus, Amadeo could only have reigned effectively if he were to do so anti-constitutionally or get the support of the opposition parties. The Alphonsists championed Isabella's son, Prince Alfonso, and had their support in the wealth of the high aristocracy and had time on their side. They were led by Antonio Cánovas del Castillo, who throughout the Sexennium had held back from conspiring with the army, focusing instead on growing political support amongst the propertied classes.[45] Amadeo had no chance with the Carlists and Federalists, who both used xenophobia to portray their opposition. For the Carlists, Amadeo was a member of an anti-papal Masonic House of Savoy, and for the Federalists, he was an 'English puppet'. Amadeo's monarchy provoked Old Carlist demands for a rising, even though the Carlist leader, Nocedal, was still committed to playing parliamentary politics, believing that civil war was out of date.

Pi, like Nocedal, was under increasing pressure to abandon legal opposition for violence. But Federalists were disappointed at the lack of international solidarity which was being exposed precisely as a myth. The ageing Democrat revolutionary, Giuseppe Mazzini, condemned not only the Paris Commune but also federalism and socialism as well. Thus, the tactics of the Federalists split into 'benevolent' and 'intransigent' camps, the former backed by Pi and open to backing Ruiz Zorrilla's ministry as long as Zorrilla was prepared to expel the rightist progresista members. The intransigents, by contrast, rejected any sort of understanding with the monarchical parties. These were the characteristic adventurers, place-seekers and opportunists who saw social discontent only as a means to power rather than an end to be solved in itself. The intransigents clung to the outdated belief in 'spontaneous revolution' and saw federalism only as an excuse for adventure and conspiracy or as a means of widening government patronage. Both Federalist factions, meanwhile, were challenged by the Socialist International, which, in 1871, pointedly refused to send observers to the Directory's deliberations claiming that whereas the republicans only want to ameliorate the lot of the workers, the International wanted to overthrow the existing social structure. Marx's son-in-law, Lafargue, a refugee from the Commune, was depressed by Pi's probably accurate judgement that the Spanish workers were uninterested in political action.

But there were also more customary revolutionaries in the army who found that federal republicanism could be just as effective a promoter of rank and salary as the dynastic parties of old. On 12 October 1872, the garrison and naval arsenal at El Ferrol (Galicia) rose in the name of the 'Federal Republic'. Another round of conscription added to radical feeling. The British consul in Barcelona reported 'the perfect insubordination of the troops who refuse to obey, or even salute, their officers'.[46] Federalist risings were now unstoppable, including a particularly serious one in Madrid on 11 December 1872. The Ruiz Zorrilla ministry was exposed as a sham and Amadeo, a king manipulated by politicians, deprived of a serious party. Distraught by a failed attempt on his life and an artillerymen's rising in Galicia led by a disgruntled survivor of the 1866 San Gil rising, Amadeo abdicated his throne on 11 February 1873. Zorrilla's rivals, Martos and Rivero, had their revenge, but this merely hastened the demise of the Radical Party. The Federalists were now the heirs to Amadeo's despair, and the Radicals disappeared from front-line politics.[47] Federal Republicans were divided between moderate centralists such as Emilio Castelar and Nicolás Salmerón, top-down federalists under Pi y Margall and Estanislao Figueras, and bottom-up federalists such as Nicolás Estévanez, Roque Barcia, Manuel Fernández Herrero, Juan Contreras, and Blas Pierrard.

Despite the radicalism of popular politics, the proclamation of the republic in February 1873 was formally the only peaceful transfer of power between 1814 and 1875, albeit in the context of a complete legal vacuum (not least in violating the monarchism of the 1869 Constitution). The republic was proclaimed amidst widespread festivities. In Málaga, revolutionaries seized control of the hated customs house and made a huge bonfire of tariff invoices.[48] The Federal-Republican Party, which found itself with a commanding majority in the Cortes of May 1873 due to the abstention of most other parties, began the debate on a new constitution. It passed autonomy legislation for Cuba, in the teeth of bitter opposition from Cánovas's *alfonsinos*, as well as legislation proscribing child labour, slavery, and more legislation separating church and state, formulating a constitution, restoring government finances and army discipline.[49] Impatient with the centralising direction of debate, Intransigentes launched the Cantonalist (or federalist) rebellion in July 1873, bringing down the government of Pi, who had replaced Estanisalo Figueras becoming Spain's second-ever president a month before. Castelar assumed the presidency and suspended the Cortes in August. Amidst the growing Carlist revolt in the north and the federalist revolt in the south, Castelar toured the country offering propaganda speeches about the benefits of political equality whilst also planning strategies to defeat the more radical form of democracy, the cantonalist revolt.[50] Castelar's oratory faced an uphill task. Catalonia was gripped by armed Carlism as assuredly as the dark days of 1836. Matters were not helped by Marshal MacMahon's virtual pro-Carlist policy concerning France's border with Spain. The federalists were disappointed at the limited support they secured from the brief Paris Commune. It was the Carlists, rather than the Federalists, who benefitted from French support in the wake of the French defeat to Prussia and brutal repression of the Commune in May 1871. President Thiers feared revolution and turned a blind eye to Carlists hatching conspiracies and sourcing arms in southern France.

Carlists, Cantonalists, and Cubans

The republic had no honeymoon, having to face as many as three wars during its tenure. The hitherto furtive Carlist revolt in the north turned into a full-fledged rising. The same regions were restive as they had been during the 1830s war, and the motives for support for the insurgency remained similar, albeit conditioned by forty years of uneven economic development. One difference was the cultural impetus offered by revolution to a declining Carlist movement. Whereas in 1833 only the dynastic issue ignited revolt, the collapse of the monarchy in 1868, liberal Constitution of 1869, and ultimately the republic of 1873, offered greater provocations. Ruiz Zorrilla's requirement for public office holders to swear allegiance to the 1869 constitution provoked a cultural war as teachers in rural Catalonia had to choose either to bow to Carlist pressure to quit or face reprisals.[51] A failed Carlist rising in 1872 signalled the end of Nocedal's legalist opposition to insurrection. The Carlist manifesto of 1872 promised the restoration of the Habsburg autonomies of Catalonia, as part of a general programme of decentralisation. The medieval-ist message of Carlos VII ironically chimed with the futuristic ideas of federal-ism and this led to an ironic de facto alliance between the two extremes for opportunistic reasons, just as between 1846 and 1849. The Carlists turned Estella into their de facto capital once more, with an itinerant court as well; controlled a press and a mint; and had a penal code and a limited railway and telegraph network that connected Carlist territory with Hendaye and the out-side world. Even though Carlos VII, like his grandfather before him, swore an oath under the Tree of Gernika to respect the *fueros* and Basque liberties, the Basque villagers might barely have noticed, as forced loans were imposed from 1874 to fund the war effort.[52]

The May 1872 Carlist defeat at Oroquieta ended the rising that year, and General Serrano's pledge to respect what remained of the Basque *fueros* under-mined Carlist militants. But the advent of the republic nine months later was a godsend to the militant Carlists accustomed to seeing their enemy in apocalyptic terms, especially given that the parliamentary option for Carl-ism of Nocedal had been discredited by rigged elections during the last elec-tions of the Amadeo monarchy. In the summer of 1873, Don Carlos crossed once more into Spain. At Guernica, he swore to protect the *fueros*, and he soon led an army of thirty-three thousand in the Basque country, supported by perhaps ten thousand armed Carlists elsewhere. Remarkably, Carlists dis-played the same strategic strengths and weaknesses as in the 1830s. They won defensive victories at Estella and elsewhere while also making the same disastrous decision as in 1835 to besiege Bilbao.[53] Carlist General Elío over-ruled plans from subordinates to mount a general invasion of Castile, just as Zumalacárregui had been fatally overruled in 1835. The result was a Carlist war that was confined mostly to its traditional areas of support, especially upland Navarra and the Basque provinces, where the insurgents' champion-ing of traditional land tenure led Karl Marx to call Carlism a form of 'feudal socialism'.[54] Extraneous factors, such as economic decline and the behaviour of Republican troops, tended to sway villages behind Carlism in the Catalan far west. In July 1873, Carlist forces, led by the famous Catalan guerrilla captain Francisco Savalls, successfully ambushed a 1,200-strong Republi-can column at Alpens, 40 kilometres north of Vic (Catalonia). The villagers of Alpens supported the Carlists in large part because of news of outrages committed by ill-disciplined Republican troops at the nearby village of Sant Quirze de Besora.[55]

Carlist efforts were aided not just by Republican ill discipline but also by Madrid's military distractions in Cuba, the cantonalist littoral, and by the lack of a single Republican command in the north to coordinate com-plex manoeuvres on land and sea. Even several army officers of the govern-ment army defected to the Carlist side (something never witnessed during the 1830s). Just like during the 1830s, Pamplona suffered a Carlist blockade, as only heavily guarded relief convoys could reach the city. Just as during the 1830s, the Carlists' inferior numbers were offset by the usual advantage of internal lines, along with the march of technology including a sophisticated system of fortifications supported by telegraphs.[56]

Even humanitarianism showed parallels with the 1830s. The newly formed Red Cross intervened offering its own volunteers and hospitals, which was much more than the dead letter of the Eliot Treaty in the 1830s. A similar rhetoric arose in radical circles that foreign humanitarian intervention was once more giving unfair advantages to the Carlists. The frequent visits to Carlist territory by British Red Cross agent Vincent Kennett-Barrington aroused the suspicion of a Madrid republican journalist who alleged that Barrington's visit to government headquarters at Logroño was designed to support for the anti-Republican Pavía coup of January 1874. Barrington, who had no desire for exposure in the press as he was about to enter Carlist territory, grew paranoid about the rumours that he was to be set up as a Carlist sacrifice to buoy up the Republican war effort.[57]

The government war effort against the Carlists was hamstrung by some similar and some new impediments that had pertained in the 1830s. Government cavalry remained superior in numbers and quality, even though the topography of fighting in the main Basque–Navarra front did not play to this arm's strengths. Artillery, by contrast, was poor, not because of a lack of guns but because of the policy driven by Ruiz Zorrilla culminating in 1873 with a complete overhaul of the artillery arm. Ruiz Zorrilla represented a pro-militarist current of republican thought that would endure until Alejandro Lerroux in the 1930s.[58] But the same current also wanted to remake the army in a republican image, and the artillery was riven with Carlist sympathisers and anti-abolitionists and was, above all, impenetrable to the politicians, as it alone of all the arms of Spanish service maintained a promotion system based solely on seniority rather than on political favouritism. The republican artillery reforms thus produced cadres of inexperienced officers inferior in quality to their Carlist opponents. As in all wars, the lion's share of the fighting fell to the infantry to perform. Yet despite nominally superior numbers and the implementation of light infantry tactics, government units could not usually bring their firepower to bear as the usual topographical advantages told in favour of the Carlists.

The Republicans also faced similar problems with morale and discipline as their Cristino predecessors. The incoming Pi y Margall presidency implemented Prim's broken promise to abolish conscription, and although it was later countermanded, this uncertainty threatened to cut off future drafts and dismayed serving conscripts who had missed out and were even more prone to desert, defect, or riot. At Igualada (Catalonia) on 5 June 1873, five thousand troops who should have been pursuing the Carlists killed several of their officers, proclaimed the Federal Republic, and intimidated loyal elements in the cavalry and artillery into fleeing.[59] With conscripts susceptible to politicised desertion, little relief could be expected from the Volunteers for Liberty, who proved prone to shirk actual fighting.[60]

The Madrid Radicals were beset not just by northern Carlism but also by the cantonalist (or federalist) revolt launched in July 1873 by disaffected *intransigente* Republicans in response to President Pi's panicked suspension of constitutional guarantees. Pi said that this measure targeted the Carlists, but the intransigents feared it could be turned against them, and their poor showing in the 12 July 1873 municipal election results drove them to rise. At first, Pi managed to stave off a federalist rising, including one at Barbastro which had been in an advanced state of conspiracy with local Carlists. But very soon most towns along the southern and eastern coast, as well as several provincial capitals inland, had risen in revolt. Revolution appeared to be sweeping Barcelona, where the British consul reported 'strongly accented Internationalists or Communists . . . delivering speeches highly seasoned with appeals to incendiarism, murder and the confiscation of private property'.[61] But the proximity of victorious Carlists in the Catalan far west drove loyalty to the central government, and cantonalists failed to take Spain's industrial capital. In fact, cantonalists proved most likely to rise in those parts of Spain (especially in the south) which Madrid had stripped of garrisons in order to wage war against Carlists and Cubans. The government forces suppressed the revolt, including in sea engagements in response to the launching of a few warships by the cantonalists at Cartagena. Even British and German ships seized some of these cantonalist vessels before handing them over to Spanish representatives at Gibraltar.[62]

In some ways, the chaotic cantonalist movement was a genuine attempt to rebuild government from the municipal and provincial levels in ways that would accord with the ideals of popular sovereignty initially expressed in Cádiz in 1812. Cantons also implemented progressive legislation controlling rents, abolishing consumption taxes, curtailing the church, and regulating working conditions. But in most places, cantonalist leaders placed clear limits on the revolution or, at least, died in the attempt to do so, as was the case of Agustí Albors, mayor of Alcoy, who was killed by militants of the general strike that had been declared in his city by the International. Only in certain cities, such as Cartagena (Murcia) under the influence of the First International, was cantonalism markedly radical, enveloping the military's 'shop stewards' of revolution, the navy, whose frigate *Numancia* Cantonalists turned into their flagship. Conscripts detailed to fight the Carlists rioted in Mallorca, a conservative island already panicked by the cantonalist rising of the sailors at Cartagena.[63] For the most part, however, provincial and local authorities succeeded in controlling extremist elements (just like in 1835), often expelling Internationalists. In Málaga, where cantonalism embraced the province's radical traditions, the canton survived longer than others because the provincial government succeeded in controlling political extremes whilst maintaining good relations with Madrid. Confined principally to the Levant and the south, the movement eventually lost momentum, weakened by the distraction of cantonalists in Catalonia by the need to fight the Carlists. As the moderate republican presidencies of Salmerón and Castelar wrestled with trying to attract cantonalists back into the fold, the general sent to restore order in Andalucía, Manuel Pavía, took power into his own hands. In January 1874, Pavía led a coup which removed Castelar's Federal-Republican government and restored Francisco Serrano as caretaker president of the republic until the *pronunciamiento* of December which, in turn, restored a Bourbon monarch to the throne of Spain.

In contrast to cantonalist and even to Carlist wars, the Cuban revolt, known as the 'Ten Years' War' (1868–78), presented both the Revolutionary and subsequent Alfonsine regime with insoluble problems. Cuba, which imperialists cherished as the 'ever-faithful isle', had remained loyal to the Spanish crown.[64] By 1868, Cuban sugar production represented almost 30 per cent of the world's sugar.[65] But Cuba's economic success barely obscured opposition to Spanish imperialism. Spanish attempts in the 1860s to tax the east of the island in a 'modern' way interfered with free-roaming cattle and common law property customs.[66] The captain general silenced the opposition press and maintained the steep imports tariffs against foreign imports, creating a false economy as Cuba's huge coastline proved vulnerable to smuggling all the same.[67] The Cuban revolt, which began on 10 October 1868, would become known as the Ten Years' War and arose when Cuban-born natives and planters joined a coalition for maximum autonomy. It was led by Carlos Manuel de Céspedes, a Cuban-born lawyer and plantation owner who had famously freed his slaves. Labra's leadership of the abolitionist movement posited that abolition would ease the growing insurrection in Cuba and win over the loyalty of the Creoles and former slaves to the First Republic.[68] The Cuban struggle was exploited by the Spanish left in an opportunistic rather than doctrinaire fashion. Diplomatic pressure weighed on Spain, especially from the United States via its ambassador to Madrid who was known openly to support Spanish republicans mainly in order to open up the United States' own imperial interests in Cuba. For their part, Spanish republicans tended to have a benign view of the United States as a land of progress and modernity in contrast to what they perceived as the entrenched backwardness of Spain.[69] In the end, Sexenio governments of all stripes managed to prevent any international recognition of the Cuban rebellion, improving diplomatic relations with the Americas more generally in the wake of O'Donnellite adventurism in the hemisphere.[70]

But the war dragged on, critically undermining the Spanish revolutionaries' opposition to conscription whilst poisoning conscripts' attitudes towards politicians who claimed to represent their interests. The mortality rate for Spanish soldiers sent on campaigns between 1866 and 1877 was about 50 per cent. The miseries inflicted on conscripts by disease, hunger and enemy action compounded those of their poverty-stricken families they had left behind in Spain. These families had lost a producer and could not even rest assured that returned conscripts who had served their term might not yet be called into service again, given the rules regulating 'reserve' status.[71] These brutal-ised conscripts, in turn, committed excesses against Cuban rebels, destroy-ing property and lives in a counter-insurgency which anticipated the more famous conflict of the 1890s. The Spanish forces constructed a *'trocha'* (forti-fied line) dividing the rebellious and underdeveloped east of the island from the west, linking Morón on the northern coast with Júcaro on the southern coast. It was a more humanitarian alternative to a radical plan proposed in 1872 to depopulate the central part of Cuba in order to provide a human desert between the elite west and rebellious east.[72] All the same, by 1878, it is estimated that more than 150,000 people died from combat-related deaths, disease, injuries, or from starvation.[73] Upon visiting Cuba at the end of the Ten Years' War, notable physician Federico de Córdova compared the island's appearance to that of a 'cemetery in a desert'.[74] As Cuba was one of Spain's most important, and profitable, remaining colonies, the war was disastrous for Spain. Although initially Cuba's savage revolt had a limited impact on daily life in Spain, the war caused further strain, economically, politically, and socially, on a very fragile political system. Historians agree that Cuba's Ten Years War decisively undermined successive Sexennium regimes by bitterly dividing opinion and military resources sorely required in Spain itself. The Ten Years War, which had originated in the abuses of the Isabelline monarchy and persisted during the ineptitude of the Revolutionary Sexennium, would be brought to an end by a more efficient monarchy. In 1878, Spain's restored Bourbon dynasty made peace in Cuba via the Peace of Zanjón, which set the course toward abolishing all slavery and restoring Cortes representation to the island.

The restoration of the monarchy in the form of Alfonso XII dealt a mortal blow to Carlism. The cult of the 'soldier-king', inspired, in part, by the Bis-marckian statue fever in newly unified Germany, moulded the Crown and the army closer together and provided the environment for an incipient praeto-rianism to flourish. A law passed in 1878 empowered the king to bypass his cabinet on military matters entirely whenever he chose to take sole command of the armed forces, and in the same year, the Civil Guard was made an inte-gral part of the army.[75] This conservative praetorianism would prove cata-strophic for Carlism. Army loyalty was reaffirmed, and Alfonso's ostentatious defence of Catholicism undermined support for armed Carlism at exactly the moment when the Pretender's armies were being defeated in Catalonia and the Basque country. Alfonsine Catholicism also rallied the middle classes who had bristled at the Republic's indulgence of religious liberty. Protestant mis-sionaries had managed to establish by 1874 only some thirty-six chapels and forty-three schools throughout Spain. But foreign missionary work some-times provoked reprisals, such as the burning of Bibles and a chapel by a mob in Granada which had been provoked by Protestant preaching outside the cathedral.[76] During 1875, Alfonsine forces under the command of Fernando Primo de Rivera (uncle of the 1920s' dictator) pacified Catalonia and Aragón and gradually reduced northern Carlist fortresses. By February 1876, it was all over. On 19 February 1876, Alfonsine forces occupied Estella, and nine days later Don Carlos went into exile. The Third Carlist War was over. Navarra's autonomy was drastically reduced as Madrid's concessions were negligible. The liberals of both republican and monarchical stripes had portrayed the civil war as a 'nationalising' conflict to convert the cancerous territories of Navarra and the Basque provinces from being a site of martyrdom into a site of Spanish nation building.[77] Accordingly, defeated Navarra's concessions amounted to little more than granting the Pamplona authorities the power to calculate their own taxes payable to the central government (the *concierto económico*).

Notes

1 Antonio Manuel Moral Roncal, '1868 en la memoria carlista de 1931: dos revoluciones anticlericales y un paralelo', *Hispania Sacra*, Vol. LIX, No. 119 (enero–junio 2007), pp. 337–61.
2 Rafael Pérez Cabanes, 'Galdós, una perspectiva del carlisme', in Montañà i Rafart (eds.), *El carlisme ahir i avui*, p. 148.
3 Eiras Roel, *El Partido demócrata*, pp. 362–80; Palacio Atard, *La España del siglo XIX*, pp. 373–4, 391.
4 Monge, *Revolucionarios de 1868*, pp. 243–5.
5 Eiras Roel, *El Partido demócrata*, pp. 408–9.
6 Palacio Atard, *España del siglo XIX*, p. 372.
7 Santiago de Miguel Salanova, 'De súbditos a ciudadanos. La emergencia de nuevas prácticas electorales del Madrid de 1868', *El Futuro del Pasado*, Vol. 8 (2017), pp. 399–443, 400–6, 415–17, 424.
8 Hennessy, *The Federal Republic in Spain*, pp. 28–49.
9 Jose Luis Vila-San-Juan, *Amadeo I: El Rey Caballero* (Barcelona: Planeta, 1997), pp. 83–5.
10 Edward Henry Strobel, *The Spanish Revolution, 1868–1875* (Boston: Small, Manard and Co., 1898), p. 115.
11 José A. Piqueras Arenas, *La revolución democrática, 1868–1874: cuestión social, colonialismo y grupos de presión* (Madrid: Ministerio de Trabajo, 1992), p. 402.
12 María Dolores Domingo Acebrón, *Rafael María de Labra: Cuba, Puerto Rico, Las Filipinas, Europa y Marruecos, en la España del sexenio democrático y la restauración, 1871–1918* (Madrid: Consejo Superior de Investigaciones Científicas, 2006), pp. 27–30, 159.
13 Rafael María de Labra, *La crisis colonial de España (1868 a 1898): estudios de política palpitante y discursos parlamentarios* (Madrid: Tipografía Sindicato de Publicidad, 1901), p. viii.
14 Rafael María de Labra, *América y la Constitución española de 1812: Cortes de Cádiz de 1810–1813* (Madrid: Sindicato de Publicidad, 1914), p. 183.
15 Labra, *La crisis colonial de España* (1901), pp. 61–6.
16 Rafael María de Labra, *La abolición de la esclavitud en el orden económico* (Madrid: Sociedad Abolicionista Española, 1874), p. 458.
17 Christopher Schmidt-Nowara, 'Imperio y crisis colonial', in Juan Pan-Montojo (ed.), *Más se perdió en Cuba* (Madrid: Alianza, 1998), p. 38.
18 Marichal, *El secreto de España*, p. 109.

19 Aurora G. Morcillo, 'Gender', in Shubert and Alvarez-Junco (eds.), *The History of Modern Spain*, pp. 167–9.
20 Isabel Burdiel, 'Emilia Pardo Bazán', in Shubert and Alvarez-Junco (eds.), *The History of Modern Spain*, pp. 401–6.
21 Hennessy, *The Federal Republic in Spain*, pp. 5–7.
22 Cit. Carlos Dardé, *Historia de España: La Restauración, 1875–1902* (Madrid: Ediciones Temas de Hoy, 1997), p. 67.
23 Hennessy, *The Federal Republic in Spain*, pp. 7–14.
24 Pilar Salomón Chéliz, 'El discurso anticlerical en la construcción de una identidad nacional española republicana (1898–1936)', *Hispania Sacra*, Vol. 54, No. 110 (2002), pp. 485–98.
25 Hennessy, *The Federal Republic in Spain*, p. 75.
26 José Tomás Raga Gil, 'Cánovas ante la Gloriosa', in de Mendoza and Togores (eds.), *Cánovas y su época*, 2 vols., Vol. I, p. 40.
27 Francisco Pí y Margall, *La reacción y la revolución: estudios políticos y sociales* (Madrid: Imprenta y Estereotipa de M. Rivadeneira, 1854), p. 200.
28 Hennessy, *The Federal Republic in Spain*, p. 88.
29 Fernando Garrido, *El socialismo y la democracia* (London Unknown Publisher, 1862), pp. 11, 26–31.
30 Hennessy, *The Federal Republic in Spain*, pp. 14–27.
31 Díaz del Moral, *Historia de las agitaciones campesinas andaluzas* (Madrid, 1928); Brenan, *The Spanish Labyrinth* (1943).
32 Eric J. Hobsbawm, *Primitive Rebels: Studies in Archaic Forms of Social Movement in the 19th and 20th Centuries* (London: Norton and Co.,1959).
33 Temma Kaplan, *The Anarchists of Andalucía, 1868–1903* (Princeton: Princeton University Press, 1977); George Esenwein, *Anarchist Ideology and the Working-Class Movement in Spain* (Oxford: Oxford University Press, 1989).
34 Vila-San-Juan, *Amadeo I*, pp. 134–5.
35 Comellas García-Llera, *Los Moderados en el poder*, p. 154.
36 Hennessy, *The Federal Republic in Spain*, pp. 73–102.
37 Trías and Elorza, *Federalismo y reforma social*, p. 37; Sarría Muñoz, *Historia de Málaga*, pp. 85–9.
38 Hennessy, *The Federal Republic in Spain*, pp. 101–24.
39 Vila-San-Juan, *Amadeo I*, pp. 58–61.
40 Manuel Suárez Cortina, 'Republicanismos y Democracia en la España del siglo XIX', in Manuel Suárez Cortina and Maurizio Ridolfi (eds.), *El Estado y la Nación: Cuestión nacional, centralismo y federalismo en la Europa del Sur* (Santander: Edición Universidad Cantabria, 2014), pp. 230–2.
41 Javier Moreno-Luzón, *Modernizing the Nation* (Sussex: Sussex Academic Press, 2016), p. 31.
42 Hennessy, *The Federal Republic in Spain*, pp. 125–42.
43 Cepeda Gómez, *Los pronunciamientos en la España del siglo XIX*, pp. 31–2.
44 Vila-San-Juan, *Amadeo I*, pp. 99–105.
45 Jorge Vilches García, 'Cánovas: Político del Sexenio Revolucionario', *Hispania: Revista Española de Historia*, Vol. 57, No. 3 (septiembre 1997), pp. 1107–29.
46 T.N.A., FO 72/1350: 7 March 1873 letter from Acting Consul William Leigh to British Foreign Office.
47 Hennessy, *The Federal Republic in Spain*, pp. 143–69.
48 Sarría Muñoz, *Breve historia de Málaga*, p. 83.
49 Trías and Elorza, *Federalismo y reforma social*, pp. 50–74; Palacio Atard, *España del siglo XIX*, pp. 374–5.
50 Leandro Nagore, *Apuntes para la historia: memorias de un pamplonés en la segunda guerra carlista* (Pamplona: Institución Príncipe de Viana, 1964), pp. 26–8.

51 Tura Clarà Vallès, 'Els mestres d'escola durant la darrera carlinada', in Montañà i Rafart (eds.), *El carlisme ahir i avui*, p. 142.
52 Jesús Martín Alías, 'Elementos de organización del estado carlista (1873–1876)', Montañà and Rafart (eds.), *Estat carlista*, pp. 155–61.
53 Holt, *Carlist Wars*, pp. 250–64.
54 Clemente, *Las guerras carlistas*, p. 291.
55 T.N.A., FO 72/1350: 12 July 1873 letter ('consular no. 15') from British Consul to Barcelona to Earl Granville.
56 José María Ocáriz Bassarte e Iban Roldán Bergaraetxea, 'Fortificaciones en el frente de Estella durante la tercera Guerra carlista', in Daniel Montañà and Josep Rafart (eds.), *Propaganda carlista, religió, literatura i operacions militars* (III Simposi d'Història del Carlisme, 9 de maig de 2015), pp. 172–8.
57 Alice L. Lascelles and J. M. Alberich (eds.), *Sir Vincent Kennett-Barrington: Letters from the Carlist War (1874–1876)* (Exeter: University of Exeter Press, 1987), pp. 46–9.
58 Stanley Payne, *Politics and the Military* (Stanford: Stanford University Press, 1967), p. 300.
59 T.N.A., FO 72/1350: 7 June 1873 letter from British Consul to Barcelona to Earl Granville.
60 Daniel Headrick, *Ejército y política en España (1868–1898)* (Madrid: Editorial Tecnos, 1981), pp. 186–92.
61 T.N.A., FO 72/1350: 18 July 1873 letter from British Consul to Barcelona to Earl Granville.
62 Hannay, *Don Emilio Castelar*, pp. 189–95.
63 Sevilla Andrés, *Antonio Maura*, p. 34.
64 Ada Ferrer, *Insurgent Cuba: Race, Nation, and Revolution, 1868–1898* (Chapel Hill: University of North Carolina Press, 1999), pp. 1–2.
65 Louis A. Pérez, *Cuba: Between Reform and Revolution* (Oxford: Oxford University Press, 2011), pp. 73–7.
66 Lawrence Tone, *War and Genocide in Cuba, 1895–1898* (Chapel Hill, NC: University of North Carolina Press, 2006), pp. 22–3.
67 Pérez, *Cuba: Between Reform and Revolution*, pp. 91–2.
68 Christopher Schmidt-Nowara, *Empire and Antislavery: Spain, Cuba, and Puerto Rico, 1833–1874* (Pittsburgh, PA: University of Pittsburgh Press, 1999), p. 140.
69 Kate Ferris, *Imagining 'America' in Late Nineteenth Century Spain* (Basingstoke: Palgrave Macmillan, 2016), pp. 13–15.
70 Agustín S. Andrés, 'Colonial Crisis and Spanish Diplomacy in the Caribbean during the Sexenio Revolucionario, 1868–74', *Bulletin of Latin American Research*, Vol. 28, No. 3 (June 2009), pp. 325–42.
71 Enrique Bernad Royo, 'El ejército español en la Guerra de la Independencia: una mirada desde el siglo XIX', in Álvarez Jímenez and Juan Antonio (foreword), *La Guerra de la Independencia Española: una visión militar. VI Congreso de Historia Militar (Zaragoza, marzo-abril 2008)* (Madrid: Ministerio de Defensa, 2009), Vol. I, pp. 156–7.
72 Andreas Stucki, '¿Guerra entre hermanos en la gran Antilla?' in Xosé M. Núñez Seixas and Francisco Sevillano (eds.), *Los enemigos de España: Imagen del otro, conflictos bélicos y disputas nacionales (siglos XVI-XX)* (Madrid, 2010), p. 273.
73 Antonio Pirala, *Anales de la guerra de Cuba*, Vol. 3 (Madrid: Felipe Gonzalez Rojas, 1898).
74 Ramiro Guerra, *A History of the Cuban Nation: The Ten Years War and other revolutionary activities from 1868–1892* (Havana: Editorial Historia de la Nación Cubana, 1958), p. 245.
75 Jensen, 'War and the Military', in Shubert and Álvarez-Junco (eds.), *The History of Modern Spain*, pp. 336–7.
76 Gregorio Alonso, *Nación en capilla*, pp. 318–19.
77 Xosé M. Núñez Seixas and Francisco Sevillano, 'Introducción: Las Españas y sus enemigos', in Seixas and Sevillano (eds.), *Los enemigos de España*, p. 18.

Chapter 6

1876–98: imagining the nation

This final chapter explains the emergence of the Spanish state in its modern form, in particular the first half of the restored Bourbon constitutional monarchy. It explains the emergence of the Cánovas system of authoritarian yet constitutional politics dominated by two parties peacefully alternating in power. It explains the abuses of this system, especially the immunity of political bosses (*caciques*), electoral fraud, and judicial corruption. It also explains how, despite the unyielding political environment, including a reinvigorated Catholic Church, a 'silver age' emerged in Spanish culture and how such new political ideas as Marxism, positivism, National Catholicism, regional nationalism, Darwinism, and, above all, Regenerationism, either reinforced or challenged the political settlement. Above all, this chapter explains how the strength of the Canovine political settlement – so strong that the army did not need to make major interventions – excluded any legal recourse to major social reforms, to say nothing of the revolution demanded by the anarchists and socialists. Thus, the outward image of stability barely concealed an ever more polarised class society whose contours stretched from the timeless divisions of landless labourers and landowners to the modernity of the winners and losers from urban capitalism. The strength of the political system would come under strain due to Spain's military defeat to the United States in 1898. The chapter thus concludes with the theme of the lost empire with which the book started.

Until the 1990s, the Spanish Restoration was seen as an era of social and political rigidity, on one hand, and gradual economic growth, on the other.[1] In 1997, the conservative prime minister of Spain, José María Aznar, marked the centenary of Cánovas's assassination with a speech comparing the statesman's political system favourably with the 1930s' Second Republic, not least because Cánovas was a 'champion of universal suffrage'.[2] A centenary essay even celebrated Cánovas's Restoration as 'Regenerationist', bringing forward the era of national renewal twenty years before the crisis of 1898.[3] Raymond Carr, Shlomo Ben-Ami, and Stanley Payne are amongst leading historians who have viewed the 1875–1923 Restoration in an optimistic fashion, Carr even venturing that the Primo coup of 1923, far from killing of a 'diseased body, in fact strangled a new birth'.[4] Certainly there were contemporary reasons why right-wing politicians and historians have been praising the Restoration. They interpreted this era as one of gradual democratisation frustrated by an intolerant and sectarian Second Republic. Economic progress, they claimed, was restored only under Franco, whose dictatorship created the necessary conditions for the late-1970s transition to democracy.[5] Even liberal historians have also reappraised how the Restoration, for all its corruption and repression, also allowed most political forces, even Carlists, republicans, and regional nationalists, periodic access to power.[6]

The Restoration certainly witnessed a flourishing of political ideas, especially those concerned with the proper form of the 'nation'. The Alfonsine Restoration was cemented by what proved to be the most enduring constitution in modern Spanish history. In many ways, the reign of Alfonso XII showed similarities with that of his exiled mother. But there were three key differences. Unlike his mother, Alfonso used the royal pregoative as an exception rather than a rule, the political parties wanted Alfonso to reign and to govern as little as possible, and unlike his mother, Alfonso never allowed himself to be 'captured' by any single political party.[7] The Constitution of 1876 balanced sovereignty between the nation and the king, allowing monarchist and liberal traditions an equal voice in a constitutional fudge which declared sovereignty to reside 'in the Cortes with the king', and which split the Cortes itself into two chambers, with the upper chamber, the Senate, composed partly of hereditary senators and (in a nod to the demands of the Krausists) partly of men nominated from the arts, sciences, and professions.[8] Cánovas ironically commented that 'together with the Republicans I have re-established the monarchy'.[9] He was inspired by the British parliamentary system. In a speech he gave at the Ateneo in 1870, Cánovas spoke of his 'envy' for the Anglo-Saxon countries which know how to 'marry order with liberty', unlike the Latin countries which he knew suffered from overly abstract political theories leading to failure or anarchy and from a confusion of liberty with licence.[10] But the British system rested on aristocrat parliamentarians whose local and regional loyalties, for good or ill, often exceeded the party politics to which they subscribed. Spain, by contrast, had fewer landed parliamentarians. The Canovine Restoration tried to cement its oligarchy by conferring noble titles on loyal politicians to an unprecedented degree. But many of these new nobles were absentee landlords just like the old nobles, especially in relation to the huge estates of the south. Thus, Cánovas's system had to depend on a powerful Ministry of the Interior, the cooperation of regional *caciques*, and eventually the alternation in power of two dynastic parties (Liberals and Conservatives) in a political dance that involved wide-ranging corruption and coercion.

There were strong arguments in favour of both abuses, given the chaos of the preceding decades, and given Cánovas's mostly successful aim of burying the *pronunciamiento* tradition. Cánovas and his fellow Restoration politicians did not identify the *caciques* as the problem as such, but 'bad government' riding roughshod over a weak civil society. The 1878 electoral law which restricted the national vote to only one-fifth of the male population was justified in terms of making voters *less* manipulable by *caciques*.[11] Liberal historians writing during the Restoration accepted that their century's political parties held little mass appeal, with the exception of the recent and unique experience of the Sexenio.[12] Only later in the Restoration did demands for an 'iron surgeon' to restrain the *caciques* emerge, especially once universal suffrage was achieved. The politics of 'order' was also justified by adherence to the positivism of Auguste Comte (1798–1857), the political implications of which found favour with conservatives across the late nineteenth-century Latin world. Cánovas's contemporary, Porfirio Díaz, positivist dictator of Mexico, demanded *poca política, mucha administración* (no politics but plenty of governing).[13] Cánovas thought that the Spanish countryside was naturally conservative and would respond well to the politics of coercion and development. Carlism, after all, had spread so easily through Spain in large part because of the previous existence of a strong canon of anti-liberal thought and culture.[14] An alliance of Crown and conservative people would perform the trick of keeping the military as the subdued third in the triarchy of Crown, the army, and Cortes. Cánovas quipped, '[I]f we can keep the army out of politics for 50 years we will end up being a normal nation'.[15] But Cánovas could not hide the fact that his demilitarised Restoration owed its birth to the *pronunciamiento* launched by Alfonso XII's Sandhurst Manifesto. Cánovas also put the cart before the horse. The neo-Catholic, Jaime Balmes, observed that '[c]ivil power is not weak because military power is strong, rather military power is strong because the civil power is weak'.[16]

Nation, producers, and consumers

The post-1876 stability of dynastic politics, combined with a growing state, inspired contemporary politicians to imagine the nation. The conservative architect of Restoration politics, Cánovas del Castillo, stressed the ongoing role of Spain's 'imperial destiny', forged by race, religion, and language. Spanish American independence had involved civil wars amongst American-born Spaniards and was therefore no threat to Spain's imperial identity. Above all, the Spanish nation was 'God-given', not an expression of 'will', as Ernest Renan argued in 1883. So any threat to the nation was a defiance of God.[17] On the radical left, Pi y Margall, former president of the republic, contested Cánovas's *Discurso sobre la nación* with his own treatise, *Las nacionalidades*, published in 1887. Pi y Margall believed that the liberal regime of the First Spanish Republic was a time of national regeneration in Spain; by reframing the nation's political, economic, and social structure, the liberal Sexennium modernised the country and broke Spain's 'intellectual isolationism'.[18]

Throughout *Las nacionalidades*, Pi y Margall closely examined the 'true' form of nationalism while at the same time justifying his progressive ideals.[19]

Like all positivists, Cánovas hoped that economic progress would satisfy material interests and displace the need for political mobilisation. But economic expansion was highly uneven in terms of region and class. There were only four years between 1845 and 1899 in which Spanish governments avoided budget deficits, owing to the need to pay accumulated debt interest, which, in turn, meant that governments were stuck in the trap of having to issue short-term bonds in order to raise money to pay existing debt interest.[20] Growing the overall economy was the best hope of surmounting the debt problem. There was early promise in the 2,750 kilometres of railway track laid in Spain before the railway bubble burst in 1866.[21] But the involvement of foreign, especially French, capital in railway construction prioritised international railways connections over regional trunk lines which might have consolidated economic growth. The structural weaknesses in population growth and employment remained apparent. Even though Spain's population during the last quarter of the century expanded from 16.5 million to 18.6 million, the proportion working in agriculture remained the same (about 65 per cent), accounting for about half of economic output. Only industrialising areas in Catalonia and the Basque country witnessed major structural changes before 1900.[22]

Landowning interests, including the socially dire *latifundia*, dominated politics, entrenching the *cacique* system and making Spain one of the most protectionist economies in Europe. From the 1880s, agricultural chambers (*Cámaras agrícolas*) had sprung up to defend agrarian productionist interests.[23] But protectionism did little to improve the precarious starvation wages facing southern day labourers. During the same decade of the 1880s, some 420,000 Spaniards emigrated to Latin America.[24] Mass emigration from Loja (Andalucía) fractured *jornalero* society and alienated the tradition of landowners to offer shelter (*alojamientos*) in times of dearth.[25] By 1891, in response to a decade of low grain prices caused by the sudden expansion of global wheatlands, the landowners had lobbied the Cánovas government to erect one of Europe's highest grain tariffs, boosting the production of the landowners and keeping prices inflated for consumers. Catalan industrialists were likewise protected by tariffs, especially in relation to the Cuban market. While the wealthy classes of Barcelona enjoyed the highest standard of living in Spain, the surrounding countryside was struck by the *rabassa morta* crisis. Viticultralist sharecroppers (*rabassers*) who had traditionally enjoyed the lifelong harvesting rights to long-lived vines were devastated when the global phylloxera epidemic reached Spain in the late 1880s, wiping out local vines which had to be replaced by faster-growing (and shorter-lived) North American strains. Yet the contracts remained unchanged, turning the viticultarlists into proletarians, whose cause in the Penedès wine region was championed by Republicans in a rare success for a party which was still reeling in the wake of the Sexenio.[26]

In the cities, economic growth was more widely shared as Spain's middle classes became consumerist. In 1885, Spain's first department store opened in Barcelona.[27] But rapid urbanisation could also impair the quality of life for city dwellers. The pleasure gardens which developed in Spanish cities after 1821 had mostly disappeared by the end of the century, owing to urban sprawl.[28] As early as 1843, Mendizábal had started expanding Madrid beyond the Puerta de Alcalá, and Mesonero Romanos had begun more ambitious expansions after 1846. Pumped gas reached private houses in Madrid in 1848, and public lavatories appeared in the Puerta del Sol in the same year.[29] As city walls were demolished beginning in the 1850s, the working-class population spread along suburban roadsides, and public services were slow to follow up. Even though Madrid got its first public water supply in 1858 (when Isabel II inaugurated a canal), driving the picturesque water sellers (*aguadores*) out of work, epidemics remained regular occurrences until the end of the century.[30] Infant mortality rates remained much higher in Madrid than in other European capitals, being known as the 'city of death'.

From 1860, major urban expansions gathered apace, as projected in the 1859 Plan Cerdá for Barcelona and the 1860 Plan Castro for Madrid. City walls were torn down to make way for urban expansion. Madrid's expansion (*ensanche*) began with the Salamanca residential district constructed from 1860 to the east of the old city. Constructed like Barcelona's Example district in a grid-like fashion with wide avenues, Salamanca offered the capital's rising middle classes refuge from the dense, cholera-prone, and unpoliceable old town. Electricity began to reach private homes in the 1880s, half a century before a nationwide grid was established.[31] From the 1880s, the authorities started protecting polite society's 'aural hygiene' by banning the music (derided as 'noise') of working-class music flamencos and organ-grinding.[32] Rapid urbanisation also led to moral panic caused by fears of homosocial and homosexual underworlds flourishing on the stream of young men migrating to Madrid, Catalonia, and the Basque country.[33] Whereas in Madrid the levelling of the city walls offered the wealthy classes hope, in Valencia urban development inspired fear. The Valencian poet Teodoro Llorente recounted the sleepless nights suffered in Valencia after its walls were demolished in 1865. The Valencian *huerta* had suffered some of Spain's sharpest abuses under feudalism and capitalism alike, turning town and country into mutual enemies. The city walls, Llorente observed, defended the city against the countryside, not against any enemy army.[34]

Against the system

Cánovas's demand for political stability stemmed from his doleful analysis of the 'administrative paralysis' and 'backwardness' evident in Spain's recent civil wars and turmoil.[35] There were two advantages to the *turno pacífico* system: (1) it privileged the maintenance of strong and orderly parties by obliging the king and the executive to pick strong and united parties for the purpose of governing the country, no matter what the parliamentary arithmetic might be, and (2) this system generally obliged the king not to act in an arbitrary manner. However, the disadvantages were obvious. Its reliance on the *caciques* belied Cánovas's hope that they might safeguard the interests of the 'real country' against the 'legal country'. Indeed, as the *caciques* controlled networks of social power that distorted and often usurped the law, such a distinction became artificial. There was systematic fraud, and unlike in proper constitutional systems where the majorities made the executive, in Spain it was the executive which made the majority.

Such a fraudulent and corrupt system could survive only as long as most of Spain continued to experience low levels of political education and participation.[36] Illiteracy rates in Málaga, for example, declined only slowly, from 83.9 per cent in 1840, to 78 per cent in 1860 and 74.5 per cent in 1877.[37] Given the low development of civil society and literacy, and the toothlessness of the Cortes, great oratory (or posturing) by parliamentarians held more of a premium in Spain than most other European countries. A foreign traveller from reserved northern Europe had marvelled at the peculiarly Spanish gift for political hyperbole: 'maddened orators leap to every elevated point . . . words of fury and revenge are poured forth like lava on the multitude . . . until the passions of the crowd are let slip and the terrible '*¡muera!* bursts forth from 100 voices'.[38] Even as parliamentary politics became more harmonious in the Restoration, speeches remained the one effective way of making and breaking reputations.[39] But they also exasperated leading figures listening to parliamentary debates like the novelist Pérez Galdós. Pérez Galdós, Spain's first substantial historical novelist had in 1873 published the first of his *Episodios Nacionales*, establishing realism as the ascendant literary current. Romanticism was now dead, but this fact seemed lost on the speechifying politicians. Although Galdós celebrated the 'brotherhood' reigning between the dynastic parties, in marked contrast to the *moderados* and *progresistas* of old, he nonetheless complained that 'government action is drowned in a flood of words'.[40]

Those who were unsatisfied by rhetoric discovered that there were few legal avenues to resist the Cánovas system. As leader of the 'possibilist' Democrats between 1876 and 1890, Emilio Castelar collaborated with the Canovine system, demonstrating that Castelar's regionalised and institutionalised powerbase was focused increasingly on the personality of leaders rather than on strict points of ideology.[41] Castelar's flexibility was challenged by intransigent republicans whose policy of *retraimiento* (electoral boycotts) after 1878 nonetheless failed on account of a lack of military support. As the Canovine settlement so effectively divided and ruled over the opposition, the left faced a shrinking number of issues to rally consensus. Anti-clericalism remained such an issue uniting old Liberals with new anarchists, as the moral panic whipped up in the leftist press against pederast priests attests.[42]

The Canovine settlement was also largely immune from the political challenge posed by Catalan and the Basque nationalism, in large part due to the rise of a centralised version of Spanish nationalism. The extent of Spanish nation building was usually downplayed by intellectuals writing after the 'Disaster' of 1898. José Ortega y Gasset believed that Basque and Catalan 'sectionalism' was a by-product of the corruption of an 'invertebrate' centralising power: 'Castile made Spain, and Castile has unmade it'.[43] The first explicitly separatist manifesto in Catalonia, the 1892 *Bases de Manresa*, had been foreshadowed by such barbed attacks on Madrid's 'lethargic' centralisation as Mañé y Flaquer's *El regionalismo* (1887). The Basque country also developed separatist nationalism in the 1890s. Even Galicia witnessed friction with Madrid in respect of its provincialism (from 1840 to 1885) and regionalism (1885–1915) thereafter. Yet Galicia's middle classes, unlike in Catalonia and even parts of the Basque country, failed by the end of the century to develop a political identity separate to the rest of Spain. Even in the Basque country Sabino Arana's Basque Nationalist Party (PNV), founded in 1895, barely made any progress beyond countryside districts in Vizcaya where its message of Catholicism and ethnic nationalism could yet appeal to villagers of Carlist heritage who were still innocent of the socialism and secularism of the cities. Whereas Basque nationalism was largely a reaction against modernisation, Catalan nationalism was largely an embrace of it. Against this bifurcated nationalism, the Spanish state itself asserted a centralising model. Spanish nationalism evolved away from mere extraction (conscription, taxation) and towards more benign features like government regulation of society and the environment.[44]

The obstacles to defying Canovine 'sham constitutionalism' were immense, and perhaps the greatest was the popular indifference towards dynastic politics as something to be experienced and reformed. Raymond Carr wrote that 'politics ran, like an express train, through the desolate townships and villages of Spain, stopping only at election times'.[45] Regional nationalism, along with socialism and anarchism, and the Carlists were anti-system forces held in check by a corrupt constitutional settlement of 'managed' elections and a perverted judiciary. Key to Cánovas's *turno pacífico* (formalised in the 1885 Pact of El Pardo) were the *caciques*, regional bosses whose webs of patronage ultimately answered to the Ministry of the Interior and kept most voters in a state of alienation. Political repression did not have to be physical or systematic but was often selective and reliant on local power networks (*cacicazgos*).[46] The south-eastern province of Murcia operated this sham constitutionalism to perfection. The conservative landowning and mining magnate, Juan de la Cierva (1864–1938), dominated this region with the highest illiteracy rates in Spain, controlling the judicial and electoral processes by appointing decision-makers who then bribed or threatened juries and voters.[47] So complete was *cacique* control in Murcia that it became a byword for impunity for wrongdoing with the saying 'If you kill the king, flee to Murcia'. In such an environment, the Liberal government's (1885–90) nominally progressive reforms introducing trial by jury (1888) and universal male suffrage (1890) ended up entrenching the *cacique* system. Blackmail details implicating Sagasta's wife in corrupt Cuban railway concessions obliged the architect of universal suffrage to resign in 1890. But his reform remained in place, ironically considering the disapproval Sagasta had repeatedly expressed for the principle universal suffrage. Yet Sagasta realised its value as a last hurrah for 'progressive' liberalism and for uniting all wings of the party and peeling off Castelar's middle-class 'possibilist' republicans from Pi y Margall's federalists. Even though the size of the electorate in the 1891 elections was six times greater than in those held in 1886–4.8 million voters instead of 800,000 – the incumbent government which 'made' the elections always 'won' it all the same. The only difference was that winning majorities became smaller with each election.[48] At no point during the Restoration system would such anti-system parties as the Socialists, Carlists, Republicans, and regional nationalists win more than a handful of Cortes seats.[49] But Republicans were not entirely excluded from political spoils, occasionally controlling town and city councils and even provincial governorships. Socialists, the International, and Basque and Catalan nationalists, however, were left out in the cold, ominous considering that many workers and agricultural labourers in Catalonia and Andalucía were turning to anarchism. Anarchism itself was split by rival 1880s strategies of propaganda by word (syndicalism) and by deed (violence). Harsh government reprisals solidified support for violence, and a series of spectacular anarchist risings (Jérez 1892) and assassinations which incited heavy reprisals and the unending militarisation of public order in Barcelona.

Apart from its suppression of anarchism, the state's coercion was so complete as to be invisible. Whenever force had to be used against political dissent, the Restoration state found that it was well equipped. The 1885 Cassola reforms set the course for a smaller army better supplied with fortifications and *materiél*.[50] There was a general consensus behind the need to modernise the armed forces. In 1883 the Krausist Free Institute of Education recommended that Spain's conscripts be given physical and moral training. Gymnastics, sports, excursions, and games would forge a harmonious bond between the army and the poverty-stricken civilian environment from which conscripts came.[51] Yet military and political inertia prevented most of the Cassola reforms, especially the planned reduction in conscription, from taking place, and few reforms were implemented to benefit the condition of the conscripts who had to serve as before. More attention was devoted to officers. The creation of the General Military Academy in 1882 modernised officers' training and established an army whose future officers would shape the wars of the twentieth century.[52]

For all the concern about its war-fighting potential, the army continued to be the backstop for public order. In 1886, the military was empowered to have jurisdiction over cases involving military rebellion or desertion by civilians, including the power of execution, and in 1890 a law was passed prohibiting offence, either written or verbal, against the military authorities and institutions.[53] Militarised public order loomed large as in the 1880s only Madrid had a perfectly organised police force, along with a municipal force accountable to local government, supported by the Civil Guard under orders of the War Ministry. In general, the Restoration did not replace a fundamentally militarised conception of public order with anything professionalised. Whenever policing was unable to suppress dissent, such as during highly contested elections, *caciques* could apply 'moral pressure' via proxies. Hired toughs, known as the partido de la porra (parties of the truncheon), terrorised opposition voters and presses, and both left-wing and right-wing groups made liberal use of them.[54] The '*porra*' was in use a great deal between 1869 and 1870 as constitutional guarantees were suspended and republicans used targeted violence to control public spaces and suppress adversary opinions.[55]

While such educated politicians as Joaquín Costa and Maura demanded changes to this 'sham constitutionalism', little more than cosmetic change was enacted this century. Costa and his fellow graduate of the Free Institute of Education, Rafael Altamira, spoke of the need to 'regenerate Spain' in order to end the grip of the cacqiues. At the heart of Costa's critique was his defence of small producers whose rights had been eroded by the demise of old law codes in his native Aragón and in Catalonia and by the march of the *caciques* of big capitalism in the cities and of large estates in the countryside grown even larger thanks to repeated liberal disentailment of church and common lands. Costa was the pioneer of Regenerationism, an intellectual current more usually discussed in the context of Spain's post-1898 history when a *revanchiste* right would look for an 'iron surgeon'.[56] But the 1898 'Disaster', in fact, did not represent a sudden break in political and literary thought but, rather, an acceleration of currents already visible during the last quarter of the century.[57] The paleontogologist Lucas Mallada, author of his withering *Males de la patria y la futura de la revolución española* (1890), opened Spain's *fin-de-siècle* intellectual crisis in arguing that Spain's barren soils were the origins of its atrophy, leading to a history marked by pride, ignorance, laziness, and a lack of practicality not compensated by imaginativeness.[58]

Restoration intellectuals certainly tried to address the burdens of geography and religion. The Krausist Free Institute of Education offered an intellectual counter-culture to the growth of clericalism. Its academics were dubbed the 'lay Jesuits' by Madrid wags, on account of their beards, dark attire, and their social habits.[59] By the end of the century, the Iberian landscape had come to shape Spanish intellectual currents, especially Krausism, as well as the official linking of landscape with nation building. Krausists working at the Free Institute in 1881 began a series of excursions for their students, designed to teach them the diversity and 'harmony' of Spain's social geography. The early success of excursions to sites of historical interest around Madrid led to visits to more far-flung parts of the peninsula, where students on visits lasting as long as five weeks would study botany, geography, geology, and religious customs.[60] The legacy of promoting public heritage would be evident in 1918 when Covadonga, a symbol of Spanishness as much as the mountain of Montserrat came to symbolise Catalanism, was upgraded in status from a national monument to a national park.[61]

Cultural and intellectual initiatives flourished in a constitutional system sealed off to radical political challenge. Two dozen typesetters, medical students and artisans in 1879 founded the Spanish Socialist Party (PSOE), a Madrid-centric party which performed significant protests (a typesetters' strike in Madrid in 1881) but very few significant contributions to Marxist theory.[62] Unlike the Spanish nationalism of the dynastic parties, and even the Republicans, the PSOE flaunted its universalism at its inaugural banquet. Universalism also characterised the anarchists, albeit for quasi-theological rather than materialistic reasons. As anarchists drew support above all from the proletariat in rural Andalucía and the workers of Barcelona, their cause would not flourish until the twentieth century. A concerted effort to use terrorism (known as anarchism by deed) in the 1890s certainly led to high-profile victims. But whereas it ignited no social revolution beyond such temporary revolts as Jérez in 1891, it always ignited a brutal response by the regime's Civil Guard and army besides.

Religion and empire

Whilst radical parties expanded on the left, on the right, the Catholic Church experienced a revival of its own. The revival of church power and influence was very marked, even though the 1876 constitution tolerated private non-Catholic worship. From 1880 the Catholic Church founded new Jesuit colleges and two private universities, extending its control over education in a manner which forged future intellectuals (the 'Generation of 1914'). This reinvigorated clericalism grew alongside the 1886–1936 'silver age' in Spanish art and literature.[63]

The ending of the revolution in 1874 found the social presence of the Catholic Church to be lopsided, with a significant presence in the north, especially the Basque country, and little presence in the south, thanks in large part to decades of disentailment that had stripped the church of most property short of the personal residences of priests and bishops. The church preached to the converted, and the farther south one went, the fewer these converts were (and the more likely they were to be propertied and ruralised). And yet, Spain was still culturally 'Catholic', as religious print culture boomed and feminised cults and devotion dominated the private sphere, especially of the middle classes. Even if the 1830s had destroyed the missionary church for good, from the 1850s, individualistic homilies proliferated, as Father Claret's publishing house demonstrated. Even a late nineteenth-century brothel in Almería had pictures of the Virgin Mary above its beds.[64] The growth in the religious private sphere ironically mirrored nineteenth-century liberalism's individualist public sphere.[65] And the favourable Restoration climate, in turn, emboldened Catholics to occupy the public sphere. The Restoration Catholic revival took various cultural and intellectual forms. Menéndez y Pelayo was the era's most insightful traditionalist thinker whose study of Spanish 'heterodoxies' lionised the era of Habsburg Spain and attributed all the ills of his era to the corrupting influence of the Bourbons, the Enlightenment, and the liberalism it spawned, with its side effects of Protestantism, free-thinking and licence.[66] Menéndez Pelayo could not forgive Ferdinand VII for refusing to restore the Inquisition. The Inquisition would have stopped the so-called Second Protestant Reformation arriving in Spain in the 1830s amongst handfuls of converts in lower Andalucía and Catalonia who listened to the Bible preachings of British missionaries.[67] The absence of the Holy Office, according to Menéndez Pelayo, led to revolution being possible after the king's death, just as soon as it found its man to destroy the basis of Catholicism, namely Mendizábal.[68]

Pelayo's intellectualism fuelled a reactionary clerical culture which promoted such phenomena as the intolerant Cult of the Sacred Heart, a large Marian procession in the Basque country timed in 1889 in opposition to the 'diabolical' centenary of France's proclamation of the rights of man, and a growing tendency for the faithful to hold ostentatious public ceremonies and processions protected by the authorities but often attacked by the anti-clerical working classes.[69] For all the energy of clericalism, it contained remarkably little criticism or self-reflection when compared to the Marian revival elsewhere in Europe. Spanish theology remained dogmatic and apologetic; only one Catholic novel, Luis Coloma's *Pequeñeces* (1890), could be considered to approach the high standard of 'silver age' literature, and the moderating and 'Social Catholic' doctrines of Pope Leo XIII gained comparatively little support in the Spanish clergy.[70] Yet for all its intellectual mediocrity, the church performed important social roles in welfare and education, as legislation universalising primary school education (1857) and increasing state interest in welfare were chronically underfunded and could not be made to work without clerical volunteers, usually women.[71]

The Spanish Church also developed its political voice. The involvement of some clerics in the failed Carlist rising of 1869 prompted the liberal press to rehearse old arguments and to push for religious liberty: 'Spanish clerics extract two thousand millions from our citizens annually . . . and yet they obey their king in Rome. What an incredible situation we face having two kings in the same country'.[72] The 1869 Cortes had contained only three very vocal clerical members who distinguished themselves with their intolerance of all opinions not derived from Catholicism.[73] In the regions, priests were mostly Carlists in rural Catalonia and the Basque country until the late nineteenth century when regional nationalist movements offered more modern ways to protect regional religious customs. Only rural upland Navarra thereafter remained true to Carlism. As the Alfonsine state was generous to Catholicism it proved harder to develop non-Carlist confessional politics on a nationwide basis. Carlist traditions were rooted in the north and accepted, even relished, violence as a logical form of protest. Even though traditionalists like Nocedal, Balmes, and Donoso Cortes had been expounding an ideological canon since the 1860s, this amounted to little more to homilies condemning the abuses of capitalism. The military defeat of 1876 set Carlism on a course of decline which could not easily be mitigated by participation in modern politics, especially when Carlists continued to cling to quaint traditions of martyrs, traitors and righteous violence.[74] In 1888, amidst a bitter civil war of words in the Carlist press, Carlism itself suffered a schism as Cándido Nocedal's son created an implacably theocratic movement known as Integrism, very much like the ultramontane currents which flourished amongst the Catholic Right elsewhere in Europe.

The Bourbon Restoration developed links between industrialisation and 'new imperialism'. Catalonia's industrial lead within Spain remained during the last quarter of the century, although the rapid expansion of Basque iron and steel from the 1870s was catching up. Basque industrialisation was recognisably modern, being financed by the region's modern banking system and being much less dependent on family ownership than was the case in Catalonia. As Catalan industry was less competitive, Restoration politicians from Barcelona maintained pressure on the Madrid government not only to keep import tariffs high in Spain itself but also to use tariffs to maintain Cuba as a captive market for Catalan textile exports.[75] The brutal Ten Years' War in Cuba (1868–78) demonstrated the persistence of Spanish imperialism. In 1883 the Sociedad de Africanistas y Colonistas was set up, and trade and investment interests grew in Morocco even before a formal Spanish protectorate was declared there in the next century.[76] The following year, Covadonga (Asturias), site where the Christian 'Reconquest' of Islamic Spain was believed to have begun, was designated as a national monument, weaving national, Catholic, and imperial identity into one.[77]

The consolidation of empire took on added poignancy given the rise of new and larger imperial powers in the late nineteenth century. In the 1880s, the Regenerationist Conservative Antonio Maura campaigned for an expanded high-seas fleet to project Spanish imperial interests.[78] But Cánovas had never shown much interest in naval matters, and the 1885 Carolinas crisis with Germany found the Spanish navy unprepared. The diplomatic standoff over the Caroline Islands ended up being diffused by Holy See mediation, so the antiquated squadron Spain assembled at Menorca never had to be tested in war.[79] The Spanish–German spat was anomalous. Only eight years earlier the authoritarian German Empire had appealed enough to Cánovas for him to ask Chancellor Bismarck for a Spanish–German military alliance. Bismarck's new German Empire, after all, had supported Spain in its Ten Years' War in Cuba and condemned Carlist efforts at the same time. But Bismarck snubbed his entreaties in the knowledge that internal divisions would make Spain a liability in any future joint war with France.[80] Even so, in 1887 the free-trade Liberal foreign minister, Segismundo Moret, faced down widespread pro-neutral opposition in the press by aligning Spain loosely with Germany's Triple Alliance.[81] During the 1892 four-hundredth anniversary celebrations of Columbus's 'discovery' of America, Spain flaunted the pan-Hispanic idea of the *magna patria*. Prime Minister Cánovas disbursed 2 million *pesetas* from his meagre treasury to hold exhibitions, parades, and poorly attended lectures, celebrating the 'Discovery'.[82] Yet Cánovas could not control the narrative about the quatercentenary. In 1891 the Cuban writer and leader of the Cuban Revolutionary Party, José Martí (1853–95), published his widely read essay, 'Nuestra América' ('America Is Ours'). Martí condemned foreign imperialism, both from Spain and from what he called the 'tiger at the door', the United States, and defended the cause of Cuban independence and Latin pan-Americanism.[83] The 1892 quatercentenary, for all its pan-Hispanist exhibitions, was a last hurrah for a Spanish imperial establishment soon to be engulfed by an anti-colonial revolt in its last serious colony and imperial rivalry from across the Atlantic.

End of empire

Spain's imperial grandeur came crashing down in the three years following the Cuban independence revolt of 1895. A Cuban insurrection which may yet have been defeated as late as 1897 would become the focus for the loss of Spain's remaining empire to a rising foreign power and the cause and effect of political turmoil in Spain itself. The historiography of this war has been insufficient for two reasons. First, military historians have ignored it because it produced no great battles, which means that only the US intervention at the end has interested them. Second, most scholars have tended to see the 1895 uprising and the defeat as products of underlying forces and long-term trends, the war itself being not much more than a footnote.[84] For many readers, the of 1895–98 Cuban war is really a war of 1898 between Spain and the United States. Generations of historians assumed US superiority against Spanish 'decadence' or accepted at face value Cuban nationalist arguments about unbeatable 'people's war'. But in reality, the war was more complex, as John Lawrence Tone's comprehensive study reveals, and Spanish defeat and even US intervention was not pre-ordained.

That said, the Cuban rebels now wanted outright independence from Spain, as set out in the 24 February 1895 Proclamation of Baire, a village in pro-rebel eastern Cuba. Also, the Spanish military was poorly prepared, the '*trocha*' of the 1870s having become run-down and overtaken by jungle. The old *trocha* was an unlikely focus for what would become the biggest European colonial effort of the age of 'new' imperialism. Over the course of the ensuing war, some 190,000 Spanish troops would be employed against the

Cuban Liberation Army, which never exceeded 40,000 (indeed, it was usually much smaller and made a point of avoiding major battles). This was thus the largest colonial campaign launched by a European power hitherto. Fewer than 4,000 Spanish soldiers died in actual combat with insurgents, but some 41,288 died from disease (i.e. 93 per cent of all Spanish fatalities and 22 per cent of all Spanish military personnel sent to Cuba). Figures of 90 per cent and above were recorded in terms of killing of livestock as part of the economic war, and perhaps some 170,000 Cuban civilians died (10 per cent of the population).

Whereas rebellious eastern Cuba had socio-economic conditions including popular relationships to rural land use, western Cuba had a much greater slave plantation legacy (slavery only having been definitively abolished on the island in 1886).[85] Since 1886, Cuban planters had been encouraging contract migration from Spain, the 'swallows' (*golondrinas*) who would spend six months harvesting Cuban sugar during the annual dearth in Spain. Given the climate of racism, Cuba's plantocracy tended to welcome the presence of white labourers. But the economic interests of the planters outweighed their racism as they refused to offer land for permanent settlement.[86] Matters got worse as sugar beet began to displace cane sugar from the late nineteenth century, threatening Cuba's premier product. At the same time, the west of the island became whiter as Spanish immigration increased. Indeed, some scholars have stressed the 1895 war as a racial war between a whiter west and a blacker east. In 1894 a severe hurricane exacerbated the traditional banditry of the east. Some scholars see 1868 through 1898 as a 'Thirty Years' War', with *criollo* elites coming down on the side of independence as the 1870s and 1880s process of abolishing slavery removed the final reason for benefitting from the rule of Madrid.[87] Certainly both Prime Minister Cánovas and Captian General of Cuba Polavieja, during 1895–1896, pressed hard, essentially trying to return Cuba to its pre-1868 prostration, albeit now with Cortes representation (one of the gains of the 1876 Zanjón agreement) and without slavery.[88]

Veterans of the Ten Years' War, Maceo and Gómez, would fall out in the 1880s, but relations were repaired in the 1890s under the leadership of José Martí, whose independence manifesto included a social dimension demanding better wages and land reform for the descendants of slavery. Martí had a Jeffersonian or Mazzinian belief in innate and natural Cuban national feeling and in the incorrigible decadence of Spain. He believed that Cuban nationalism could also bridge the island's racial divides.

The 1890s' Spanish captain general of Cuba, Calleja, and Miguel Maura in the Spanish government tried to institute Maura's 1893 Cuban autonomy plan. This might have worked but was delayed by a colonial disaster in Morocco which diverted Spanish parliamentary attention until it was too late (an amended version of the autonomy law was introduced only in 1895), and Sagasta was never really interested in Cuba anyway.[89] When Cánovas declared that Spain would fight to keep Cuba until 'the last peseta and the last drop of blood' before relinquishing any control of the island, Sagasta's retort was 'not a man nor peseta more'.[90] Anti-war demonstrations were spreading throughout Spain, as youngsters in Barcelona and Valencia trailed banners reading 'Long Live Spain! Send no more soldiers to Cuba!'[91] Both Cánovas and Sagasta were aware of how tightly constrained any Madrid policy towards Cuba could be in terms of autonomy. Any loosening of Spanish control would logically propel the island towards the United States, the economic giant only 120 kilometres away and destination by the 1890s for 90 per cent of exports. Spain, by contrast, lay 9,000 kilometres distant and bought only 3.7 per cent of exports. Spain, as one historian commented, was a 'parasite extracting resources who could only offer its culture in return'.[92]

Martí's March 1895 death in action ended the chance of a liberal-democratic Cuban nationalism. Command of the Cuban Liberation Army (CLA) was taken over by the more authoritarian Gómez who demanded total war (and banning any compromise like the hated Zanjón Treaty of 1876). Economic war was waged against Spanish-held parts of the island, the idea being to turn Cuba's wealth into a mortal weapon. The infamous Spanish 'reconcentration' policy thus originated in part in the rebels' own actions (the flight of refugees from devastated areas to Spanish centres of control).[93] In practice, Máximo Gómez's extreme line was moderated by commanders on the spot, especially in the friendlier east.

The 14 July 1895 Cuban victory at Peralejo was a great turning point and was partly a result of the inspired leadership of General Antonio Maceo, a mulatto of Venezuelan heritage (at a time when the vast majority of officers in Cuba were white and the soldiers black). Maceo's strategy of guerrilla war played on Cuban strengths, especially their superior numbers of horses which had the effect of driving out pro-Spanish communities in the east, compounding Spanish logistical difficulties and increasing reconcentration. Matters were made worse for the Spaniards by their greater weakness with malaria and yellow fever and by the employment of outdated Napoleonic tactics of squares and volleys in the age of efficient and accurate rifle fire and Cuban dum-dum bullets. Thus, the colonial Cubans won at Peralejo using modern and appropriate tactics against a supposedly superior metropolitan power.[94]

Cuban independence victories at Peralejo and later at Mal Tiempo could not obscure the fact that Cuba's war was also a civil war. Some sixty thousand Cubans (mainly from the anti-rebel west) served in the Spanish forces. Yet over the course of 1895–1896, Spanish captain general Martínez Campos dissipated his combat strength by garrisoning even small settlements in order to placate Cuban loyalism, a strategy which invariably squandered resources as small detachments were detailed to defend plantations and timber yards.[95] The shortcoming in Campos's strategy was laid bare by Cuban victories. The December 1895 Cuban victory at Mal Tiempo was the most important victory before the US victory at Santiago in July 1898 and led

Spanish commander-in-chief Martínez Campos to resign his command.[96] Mal Tiempo helped create the myth of the machete as terror for Spaniards and people's war symbol for Cubans. But, in fact, the Cubans used rifles just as much as the Spaniards. Despite early twentieth-century Cuban interpretations of the 1890s war as a 'people's war', Cubans reached for technology and militarization, and only some 3 per cent of the male population enlisted in the Liberation Army, and even these figures were skewed towards the closing months of the war.[97]

Empire fights back

Madrid replaced Campos with a hard-bitten soldier. When Valeriano Weyler was given the post of governor and commander-in-chief of Cuba, he vowed that he would 'answer war with war'. After his nomination, Weyler took the train from Madrid to Barcelona in a journey marked by waving crowds along the way. Barcelona welcomed him with more crowds and a mass conferring him the protection of the Virgin. The former commander of Cuba, Martínez Campos, by contrast, was booed and ridiculed upon his return to Spain. Spanish nationalism swept the literate classes in recognisably modern ways. The aristocratic novelist and feminist Emilia Pardo Bazán filled almost the entire 20 December 1896 edition of *El Liberal* newspaper with 'Página suelta', a short story laced with religious and racist overtones praising the loyalty of loyal Spanish soldiers fighting Philippine insurgents.[98] Weyler set sail for Cuba on 23 January 1896, and on reaching the embattled island, it became clear exactly what he had in mind 'answering war with war'.[99] General Weyler's three-point counter-insurgency strategy involved (1) consolidation of hitherto scattered garrisons and detachments (hence, the objective would no longer be protection of property but the destruction of the Liberation Army), (2) he would expend his resources on one part of Cuba at a time, and (3) Weyler would relocate civilians from the countryside to the towns where he could shield them from rebel demands for supplies (and end the need for isolated garrisons).[100] This strategy was supported by the largest yet dispatched from Europe to a non-European theatre of operations. Over the course of the 1868–78 and 1895–98 Cuban wars, some four hundred thousand Spanish troops were dispatched to the island, nine times more than the total amount of peninsular forces sent to quell the entire Spanish American continent during the 1810–21 independence movements.[101] Weyler's resolve to destroy the enemy rather than protect property denuded the countryside of garrisons and therefore forced loyalists to side with the CLA. Yet Weyler's brutalising field army at least was scoring military victories.

The Cubans scored a limited victory at Ceja del Negro on 4 October 1896. Yet the tides turned in favour of Weyler as in December 1896 Antonio Maceo was killed in action. This set off jingoistic celebrations in Havana and Madrid and hopes that the war would soon end. At the time of Maceo's death, the west of the island was 'almost' pacified (there were always still armed groups), which meant the the Cubans' economic war was no longer effective. Given the Spanish military superiority, horses were turned over to them rather than to the CLA, and the death penalty issued by the CLA against any Cuban caught with Spanish identification documents was recognised as a dead letter as Weyler continued his gains.

Weyler's most notorious counter-insurgency strategy was 'reconcentration'. It is often overlooked that reconcentration operated in tandem with rebel 'deconcentration'. The practice was hardest on women and children, as the vast majority were poor and could not buy their way out of forced reset-tlement. There was a certain logic to civilian suffering in CLA war strategy, as the CLA always wanted economic war and did not think it could defeat the Spanish Army in formal battle. Also, driving off refugees into Spanish areas of control helped with the war effort as the Spaniards suffered over-burdened food supplies and logistics and civilian suffering aided the rebels' propaganda agenda. Lands were denied to reconcentrated families if they had family members fighting with the insurgents, which proved a virtual death sentence. The urgency of reallocating lands, in any case, was lost on the Span-ish military command. Spanish officers were Spanish nationalists representing the colonial order. And in Cuba, despite the abolition of slavery, property remained more valuable than people.[102]

The horrors of war created scandals in both Spain and the United States. Both Spanish Liberals (such as Canalejas's investigation in 1897) and US jin-goists exaggerated the death toll of Cuban civilians as as much as three hun-dred to four hundred thousand, and these contemporary investigation figures have also been repeated uncritically by scholars. In fact, a figure between sixty thousand and two hundred thousand is likely to be accurate, and according to the authoritative historian Jordi Maluquer de Motes, it was, in fact, between 155,000 and 170,000. Fatalities were higher in the middle of the island (Santa Clara province) as it was a grey area between the Spanish-controlled west (where reconcentration could be ameliorated by economic recovery) and the rebel-controlled east.[103] But the controversy of the war reached its peak when Weyler's Conservative backers in Spain fell from power in August 1897. The assassination of Cánovas at the hands of an anarchist on 4 October 1897 was followed by the formation of a Liberal ministry under Sagasta. Sagasta sacked Weyler, whose counter-insurgency been the subject of vitriol in the Spanish and foreign press, and drafted an autonomy statute for Cuba which entered into force on 1 January 1898.

The Sagasta government's recall of Weyler did not immediately halt the reconcentration policy, and during the many weeks it had left to run, recon-centration claimed its highest number of victims. Returning farmers faced the same policy in reverse, as the CLA itself reconcentrated refugees deep inside Cuba Libre or expelled them back into Spanish zones of control.

The incoming Liberal regime in Madrid ushered in a limited form of autonomy for Cuba, with a devolved administration taking power on

1 January 1898 running its own affairs short of foreign policy, and military and budgetary powers which remained reserved to Madrid. Elections on the island were called for May 1898. These reforms clearly presented a threat to the CLA which, in response, drafted its own constitution, partly in order to convince the United States that the Gómez insurgency was not presiding over a permanent military dictatorship. Spanish reforms in Cuba by late 1897 had led the Spanish ambassador to Washington to believe that President McKinley would not intervene in Cuba. Thus, the assassination of Cánovas the hardliner actually tipped the scales in favour of US armed intervention. Madrid's recall of General Weyler frustrated what had been an effective, if brutal, counter-insurgency, and half-baked offers of autonomy to Cuba emboldened the CLA.[104]

The trigger for the US declaration of war on 25 April 1898 Spain was the infamous sinking of the US battleship *Maine* in Havana harbour. The source of the explosion of the *Maine* was most likely negligence, probably a coal fire near the ammunition store. But the combination of jingoism in the United States, enraged Spanish loyalism in western Cuba, and political calculations in Madrid escalated this incident into the Spanish–American War (April–August 1898). On 21 April 1898, the United States declared war on Spain.[105]

The instability of Spain's domestic politics had obliged the Madrid government to be intransigent towards the United States. Popular Spanish nationalism, something largely absent in 1808 and partly confected in the colonial wars of the 1860s, swept the country, boosted to some extent by droughts and high food prices.[106] The Spanish government felt itself pulled in a nationalistic direction. Rumours gripped Madrid that even the Carlists, very much a spent force since 1876, would mount a rebellion if Madrid failed to defend *Hispanidad*. In September 1895, the bishop of Oviedo linked his native Covadonga, supposed site of the Christian 'Reconquest' of Spain, with the defence of Columbus's legacy in Cuba. Once war with the United States was joined, the patriotic-religious fervour bubbled over. On 2 May 1898, a sermon read out in Madrid Cathedral linked the Second of May uprising against the French with the war recently declared with the United States and condemned the United States as 'greedy barbarians riding high on steam engines, armed with electricity, disguised as Europeans'.[107] The clericalised nationalism appeared propitious for a Carlist effort. In fact, in October 1900, some sixty armed Carlists led by Josep Torrents did lead a failed attack on a Civil Guard barracks at Badalona near Barcelona. But the threat had been exaggerated as authorities deployed extra troops and closed suspicious Traditionalist clubs with apparent ease.[108] What decisively drove Madrid to opt to accept war with the United States instead of surrender was the fear that a *pronunciamiento* in Spain would ensue, overthrowing the teetering Restoration system.[109]

The Spanish government under Cánovas had censored the wartime press, even establishing a 'Black Cabinet' adjoined to the Interior Ministry tasked with cutting off all telegramme and telephone communications the moment they relayed militarily sensitive information.[110] Sagasta's Liberal ministry retained strict censorship over communications between Cuba and Spain but relaxed it in respect of both Spanish and foreign newspapers circulating in Spain itself. Thus, the United States, after its declaration of war in April 1898, benefitted from several weeks of uncensored access to and from Spain. Once constitutional guarantees were suspended across Spain in July 1898, Sagasta was attacked by Conservatives and Republicans alike for using censorship to protect himself and party from criticism. As one historian has recently argued, both Conservatives and Liberals stopped liking the freedom of the press as soon as it criticised them.[111]

Whilst domestic Spanish politics were in turmoil, the military contest in Cuba and the Philippines went America's way. The United States scored devastating naval victories in both theatres. Even though the Americans worried that they were still a 'brown-water' naval power, their modern fleet made short work of the antiquated and smaller vessels deployed by Spain.[112] Spain had committed itself to the *jeune ecole* theory of naval warfare, investing in smaller vessels and raiding tactics as a type of 'guerrilla war at sea', as one Spanish naval officer put it.[113] But Spain's faith in the *jeune ecole* ideas of Hyacinthe Aube proved catastrophically misplaced, as its fleet was annihilated by the larger, blue-water vessels of the Americans which had been designed very much in the 'power projection' image of the influential US naval officer Alfred Thayer Mahan. On land, Spain also suffered from a self-defeating guerrilla myth, according to which, in brief, Spain was supposedly a martial race intrinsically superior to the money-obsessed Anglo-Saxons. In fact, the Spanish army inflicted heavy casualties on the Americans, and to the end, its garrison at Havana was undefeated. But the Spanish Army was still wrong-footed by the sudden need to wage symmetrical warfare against the US invasion after three years of counter-insurgency operations.[114]

US naval supremacy rendered continued Spanish resistance hopeless, and by August the Madrid government accepted that it was defeated. The subsequent Treaty of Paris surrendered Cuba, Puerto Rico, and the Philippines to US control, and Spain's last remaining island possessions in the Pacific would be sold to Germany soon afterwards. The Cuban War ushered in 1898 as the 'Disaster' year that ended Spain's nineteenth century. Historians now find dates unfashionable, but the series of macro-structural changes in Spanish politics, culture, and society after 1898 rightly demarcate the centuries along 'Disaster' lines. Spain's nineteenth century, which had begun with a crisis of empire at home and abroad, thus ended in a similar fashion.

Notes

1 Dardé, *Historia de España*; Nigel Townson, 'The Contested Quest for Modernization, 1914–1936', in Shubert and Alvarez-Junco (eds.), *The History of Modern Spain*, p. 64.
2 Javier Moreno Luzón, 'El mosaico de la Restauración', *Revista de libros*, No. 34 (Octubre 1999), pp. 10–11.

3 José Luis Martínez Sanz, 'Los proto-regeneracionistas', in de Mendoza and Togores (eds.), *Cánovas y su época*, 2 vols., Vol. II, p. 845.

4 Carr, *Spain, 1808–1939*, p. 523; Moreno-Luzón, *Modernizing the Nation*, p. 138. Yet Carlos Seco Serrano and Javier Tusell were pessimists, arguing that by the time of 1923 coup the Restoration was indeed 'exhausted'.

5 Pamela Beth-Radcliff, 'From Democratic Transition to Consolidation and *Crispación*: 1970s-Present', in Shubert and Alvarez-Junco (eds.), *The History of Modern Spain*, p. 127.

6 Jesús Millán and María Cruz Romeo, 'Was the Liberal Revolution Important to Modern Spain? Political Cultures and Citizenship in Spanish history', *Social History*, Vol. 29, No. 3 (2004), pp. 284–300, 296–8.

7 Carlos Dardé, 'Ideas acerca de la monarquía y las funciones del monarca', in Encarna García Monerris, Mónica Moreno Seco, and Juan I. Marcuello Benedicto (eds.), *Culturas políticas en la España liberal*, pp. 335–6.

8 Dardé, *Historia de España*, p. 16.

9 José Luis Comellas García-Llera, *Cánovas* (Madrid: Ediciones Cid, 1965), p. 165.

10 José Luis Comellas García-Llera, 'Sobre los discursos de Cánovas en el Ateneo', in de Mendoza and Togores (eds.), *Cánovas y su época*, 2 vols., Vol. I, p. 95.

11 Dardé, *Historia de España*, pp. 28–9.

12 Millán and Romeo, 'Was the Liberal Revolution Important to Modern Spain?' pp. 284–300, 289–300.

13 Paul Garner, 'Porifirio Díaz and Personalist Politics in Mexico', in Will Fowler (ed.), *Authoritarianism in Latin America Since Independence* (London: Praeger, 1996), pp. 33–4.

14 Pedro Rújula, 'El antiliberalismo reaccionario', in María Cruz Romeo and María Sierra (eds.), *La España liberal: 1833–1874* (Madrid: Marcial Pons, 2014), p. 387.

15 Dardé, *Historia de España*, p. 30.

16 Carlos Seco Serrano, 'El sistema político de la Restauración', in de Mendoza and Togores (eds.), *Cánovas y su época*, 2 vols., Vol. I, p. 389.

17 Antonio Cánovas del Castillo, *Discurso sobre la nación* (Madrid: Impresa Central, 1882), pp. 130–2.

18 Hennessy, *The Federal Republic in Spain*, pp. 9–11.

19 Pí y Margall, *La reacción y la revolución*, p. 263.

20 Francisco Comín Comín, *Las crisis de la deuda soberana en España (1500–2015)* (Madrid: Catarata, 2016), p. 182.

21 Manuel Santirso, *España en la Europa liberal (1830–1870)* (Barcelona: Ariel, 2012), p. 255.

22 Dardé, *Historia de España*, pp. 38–40.

23 Moreno-Luzón, *Modernizing the Nation*, p. 34.

24 Eiras Roel, *La Emigración española a ultramar*.

25 Thomson, *Birth of Modern Politics*, pp. 266–7.

26 Josep Colomé Ferrer, 'L'ofensiva dels propietaris contra el contracte de rabassa morta a la comarca del Penedès, 1850–1910', *Recerques*, Vol. 67 (2013), pp. 115–40.

27 Jesús Cruz, 'Ways of Life: Cities, Towns and Villages', in Shubert and Alvarez-Junco (eds.), *The History of Modern Spain*, p. 185.

28 *Ibid.*, p. 187.

29 Comellas García-Llera, *Los Moderados en el poder*, p. 59.

30 Josefina Gómez de Mendoza, 'The Environment', in Shubert and Alvarez-Junco (eds.), *The History of Modern Spain*, pp. 225–6.

31 Cruz, 'Ways of Life', in Shubert and Alvarez-Junco (eds.), *The History of Modern Spain*, p. 191.

32 Samuel Llano, *Discordant Notes: Marginality and Social Control in Madrid, 1850–1930* (Oxford: Oxford University Press, 2018), pp. 1–11.

33 Cleminson and Vázquez García, '*Los invisibles*', p. 67.

34 Ardit Lucas, *Revolución liberal y revuelta campesina*, p. 70.
35 Antonio Cánovas del Castillo, *Discursos parlamentarios* (Madrid: Congreso de los Diputados, 1854).
36 Javier Moreno-Luzón, 'The Restoration, 1874–1914', in Shubert and Alvarez-Junco (eds.), *The History of Modern Spain*, pp. 50–1.
37 Emilio Ortega Berenguer, *La enseñanza en Málaga, 1833–1933* (Málaga: Universidad de Málaga, 1985), p. 58.
38 Hughes, *Revelations of Spain in 1845*, Vol. I, p. 252.
39 Moreno-Luzón, 'The Restoration, 1874–1914', in Shubert and Alvarez-Junco (eds.), *The History of Modern Spain*, p. 52.
40 Miguel Martorell Linares, 'Legislation, Accountability and Consensus in the Spanish Parliament', in Pedro Tavares de Almeida and Javier Moreno Luzón (eds.), *The Politics of Representation* (Sussex: Sussex Academic Press, 2018), pp. 57–8.
41 Thomson, *Birth of Modern Politics*, p. 225.
42 Francisco Vázquez García, 'La campaña contra los sacerdotes pederastas (1880–1912): un ejemplo de "pánico moral" en la España de la Restauración', *Hispania*, 2018, Vol. LXXVIII, No. 260 (septiembre–diciembre), pp. 759–86.
43 José Ortega y Gasset, *La España Invertebrada* (Madrid: Calpe, 1922), pp. 64–5.
44 Justo Beramendi, 'Algunos aspectos del *nation-building* español en la Galicia del siglo XIX', in Moreno Luzón (ed.), *Construir España*, pp. 59–82; Ramón Villares, *Historia de Galicia* (Barcelona: Galaxia, 2014).
45 Carr, *Spain, 1808–1975*, p. 369.
46 Eduardo González Calleja, *La razón de la fuerza: orden público, subversión y violencia política en la España de la Restauración (1875–1917)* (Madrid: CSIC, 1998), p. 53.
47 Pedro María Egea Bruno, 'Mata al rey y vete a Murcia. La corrupción de la justicia en la España de la Restauración', *Studia Historia Contemporánea*, Vol. 33 (2015), pp. 159–92.
48 Carlos Dardé, 'Elections in Spain', in de Almeida and Moreno Luzón (eds.), *The Politics of Representation*, p. 50.
49 Dardé, *Historia de España*, pp. 82–4.
50 Conde Fernández-Oliva, 'Sobre el pensamiento en relación a as fuerzas armadas de Cánovas del Castillo', in de Mendoza and Togores (eds.), *Cánovas y su época*, 2 vols., Vol. I, p. 147.
51 Carlos Blanco Escolá, *La Academia General Militar de Zaragoza (1928–1931)* (Barcelona: Labor, 1989), p. 147.
52 Roberto Sánchez Abal, 'La restauración y la reforma de la enseñanza militar', in de Mendoza and Togores (eds.), *Cánovas y su época*, 2 vols., Vol. II, pp. 934–42.
53 Eduardo Calleja, *La razón de la fuerza*, p. 33.
54 *Ibid.*, pp. 27–9, 39, 51.
55 Vila-San-Juan, *Amadeo I*, pp. 64–5.
56 Alejandro Quiroga and Miguel Angel del Arco (eds.), *Right-wing Spain in the Civil War Era: Soldiers of God and Apostles of the Fatherland, 1914–45* (London: Continuum, 2012), pp. 1–18.
57 Ginger, 'How to Be Universal', in Ginger and Lawless (eds.), *Spain in the Nineteenth Century*, pp. 78–9.
58 Fox, *La invención de España*, pp. 58, 63.
59 Marichal, *El secreto de España*, p. 161.
60 Fox, *La invención de España*, pp. 32–3.
61 de Mendoza, 'The Environment', in Shubert and Alvarez-Junco (eds.), *The History of Modern Spain*, pp. 220–2.
62 José Alvarez-Junco, 'Pablo Iglesias', in Shubert and Alvarez-Junco (eds.), *The History of Modern Spain*, pp. 415–17.
63 Marichal, *El secreto de España*, pp. 136, 291.
64 Frances Lannon, *Privilege, Persecution, and Prophecy: The Catholic Church in Spain, 1875–1975* (Oxford: Oxford University Press, 1987), pp. 2–4, 22.

65 Callahan, *Church, Politics and Society*, pp. 235–6.
66 Lannon, *Privilege and Prophecy*, pp. 37–8.
67 Gregorio Alonso, *Nación en capilla*, pp. 207, 238.
68 Monerris and Rosa, 'Apologistas y detractores', in Moerris, Frasquet, and Monerris (eds.), *Cuando todo era posible*, pp. 43–4.
69 Lannon, *Privilege and Prophecy*, pp. 29–32.
70 *Ibid.*, pp. 44, 94–100.
71 *Ibid.*, pp. 63–6.
72 María Pilar Salamón Chéliz, 'La Iglesia y el Vaticano, enemigos de la España liberal', in Seixas and Sevillano (eds.), *Los enemigos de España*, p. 196.
73 Lannon, *Privilege and Prophecy*, pp. 99–100.
74 Martin Blinkhorn, *Carlism in Crisis* (Oxford: Oxford University Press, 1975), pp. 20–37.
75 Dardé, *Historia de España*, pp. 44–50.
76 Moreno-Luzón, *Modernizing the Nation*, p. 66.
77 Mary Vincent, *Spain: 1833–2002* (Oxford: Oxford University Press, 2007), p. 51.
78 Melchor Fernández Almagro, 'Prólogo' to Sevilla Andrés, *Antonio Maura*, p. 14.
79 Agustín Ramón Rodríguez González, 'Cánovas y la política naval de la Restauración', in de Mendoza and Togores (eds.), *Cánovas y su época*, 2 vols., Vol. I, pp. 492–7; Rodríguez González, 'La crisis de las Carolinas', *Cuadernos de Historia Contemporánea*, Vol. 13 (1991), pp. 25–46.
80 Julio Salom Costa, 'La política exterior u ultramarina de Cánovas', in de Mendoza and Togores (eds.), *Cánovas y su época*, 2 vols., Vol. II, p. 1126.
81 *Ibid.*, pp. 1118–19.
82 Marichal, *El secreto de España*, p. 216; Krauel, *Imperial Emotions*, pp. 51–6.
83 José Martí, 'Nuestra América', *La Revista illustrada* (New York, 10 January 1891).
84 Tone, *War and Genocide in Cuba, 1895–1898*, pp. 3–13.
85 *Ibid.*, p. 20.
86 Albert Garcia-Balañà, 'Migración y milicia en la España transatlántica del siglo XIX: quge y caída del imperialismo popular', *Storicamente*, Vol. 12, No. 1 (2016), pp. 1–24, 8–9.
87 Tone, *War and Genocide in Cuba, 1895–1898*, pp. 25–9.
88 Schmidt-Nowara, 'Imperio y crisis colonial', in Pan-Montojo (ed.), *Más se perdió en Cuba*, p. 49.
89 Tone, *War and Genocide in Cuba, 1895–1898*, pp. 34–49.
90 *Ibid.*, p. 49.
91 Manuel Pérez Ledesma, 'La sociedad española, la guerra y la derrota', in Juan Pan-Montojo (ed.), *Más se perdió en Cuba*, pp. 115–16.
92 Manuel Moreno Fraginals, *Cuba/España – España-Cuba: Historia Común* (Barcelona: Grijalbo Mondadori, 1995), p. 294.
93 Tone, *War and Genocide in Cuba, 1895–1898*, pp. 54–8.
94 *Ibid.*, pp. 64–80.
95 *Ibid.*, pp. 93, 113–18.
96 Stucki, '¿Guerra entre hermanos en la gran Antilla?' in Seixas and Sevillano (eds.), *Los enemigos de España*, p. 283.
97 Tone, *War and Genocide in Cuba, 1895–1898*, pp. 125–44.
98 Susana Bardavío Estevan, '"¡España es también aquí!": Nación e imaginario colonial en los cuentos de Emilia Pardo Bazán', *Castilla: Estudios de Literatura*, No. 9 (2018), pp. 176–203, 180–2.
99 Ledesma, 'La sociedad española, la guerra y la derrota', in Pan-Montojo (ed.), *Más se perdió en Cuba*, pp. 95–6.
100 Tone, *War and Genocide in Cuba, 1895–1898*, p. 160.
101 Schmidt-Nowara, 'Imperio y crisis colonial', in Pan-Montojo (ed.), *Más se perdió en Cuba*, p. 33.
102 Tone, *War and Genocide in Cuba, 1895–1898*, pp. 81–5, 181–208.

103 *Ibid.*, pp. 209–15.
104 Luis Navarro García, '1898, la incierta victoria de Cuba', *Anuario de Estudios Americanos*, Vol. 55, No. 1 (1998), pp. 165–87.
105 Tone, *War and Genocide in Cuba, 1895–1898*, pp. 216–49.
106 Sebastian Balfour, 'Riot, Regenration and Reaction: Spain in the Aftermath of the 1898 Disaster', *The Historical Journal*, Vol. 38, No. 2 (1995), pp. 405–23.
107 Ledesma, 'La sociedad española, la guerra y la derrota', in Pan-Montojo (ed.), *Más se perdió en Cuba*, pp. 104–6.
108 Xavier Tornafoch Yuste, 'De la insureción ó a les urnes: La consolidació electoral del carlisme a Vic (1900–1909)', in Montañà and Rafart (eds.), *Propaganda carlista, religió, literatura i operacions militars*, pp. 200–2.
109 José Alvarez-Junco, 'La nación en duda', in Pan-Montojo (ed.), *Más se perdió en Cuba*, p. 409.
110 María López de Ramón, 'Influencia del poder politico en la libertad de prensa: la guerra de Cuba (1895–98)', *Revista Jurídica de la Universidad Autónoma de Madrid*, Vol. 33 2016, pp. 143–64, 146.
111 *Ibid.*, pp. 143–64, 148–56.
112 Tone, *War and Genocide in Cuba, 1895–1898*, pp. 259–61.
113 *Ibid.*, p. 262.
114 *Ibid.*, p. 274.

Conclusion

The Liberal prime minister Práxedes Sagasta explained the defeat of 1898 by the fact that 'Spain was a poor country'. Britain's prime minister, Lord Salisbury, called Spain 'moribund'. Yet it was a poor country which had invested heavily in Cuba, the 'pearl of the Caribbean', having sent more soldiers, slaves, and emigrants to that island during the nineteenth century than in any previous century. After 1898, Spain's colonial legacy persisted on the island, even with the connivance of the US imperialists. After the war, the victorious US colonial authorities, gripped like other Western powers by scientific racism and despite the recent Hispanophobic propaganda of Chicago's 'yellow press', rediscovered the benefits of Spanish whiteness and its 'superiority' in both Cuba and the Philippines.[1]

But within Spain, the sight of returning veterans gave sharp relief to the ongoing bread riots of 1899. A shoemaker killed by the Civil Guard during riots in Zaragoza in 1899 had his corpse reclaimed by his father who cried, 'He came from Cuba! He was a sergeant! He didn't get his back-pay and was protesting against the government!'[2] Disturbances involving post-war veterans belied the official commemorations, part of which centred on the statue in the Rastro (Madrid) honouring the everyman Eloy Gonzalo. Gonzalo had been a marginalised child who, as an adolescent at his wits' end, joined the army and later became a posthumous hero after being killed in action in a minor action against Cuban insurgents. His public commemoration was 'nationalised' by a mournful nation after the defeat of 1898. Thus, Cuba had not been the last vestige of an empire stuck in the sixteenth century, as several commentators in the United States claimed, but the object of a new imperial project whose loss after 1898 would become the focus for ill-focused revanchism.[3]

In some ways, the 'boomerang effect' of imperialism on the homeland, which the German Jewish philosopher Hannah Arendt identified as a factor in driving European totalitarianism,[4] would be evident in Spain as army politics developed *revanchism* after 1898. And since the 1898 defeat, the most violently creative part of the Spanish Army, the *africanistas*, would 'internalise empire', viewing metropolitan, Peninsular Spain as its muse and acting out for themselves a role as a conservative unifying force in domestic politics.[5]

Army officers in 1898 were unanimous in blaming the defeat on politicians, and their subsequent 'internalisation of empire' had very limited toleration for the regionalist aspirations of Catalonia and the Basque country. The 'Disaster' boosted regional nationalism in both these areas, although in the case of the Basque country nationalism was still only really 'Biscayism'. Bilbao continued to attract growing numbers of 'immigrant' Spaniards (dubbed *maketos*) who worked for Basque factory owners, banished Euskeran from the towns and cities, refused to go to Mass, and voted Socialist. The Catholic, ethnic, and ruralist nationalism of Arana's Basque National Party (PNV) thus took hold in the country districts of Vizcaya where it began to rival Carlism. Much more imposing, however, was Catalanism, even though the PNV founder, Sabino Arana, was convinced that, whereas the Basque country only formed part of 'Iberia', Catalonia actually formed part of 'Spain'. Part of the Catalanist current shared Arana's medievalist and rural revolt against the centralising *caciques* and capitalism of Castile. Enric Prat de la Riba, who had founded the conservative wing of Catalanism, the Unió Catalanista, in 1891, would do to Carlism in rural Catalonia what Sabino Arana would to do rural Vizcaya. Prat's medievalism shared a worldview with Joaquín Costa, whose regenerationism railed against the dead hand of Castile and its *caciques*. It was also inspired by the neo-Catholic Jaime Balmes, who had argued in proto-Catalan nationalist terms that Madrid had 'no sea, no river, [it exists] in the heart of a desert, with no industry, no life of its own . . .' But Prat's medievalism was outweighed by the industrial Catalanism of the Francesc Cambó, which was boosted after 1898 by the loss of Catalonia's captive market in Cuba and which early in the twentieth century would dominate the agenda of the overarching Catalanist party known as the Lliga Regionalista.[6]

Other critics of the Disaster lobbied for political 'Regeneration'. Joaquín Costa in 1900–1902 published works on 'Europeanising' Spain and abolishing 'oligarchy and caciquism'.[7] The loss of empire aggravated Spain's intellectual crisis, forging such 'silver age' pessimists as Joaquín Costa and Miguel de Unamuno, who would soon become known as the 'Generation of 1898'. Costa defended his country's right and responsibility to 'improve' Morocco via colonialism, citing the common history and even race binding the two sides of the Mediterranean, even though he remained a cultural pessimist. Yet Spain's crisis also mirrored a wider European nihilism which was rejecting the supposed progress inherent in positivism and industrial society just as assuredly as earlier generations rejected the unifying vision of religion.[8]

Spain's nineteenth century thus witnessed a complex process of war, pendulum swings in politics, and nation building. The foundations of a modern society and economy were set, and the personalist *cacique* style of politics would be superseded in the twentieth century by corporate relationships between elites and the masses. The persistent tension between the centre and the periphery, between town and country, and between progress and tradition would be played out on a more sophisticated canvas of a half-industrialised society. Pendulum swings would prove to be much more extreme in Spain, even for a country which would remain neutral in both world wars. Macrostructural changes in the economy and society would unfold alongside a brutalisation of political discourse, surpassing anything witnessed during the horrors of nineteenth-century national, civil, and colonial wars. Given the horrors of colonial campaigning in Spain's substitute colony in Morocco, the polarisation of the 1930s and the ensuing extremes of violence during the Spanish Civil War (1936–39), and given the persistence of Western Europe's last dictatorship (the Franco regime, 1939–75), one is given to wonder why the nineteenth century retained such a calamitous reputation for generations of Spaniards.

Notes

1 Schmidt-Nowara, 'Imperio y crisis colonial', in Pan-Montojo (ed.), *Más se perdió en Cuba*, pp. 76–82.
2 Ledesma, 'La sociedad española, la guerra y la derrota', in Pan-Montojo (ed.), *Más se perdió en Cuba*, p. 123.
3 Schmidt-Nowara, 'Imperio y crisis colonial', in Pan-Montojo (ed.), *Más se perdió en Cuba*, pp. 31–2.
4 Hannah Arendt, *The Origins of Totalitarianism* (New York: Harcourt Brace Jovanovich, 1973), p. 155.
5 Paul Preston, *The Spanish Civil War: Reaction, Revolution and Revenge* (London: Harper Perennial, 2006), p. 56.
6 Stanley Payne, *Basque Nationalism* (Reno: University of Nevada Press, 1975), pp. 75–9; Smith, *Origins of Catalan Nationalism*.
7 Juan Pro Ruiz, 'La política en tiempos del *Desastre*', in Pan-Montojo (ed.), *Más se perdió en Cuba*, p. 208.
8 Pedro Cerezo Galán, *El mal del siglo: el conflicto entre Ilustración y Romanticismo en la crisis finisecular del siglo XIX* (Madrid: Biblioteca Nueva, 2013), pp. 19–22.

Sources and bibliography

Archives

A.C. (Archivo Congreso de Diputados, Madrid)
A.G.P. (Archivo General de Palacio, Madrid)
A.H.N. (Archivo Histórico Nacional, Madrid)
A.M.M. (Archivo Municipal de Málaga)
British Library (London)
B.U.Z. (Biblioteca de la Universiad de Zaragoza)
R.A.H. (Real Academia de la Historia, Madrid)
S.J.L. (Sydney Jones Library, Special Collections, University of Liverpool)
T.N.A. (The National Archives, London)

Newspapers/pamphlets

Diario de Sesiones de Cortes
El Castellano
El Ciudadano por la Constitución
El Correo Nacional
El Eco del Comercio
El Español
El Espectador
El Huracán
El Mundo: Diario del Pueblo
Illustrated London News
El Observador
La Gaceta de Madrid
La Revista Española
El Robespierre Español (Amigo de las Leyes ó Questiones Atrevidas sobre la España)
The Times
El Universal
El Universal Observador Español
Manifiesto de la conducta y servicios hechos a la patria en el tiempo de nuestra gloriosa revolución, por Pablo López (Madrid, 1814)
Semanario Político, Histórico y Literario de la Coruña

Published primary sources

Alcalá Galiano, Antonio, *Memorias de D. Antonio Alcalá Galiano*, 2 vols. (Madrid: Imprenta de Enrique Rubiños, 1886)

Barado y Font, Francisco, *Literatura militar española en el siglo XIX* (Madrid: Administración, Florida 14, 1889)

Bunbury, Thomas, *Reminiscences of a Veteran Being Personal and Military Adventures in Portugal, Spain, France, Malta, New South Wales, Norfolk Island, New Zealand, Andaman Islands and India* (London: C J Skeet, 1861)

Burke Honan, Michael, *The Court and Camp of Don Carlos: Being the Results of a Late Tour in the Basque Provinces, and Parts of Catalonia, Aragón, Castile, and Estramadura* (London: John Macrone, 1836)

Cánovas del Castillo, Antonio, *Discursos parlamentarios* (Madrid: Congreso de los Diputados, 1854)

Cánovas del Castillo, Antonio, *Discurso sobre la nación* (Madrid: Impresa Central, 1882)

Dembowski, Carlos, *Dos años en España durante la guerra civil, 1838–40* (Madrid: Crítica, 2008)

García Tejero, Alfonso, *Historia politico-administrativa de Mendizábal*, 2 vols. (Madrid: Ortigosa, 1858)

Garrido, Fernando, *El socialismo y la democracia ante sus adversarios* (London: Unknown Publisher, 1862)

Güell y Renté, José, *Paralelo entre las reinas catolicas Doña Isabel Iª y Doña Isabel II* (Paris: Imprenta de Jules Claye, 1858)

Hilen, Andrew, *The Letters of Henry Wadsworth Longfellow*, Vol. 1 (Cambridge, MA: Harvard University Press, 2014)

Hughes, Terence McMahon, *Revelations of Spain in 1845*, 2 vols. (London: Henry Colburn, 1845)

Ilchester, Earl of (ed.), *The Spanish Journal of Elizabeth Lady Holland (1791–1811)* (London: Longman, Greens and CO., 1909)

Labra, Rafael María de, *La abolición de la esclavitud en el orden económico* (Madrid: Sociedad Abolicionista Española, 1874)

Labra, Rafael María de, *La crisis colonial de España (1868 a 1898): estudios de política palpitante y discursos parlamentarios* (Madrid: Tipografía Sindicato de Publicidad, 1901)

Lascelles, Alice L. and Alberich, J. M. (eds.), *Sir Vincent Kennett-Barrington: Letters from the Carlist War (1874–1876)* (Exeter: University of Exeter Press, 1987)

le Brun, Carlos, *Retratos políticos de la revolución de España* (Philadelphia, 1826)

Leslie, Charles, *Military Journal of Colonel Leslie of Balquhain* (Aberdeen: Aberdeen University Press, 1887)

Lichnowsky, Felix, *Erinnerungen aus den Jahren 1837, 1838 und 1839*, 2 vols. (Frankfurt-am-Main: Johann David Sauerländer, 1841)

Martí, José, 'Nuestra América', *La Revista iIlustrada* (New York, 10 January 1891)

Miraflorres, Marqués de, *Apuntes histórico-críticos para escribir la historia de la revolución de España desde el año 1820 hasta 1823* (London: Oficina de Ricardo Taylor, 1834)

Nagore, Leandro, *Apuntes para la historia: memorias de un pamplonés en la segunda guerra carlista* (Pamplona: Institución Príncipe de Viana, 1964)

Pirala, Antonio, *Anales de la guerra de Cuba*, 3 vols. (Madrid: Felipe Gonzalez Rojas, 1898)

Pí y Margall, Francisco, *La reacción y la revolución: estudios políticos y sociales* (Madrid: Imprenta y Estereotipa de M. Rivadeneira, 1854)

Poco Mas, *Scenes and Adevntures in Spain, 1835 to 1840*, 2 vols. (Philadelphia: J. W. Moore, 1846)

Pombo, Nemesio de, *Situación de España a fines del año 1842* (Madrid: Imprenta Hernández, 1843)

Renouard, Jules, *Narración de D. Juan Van Halen, Gefe de Estado Mayor de una de las divisiones de Mina en 1822 y 1823, ó relación circunstanciada de su cautividad en los calabozos de la Inquisición, su evasión y su emigración*, 2 vols. (Paris, 1828)

Romero Alpuente, Juan, *El grito de la razón al español invencible* (Zaragoza, 1808)

Romero Alpuente, Juan, *Pensamientos diversos sobre la conservación y felicidad de la patria* (Granada, 1814)

Romero Alpuente, Juan, *Wellington en España y Ballesteros en Ceuta* (Cádiz, 1813)

Strobel, Edward Henry, *The Spanish Revolution, 1868–1875* (Boston: Small, Manard and Co. 1898)

Ticknor, George, *Life, Letters and Journals of George Ticknor* (Boston: James R. Osgood and Company, 1876)

Secondary sources

Aguilar Fernández, Paloma, *Políticas de la memoria y memorias de la política* (Madrid: Alianza Editorial, 2008)

Alonso, Gregorio, *La nación en capilla: ciudadanía católica y cuestión religiosa, 1793–1874* (Granada: Comares, 2014)

Alonso, José Antonio (foreword), *La Guerra de la Independencia (1808–1814): el pueblo español, su ejército y sus aliados frente a la ocupación napoleónica* (Madrid: Ministerio de Defensa, 2007)

Álvarez del Vayo, Julio, *The Last Optimist* (London: Putnam, 1950)

Álvarez Jímenez, Juan Antonio (foreword), *La Guerra de la Independencia Española: una visión militar. VI Congreso de Historia Militar (Zaragoza, marzo-abril 2008)*, 2 vols. (Madrid: Ministerio de Defensa, 2009)

Álvarez-Junco, José, *Mater Dolorosa: la idea de España en el siglo XIX* (Madrid: Taurus, 2001)

Álvarez-Junco, José (ed.), *Populismo, caudillaje y discurso demagógico* (Madrid: Siglo XXI de España, 1987)

Álvarez-Junco, José, *Spanish Identity in the Age of Nations* (Manchester: Manchester University Press, 2011)

Álvarez Junco, José and Shubert, Adrian (eds.), *Nueva historia de la España contemporánea (1808–2018)* (Barcelona: Galaxia Gutenberg, 2018)

Andrés, Agustín S., 'Colonial Crisis and Spanish Diplomacy in the Caribbean during the Sexenio Revolucionario, 1868–74', *Bulletin of Latin American Research*, Vol. 28, No. 3 (June 2009), 325–42

Anes y Álvarez de Castrillón, Gonzalo (ed.), *Economía, sociedad, política y cultura en la España de Isabel II* (Madrid: Real Academia de Historia, 2004)

Ardit Lucas, Manuel, *Revolución liberal y revuelta campesina* (Barcelona: Ariel, 1977)

Arendt, Hannah, *The Origins of Totalitarianism* (New York: Harcourt Brace Jovanovich, 1973)

Aróstegui, Julio, Canal, Jordi and Calleja, Eduardo G., *Las guerras carlistas: hechos, hombres e ideas* (Madrid: La Esfera de los Libros, 2003)

Artola-Gallego, Manuel, *Los afrancesados* (Madrid: Editorial Turner, 1976)

Artola-Gallego, Mguel, *Partidos y programas políticos, 1808–1936* (Madrid: Aguilar, 1974)

Artola-Gallego, Miguel, *La burguesía revolucionaria (1808–1874)* (Madrid: Alianza, 1974)

Artola-Gallego, Miguel, *La España de Fernando VII* (Madrid: Espasa, 1999)

Balfour, Sebastian, 'Riot, Regeneration and Reaction: Spain in the Aftermath of the 1898 Disaster', *The Historical Journal*, Vol. 38, No. 2 (1995), 405–23

Banfield, Edward C., *The Moral Basis of a Backward Society* (Chicago: Free Press, 1958)

Bardavío Estevan, Susana, ' "!España es también aquí!": Nación e imaginario colonial en los cuentos de Emilia Pardo Bazán', *Castilla: Estudios de Literatura*, No. 9 (2018), 176–203

Baroja, Pío, *Siluetas Románticas (y otras historias de pillos y de extravagantes)* (Madrid: Espasa-Calpe, 1934)

Barrio Gozao, Maximiliano, 'La segunda restauración española a través de los despachos del nuncio Giustiniani (1823–1827)', *Pasado y Memoria. Revista de Historia Contemporánea*, Vol. 16 (2017), 121–48

Bautista Vilar, Juan, *El despegue de la revolución industrial en España, 1827–1869* (Madrid: Istmo., 1990)

Berenguer Barceló, Julio, *Historia de Alcoy* (Alcoy: Llorens Distribuidor, 1977)

Bernal, Antonio Miguel, *La lucha por la tierra en la crisis del antiguo régimen* (Madrid: Taurus, 1979)

Bernecker, Walther L., *España entre tradición y modernidad: política, economía y sociedad (siglos XIX y XX)* (Madrid: Siglo XXI, 1999)

Blanco, Alda and Thomson, Guy (eds.), *Visiones del liberalismo: política, identidad y cultura en la España del siglo XIX* (Valencia: Universitat de València, 2008)

Blanco Escolá, Carlos, *La Academia General Militar de Zaragoza (1928–1931)* (Barcelona: Labor, 1989)

Blinkhorn, Martin, *Carlism in Crisis in Spain, 1931–1939* (Oxford: Oxford University Press, 1975)

Bowen, Wayne H., *Spain and the American Civil War* (Columbia: University of Missouri Press, 2011)

Bowen, Wayne H. and Alvarez, José E (eds.), *A Military History of Modern Spain: From the Napoleonic Era to the International War on Terror* (Westport: Praeger, 2007)

Brenan, Gerald, *The Spanish Labyrinth: An Account of the Social and Political Background of the Spanish Civil War* (London: Cambridge University Press, 1943)

Brett, Edward, *The British Auxiliary Legion in the First Carlist War, 1835–38* (Dublin: Four Courts Press, 2005)

Bridenthal, Renate, Mosher Stuard, Susan and Wiesner, Merry E. (eds.), *Becoming Visible: Women in European History* (New York: Houghton Mifflin, 1988)

Broers, Michael, *The Napoleonic Mediterranean: Enlightenment, Revolution and Empire* (London: I.B. Tauris, 2016)

Broers, Michael, Caiani, Ambrogio and Bann, Stephen (eds.), *A History of the European Restorations: Culture, Society and Religion*, Vol. 2 (London: Bloomsbury, 2019)

Bullón de Mendoza, Alfonso, 'La primera guerra carlista' (doctoral theses, Universdad Complutense de Madrid, 1991)

Bullón de Mendoza, Alfonso, *La primera guerra carlista* (Madrid: Actas, 1992)

Bullón de Mendoza, Alfonso and Togores, Luis E. (eds.), *Cánovas y su época*, 2 vols. (Madrid: Siglo XXI, 1999)

Burdiel, Isabel, *Isabel II: no se puede reinar inocentemente* (Madrid: Espasa Calpe Mexicana, 2004)

Burdiel, Isabel, *La política de los notables: moderados y avanzados durante el régimen del Estatuto Real (1834–36)* (Valencia: Edicions Alfons el Magnànim, 1987)

Burdiel, Isabel, *La política en el reinado de Isabel II* (Madrid: Marcial Pons, 1998)

Burdiel, Isabel, "The Queen, the Woman and the Middle Class. The Symbolic Failure of Isabel II in Spain", *Social History*, Vol. 29, No. 3, Spain (August 2004), 301–19

Burdiel, Isabel, Ledesma, Manuel and Pérez, Manuel (eds.), *Liberales, agitadores y conspiradores: Biografías heterodoxas del siglo XIX* (Madrid: Espasa Calpe, 2000)

Caballé, Anna, *Concepción Arenal: la caminante y su sombra* (Barcelona: Taurus, 2018)

Cabral Chamorro, Antonio, *Socialismo utópico y revolución burguesa: el fourierismo gaditano, 1834–1848* (Cádiz: Diputación Provincial de Cádiz, 1990)

Cacho Viu, Vicente, *La Institución Libre de Enseñanza* (Madrid: Rialp, 1962)

Callahan, William J., *Church, Politics and Society in Spain, 1750–1874* (Cambridge: Harvard University Press, 1984)

Calleja, Eduardo, *La violencia en la política: perspectivas teóricas sobre el empelo deliberado de la fuerza en los conflictos de poder* (Madrid: Consejo Superior de Investigaciones Científicas, 2003)

Campoy-Cubillo, Adolfo, *Memories of the Maghreb: Transnational Identities in Spanish Cultural Production* (Basingstoke: Palgrave Macmillan, 2012)

Cárcel Ortí, Vicente, 'Un siglo de relaciones diplomáticas entre España y la Santa Sede (1834–1931)', *Anales de História Contemporánea* (febrero 2009), 313–31

Caridad Salvador, Antonio, 'El carlismo aragonés en armas. La revuelta de 1855', *Cuadernos de Historia Contemporánea*, Vol. 36 (2014), 165–88

Caridad Salvador, Antonio, *El ejército y las partidas carlistas en Valencia y Aragón (1833–1840)* (Valencia: Universitat de València, 2013)

Caridad Salvador, Antonio, 'Las consecuencias socioeconómicas directas de la Primera Guerra Carlista', *Cuadernos de Historia Contemporanea*, Vol. 40 (2017), 149–67

Caridad Salvador, Antonio, 'Los carlistas de Valencia. La reacción en una ciudad liberal (1833–40), *BROCAR*, Vol. 36 (2012), 161–83

Carr, Raymond, *Spain, 1808–1939* (Oxford: Oxford University Press, 1966)

Castells, Irene, *La utopía insurreccional del liberalismo: Torrijos y las conspiraciones liberales de la década ominosa* (Barcelona: Crítica, 1989)

Castells, Irene and Moliner Prada, Antonio, *Crisis del antiguo régimen y revolución liberal en España (1789–1845)* (Barcelona: Ariel, 2000)

Cepeda Gómez, José, *El ejército español en la política española (1789–1843): conspiraciones y pronunciamientos en los comienzos de la España liberal* (Madrid: Fundación Universitaria Española, 1990)

Cepeda Gómez, José, *Los pronunciamientos en la España del siglo XIX* (Madrid: Arco Libros, 1999)

Cerezo Galán, Pedro, *El mal del siglo: el conflicto entre Ilustración y Romanticismo en la crisis finisecular del siglo XIX* (Madrid: Biblioteca Nueva, 2013)

Chavarri Sidera, Pilar, *Las elecciones de diputados a las Cortes Generales y Extraordinarias (1810–1813)* (Madrid: Centro de Estudios Constitucionales, 1988)

Christiansen, Eric, *The Origins of Military Power in Spain, 1800–1854* (Oxford: Oxford University Press, 1967)

Clemente, Josep Carles, *Las guerras carlistas* (Barcelona: Península, 1982)

Cleminson, Richard and Vázquez García, Francisco, *'Los invisibles': A History of Male Homosexuality in Spain, 1850–1940* (Cardiff: University of Wales Press, 2007)

Colley, Linda, *Britons: Forging the Nation, 1707–1837* (New Haven: Yale University Press, 1992)

Colomé Ferrer, Josep, 'L'ofensiva dels propietaris contra el contracte de rabassa morta a la comarca del Penedès, 1850–1910', *Recerques*, Vol. 67 (2013), 115–40

Comellas García-Llera, José Luis *Cánovas* (Madrid: Ediciones Cid, 1965)

Comellas García-Llera, José Luis, *El trienio constitucional* (Pamplona: Ediciones Universidad de Navarra, 1963)

Comellas García-Llera, José Luis, *Los moderados en el poder, 1844–54* (Madrid: CSIC, 1970)

Comellas García-Llera, José Luis, *Los primeros pronunciamientos en España, 1814–1820* (Madrid: Consejo Superior de Investigaciones Científicas, 1958)

Comellas, José Luis, Martínez Gallego, Francesc, Ortuzar, Trinidad, Poveda, Angee Ramón and Rueda, Germán (eds.), *Los generales de Isabel II* (Madrid: Ediciones 19, 2016)

Cruz, Jesús, *Gentlemen, Bourgeois, Revolutionaries: Political Change and Cultural Persistence among the Spanish Dominant Groups, 1759–1850* (Cambridge: Cambridge University Press, 1996)

Cruz, Jesús, *Los notables de Madrid: las bases sociales de la revolución liberal española* (Alianza Editorial: Madrid, 2000)

Cruz, Jesús, *The Rise of Middle-Class Culture in Nineteenth-Century Spain* (Shreveport: Louisana State University Press, 2011)

Cuenca Toribio, José Manuel, *La iglesia espanola ante la revolucion liberal* (Madrid: Ediciojnes Rialp, 1971)

Daly, Gavin, "Barbarity More Suited to Savages': British Soldiers' Views of Spanish and Portuguese Violence During the Peninsular War, 1808–1814', *War and Society*, Vol. 35, No. 4 (October 2016), 242–58

Dardé, Carlos, *La Restauración, 1875–1902: Alfonso XII y la regencia de María Cristina (Historia de España)* (Madrid: Temas de Hoy, 1997)

del Burgo, Jaime, *Para la historia de la primera guerra carlista: Comentarios y acotaciones a un manuscrito de la época 1834–1839* (Pamplona: Institución Príncipe de Viana, 1981)

Díaz del Moral, Juan, *Historia de las agitaciones campesinas andaluzas: Córdoba (antecedentes para una reforma agraria)* (Madrid: Alianza, 1973)

Domingo Acebrón, María Dolores, *Rafael María de Labra: Cuba, Puerto Rico, Las Filipinas, Europa y Marruecos, en la España del sexenio democrático y la restauración, 1871–1918* (Madrid: Consejo Superior de Investigaciones Científicas, 2006)

Dwyer, Philip G., 'It Still Makes Me Shudder: Memories of Massacres and Atrocities during the Revolutionary and Napoleonic Wars', *War in History*, Vol. 16, No.4 (2009)

Egea Bruno, Pedro María, 'Mata al rey y vete a Murcia. La corrupción de la justicia en la España de la Restauración', *Studia Historia Contemporánea*, Vol. 33 (2015), 159–92

Eiras Roel, Antonio, *El partido demócrata español (1849–1868)* (Madrid: Rialp, 1961)

Eiras Roel, Antonio (ed.), *La emigración española a ultramar, 1492–1914* (Madrid: Tabapress, 1991)

Eiras Roel, Antonio, *Las sociedades secretas republicanas en el reinado de Isabel II* (Madrid: Instituto Jerónimo Zurita, 1962)

Esdaile, Charles J., *Fighting Napoleon: Guerrillas, Bandits and Adventurers in Spain 1808–1814* (London: Yale University Press, 2004)

Esdaile, Charles J., *Outpost of Empire: The Napoleonic Occupation of Andalucíam, 1810–1812* (Oklahoma: Oklahoma University Press, 2012)

Esdaile, Charles J., *The Peninsular War: A New History* (London: Penguin, 2003)

Esdaile, Charles J., *Popular Resistance in the French Wars: Patriots, Partisans and Land Pirates* (Basingstoke: Palgrave Macmillan, 2004)

Esenwein, George, *Anarchist Ideology and the Working-Class Movement in Spain, 1868–1898* (Oxford: Oxford University Press, 1989)

Espadas Burgos, Manuel, *Baldomero Espartero: un candidato al trono de España* (Madrid: Biblioteca de Autores Manchegos, 1986)

Esteban Navarro, Miguel Ángel, 'La formación del pensamiento político y social del radicalismo español (1834–1874)' (doctoral thesis, Universidad de Zaragoza, 1995)

Fehrenbach, Charles Wentz, 'Moderados and Exaltados: The Liberal Opposition to Ferdinand VII, 1814–1823', *The Hispanic American Historical Review*, Vol. 50, No. 1 (February 1970)

Fernández Benítez, Vicente, *Burguesía y revolución liberal: Santander, 1812–1840* (Santander: Estudio Librería, 1989)

Fernández Vargas, Valentina, *Las militares españolas: un nuevo grupo profesional* (Madrid: Biblioteca Nueva, 1997)

Ferrer, Ada, *Insurgent Cuba: Race, Nation, and Revolution, 1868–1898* (Chapel Hill: University of North Carolina Press, 1999)

Ferris, Kate, *Imagining 'America' in Late Nineteenth Century Spain* (Basingstoke: Palgrave Macmillan, 2016)

Fletcher, Ian (ed.), *For King and Country: The Letters and Diaries of John Mills, Coldstream Guards. 1811–14* (Staplehurst: Spellmount Publishers, 1995)

Fontana, Josep, *De en medio del tiempo: la segunda restauración española, 1823–1834* (Barcelona: Crítica, 2006)

Fontana, Josep, *La crisis del antiguo régimen, 1808–1833* (Barcelona: Editorial Crítica, 1992)

Fontana, Josep and Villares, Ramón (eds.), *Historia general de España*, 8 vols. (Barcelona: Crítica, 2007)

Forrest, Alan, Hagemann, Karen and Rendall, Jane (eds.), *Soldiers, Citizens and Civilians: Experiences and Perceptions of the Revolutionary and Napoleonic Wars, 1790–1820* (Basingstoke: Palgrave Macmillan, 2009)

Fowler, Will (ed.), *Authoritarianism in Latin America Since Independence* (London: Praeger, 1996)

Fox, Inman, *La invención de España: nacionalismo liberal e identidad nacional* (Madrid: Cátedra, 1997)

Fradera, Josep M., 'La importancia de tenir colonias', in *Catalunya i ultramar: poder i negoci a les colònies espanyoles* (Barcelona: Ambit Serveis, 1995)

Fraser, Ronald, *La maldita guerra de España: historia social de la Guerra de la Independencia, 1808–1814* (Madrid: Editorial Crítica, 2013)

Fraser, Ronald, *Napoleon's Cursed War: Popular Resistance in the Spanish Peninsular War* (London: Verso, 2008)

Fuente Monge, Gregorio de la, *Los revolucionarios de 1868: élites y poder en la España liberal* (Madrid: Marcial Pons, 2000)

Fuentes, Juan Francisco and Roura i Aulinas, Lluís (eds.), *Sociabilidad y liberalismo en la España del siglo XIX* (Lleida: Editorial Milenio, 2001)

Furet, François, *Revolutionary France, 1770–1880* (Oxford: Oxford University Press, 1992)

Fusi, Juan Pablo and Palafox, Jordi, *España: 1808–1996. El desafío de la modernidad* (Madrid: Espasa, 1997)

Garcia-Balañà, Albert, 'Migración y milicia en la España transatlántica del siglo XIX: quge y caída del imperialismo popular', *Storicamente*, Vol. 12, No. 1 (2016), 1–24

García Cárcel, Ricardo, *El sueño de la nación indomable: los mitos de la Guerra de la Independencia* (Madrid: Temas de Hoy, 2007)

García Fernández, Javier, *El orígen del municipio constitucional: autonomía y centralización en Francia y en España* (Madrid: Instituto de Estudios de Administración Local, 1983)

García Sánchez, Fernando, *Las campañas militares del general Prim en el exterior (1853–1862)* (Granada: Universidad de Granada, 2018)

Getz, Trevor R., *The Long Nineteenth Century, 1750–1914* (London: Bloomsbury, 2018)

Gil Cremades, Juan José, *Krausistas y liberales* (Madrid: Seminarios y Ediciones, 1975)

Gil Novales, Alberto (ed.), *Juan Romero Alpuente: historia de la revolución española y otros escritos*, 2 vols. (Madrid: Centro de Estudios Constitucionales, 1989)

Gil Novales, Alberto, *Las sociedades patrióticas (1820–1823)* (Madrid: Editorial Tecnos, 1975)

Gil Novales, Alberto (ed.), *Rafael del Riego, La revolución de 1820, día a día: cartas, escritos y discursos* (Madrid: Editorial Tecnos, 1976)

Gil Novales, Alberto, *Textos exaltados del Trienio Liberal* (Madrid: Ediciones Júcar, 1978)

Ginger, Andrew and Lawless, Geraldine (eds.), *Spain in the Nineteenth Century: New Essays on Experiences of Culture and Society* (Manchester: Manchester University Press, 2018)

Glover, Michael, *Legacy of Glory: The Bonaparte Kingdom of Spain* (New York: Leo Cooper, 1971)

Gómez Oliver, Miguel, *La desamortización de Mendizábal en Granada* (Granada: Excma. Diputación Provincial de Granada, 1983)

Gómez Urdáñez, Gracia, *Salustiano de Olózaga: élites políticas en el liberalismo español 1805–1843* (Logroño: Universidad de La Rioja, 1999)

Graham, John, *Donoso Cortes: Utopian Romanticist and Political Realist* (Columbia: University of Missouri Press, 1974)

Gribble, Francis, *The Tragedy of Isabella II* (London: Chapman and Hall, 1913)

Guerra, Ramiro, *A History of the Cuban Nation: The Ten Years War and Other Revolutionary Activities from 1868–1892* (Havana: Editorial Historia de la Nación Cubana, 1958)

Hamnett, Brian, 'Process and Pattern: A Re-examination of the Ibero-American Independence Movements, 1808–1826', *Journal of Latin American Studies*, Vol. 29, No. 2 (May 1997), 279–328

Hannay, David, *Don Emilio Castelar* (London: Bliss, Sands and Foster, 1896)

Hargreaves-Mawdsley, William Norman (ed.), *Spain Under the Bourbons, 1700–1833: A Collection of Documents* (London: Palgrave Macmillan, 1973)

Headrick, Daniel, *Ejército y política en España (1868–1898)* (Madrid: Editorial Tecnos, 1981)

Headrick, Daniel, 'Spain and the Revolutions of 1848', *European Studies Review*, Vol. 6 (1976), 197–223

Hennessy, Charles, *The Federal Republic in Spain: Pi y Margall and the Federal Republican Movement 1868–1874* (Oxford: Oxford University Press, 1962)

Hernández Montalbán, Francisco J., *La abolición de los señoríos en España (1811–1837)* (Valencia: Universitat de Valencia, 1999)

Herr, Richard (ed.), *Memorias del cura liberal don Juan Antonio Posse con su discurso sobre la Constitución de 1812* (Madrid: Centro de Investigaciones Sociológicas, 1984)

Herráiz de Miota, César, 'Los montepíos militares del siglo XVIII como origen del sistema de clases pasivas del estado', *Revista del Ministerio del Trabajo y Asuntos Sociales*, Vol. 56 (January 2005), 107–208

Herrero, Javier, *Los orígenes del pensamiento reaccionario español* (Madrid: Alianza, 1973)

Hobsbawm, Eric J., *Primitive Rebels: Studies in Archaic Forms of Social Movement in the 19th and 20th Centuries* (London: Norton and Co.,1959)

Holt, Edgar, *The Carlist Wars in Spain* (London: Putnam, 1967)

Inarejos Muñoz, Juan Antonio, *Intervenciones coloniales y nacionalismo español* (Madrid: Sílex, 2010)

Innes, Joanna and Philp, Mark, *Re-Imagining Democracy in the Mediterranean, 1780–1860* (Oxford: Oxford University Press, 2018)

Iribarren, José María, *Espoz y Mina: el Liberal* (Madrid: Editorial Aguilar, 1967)

Janke, Peter, *Mendizábal y la instaración de la monarquía constitucional en España, 1790–1853* (Madrid: Siglo Veintiuno, 1974)

Jiménez Guerrero, José, *El reclutamiento militar en el siglo XIX: las quintas de Málaga (1837–1868)* (Málaga: Fundación Unicaja, 2001)

Jones Parry, Ernest, *The Spanish Marriages, 1841–1846* (London: Palgrave Macmillan, 1936)

Jover Zamora, José María, *España en la política internacional* (Madrid: Marcial Pons, 1999)

Kagan, Richard L., 'Prescott's Paradigm: American Historical Scholarship and the Decline of Spain', *The American Historical Review*, Vol. 101, No. 2 (April 1996), 430–1

Kamen, Henry, *The War of Succession in Spain, 1700–1715* (London: Littlehampton Book Services, 1969)

Kaplan, Temma, *The Anarchists of Andalucía, 1868–1903* (Princeton: Princeton University Press, 1977)

Kern, Robert W., *Liberals, Reformers and Caciques in Restoration Spain, 1875–1909* (New Mexico: University of New Mexico Press, 1974)

Kiernan, Victor, *The Revolution of 1854 in Spanish History* (Oxford: Oxford University Press, 1966)

Krauel, Javier, *Imperial Emotions: Cultural Responses to Myths of Empire in fin-de-siècle Spain* (Liverpool: Liverpool University Press, 2013)

La abolición de la Inquisición Española: Discurso leído el día 2 de diciembre de 1991, en su recepción pública, por el Excmo. Señor D. José Antonio Escudero y contestación del Excmo. Señor D. Alfonso García Gallo de Diego (Madrid: Real Academia de Jurisprudencia y Legislación, 1991)

Labra, Rafael María de, *América y la Constitución española de 1812: Cortes de Cádiz de 1810–1813* (Madrid: Sindicato de Publicidad, 1914)

La Comba, Juan Antonio, *Sociedad y política en Málaga en la primera mitad del siglo XIX* (Málaga: Librería Ágora, 1989)

Laven, David and Riall, Lucy (eds.), *Napoleon's Legacy: Problems of Government in Restoration Europe* (Oxford: Berg, 2000)

Lawrence, Mark, 'Poachers Turned Gamekeepers', *Small Wars and Insurgencies*, Vol. 25, No. 4 (2014), 843–57

Lawrence, Mark, 'Popular Radicalism in Spain, 1808–1844' (unpublished PhD thesis, University of Liverpool, 2008)

Lawrence, Mark, *Spain's First Carlist War, 1833–1840* (Basingstoke: Palgrave Macmillan, 2014)

Lawrence, Mark, *The Spanish Civil Wars: A Comparative History of the First Carlist War and the Conflict of the 1930s* (London: Bloomsbury, 2017)

Lawrence Tone, John, *War and Genocide in Cuba, 1895–1898* (Chapel Hill: University of North Carolina Press, 2006)

Lida, Clara, *Anarquismo y revolución en la España del siglo XIX* (Madrid: Siglo XXI, 1972)

Llano, Samuel, *Discordant Notes: Marginality and Social Control in Madrid, 1850–1930* (Oxford: Oxford University Press, 2018)

López de Ramón, María 'Influencia del poder politico en la libertad de prensa: la guerra de Cuba (1895–98)', *Revista Jurídica de la Universidad Autónoma de Madrid*, Vol. 33 (2016), 143–64

López Garrido, Diego, *La Guardia Civil y los orígenes del estado centralista* (Madrid: Crítica, 1982)

López-Portillo, Raúl Pérez, *La España de Riego* (Madrid: Silex, 2005)

Lovett, Gabriel, *Napoleon and the Birth of Modern Spain: The Challenge to the Old Order*, 2 vols. (New York: New York University Press, 1965)

Luengo Sánchez, Jorge, *El nacimiento de una ciudad progresista: Valladolid durante la regencia de Espartero (1840–1843)* (Valladolid: Ayuntamiento de Valladolid, 2005)

Maestrojuán Catalán, Francisco Javier, *Ciudad de vasallos, Nación de heroes (Zaragoza: 1809–1814)* (Zaragoza: Institución 'Fernando el Católico', 2003)

Maestrojuán Catalán, Francisco Javier (ed.), *La Guerra de la Independencia en el Valle Medio del Ebro* (Segundo curso de verano de Tudela 9 al 13 de Julio de 2001, Ayuntamiento de Tudela, Universidad SEK de Segovia)

Maluquer de Motes, Jordi, *El socialismo en España, 1833–1868* (Barcelona: Crítica, 1977)

Marichal, Carlos, *Spain (1834–1844): A New Society* (London: Támesis, 1977)

Marichal, Juan, *El secreto de España* (Madrid: Taurus, 1995)

Martín-Portugues, Isidoro Lara, *Jaén: la lucha por la libertad durante el trienio constitucional (1820–1823)* (Jaén: Ayuntamiento de Jaén, 1996)

Martínez-Gallego, Francesc A., *Conservar progresando: la Unión Liberal, 1856–1868* (Valencia: Centro Francoscio Tomás Valiente, 2001)

Martínez Martín, Manuel, *Revolución liberal y cambio agrario en la alta Andalucía* (Granada: Universidad de Granada, 1995)

McCoy, Alfred W., Fradera, Josep M. and Jacobson, Stephen (eds.), *Endless Empire: Spain's Retreat, Europe's Eclipse, America's Decline* (Madison: University of Wisconsin Press, 2012)

Melgar, Francisco, *Pequeña historia de las guerras carlistas* (Madrid: Gómez, 1958)

Meyer Forsting, Richard, *Raising Heirs to the Throne on Nineteenth-century Spain* (Basingstoke: Palgrave Macmillan, 2018)

Milán, José R., *Sagasta, o el arte de hacer política* (Madrid: Biblioteca Nueva, 2001)

Millán, Jesús and Romeo, María Cruz, 'Was the Liberal Revolution Important to Modern Spain? Political Cultures and Citizenship in Spanish History', *Social History*, Vol. 29, No. 3 (2004), 284–300

Moliner Prada, Antonio, 'La conflictividad social en la Guerra de la Independencia', *Trienio: Ilustración y Liberalismo*, Vol. 35 (Madrid, May 2000), 81–155. ISSN 0212-4025.

Moliner Prada, Antonio (ed.), *La Guerra de la Inependencia en España (1808–1814)* (Barcelona: Nabla Ediciones, 2007)

Moliner Prada, Antonio, *La guerrilla en la Guerra de la Independencia* (Madrid: Colección Adalid, 2004)

Moliner Prada, Antonio, *Revolución burguesa y movimiento juntero en España* (Lleida: Milenio, 1997)

Monerris, Encarna García, Frasquet, Ivana and Monerris, Carmen G. (eds.), *Cuando todo era posible: liberalismo y antiliberalismo en España e Hispanoamérica (1780–1842)* (Madrid: Sílex Ediciones S. L., 2016)

Monerris, Encarna García, Moreno Seco, Mónica and Marcuello Benedicto, Juan I. (eds.), *Culturas políticas en la España liberal: discursos, representaciones y prácticas (1808–1902)* (Valencia: Universitat de València, 2013)

Montaña, Daniel, i Rafart, Josep (eds.), *El carlisme ahir i avui* (I Simposi d'Història del Carlisme, 11 de maig de 2013)

Montañà, Daniel and Rafart, Josep (eds.), *Estat carlista: tradició i furs* (II Simposi d'Història del carlisme, 10 maig de 2014)

Montañà, Daniel and Rafart, Josep (eds.), *Propaganda carlista, religió, literatura i operacions militars* (III Simposi d'Història del Carlisme, 9 de maig de 2015)

Moral Roncal, Antonio Manuel, '1868 en la memoria carlista de 1931: dos revoluciones anticlericales y un paralelo', *Hispania Sacra*, Vol. LIX, No. 119 (enero–junio 2007), 337–61

Morange, Claude, 'Sebastián de Miñano durante la Guerra de la Independencia', *Trienio*, No. 35 (May 2000, Madrid)

Moreno Alonso, Manuel, *Blanco White: la obsesión de España* (Sevilla: Ediciones Alfar, 1998)

Moreno Alonso, Manuel, *La forja del liberalismo en España: los amigos españoles de Lord Holland, 1793–1840* (Madrid: Congreso de Diputados, 1997)

Moreno Alonso, Manuel, *La Junta Suprema de Sevilla* (Sevilla: Ediciones Alfar, 2001)

Moreno Alonso, Manuel, *La revolución 'santa' de Sevilla (la revuelta popular de 1808)* (Sevilla: Caja San Fernando de Sevilla y Jerez, 1997)

Moreno Fraginals, Manuel, *Cuba/España – España-Cuba: Historia Común* (Barcelona: Grijalbo Mondadori, 1995)

Moreno Luzón, Javier (ed.), *Construir España: Nacionalismo español y procesos de nacionalización* (Madrid: Centro de Estudios Políticos y Constitucionales, 2007)

Moreno Luzón, Javier, 'El mosaico de la Restauración', *Revista de libros*, No. 34 (Octubre 1999)

Moreno-Luzón, Javier, *Modernizing the Nation: Spain During the Reign of Alfonso XIII, 1902–1931* (Sussex: Sussex Academic Press, 2016)

Morgan, John, 'War Feeding War? The Impact of Logistics Upon the Occupation of Catalonia', *Journal of Military History*, Vol. 73, No. 1 (2009), 83–116

Navarro García, Luis, '1898, la incierta victoria de Cuba', *Anuario de Estudios Americanos*, Vol. 55, No. 1 (1998), 165–87

Núñez Seixas, Xosé M. (ed.), *Historia Mundial de España* (Barcelona: Destino, 2018)

Núñez Seixas, Xosé M. and Sevillano, Francisco (eds.), *Los enemigos de España: Imagen del otro, conflictos bélicos y disputas nacionales (siglos XVI–XX)* (Madrid: Centro de Estudios Políticos y Constitucionales, 2010)

Ofer, Inbal, 'Class, Space and Urban Development: Madrid, 1860–1936', *Cuadernos de Historia Contemporánea*, Vol. 39 (2017), 339–44

Oman, Charles, *A History of the Peninsular War*, 1–6 vols. (London, 1902, reprinted London: Greenhill Books, 2004)

Ortega Berenguer, Emilio *La enseñanza en Málaga, 1833–1933* (Málaga: Universidad de Málaga, 1985)

Ortega y Gasset, José, *La España Invertebrada* (Madrid: Calpe, 1922)

Oyarzun, Román, *Historia del carlismo* (Madrid: Maxtor, 1965)

Palacio Atard, Vicente, *La España del siglo XIX* (Madrid: Espasa-Calpe, 1978)

Pan-Montojo, Juan and Álvarez Junco, José (eds.), *Más se perdió en Cuba: España 1898 y la crisis de fin de siglo* (Madrid: Alianza, 1998)

Payne, Stanley, *Basque Nationalism* (Reno: University of Nevada Press, 1975)

Payne, Stanley, *Politics and the Military in Modern Spain* (Stanford: Stanford University Press, 1967)

Pegenaute, Pedro, *Represión política en el reinado de Fernando VII: las comisiones militares* (Pamplona: Universidad de Navarra, 1974)

Penson, Lillian M. and Temperley, Harold, *Foundations of British Foreign Policy, 1792–1902* (Abingdon: Routledge, 1966)

Pereira, Juan Carlos (ed.), *La política exterior de España (1800–2003)* (Madrid: Ariel, 2003)

Pérez Galdós, Benito, *Un faccioso más . . . y algunos frailes menos* (Episodios Nacionales, 20, Segunda Serie) (Madrid: Alianza, 2005)

Pérez Garzón, Juan Sisinio, *Milicia Nacional y revolución burguesa: el prototipo madrileño 1808–1874* (Madrid: Consejo Superior de Investigaciones Científicas, 1978)

Pérez, Louis A., *Cuba: Between Reform and Revolution* (Oxford: Oxford University Press, 2011)

Pérez Núñez, Javier, 'La revolución de 1840: la culminación del Madrid progresista', *Cuadernos de Historia Contemporánea*, Vol. 36 (2014), 141–64

Pérez-Reverte, Arturo, *Un día de cólera* (Madrid: Debolsillo, 2007)

Peyrou, Florencia, *El republicanismo popular en España 1840–1843* (Cádiz: Universidad de Cádiz, 2002)

Peyrou, Florencia, 'A Great Family of Sovereign Men: Democratic Discourse in Nineteenth-century Spain', *European History Quarterly*, Vol. 43, No. 2 (2013), 235–56

Piqueras Arenas, José A., *La revolución democrática, 1868–1874: cuestión social, colonialismo y grupos de presión* (Madrid: Ministerio de Trabajo, 1992)

Piqueras, José A. and Chust, Manuel (eds.), *Republicanos y repúblicas en España* (Madrid: Siglo XXI, 1996)

Pirala, Antonio, *Historia de la guerra civil y de los partidos liberal y carlista*, 6 vols. (Madrid: Turner/Historia, 1984)

Prescott, William H., *History of the Reign of Ferdinand and Isabella, the Catholic*, Vol. 1 (New York: A. L. Burt Publisher, 1837)

Preston, Paul, *Juan Carlos: A People's King* (London: Harper Collins, 2004)

Preston, Paul, *The Spanish Civil War: Reaction, Revolution and Revenge* (London: Harper Perennial, 2006)

Queipo de Llano, José María (Conde de Toreno), *Historia del levantamiento, guerra y revolución de España* (Madrid: Imprenta de Berenguillo, 1953)

Quennell, Peter, *Byron: The Years of Fame, Byron in Italy* (London: Harper Collins, 1974)

Quiroga, Alejandro and Ángel del Arco, Miguel (eds.), *Right-wing Spain in the Civil War Era: Soldiers of God and Apostles of the Fatherland, 1914–45* (London: Continuum, 2012)

Ramos Rodríguez, María del Pilar, *La conspiración del Triángulo* (Sevilla: Universidad de Sevilla, 1970)

Regueiro Salgado, Begoña, 'Una nueva forma de orientalismo romántico: presencia y valores de lo oriental en la obra de Gustavo Adolfo Bécquer', *Bulletin of Spanish Studies*, Vol. 90, No. 2 (2013), 177–94, 186–8

Révesz, Andrés, *Narváez: un dictador liberal* (Madrid: Aguilar, 1953)

Ringrose, David, *Spain, Europe and the 'Spanish Miracle', 1700–1900* (Cambridge: Cambridge University Press, 1998)

Risco, P. Alberto, *Zumalacárregui en campaña* (Madrid: Imprenta de José Murillo, 1935)

Rodríguez González, Ramón, 'La crisis de las Carolinas', *Cuadernos de Historia Contemporánea*, Vol. 13 (1991), 25–46

Rodríguez, Laura, 'The Spanish Riots of 1766', *Past and Present*, No. 59 (May 1973), 117–46

Rodríguez O. Jaime E., *"We are now the True Spaniards": Sovereignty, Revolution, Independence, and the Emergence of the Federal Republic of Mexico, 1808–1824* (Stanford: Stanford University Press, 2012)

Romeo Mateo, María Cruz, *Entre el orden y la revolución* (Alicante: Instituto de Cultura, 1993)

Romeo Mateo, María Cruz and Sierra, María (eds.), *La España liberal: 1833–1874* (Madrid: Marcial Pons, 2014)

Ross, Michael, *The Reluctant King: Joseph Bonaparte, King of the Two Sicilies and Spain* (London: Sidgwick and Jackson, 1976)

Roura i Aulinas, Lluís and Castells, Irene (eds.), *Revolución y democracia: el jacobinismo europeo* (Madrid: Ediciones del Orto, 1995)

Rubio Pobes, Coro, *Revolución y tradición: el país vasco ante la revolución liberal y la construcción del estado liberal, 1808–1868* (Madrid: Siglo XXI de España Editores, 1996)

Rújula, Pedro, *Constitución o Muerte: el trienio liberal y los levantamientos realistas en Aragón (1820–1823)* (Zaragoza: Edizións de l'Astral, 2000)

Rújula, Pedro, 'El mito contrarrevolucionario de la Restauración', *Pasado y Memoria*, Vol. 13 (2014), 79–94

Rújula, Pedro (ed.), *Historia de la guerra última en Aragón y Valencia (escrita por F. Cabello, F. Santa Cruz y R. M. Temprado)* (Zaragoza: Institución 'Fernando el Católico', 2006)

Salanova, Santiago de Miguel, 'De súbditos a ciudadanos. La emergencia de nuevas prácticas electorales del Madrid de 1868', *El Futuro del Pasado*, Vol. 8 (2017), 399–443

Salomón Chéliz, Pilar, 'El discurso anticlerical en la construcción de una identidad nacional española republicana (1898–1936)', *Hispania Sacra*, Vol. 54, No. 110 (2002), 485–98

Sánchez-Albornoz, Nicolás, *Las crisis de subsistencias de España en el siglo XIX* (Rosario: Universidad Nacional del Litoral, 1963)

Sánchez-Albornoz, Sonsoles Cabeza, *Los sucesos de 1848 en España* (Madrid: Fundación Universitaria Española, 1981)

Sarría Muñoz, Andrés, *Breve historia de Málaga* (Málaga: Editorial Sarría, 1995)

Saurin de la Iglesia, María Rosa (ed.), *Manuel Pardo de Andrade: Semanario Político, Histórico y Literario de la Coruña (1809–1810)*, II (La Coruña: edición facsímile, Fundación Pedro Barrie de la Maza, 1996)

Schmidt-Nowara, Christopher, *The Conquest of History: Spanish Colonialism and National Histories in the Nineteenth Century* (Pittsburgh: University of Pittsburgh Press, 2006)

Schmidt-Nowara, Christopher, *Empire and Antislavery: Spain, Cuba, and Puerto Rico, 1833–1874* (Pittsburgh, PA: University of Pittsburgh Press, 1999)

Schmidt-Nowara, Christopher, 'La España ultramarina: Colonialism and Nation-Building in Nineteenth-century Spain', *European History Quarterly*, Vol. 34, No. 2 (2004), 191–214

Schneid, Frederick (ed.), *European Armies of the French Revolution, 1792–1802* (Oklahoma: University of Oklahoma Press, 2015)

Sevilla Andrés, Diego, *Antonio Maura: la revolución desde arriba* (Barcelona: Aedos, 1954)

Shubert, Adrian and Álvarez Junco, José (eds.), *The History of Modern Spain: Chronologies, Themes, Individuals* (London: Bloomsbury, 2018)

Shubert, Adrian and Álvarez Junco, José (eds.), *Spanish History Since 1808* (New York: Bloomsbury, 2000)

Smith, Angel, *The Origins of Catalan Nationalism, 1770–1898* (Basingstoke: Palgrave Macmillan, 2014)

Sobrevilla, Natalia, 'From Europe to the Andes and Back: Becoming "Los Ayacuchos"', *European History Quarterly*, Vol. 41, No. 3 (July 2011), 472–88

Suárez Cortina, Manuel and Ridolfi, Maurizio (eds.), *El Estado y la Nación: Cuestión nacional, centralismo y federalismo en la Europa del Sur* (Santander: Edición Universidad Cantabria, 2014)

Suárez Verdeguer, Federico, *Las Cortes de Cádiz* (Madrid: Ediciones Rialp, 2002)

Tavares de Almeida, Pedro and Moreno Luzón, Javier (eds.), *The Politics of Representation* (Sussex: Sussex Academic Press, 2018)

Temperley, Harold, *The Foreign Policy of Canning: 1822–1827* (Abingdon: Routledge, 2006)

Thompson, Edward P., *Customs in Common* (London: Penguin, 1993)

Thomson, Guy, *The Birth of Modern Politics in Spain: Democracy, Association and Revolution, 1854–75* (Basingstoke: Palgrave Macmillan, 2009)

Thomson, Guy, '*Democracia*: The Cult of Heroic Self-Sacrifice and Popular Mobilization in Southern Spain, 1849–1869', *Bulletin of Spanish Studies*, Vol. 94, No. 6 (2017), 927–53

Thomson, Guy, 'Garibaldi and the Legacy of the Revolutions of 1848 in Southern Spain', *European History Quarterly*, Vol. 31, No. 3 (2001), 353–95

Torras, Jaime Elías, *La guerra de los Agraviados* (Barcelona: Cátedra de Historia general de España, 1967)

Torras, Jaime Elías, *Liberalismo y rebeldía campesina (1820–1823)* (Barcelona: Ariel, 1976)

Townson, Nigel (ed.), *Is Spain Different? A Comparative Look at the Nineteenth and Twentieth Centuries* (Sussex: Sussex Academic Press, 2015)

Trías, Juan J. and Elorza, Antonio, *Federalismo y reforma social en España (1840–1870)* (Madrid: Seminarios y Ediciones, 1975)

Tuñón de Lara, Maunel, *El movimiento obrero en la historia de España*, 2 vols. (Madrid: Sarpe, 1985)

Tuñón de Lara, Manuel, *Historia de España* (Madrid: Ámbito, 1988)

Vázquez García, Francisco, 'La campaña contra los sacerdotes pederastas (1880–1912): un ejemplode "pánico moral" en la España de la Restauración', *Hispania*, Vol. LXXVIII, No. 260 (septiembre–diciembre 2018), 759–86

Vicens Vives, Jaime *Historia de España y América*, 5 vols. (Barcelona: Vicens Vives, 1971)

Vila-San-Juan, Jose Luis, *Amadeo I: El Rey Caballero* (Barcelona: Planeta, 1997)

Vilches García, Jorge, 'Cánovas: Político del Sexenio Revolucionario', *Hispania: Revista Española de Historia*, Vol. 57, No. 3 (septiembre 1997), 1107–29

Villares, Ramón, *Historia de Galicia* (Barcelona: Galaxia, 2014)

Viñao, Antonio (ed.), *José María Blanco White sobre educación* (Madrid: Biblioteca Nueva, 2003)

Vincent, Mary, *Spain, 1833–2002: People and State* (Oxford: Oxford University Press, 2002)

Index